Religious Diversity and American Religious History

Religious Diversity and American Religious History

STUDIES IN

TRADITIONS AND CULTURES

EDITED BY

Walter H. Conser Jr.

and

Sumner B. Twiss

The University of Georgia Press

ATHENS AND LONDON

© 1997 by the University of Georgia Press
Athens, Georgia 30602
All rights reserved
Designed by Betty Palmer McDaniel
Set in ten on twelve Electra by G & S Typesetters, Inc.
Printed and bound by Braun-Brumfield, Inc.
The paper in this book meets the guidelines for
permanence and durability of the Committee on
Production Guidelines for Book Longevity of the
Council on Library Resources.

Printed in the United States of America

01 00 99 98 97   C   5 4 3 2 1
01 00 99 98 97   P   5 4 3 2 1

Library of Congress Cataloging in Publication Data
Religious diversity and American religious history : studies in
traditions and cultures / edited by Walter H. Conser, Jr. and
Sumner B. Twiss.
p.   cm.
Includes papers presented at a national conference on new
directions in American religious history sponsored by Brown
University in March 1994.
Includes bibliographical references and index.
ISBN 0-8203-1917-1 (alk. paper). — ISBN 0-8203-1918-X (pbk. :
alk. paper)
1. United States — Religion.   2. Religious pluralism — United
States–History.   I. Conser, Walter H.   II. Twiss, Sumner B.
BL2525.R4694   1997
200'.973 — dc21   97-26767

British Library Cataloging in Publication Data available

The essay "Retelling Carter Woodson's Story" by Albert J. Raboteau
and David W. Wills, with Randall K. Burkett, Will B Gravely,
and James Melvin Washington was originally published
in the *Journal of American History* 77 (June 1990)
and is reprinted in this volume with permission.

In memory of
William G. McLoughlin

Contents

Preface

In March 1994 Brown University sponsored a national conference on new directions in American religious history, in memory of the contributions of William G. McLoughlin to the field. At the time of his death in December 1992, McLoughlin was Willard Prescott and Annie McClelland Smith Professor Emeritus of History and Religion, Professor Emeritus of History, and Chancellor's Fellow at Brown University. As one of his generation's most distinguished historians of American religion, McLoughlin examined such topics as modern revivalism, the separation of church and state in the United States, and Cherokee religion and society in the eighteenth and nineteenth centuries. The success of that conference and the participation by colleagues, former students, and friends from near and far was a fitting tribute to McLoughlin's personal influence and his wider impact on the field of American religion.

During the conference and subsequent to it, the editors discussed with many scholars the issue of whether a volume building upon the conference and extending its concern with the intersection of religious diversity and American religious history to other case studies would be useful for helping to chart the course of future inquiry in American religious history. This book is the result of those conversations and includes papers delivered at the Brown conference as well as one recently published essay and pieces specifically commissioned for this volume. The authors, all acknowledged experts in their fields, have shaped their essays so as to orient the reader to the relevant trends of historiographical interpretation and, as appropriate, to sketch out an illuminative case study of a topic or issue that would project the author's vision of how that area should be developed in the future, given what has been done (or left undone) to date.

The editors wish to thank the Departments of History, Religious Studies, American Civilization, Afro-American Studies, and Judaic Studies at Brown University as well as President Vartan Gregorian, the Francis Wayland Collegium for Liberal Learning, and the University Lectureships Committee of Brown University for their assistance with the national conference in 1994 and with the preparation of this volume.

Editorial Introduction:
Past Traditions, Future Directions

In 1854 the church historian Philip Schaff forecast that America would become the "Phenix grave" of European Christianity, giving rise to forms of religious life that would be new, vigorous, and expansive.[1] Echoes of Schaff's predictions have been heard more than once since his day. Sometimes appearing as triumphalist justifications for American exceptionalism, sometimes sounding a more elegiac tone over perceived declension from honored traditions, established standards, and revered orthodoxies, the particularity of American religious experience has become a hallmark of its interpretation.

However, where earlier commentators located its distinctiveness in institutional arrangements, such as church and state separation, or the rise of voluntary organizations, more recent interpreters of American religious history have been drawn to its pluralistic diversity. Conceding that a loosening of church and state ties and a concomitant reconfiguration of notions of personal autonomy, ecclesiastical identity, and institutional involvement have characterized modern nation states, the American pattern seems less exceptional. More distinctive of the American style has been the religious pluralism of its peoples, those Native Americans who were first on the North American continent and then the immigrants, voluntary or forced, who came from Europe, Africa, Asia, and Oceania, and who in arriving also brought their religions. Historians have debated the degree, persistence, and nature of social and ethnic heterogeneity in the various periods of American history, yet few observers would dispute the polymorphous disposition of religion on the American scene today. From the Amish to the Zoroastrians, from Buddhists to Baptists, from the Society of Pragmatic Mysticism to the Brotherhood of the Seven Rays, the spiritually fecund and sometimes exotic character of the religious landscape in America confronts dedicated members and academic witnesses alike.

The field of American religious history is one with its own historiographical traditions, its own perennial themes, and its own familiar texts and personalities.

In certain respects as old as the European settlement of North America, it is an area of scholarly activity that continues vigorously today. Four general periods characterize the historiography of the field of American religious history, and attention to these interpretive developments can help orient one to the distinctive contributions as well as characteristic problems in the current literature. The field's beginnings as a tradition of interpretation can be found, first, in a period of denominational apologetics and the pervasive tendency to see the hand of God working through the particular group about which the author was writing, and, usually to which he also belonged. Thus Cotton Mather, in his *Magnalia Christi Americana* (1702) narrated the settlement of New England, and chronicled the disputes over the colonial charter, the founding of Harvard College, and the lives and activities of the colonial governors and magistrates all as a way of extolling the accomplishments of Puritan Massachusetts Bay in bringing true and godly religion to the New World.

Roughly 150 years later, Robert Baird and Philip Schaff each took the measure of Christianity in the United States and each again discerned providential activity in the course of America's religious history. Baird, for his part, identified several of the perennial themes that have tended to shape the field in both its monographic literature and synthetic accounts. For in his book, *Religion in America*, published in 1843, Baird canvassed the significance of the legal separation of church and state, the consequent development of voluntary forms of ecclesiastical participation and support, and the, no less significant, uses of revivalism as a means of expanding church membership. All of these structures worked, in Baird's view, to hasten the coming of the Kingdom of God and thus attested to the place of America in the divine plan.

Similarly, Philip Schaff, the Swiss-born, German-educated, American historian of Christianity insisted in a series of influential books and essays written in the 1840s and 1850s that America was "the land of the future and appears more and more destined to become the chief source of world and church history." Indeed, in Schaff's view, "not in Europe . . . but on the banks of the Hudson, the Susquehannah, the Mississippi and the Sacramento" would develop the Christianity of the future. Here, then, in all three of these Protestant clerical historians, Mather, Baird, and Schaff, and the same point could be made for John Gilmary Shea, the Roman Catholic author of the four-volume *History of the Catholic Church within the Limits of the United States* (1846), their histories developed around the interpretive pivot of divine redemption through the agency of an American group or institution.[2]

It should not be forgotten, however, that this same tendency to see American experience as the unwitting agent of the sacred plan could also be easily identified in the writings of nonclerical historians of America's early history. Here the Federalists or later the Jacksonians were depicted as just exactly the same bearers of divine redemption that Mather, Baird, and Shea ascribed to their denominational protagonists. Indeed, for every Mather championing the Puritans, there was a Noah Webster defending the divine gift of the Federalist's Constitution, and Robert Baird's interpretive conclusions were more than matched by George Bancroft's Jacksonian insistence that the voice of the people was the voice of God.

By the second and third decade of the twentieth century, a second era of historiography emerged and with it an interpretive sea change in which categories of divine causation and providential intervention fell away and were replaced. Here, in the ecclesiastical counterpart to the Progressive historians such as Frederick Jackson Turner and Charles Beard, the role of environmental factors, and especially the frontier, was highlighted. Peter Mode's *The Frontier Spirit in American Christianity* (1923) captured in its title the newly privileged significance attributed to the frontier; however, William Warren Sweet's four-volume study, *Religion on the American Frontier*, stands as the mainstay of this interpretive tradition. For in Sweet's work it was the challenge of the frontier that forced American churches to innovate, experiment, and accommodate as they sought out pragmatic answers to their new, indigenously American situation. "In the new world there were few restraining forces," Sweet wrote, and thus the opportunity to experiment and to modify the old ways led to dramatic results and unexpected successes.[3] In such a context, Sweet highlighted the activism, the individualism, and the rough-and-ready tolerance toward fellow believers that he believed typified American Christianity, and he later concluded that "the story of experimentation in organized religion on the frontier constitutes one of the most significant and important aspects of the development of a new western civilization and culture."[4]

In the aftermath of World War II, the third period, that of consensus historiography, shaped the field of American religious history just as it did American political and social history more generally. Here the desire to identify the spiritual values and persistent visions of the American experience and to rescue and resuscitate them in the face of the anomie of the postwar world came to the fore. Though never one to indulge in a nationalistic boosterism, Winthrop Hudson's study, *Religion in America*, aptly illustrates this period in the historiography of the field. For here the emphasis is repeatedly upon the unity of American religious life and upon the shared national faith that Hudson claimed existed at a deeper level within the American experience.[5]

In another context, Will Herberg's *Protestant, Catholic, Jew* (1955) championed at the functional level the basic unity of American religion as rooted in what he called "the underlying presuppositions, values, and ideals that constitute the American Way of Life." For, Herberg insisted, "with the religious community as the primary context of self-identification and social location, and with Protestantism, Catholicism, and Judaism as three culturally diverse representations of the same 'spiritual values,' it becomes virtually mandatory for the American to place himself in one or another of these groups. It is not external pressure but inner necessity that compels him. For being a Protestant, a Catholic, or a Jew is understood as the specific way, and increasingly perhaps the only way, of being an American and locating oneself in American society."[6]

Since the early 1970s, a fourth era has emerged, one that has discarded the image of the melting pot for that of the salad bowl. Here pluralism is accepted, and just as the individual ingredients of the salad each contribute to the whole without losing their own identity, so too do the disparate religious traditions comprise the ethnically diverse and culturally complicated field of American religious history. Sydney E. Ahlstrom best described the interpretive challenge of this pluralism when he noted that by the 1960s the United States had become "a post-Puritan, post-Protestant, post-Christian, post-WASP America" and that future historians of religion in America would have to deal with these developments in new and fresh ways.[7]

Scholars have acknowledged the validity of Ahlstrom's description and have responded to his challenge. In his bibliographic review of the scholarship in American religious history during the 1980s, subtitled "A Decade of Achievement," Martin E. Marty noted the efflorescence of works dealing with American Catholic, American Judaic, and Afro-American religious history. With reference to the older paradigm of scholarship, centered exclusively on mainstream Protestant denominations, Marty concluded that in the 1980s, " 'outsiders' have come to have their day; the margins have moved to the historians' center."[8]

Further trends, both substantive and methodological, can be identified, developments that again reflect the situation Ahlstrom described. First, new areas of investigation are emerging onto scholarly agendas. Native American religious traditions in all their tribal complexity as well as the rich story of Asian religions and of Islam in America have all received attention. Beyond that, alternative traditions — regional, communal, and spiritualistic — have benefited from historical examination. Finally, one of the most important legacies of the 1960s has been the emergence and development of historical studies of gender generally, and, in turn, the application of these questions to American religious history.

A second trend, more methodological in nature, has been the emergence of creative approaches in social history. Here the history of people supplants the history of institutions as now the laborer and farmhands in the pew receive the kind of attention and examination that previously had been reserved for the preachers in the pulpit. On the one hand, these approaches have often utilized quantitative sources to analyze general patterns of behavior and action rather than individual actions. On the other hand, social historians have been concerned to illuminate the diversity within congregations and groups, to examine the class, gender, ideological, and ethnic divisions that are every bit as significant as nominal membership in the formation and existence of a religious tradition.

With this attempt to write history "from below" also came the desire to recover previously unheard or overlooked voices — those of women, of racial and religious minorities, of persons subordinated and suppressed — and to explore their own experiences of identity and power. One strategy for this endeavor has taken the form of postmodern semiotic analysis, an enterprise in which texts and other areas of discourse are examined to reveal their inherent disjunctions and contested relationships, their foreclosures and interstices, and their configurations of power and authority. A second strategy, influenced by the works of Clifford

Geertz, Mary Douglas, Victor Turner, and Anthony F. C. Wallace among others, has focused on cultural analysis and has attended to such topics as popular religion, devotional practices, and the dynamics and significance of religious revitalization movements. In these ways, social, semiotic, and cultural approaches to American religious history have reshaped the field, augmenting its method and shifting its focus from church history — theologically based and institutionally focused — to religious history — empirically based and socially and culturally focused.

In 1964 William G. McLoughlin spoke of a "renascence" in the study of the history of American religion, and Henry May described what he called the field's "recovery." [9] Some thirty years later, it is clear that the field of American religious history is experiencing another fresh creative surge as the pluralism of the religions of the world is now inexorably accepted as part of the history of religion in America.

The essays contained in this volume exemplify the diversity of subject matter and method engaging the field. The first three essays represent areas of research that, following Martin E. Marty's observation, have grown substantially in the last decade or so. Jonathan D. Sarna in his essay explores the meaning and impact of the late nineteenth-century Jewish immigration to America. Rejecting as simplistic and anachronistic earlier suggestions that the arrival of East European Jews was exclusively responsible for introducing changes into American Judaism, Sarna posits a multifaceted religious and cultural awakening within the American Jewish community beginning in the 1870s that reoriented and eventually transformed the Jewish community. Jay P. Dolan's essay surveys the earlier paradigms in the historiography of American Catholicism and suggests that a new one is now emerging in the field. Here the focus of the social historian on popular experience is accepted and broadened into a recognition of the importance of cultural expressions such as ritual and devotional practices or modes of belief. Utilizing a concept of religious awakening similar to Sarna's, Dolan investigates an important transition within American Catholicism occurring in the late eighteenth and early nineteenth centuries. He charts the emergence of a republican Catholicism, reasonable and democratic, and its eventual demise in the face of specific nineteenth-century challenges.

The contribution of Albert J. Raboteau and David W. Wills, with Randall K. Burkett, Will B. Gravely, and James Melvin Washington, calls for a retelling of the story of black Christian churches in the United States. While much recent scholarship has focused on popular as well as elite forms of Afro-American religious history, that has placed the institutional study of black American Christianity under what these authors call "a shadow of neglect." Citing the dearth of modern scholarship on black denominations, in contrast to the volumes devoted to denominational histories of Euro-American Protestantism, they review the major archival resources available for a fresh appraisal of the roles and meanings of the black church. Such a project would recount the history of the black churches from their emergence in the eighteenth century through to the present and, as well, would explore fundamental themes such as the black churches' engagement in social reform movements or the sustaining life of worship and music that developed under such auspices. The accomplishment of this task is a daunting one, these authors concede; however, only once appropriate attention has been given to the patterns of development and change in the black churches can the full variety and meaning of Afro-American religious history be appreciated.

The second cluster of essays deals with topics that have been less often recognized in the older scholarship but that are beginning to receive sustained attention. Regional identity, for example, has materialized as a significant factor in understanding American religion in the aftermath of the breakup of consensus historiography. Pacific slope, Upper Midwest, New England, and Great Basin are all easily identifiable areas with particular regional and religious attributes; however, it is the South that has provided the model for the study of the interplay of regional culture and religion. In his piece on southern religion, Donald G. Mathews links religion, race, and gender into a cultural analysis of southern religious history. Tracing cohesive and disjunctive consequences from the creative social processes of southern religious history, Mathews moves beyond descriptions of Baptist and Methodist regional hegemony to explicate what he calls "the compelling power of religion in the South." In Rosemary Skinner Keller's essay, the issue of gender moves to center stage. Locating her contribution in the ongoing process of historical revision concerning the presence of women and the differences their presence makes in interpreting the history of religion in America, she focuses on the biography of Georgia Harkness as one lens through which to illustrate wider cultural transformations and continuities. Charting Harkness's rise in educational and religious institutions, Keller demonstrates how she tested the boundaries of her era. Reconceiving American religious history from the standpoint of gender, Keller suggests, not only increases the events, personnel, and sites of that history, it also can reshape the field in fundamental ways.

The essays by Stephen J. Stein and Catherine L. Albanese deal with groups often considered peripheral, if not morally aberrant, by an earlier period. Where previous scholars consigned them to the ash heaps of the burned-over district or the domain of the disinherited, Stein argues that recent historians have examined indigenous sectarian communities such as the Mormons, Christian Scientists, Seventh-Day Adventists, Jehovah's Witnesses, Oneida Perfectionists, and Shakers with a more empathetic attitude. This renewed investigation has drawn attention away from perennial questions concerning origins and founders, instead, employing thematic comparative categories such as millennialism, primitivism, and gender not only to gain new insights into these movements but also to link them to wider concerns in the historiography of American religion. Catherine L. Albanese's contribution explores the dissident religious history created by the metaphysical tradition in America. With its roots identifiable in biblical as well as Platonic sources, Albanese traces this tradition from Puritanism through Transcendentalism, Spiritualism, and Theosophy in the nineteenth century to New Age teachings in the late twentieth century. Her focus is on the motif of origin and fall, and whether expressed in Puritan jeremiads of declension, in reports of the lost continent of Atlantis, or in contemporary apocalypses of technology out of control, the theme is illuminating, as is this new attention to previously marginalized groups.

The last three essays examine the religious history of the first inhabitants and the most recent immigrants in American society. Citing the prominence of Asian religions in the late twentieth-century American cultural landscape, Thomas A. Tweed probes the meaning of this presence for the teaching and writing of American religious history. Reminding us of the multiple ethnic and racial groups as well as the diverse histories comprising the Asian experience in America, Tweed surveys the current historiographical situation concerning Asian religions in America. He concludes with his own "historiographical heresy," suggesting that attention to the themes of place, identity, and contact not only provide a window into the nature and meaning of Asian-American religions but also illumine broader patterns in the general field of American religious history.

Yvonne Yazbeck Haddad also acknowledges the significance of diversity, pointing out the linguistic, cultural, and national variations within the Islamic community in America and typologizing that community over the last hundred years in terms of immigrants, converts, and sojourners. Noting the formative influence of international events, the communication revolution, and recent intellectual ferment in the crystallization of Islamic identity in America, she sketches a range of discourses, perspectives, and issues within contemporary American Islam. The presence and growth of the Muslim community in America, Haddad concludes, not only challenges scholars to rethink their descriptive and analytical categories, it also tests the public limits and meanings of authentic religious pluralism in the United States.

Christopher Vecsey's essay examines the participation of the Oglala Lakota Sioux in the faith, devotionalism, and institutions of Roman Catholicism on the Pine Ridge Reservation. On the one hand, Vecsey traces the changes in clerical consciousness culminating, controversially, in the use by several Catholic officiants of Lakota religious symbols and rituals in Christian contexts. On the other hand, in recovering and presenting the many voices and faces of Lakota Catholicism, he shows the range of religious orientations from those Sioux adopting traditional patterns of Lakota belief and practice in active opposition to Christianity, through those who syncretically blend Catholic and Lakota practices, to those Sioux who are exclusively, and sometimes quite conservatively, Catholic in their faith. Vecsey's evocation of the complexity of Lakota Catholicism underscores the concern of this volume to explore the dimensions and to understand the diversity within American religious history. In exemplifying that rambunctious and dynamic spiritual variety, these essays point out future directions for scholars in the field, at the same time in which they provide markers disclosing how we arrived at our present location. Discernment of auspicious directions has traditionally been lauded by humanistic scholars and religious seers alike; this collection and its authors chart a promising course.

Notes

1. Philip Schaff, *America: A Sketch of Its Political, Social, and Religious Character*, ed. Perry Miller (Cambridge, Mass.: Harvard University Press, 1961), 80.

2. Schaff, "Prolegomena zur Kirchengeschichte der Vereinigten Staaten," *Der Kirchenfreund* 1 (Dec. 1848): 357; Schaff, *America*, 191.

3. William Warren Sweet, *The Story of Religions in America* (New York: Harper and Brothers, 1930), 4.

4. William Warren Sweet, *Religion in the Development of American Culture, 1765–1840* (1952; rpt., Gloucester, Mass.: Peter Smith, 1963), ix.

5. See Winthrop S. Hudson, *Religion in America* (New York: Scribner's, 1965), viii, 409.

6. Will Herberg, *Protestant, Catholic, Jew* (1955; rpt., Garden City, N.Y.: Doubleday, 1960), 231, 39.

7. Sydney E. Ahlstrom, "The Problem of the History of Religion in America," *Church History* 39 (June 1970): 232.

8. Martin E. Marty, "American Religious History in the Eighties: A Decade of Achievement," *Church History* 62 (Sept. 1993): 337. Further evidence of this scholarly response can be seen in the publication of the three-volume reference work, *Encyclopedia of the American Religious Experience*, ed. Charles H. Lippy and Peter W. Williams (New York: Scribner's, 1988).

9. McLoughlin's remarks were delivered in 1964 and published as "Pietism and the American Character," *American Quarterly* 17 (Summer 1965): 163–86 (quote p. 163). Henry May's description is given in the article "The Recovery of American Religious History," *American Historical Review* 70 (Oct. 1964): 79–92.

Religious Diversity and American Religious History

The Late Nineteenth-Century American Jewish Awakening

JONATHAN D. SARNA

The years from 1881 to 1914 are generally known in American Jewish historiography as the era of mass immigration, the period when Central European Jews were overwhelmed by East European Jews and the nation's Jewish population increased twelvefold. Most historians assume that whatever else happened during these years was a response to this immigration, a subsidiary consequence to the era's main theme. Leon Jick's interpretation sums up what is essentially a consensus view:

> The tidal wave of East European Jewish immigrants which began after 1881 inundated the Jewish community and transformed the confident [R]eform majority into a defensive minority. In the wake of the radically different values and attitudes of the newcomers and the problems created by their arrival, the process of adaptation and adjustment began anew. A new burst of organizational energy led to new modes of accommodation and to the creation of the complex institutional and ideological panorama of twentieth-century American Jewry.[1]

This view is not new; indeed one finds it expressed as early as 1911 in Rabbi Solomon Schindler's famous mea culpa sermon entitled "Mistakes I Have Made." Schindler, who had by then abandoned his earlier radicalism and become a kind of born-again Jew, a *baal teshuva*, believed that post–Civil War Jews "seemed near assimilation." Anticipating contemporary scholars, he attributed subsequent changes, including his own sense of personal guilt for having formerly espoused assimilation, to what he called the "new spirit" that East European Jews had brought with them:

> A cloud came up out of the East and covered the world. It brought here to us two millions of people. Whilst they were different from us in appearance and habits, there were ties of blood between us and they brought a new spirit

1

amongst us. They surrounded us like an army. This movement from the east to the west of this great army strong in the old ideals acting upon and changing our mode of thought, demanding from us change, — this was the hand of God.[2]

The assumption, then, is that East European Jews were responsible for introducing a "new spirit" into American Jewish life. They overwhelmed the hitherto dominant Reform movement, reducing it, statistically, "to the position of a denomination of high social level representing only a fraction of the American Jews." Scholars like Nathan Glazer and Henry Feingold go so far as to argue that without this immigration, American Jews might well have assimilated and disappeared.[3]

Yet, well rooted as this view is within twentieth century American Jewish historiography, it does not stand up under close scrutiny. Nobody, of course, disputes that East European Jewish immigration had a profound historical impact. But it is extraordinarily difficult to argue that the immigration challenge is central to the whole period, sufficient in and of itself to explain all of the many changes that historians attribute to it. Three problems with the interpretation are particularly daunting.

First, the interpretation is, in many ways, anachronistic. Many of the changes attributed to mass immigration actually took place earlier, either before 1881 or before American Jews realized how portentous the immigration would be. So, for example, it is claimed that East European Jews are responsible for breathing a "new spirit" into American Judaism, resulting in a considerable movement back to tradition even among native-born Jews. Yet in fact this movement began much earlier, in the late 1870s, and was associated not with immigrants but with a core of American-born young people, particularly in Philadelphia and New York. Reports that "genuine Orthodox views are now becoming fashionable among Jewish young America" circulated as early as 1879,[4] and that same year saw the establishment of the new journalistic voice of these young people, the *American Hebrew*, described by one of its founders as "our forcible instrument for the perpetuation and elevation of Judaism."[5] By the mid-1880s — that is, before immigration's impact had fully been felt — the new conservative trend within American Judaism was already widely in evidence.[6]

New organizational forms likewise predated mass immigration. The tremendous growth of the Young Men's Hebrew Associations, to take perhaps the most significant example, began in the mid-1870s. By 1890 some 120 of the associations had been founded nationwide, many in places scarcely affected by immigration.[7] These and other religious, cultural, and organizational changes cannot be attributed to mass immigration, and are therefore not explicable according to our current understanding of late nineteenth-century developments.

Second, besides being anachronistic, the current interpretation is also extraordinarily simplistic. It assumes that a wide array of late nineteenth-century developments can all be explained by a single factor, mass migration, and that this one factor was sufficient to trigger a full-scale cultural revolution in American Jewish life. Yet, accounts of the founding of such new nationwide organizations as the Jewish Publication Society (1888), the American Jewish Historical Society (1892), Gratz College (1893), the Jewish Chautauqua Society (1893), and the National Council of Jewish Women (1893), as well as the ambitious project to produce a full-scale *Jewish Encyclopedia* in America, work on which began in earnest in 1898, demonstrate that they were *not* originally justified on the basis of the mass migration and have only limited initial connection to it. These were instead cultural and educational undertakings designed to promote Jewish learning on the part of native Jews, to promote America itself as a center of Jewish life, and to counter antisemitism.[8] Admittedly, some of these organizations subsequently changed their mission in response to the immigrant challenge. But we misunderstand a great deal if we assume, as so many today do, that immigration was the fountainhead from which all other turn-of-the-century developments flowed.

Finally, the immigrant interpretation is painfully insular. It assumes, quite wrongly, that American Jewish life in this period was largely shaped by Jewish events, and that the impact of surrounding American cultural and religious developments was negligible. It also assumes, again wrongly, that the religious history of America's Jews was exclusively shaped by immigrating East Europeans. Instead of viewing American Jewish history in its broadest context, noting parallels to developments within American society and in Europe, the interpretation reflects and encourages a lamentable tunnel vision that hinders our understanding of what the period's history was really all about.

Contemporaries understood turn-of-the-century developments in American Jewish life quite differently. They used terms like "revival," "renaissance," and "awakening" to explain what was going on in their day, and they understood these terms in much the same way that contemporary Protestants did. The *London Jewish Chronicle* thus reported in 1887 that "a strong religious revival has apparently set in among the Jews in the United States." It was especially struck by the number of American synagogues looking for rabbis and by the comparatively high salaries that rabbinic candidates were then being offered. Cyrus Adler, writing in the *American Hebrew* seven years later, described what he called an American Jewish "renaissance" and a "revival of Jewish learning." He listed a whole series of Jewish cultural and intellectual achievements in America dating back to 1879. By 1901 lawyer and communal leader Daniel P. Hays was persuaded that the previous decade had witnessed "a great awakening among our people — a realization that the Jew is not to become great by his material achievements, but by his contribution toward the higher ideals of life and by his endeavors toward the uplifting of the race." Edwin Wolf, in his presidential address to the Jewish Publication Society in 1904, carried the same theme into the future: "we are," he proclaimed, "laying the foundation for a Jewish renaissance in America."[9]

Historians of American Judaism have paid scant attention to these claims.[10] Terms such as "revival," "awakening," and "renaissance" play no part in the traditional religious vocabulary of Judaism, and in America they run counter to the standard assimilationist model that posits "linear descent," a movement over several generations of American Judaism from Orthodoxy to Reform to complete secularity.[11] Where historians of American Protestantism have long posited a cyclical pattern of revival and stagnation ("backsliding"), a model that Catholic historians have now borrowed, no such pattern has heretofore been discerned in the story of American Judaism—at least until we reach contemporary times.[12] My argument here, however, is that the explanation offered by turn-of-the-century Jews to describe the developments of their day was essentially correct. Jews *were* experiencing a period of religious and cultural awakening, parallel but by no means identical to what Protestantism experienced during the same period.[13] This multifaceted awakening—its causes, manifestations, and implications— holds the key to understanding this critical period in American Jewish history, explaining much that the regnant "immigration synthesis" cannot adequately contain.

Before proceeding to make the case for a late nineteenth-century American Jewish awakening, a methodological problem must be disposed of. In recent years, Timothy Smith, Jon Butler, and others have questioned whether "religious awakenings," at least as historians describe them, ever truly existed. Are they, in Butler's words, "interpretive fiction," perhaps "more a cycle . . . in the attention of secular writers," as Smith charges, "than in the extent of actual religious excitement?" This question was debated at length at a session held in Providence, Rhode Island, in 1982, and it seems to me that William G. McLoughlin, in his response to these challenges, had the best of the argument. "The most important current interpretations of the Awakening cycle," he wrote, "have divorced the construct from a direct connection with revivalists and revival meetings. They see revivalism and revivalists as the symptoms of the process of cultural stress and reorientation, and not as the prime movers." Borrowing concepts from anthropology and sociology, he defined an awakening as "a major cultural reorientation—a search for new meaning, order, and direction in a society which finds that rapid change and unexpected intrusions have disrupted the order of life."[14] This definition matches, quite precisely, what I see as having happened in the late nineteenth-century American Jewish community.

I shall argue in what follows that a "major cultural reorientation" began in the American Jewish community late in the 1870s and was subsequently heightened by mass immigration. The critical developments that we associate with this period—the return to religion, the heightened sense of Jewish peoplehood and particularism, the far-reaching changes that opened up new opportunities and responsibilities for women, the renewed community-wide emphasis on education and culture, the "burst of organizational energy," and the growth of Conservative Judaism and Zionism—all reflect different efforts to resolve the "crisis of beliefs and values" that had developed during these decades.[15] By 1914, American Jewry had been transformed and the awakening had run its course. The basic contours of the twentieth-century American Jewish community had by then fallen into place.

The late 1860s and early 1870s were a period of confident optimism in American Jewish life. The Central European Jews who immigrated two decades earlier had, by then, established themselves securely. The Jewish community had grown in wealth and power and now stood at about a quarter of a million strong with close to three hundred synagogues spread from coast to coast. The community had created hospitals, orphanages, schools, newspapers, magazines, several fraternal organizations, a union of synagogues, and in 1875 a rabbinical seminary. The nation was booming, liberal Jews and Protestants spoke warmly of universalism, and rabbis and ministers even occasionally traded pulpits. Small wonder that Jews looked forward with anticipation to the onset of a glorious "new era" in history, described by one rabbi in an 1874 lecture delivered "in every important city east of the Mississippi River" as a time when "the whole human race shall be led to worship one Almighty God of righteousness and truth, goodness and love," and when Jews would stand in the forefront of those ushering in "the golden age of a true universal brotherhood." [16]

Beginning in the late 1870s, this hopeful scenario was undermined by a series of unanticipated crises that disrupted American Jewish life and called many of its guiding assumptions into question. "Antisemitism" — a word coined in Germany at the end of the 1870s to describe and justify ("scientifically") anti-Jewish propaganda and discrimination — explains part of what happened. The rise of racially based anti-Jewish hatred in Germany, a land that many American Jews had close ties to and had previously revered for its liberal spirit and cultural advancement, came as a shock. Here Jews had assumed that emancipation, enlightenment, and human progress would diminish residual prejudice directed toward them, and suddenly they saw it espoused in the highest intellectual circles, and by people in whom they had placed great faith. German antisemitism was widely reported upon in the United States, covered both in the Jewish and in the general press. "What American Jews were witnessing," Naomi Cohen explains, was nothing less than "the humiliation of their Jewish parents, a spectacle that could shake their faith in Judaism itself." [17]

What made this situation even worse was that antisemitism and particularly social discrimination soon spread to America's own shores. Anti-Jewish hatred was certainly not new to America, but Jews had previously considered it something of an anachronism, alien both to the modern temper and to American democracy. Like Jews in Germany, they optimistically assumed that prejudice against them would in time wither away. The two well-publicized incidents of the late 1870s — Judge Hilton's exclusion of banker Joseph Seligman from the Grand Union Hotel (1877) and Austin Corbin's public announcement that "Jews as a class" would be unwelcome at Coney Island (1879) — proved so shocking precisely because they challenged this assumption.[18] The questions posed by Hermann Baar, superintendent of the Hebrew Orphan Asylum, in a published address to his charges responding to Corbin's outburst were the questions that Jews in all walks of life suddenly had to ask of themselves:

> In what age and country do we live? Are we going to have the times of Philip II., of Spain, repeated, or do we really live in the year 1879, in that century of progress and improvement, of education and enlightenment? Do we really live in the year 1879, in that era of moral refinement and cultured tastes, of religious toleration and social intercourse? And if we really live in this era, can such an act of injustice and bigoted ostracism happen on American soil, in this land of the free and brave, in which the homeless finds a shelter and the persecuted a resting place, in which the peaceable citizen enjoys the blessings of his labor, and the devout worshiper the full liberty of his religious conscience, and in which humanity teaches to other countries and nations the blessed code of right and justice?[19]

By brazenly defending and legitimating antisemitism on socioeconomic, racial, and legal grounds, incidents such as these paved the way for a depressing rise in antisemitic manifestations of all sorts, from social discrimination to antisemitic propaganda to efforts to stem the tide of Jewish immigrants. Over the next two decades, Jews experienced a substantial decline in their social status. "Gradually, but surely, we are being forced back into a physical and moral ghetto," thirty-five-year-old Professor Richard Gottheil of Columbia University complained, speaking in 1897 to a private meeting of the Judaeans, the cultural society of New York's Jewish elite. "Private schools are being closed against our children one by one; we are practically boycotted from all summer hotels — and our social lines run as far apart from those of our neighbors as they did in the worst days of our European degradation."[20]

Developments within American Protestantism added yet another dimension to the mood of uneasiness that I sense in the American Jewish community of this period. The spiritual crisis and internal divisions that plagued Protestant America during this era — one that confronted all American religious groups with the staggering implications of Darwinism and biblical criticism — drove Evangelicals and liberals alike to renew their particularistic calls for a "Christian America." Visions of a liberal religious alliance and of close cooperation between Jews and Unitarians gradually evaporated. Although interfaith exchanges continued, Jews came to realize that many of their Christian friends continued to harbor hopes that one day Jews would "see the light." Much to the embarrassment of Jewish leaders, some Christian liberals looked to Felix Adler's de-Judaized Ethical Culture movement as a harbinger of Judaism's future course.[21]

On the Jewish side, this period witnessed a comparable crisis of the spirit. Alarmed at religious "indifference," Jewish ignorance, some well-publicized cases of intermarriage, and Felix Adler's success in attracting young Jews to his cause, many began to question prior assumptions regarding the direction in which American Judaism should move. Was Reform Judaism really the answer?

Had the effort to modernize Judaism gone too far? Would assimilation triumph? By the 1880s the Reform movement was on the defensive facing attacks from both left and right. Its uncertainty, which as we shall see found expression in the 1885 Conference of Reform rabbis who produced the Pittsburgh Platform, was also reflected in an 1884 letter to Rabbi Bernhard Felsenthal, a pioneer of American Reform, from a confused young rabbi named David Stern, who subsequently committed suicide. Stern remarked that the religious agenda of his day was "entirely different" from what it had been before. "Then the struggle was to remove the dross; to-day it is to conserve the pearl beneath." [22]

Mass East European Jewish immigration, coming on the heels of all of these developments, added a great deal of fuel to the crisis of confidence that Jews experienced in the 1880s. In Russia, as in Germany, liberalism had been tested and found wanting; reaction followed. The resulting mass exodus strained the Jewish community's resources, heightened fears of antisemitism, stimulated an array of Americanization and revitalization efforts, and threatened to change the whole character of the American Jewish community once East European Jews gained cultural hegemony.

So visible and long-lasting was the transformation wrought by East European Jewish immigration that it eventually overshadowed all other aspects of the late nineteenth-century crisis. From the point of view of contemporaries, however, antisemitism at home and abroad, the specter of assimilation and intermarriage, and the changing religious and social environment of the United States were no less significant. Faced with all of these unexpected problems at once, American Jews began to realize that their whole optimistic vision of the future had been built on false premises. Even the usually starry-eyed Reform Jewish leader Rabbi Isaac Mayer Wise, writing in 1881, felt his faith in the future slowly ebbing away:

> There is something wrong among us optimists and humanists, sad experience upsets our beautiful theories and we stand confounded before the angry eruptions of the treacherous volcano called humanity. There is a lie in its nature which has not been overcome. Will it ever be overcome? We hope and trust that it will. Till then, we poor optimists are sadly disappointed and made false prophets. [23]

Utopia, in short, had proved more distant than expected. The universalistic prophecies of the 1860s and 1870s had failed, the hoped-for "new era" had not materialized, and conditions for Jews in America and around the world had grown worse instead of better. This posed a cultural crisis of the highest order for American Jews, and precipitated the cultural awakening that changed the face of American Jewish life forever.

Protestant awakenings, at least as historians have described them in America, operate from the top down. A revivalist, like Dwight L. Moody or Billy Sunday in the late nineteenth and early twentieth centuries, stimulated a movement of religious revitalization, usually through his preaching, and in retrospect scholars discover that he defined the cultural issues (or, less charitably, embodied the "cultural confusion") that characterized his era as a whole. Parallel Jewish awakenings, by contrast, percolated from the bottom up. Young people and others alienated from the religious establishment stood in the forefront of late nineteenth-century efforts to promote religious revitalization, and through their teachings (much more than their preaching) as well as their organizational activities they stimulated the conversions, religious excitement, schismatic conflicts, theological disputations and institutional changes that promoted the cultural transformations that we associate with a religious awakening. Jewish awakenings are somewhat more difficult to identify and characterize than Protestant ones, since one cannot easily focus on the work of individual revivalists. What one can present is evidence of revitalization on the part of a whole range of individuals aimed at promoting Jewish religious renewal.

By far the most important group seeking to promote Jewish religious renewal in the last decades of the nineteenth-century was centered in Philadelphia [24] and consisted largely of young single men. Mayer Sulzberger (1843–1923), the city's foremost Jewish citizen, was the "patriarch" of this group, and his associates (several of whom were also his relatives) included such future activists as Solomon Solis-Cohen (1857–1948), Cyrus L. Sulzberger (1858–1932), Joseph Fels (1854–1914), Samuel Fels (1860–1950), and Cyrus Adler (1863–1940). All were initially involved in the Young Men's Hebrew Association (YMHA) of Philadelphia, founded in 1875 to promote social as well as cultural activities of a Jewish nature, including lectures, literary discussions, formal Jewish classes, and the publication of a lively newsletter. Of primary significance, for our purposes, was their campaign, carried out in association with the YMHA of New York (founded in 1874), for "the Grand Revival of the Jewish National Holiday of Chanucka," complete with appropriate pageants and publicity. This was an effort "to rescue this national festival from the oblivion into which it seemed rapidly falling," and was a direct challenge to Reform Judaism, which had renounced national aspects of Judaism as antithetical to the modern spirit; presumably, the campaign also sought to counteract the evident allure of Christmas. In 1879, the "revival" proved a triumphant success. "Every worker in the cause of a revived Judaism," one of the organizers wrote, "must have felt the inspiration exuded from the enthusiastic interest evinced by such a mass of Israel's people." [25]

A few months before this "revival," on October 5, 1879, several of the young people in this circle bound themselves together in a solemn covenant "for God and Judaism," which they called *Keyam Dishmaya*, in which they pledged all in their power to bring Jews back "to the ancient faith." Solomon Solis-Cohen's papers preserve letters from a corresponding member of this group, Max Cohen, later librarian of New York's Maimonides Library, that indicate the earnestness and fervor with which these young people undertook their mission. "The great question for contemporary Judaism is whether it will continue God's work or cease to be," he wrote in one letter. His own conclusion was unambiguous: "Israel must be whatever its children make it. . . . They who wish to give Israel her true position in the world's autonomy must set a high ideal before them and abide thereby." In another letter, Cohen discussed his forthcoming lecture entitled "The Restoration of the Jews" and expressed pleasure "with the movement that is now on foot . . . to recreate the ancient Hebrew Sabbath." He hoped that the Sabbath movement would result "in the more universal observance of other Jewish ordinances and the incitement to higher spiritual life." Cohen was all of twenty-six and still living at home when he expressed these lofty sentiments. His "Israel must be" letter concluded with the hurried note, "Mother is calling that it is time to blow out my lamp." [26]

On the first anniversary of *Keyam Dishmaya*, one of its leaders, twenty-two-year-old Cyrus L. Sulzberger (1858–1932), who had just moved from Philadelphia to New York and was on the road to becoming a prominent New York merchant and communal leader (as well as the grandfather of the *New York Times* columnist C.L. Sulzberger), summed up the group's achievements and aims in a remarkable and revealing letter:

> "That fateful 5th of October night" has borne its fruit. The seed then planted fell on no barren soil. The covenant then made has not been broken. We have kept before us that vow "for God and Judaism" and with that we have used all the abilities God has given us in His sacred cause. Looking back over the first year of our *Berith* [covenant], we have cause to be grateful to God for the successful manner in which we have begun our work. We have in the American Hebrew a means of addressing the community; we, here, [in New York] have in our Bible Class a means of addressing a smaller community whom, with God's blessing, we shall redeem to the ancient faith. You in the Sunday School did good work in your address and have further good work to do; there is at least one straying sheep whom you can reclaim and there may be more. This is the kind of missionary labor in which we must engage. While we may not hope to live to see the fulfillment of all our desires, while we may not live to see the restoration of our people to the land of their inheritance, we may yet so live that we shall do our share toward hastening these events; we may so live that the work we now are doing will be taken in hand by others who profiting by our experience, our example and our lives, shall continue the good work we are in. May God grant us the ability to continue in the cause, may He raise us above the petty strifes of daily occurrences, may He strengthen us to renewed labor and renewed activity, may He bring us peace of mind wherewith to labor undisturbed, may He bless our covenant and grant us a successful issue in our labors "for God and Judaism" Amen! [27]

In this letter of 1880, Sulzberger spelled out the three cornerstones of the revival that he and his associates were trying to spawn: they sought, first, to revitalize and deepen the religious and spiritual lives of American Jews; second, to strengthen Jewish education; and third, to promote the restoration of Jews as a people, including their ultimate restoration to the land of Israel. Together, these goals signified an inward turn among young American Jews. Their response to the cultural crisis of their day was to reject universalism, assimilationism, and the redefinition of Judaism along purely religious lines — themes heavily promoted by Reform Judaism at that time — in favor of a Judaism that was in their view more closely in tune with God and Jewish historical tradition.

No movement for change can confine itself to secret societies and clandestine cells. For this reason, and in order to promote their lofty aims among the 'movers and shakers' of the American Jewish community, these young Jewish revivalists established on November 21, 1879, a lively and important highbrow Jewish newspaper in New York entitled the *American Hebrew.* "Our work," they explained to the public in their first issue, "shall consist of untiring endeavors to stir up our brethren to pride in our time-honored faith." The newspaper's publisher, Philip Cowen, recalled half a century later that "we were fully convinced that not only New York Judaism, but American Judaism, awaited its journalistic redeemers!"[28]

The nine editors of the new newspaper, some Philadelphians, some New Yorkers, were all anonymous — understandably so, since their ages ranged from twenty-one to twenty-nine. They represented a new phenomenon on the American Jewish scene: most were American-born Jews who were "strong for traditional Judaism" (two of the nine were rabbis) yet at the same time eager to accommodate Judaism to American conditions.[29] "Our proclivities . . . are toward 'reformed' Judaism and yet our disposition is toward orthodoxy," the editors admitted in their first issue. Years later Max Cohen described his associates as having been "a group of young American Jews who, while not inordinately addicted to Orthodoxy as a rigid standardization of thought and conduct, was yet opposed to the wholesale and reckless discarding of everything that was Jewish simply because it was inconvenient, oriental, or was not in conformity with Episcopalian customs."[30]

By the time he published this recollection, in 1920, Cohen and the other erstwhile members of his group had moved far beyond the *American Hebrew.* Led by the indefatigable Cyrus Adler, who had joined the editorial board of the paper in 1894, members of this cohort of New York and Philadelphia Jews established a wide range of cultural and religious institutions and involved themselves in an array of communal projects, some of them designed to strengthen what became known as Conservative Judaism, one of the most significant and far-reaching outcomes of this whole religious awakening,[31] and all of them designed to extend the work of Jewish cultural and religious renewal in new directions. In the space of a few decades they created, among other things, the Jewish Theological Seminary (1886), the Jewish Publication Society (1888), the American Jewish Historical Society (1892), Gratz College (1893), and Dropsie College (1907). They were associated with the publication of the *Jewish Encyclopedia* (1901–6), the movement to bring the renowned Jewish scholar Solomon Schechter to America (he arrived in 1902), the transfer to America's shores of the scholarly journal the *Jewish Quarterly Review* (1910), and the establishment of American Jewry's first high-quality Hebrew Press (1921). They were also involved in the Jewish Bible translation project (1893–1917) and the Schiff Library of Jewish Classics (1914–36), both specially funded projects of the Jewish Publication Society.

These highly ambitious and for the most part successful undertakings mirror the "organizing process" that Donald Mathews associated with the Protestant Second Great Awakening; they sought to provide "meaning and direction" to Jews suffering from the social and cultural strains of a transitional era.[32] Appropriately, the organizations sought to reach different audiences: some looked to scholars, some to rabbis and teachers, and some to the Jewish community at large and to non-Jews. In the case of Cyrus Adler, Naomi W. Cohen describes this multitiered cultural agenda as a conscious creation:

> On one level, Adler envisioned the modern training of Jewish scholars, abetted by appropriate library and publication resources. On a second, he aimed for the education of American rabbis and teachers who would inculcate a loyalty to historical Judaism in consonance with acculturation to American surroundings. On still a third, he worked for a community knowledgeable about its heritage, that would appreciate the value of reading books of Jewish interest, of collecting Jewish artifacts, and of keeping alert to contemporary events that involved Jewry.[33]

What these levels all had in common was the fact that they were dedicated to the same general ends. All sought to promote religious renewal, improved Jewish education, cultural revitalization, the professionalism of Jewish scholarship, the promotion of a positive Jewish image to the Gentiles, and the elevation of American Jewry to a position of greater prominence, if not preeminence among the Jews of the world.

Admittedly, the challenge posed by massive East European Jewish immigration led, for a time, to a greater rhetorical emphasis upon Americanization as a goal, but this should not be exaggerated. Promoters of Jewish renewal understood better than other Jewish leaders did that the real concern was not so much how to assimilate the East Europeans as how to ensure that all American Jews would not assimilate completely. It was this critical insight coupled with a prescient sense that American Jewry needed to prepare itself to play a central role in the affairs of world Jewry that prompted these Jews to participate in the creation of these great institutions and projects that shaped American Jewish cultural and religious life into the late twentieth century.[34]

Although this remarkable cohort of Philadelphia and New York Jews — most of them young, male, and well-educated laypeople, rather than rabbis[35] — formed the most visible leadership cadre of the late nineteenth-century awakening, they were by no means its only source of energy. In fact, more than generally realized, the awakening marked a turning point both in the history of American Jewish women and in the history of the American Jewish Reform movement.

The role of women in American Judaism had been undergoing change since the early decades of the nineteenth century. Influenced by the Second Great Awakening, Rebecca Gratz of Philadelphia introduced Jewish women into the world of Jewish philanthropy, establishing in 1819 the Female Hebrew Benevolent Society, the progenitor of many similar benevolent organizations by and for Jewish women. Previously, Jewish philanthropy had been part of the synagogue's domain and governed by men. The Jewish Sunday School movement, pioneered by Gratz in 1838, transformed the role of Jewish women still further by making them responsible for the religious education and spiritual guidance of the young. By the time Gratz died, in 1869, it can safely be estimated that the majority of American Jews who received any formal Jewish education at all learned most of what they knew from female teachers. These teachers, in turn, had to educate themselves in Judaism, which they did with the aid of new textbooks, some of them too written by women.[36] By the end of the nineteenth century, thanks to a legacy left by Rebecca Gratz's brother, Hyman, women could receive advanced training in Judaism at Gratz College, the first of a series of Hebrew teachers colleges across the United States that trained women on an equal basis with men.[37] In still another transformation, this one beginning in 1851 and confined to Reform temples, women achieved parity with their husbands in the realm of synagogue seating. No longer were they relegated to the balcony or separated from men by a physical barrier; instead, by the late 1870s, mixed seating was the rule throughout Reform congregations.[38] Now, building on these earlier developments, women experienced still more far-reaching changes as part of the late nineteenth-century American Jewish awakening.

The first woman to achieve great prominence in the awakening was the poet Emma Lazarus (1849–1887), best known for her poem "The New Colossus," composed in 1883 to help raise funds for the pedestal on which the Statue of Liberty rests.[39] Born in New York to an aristocratic Jewish family of mixed Sephardic and Ashkenazic, she had emerged at a young age as a sensitive poet (her first book was published when she was seventeen) but had never maintained close ties to the Jewish community; only a very small percentage of her early work bore on Jewish themes at all. Antisemitism and the first wave of East European Jewish immigration shocked Lazarus, and in 1882, in a burst of creative energy, she emerged as a staunch defender of Jewish rights, the poet laureate of the Jewish awakening, and as the foremost proponent of the "national-Jewish movement" aimed at "the establishment of a free Jewish State."[40] Her oft-quoted poem, "The Banner of the Jew," composed in the spring of 1882, began with the words "Wake, Israel, wake!" and ended on a militant note:

> O deem not dead that martial fire,
>   Say not the mystic flame is spent!
> With Moses' law and David's lyre,
>   Your ancient strength remains unbent.
> Let but an Ezra rise anew,
>   To lift the *Banner of the Jew!*
>
> A rag, a mock at first — erelong
>   When men have bled and women wept,
> To guard its precious folds from wrong,
>   Even they who shrunk, even they who slept,
> Shall leap to bless it, and to save.
>   Strike! for the brave revere the brave![41]

Meanwhile, her essays, notably *An Epistle to the Hebrews* (1882–83), called for "a deepening and quickening of the sources of Jewish enthusiasm" in response to the "'storm-centre' in our history" that Jews were passing through.[42]

Lazarus herself soon established close ties with the publisher of the *American Hebrew*, where much of her work now appeared, and she began studying the Hebrew language. Her interest, however, lay not in the religious revitalization of the Jews, as advocated by the members of *Keyam Dishmaya*; instead, she placed her emphasis on Jewish peoplehood, emphasizing the virtues of unity, discipline, and organization in the service of Jewish national renewal. Influenced by George Eliot's *Daniel Deronda*, Laurence Oliphant's *The Land of Gilead*, and Leon Pinsker's *Auto-Emancipation*, she abandoned her own skepticism concerning Jewish nationalism and became "one of the most devoted adherents to the new dogma." She embraced it as if it were a full-fledged religion, and in doing so she recognized that she was not alone:

> under my own eyes I have seen equally rapid and thorough conversions to the same doctrine. In the minds of mature and thoughtful men, men of prudence and of earnest purpose, little apt to be swayed by the chance enthusiasm of a popular agitation, it has taken profound root, and in some cases overturned the theories and intellectual habits of a life-time.[43]

With her untimely death of Hodgkin's disease at thirty-eight, Lazarus became something of a saint to Jews caught up in the late nineteenth-century awakening. A special issue of the *American Hebrew* memorialized her, with tributes "from the foremost literati of the age," and her *Epistle to the Hebrews*, published in pamphlet form in 1900, was kept in print for many years by the Federation of American Zionists. Even as her memory was kept alive, however, her death came as a blow to the movement for Jewish renewal. It deprived it of its first truly significant convert, its most inspiring and cosmopolitan intellectual figure, and its foremost advocate (to that time) of what would shortly become known as American Zionism — the other great movement (along with Conservative Judaism) that the late nineteenth-century American Jewish Awakening did so much to spawn.[44]

Yet another dimension of the effervescence of late nineteenth-century American Jewish religious life is suggested by the career of Ray Frank, known in her day as the "girl rabbi" and the "female messiah." While not of long-lasting significance, her brief stint as a charismatic woman Jewish revivalist demonstrates that the late nineteenth-century American Jewish crisis of expectations and faith was not confined to the East Coast, restricted to intellectual circles, or exclusively the preserve of traditionalists and proto-Zionists. It was, instead, a complex nationwide phenomenon that affected a wide range of Jews, men and women, in sometimes unpredictable ways.

Ray (Rachel) Frank (1861–1948),[45] born in San Francisco, was a schoolteacher, writer, and lecturer. Critical of the Judaism of her day, she published in 1890 a stinging critique of the American rabbinate in response to a New York Jewish newspaper's call for articles on the question "What would you do if you were a rabbi?" What she "would *not* do," she emphasized, was emulate the many abuses she considered characteristic of the pompously materialistic American rabbinate. She called on rabbis to don "the spiritual mantle of Elijah" and implied that women ("were the high office not denied us") might do the job better.[46] Shortly after this article appeared, Ray Frank achieved momentary fame when she traveled to Spokane, Washington, and became "the one Jewish woman in the world, may be the first since the time of the prophets" to preach from a synagogue pulpit on the Jewish high holidays.[47] According to the story widely reported in her day and subsequently preserved by her husband:

> It happened to be on the eve of the High Holy Days and she made inquiries concerning the location of the synagogue as she wanted to attend services. When informed that there was no synagogue and there would be no services, she called on one of the wealthy Jews in town, to whom she had letters of introduction, and expressed surprise that a town containing many well-to-do Jews should be without a place of worship. The man, who knew Ray Frank by reputation, said, "If you will deliver a sermon we shall have services tonight." Ray acquiesced. At about five o'clock on that day special editions of *Spokane Falls Gazette* appeared on the streets announcing that a young lady would preach to the Jews that evening at the Opera House. The place was crowded. After the services were read, Ray spoke on the obligations of a Jew as a Jew and a citizen. In an impassioned appeal she asked her coreligionists to drop their dissensions with regard to ceremonials and join hands in a glorious cause, that of praying to the God of their fathers. She emphasized the fact that they shirked their duty if they did not form a permanent congregation and that by being without a place of worship and all that it stands for they were doing an incalculable harm to their children. After Ray finished her sermon, a "Christian gentleman" who was in the audience arose and said that he had been very much impressed by what he heard and if the Jews would undertake the building of a synagogue, he would present them with a site to be used for that purpose.[48]

Throughout the 1890s Ray Frank delivered sermons and lectures, mostly in the West, and published articles extolling the virtues of Judaism, the Jewish family, and Jewish women. According to the memoir published by her husband after her death, people "flocked to listen" as she talked on "Heart Throbs of Israel," "Moses," "Music and Its Revelations," "Nature as a Supreme Teacher," and related topics.[49] In these lectures, she attacked divisions in Jewish life, called for peace in the pulpit, and promoted spirituality, simplicity, earnestness, and righteousness: "Give us congregational singing which comes direct from the heart and ascends as a tribute to God. . . . Give us simplicity in our rabbi, sympathy with things which practically concern us, give us earnestness, and our synagogues will no longer mourn in their loneliness."[50] On one occasion she disclosed a mystical vision, a call from God in which she was cast in the role of Moses. ("I know I hold in my hand the staff of Moses. I kneel and raise my hands in adoration of the Eternal. I pray that all knowledge be mine. . . . I go down. I will tell all I know to the world. . . . I must wherever and whenever I can preach my message.")[51] For the most part, however, hers was a conservative message. She opposed women's suffrage, spoke of motherhood as the culmination of womanhood, and reminded women "how all-important the home and the family are."[52]

Much like a Protestant revivalist, Frank was described by those who heard her as a spellbinding preacher whose enthusiasm proved infectious. "Before she had finished," the *San Francisco Chronicle* wrote of one of her lectures, "her words were dropping like sparks into the souls of aroused people before her."[53] So well known had she become that at the Jewish Women's Congress, held in Chicago in 1893, she was invited to deliver the opening prayer. Four years later, in 1897, seven thousand people reportedly turned out to hear her at the adult education Chautauqua at Gladstone Park in Portland, Oregon, on what was billed as "Ray Frank Day."[54]

In 1898, Ray Frank traveled to Europe where she met and married an economist named Simon Litman. Her marriage and sojourn abroad (the couple did not return until 1902) effectively ended her public career.[55] The success that she demonstrated during her years on the lecture circuit, however, suggests that her message struck a meaningful chord.[56] On the one hand she spoke to the spiritual concerns and traditional values of American Jews of her day; on the other hand, simply by virtue of her sex, she challenged Jews' religious and gender-based assumptions. In evoking, simultaneously, both new and old, she embodied, but in no way resolved, the cultural contradictions that underlay the religious ferment to which she herself contributed.

In raising the issue of women's role both in American society and in Judaism, Ray Frank had pointed to one of the central concerns of the late nineteenth-century American Jewish Awakening. In response to the manifold crises of the day, particularly assimilation and immigration, responsibility for "saving Judaism" came increasingly to rest upon the shoulders of women. Just as in Protestantism so too in Judaism, religion had become "feminized." The home, the synagogue, and philanthropic social work came increasingly to be seen as part of women's domain, especially among Reform Jews. As a result, women became significant players in the campaign to revitalize Judaism to meet the needs of a new era.[57]

The National Council of Jewish Women, established in 1893, was the first national Jewish organization to take up this challenge. Created at the Jewish Women's Congress of the Columbian Exposition, its original goals explicitly addressed the responsibilities of Jewish women to strengthen Jewish life:

Resolved, that the National Council of Jewish Women shall (1) seek to unite in closer relation women interested in the work of Religion, Philanthropy and Education and shall consider practical means of solving problems in these fields; shall (2) organize and encourage the study of the underlying principles of Judaism; the history, literature and customs of the Jews, and their bearing on their own and the world's history; shall (3) apply knowledge gained in this study to the improvement of the Sabbath schools, and in the work of social reform; shall (4) secure the interest and aid of influential persons in arousing general sentiment against religious persecutions, wherever, whenever and against whomever shown, and in finding means to prevent such persecutions.[58]

Faith Rogow, in her recent history of the council, points out that "no one believed more strongly in woman's ability to save Judaism than did Council women themselves." Motherhood, the primacy of the home, the extension of motherhood into the synagogue — these were the values and goals that council members proudly espoused. Indeed, "motherhood and its presumed opportunity to influence husbands and children" was touted "as the only possible savior of Jewish life in America."[59]

Through "sisterhoods of personal service," Jewish women extended the sphere of "motherhood" into new realms aimed at combating the social crisis within the Jewish community as a whole. Initiated at Temple Emanu-El of New York in 1887, sisterhoods offered Jewish women the opportunity to emulate, from within a synagogue setting, the same kind of philanthropically directed urban missionary work performed by New York's Protestant and Catholic women, as well as the women of the Ethical Culture Society. Outdoor relief, home visits, religious schooling, industrial and domestic education, day nurseries, kindergartens, employment bureaus — these and related efforts devoted "to the care of the needy and the distressed" harnessed the energies of Jewish women in ways that synagogues never had before. By 1896 practically every major uptown synagogue in New York had established a sisterhood, and in 1896 a Federation of Sisterhoods was established, in cooperation with the United Hebrew Charities. What distinguished these efforts from their more secular counterparts was their religious character. Indeed, Rabbi David de Sola Pool, recounting the activities undertaken by the Orthodox sisterhood established in 1896 at the venerable Shearith Israel Synagogue in New York, stressed its role in "the loyal conservation and transmission of Jewish religious values." Increasingly, in response to the perceived crisis of the day, women were fulfilling new roles within the Jewish community, expanding on those that they had formerly carried out almost exclusively within the home.[60]

All of these new themes — the cultural and educational work of young Jews in Philadelphia and New York, the Zionism of Emma Lazarus, the spirituality of Ray Frank, salvation through motherhood as preached by the National Council of Jewish Women, and the charity work of the Sisterhoods of Personal Service — eventually came together in what became, after the period studied here, the largest and strongest of the Jewish women's organizations created to revitalize American Jewish life: Hadassah, the Women's Zionist Organization of America. Henrietta Szold (1860–1945), who played the dominant role in the establishment of Hadassah in 1912, had been involved in the work of Jewish renewal since she was a teenager, first as an essayist and educator, later as secretary of the publication committee (editor) of the Jewish Publication Society, and still later, in addition to her other work, as a leader of the Federation of American Zionists. She served as a role model to her peers and was respected as one of the most learned and accomplished Jewish women of her day.[61] Now, in the wake of her first visit to Palestine (1909), she and a few like-minded Zionist women activists in the New York area met to form a new women's Zionist organization that, at Szold's insistence, would have both a general and a highly specific purpose: "In America, to foster Jewish ideals and make Zionist propaganda; in Palestine, to establish a system of District Visiting Nursing."[62] In many ways, the new organization did for Jewish women what foreign missions did for Protestant women: it provided them with an opportunity to participate in the "holy work" of "salvation through social, medical and educational agencies."[63] As the historian of Hadassah's early years explains, Henrietta Szold firmly believed that women, unlike men, were interested in "specific practical projects of immediate emotional appeal to their maternal and Jewish religious instincts." Szold was convinced, therefore, that "we [American Jewish women] need Zionism as much as those Jews do who need a physical home." By working to strengthen Jewish life in the land of Israel, she hoped, women's own Judaism, and American Judaism generally, would be strengthened and renewed.[64]

Reform Judaism, which by the last quarter of the nineteenth century had become firmly established in the United States, maintained an uneasy relationship with all of these proponents of Jewish renewal. This was understandable: For half a century, young progressive American Jews had marched under the Reform banner and had viewed its program as the wave of the future, the only viable direction for Judaism in the New World to follow. Led by Rabbi Isaac Mayer Wise, many Reform Jews had triumphalistically believed that their brand of Judaism would in time become *Minhag Amerika*, the rite practiced by American Jews as a whole. Now, unexpectedly, Reform Jewish leaders found this and other long-cherished assumptions of theirs called into question. Indeed, some critics argued that Reform, far from being the solution to the crisis facing American Jews, was actually part of the problem. Discounting those who had never considered Reform Judaism legitimate and favored the moderate traditionalism championed in earlier decades by Isaac Leeser,[65] Reform still found itself on the defensive. Shaken by the same crisis of confidence that transformed so much of American Jewish life during this period, it struggled to redefine itself.

The 1885 Pittsburgh Rabbinical Conference, called by Rabbi Kaufmann Kohler "for the purpose of discussing the present state of American Judaism, its pending issues and its requirements," was Reform's most significant attempt to respond to the new situation in which it found itself. Its objective was clearly stated: to unite the Reform rabbinate around "such plans and practical measures as seen demanded by the hour." Michael A. Meyer explains in his history of the Reform movement that the gathering was actually an attempt "to lay down a set of defining and definitive principles which would distinguish Reform Judaism from a wholly nonsectarian universalism on the one hand and from more traditional expressions of Judaism on the other." Under attack both from the left and from the right, the rabbis who came to Pittsburgh now sought to focus Reform Judaism on a platform bold enough and inspiring enough to, as Kohler put it, "rally our forces," "consolidate," and "build." [66]

The well-known eight-point "Pittsburgh Platform" produced by the conference succeeded in its task. It was, in Isaac Mayer Wise's famous words, a "Declaration of Independence." It defined more clearly than ever before the Reform Jewish understanding of Judaism, and it laid down the gauntlet to those who understood Judaism differently. Even, however, as the Platform distanced Reform from "Conservative Judaism" (which Kohler did not apparently distinguish from Orthodoxy),[67] the conference as a whole did address many of the same themes that animated those young people and others who, as we have seen, were self-consciously caught up in the movement for American Jewish renewal. Kohler, for example, called for greater "help and participation" by women in Jewish religious life. He also spoke out on behalf of a publication society and a periodical press to "foster Jewish life, awaken Jewish sentiment and train the Jewish minds and hearts." Criticizing his Reform colleagues for "leaving the home unprovided," he called for a revitalization of Jewish home life, including the renewed observance of Chanukah and major Jewish festivals. In addition, he and others at the conference called for educational reforms to counter the "appalling ignorance . . . which seems to constantly grow from year to year." [68]

In short, even as the Pittsburgh Platform reaffirmed Reform Judaism's opposition to Jewish nationalism ("We consider ourselves no longer a nation, but a religious community, and therefore expect neither a return to Palestine . . . nor the restoration of any of the laws concerning the Jewish state") and reiterated its abrogation of those ceremonial laws "not adapted to the views and habits of modern civilization," Reform Jewish leaders did participate wholeheartedly in other efforts to revitalize Jewish life at the end of the nineteenth century. Educational and cultural programs, measures to revitalize Jewish home life, expanded roles for women, and enhanced spirituality in worship all loomed large on the new Reform Jewish agenda. In addition, the movement participated in a general return to Jewish forms, characterized not only by a revival of certain Jewish ceremonies, like Chanukah and the synagogue celebration of Sukkot, but also by a return to distinctive Jewish terminology, such as greater use of the word "Jew" as opposed to "Hebrew" and "Israelite," and the almost complete abandonment by World War I of such once commonly used terms, borrowed from Protestantism, as the Jewish "church," the Jewish "minister," and the Jewish "Easter." [69]

Most important of all, Reform Judaism in this period offered those disaffected with synagogue life a new alternative means of actively expressing their faith.[70] Following the lead of Rabbi Emil G. Hirsch of Chicago, it called upon Jews, in the words of the Pittsburgh Platform, to help "solve, on the basis of justice and righteousness, the problems presented by the contrasts and evils of the present organization of society." [71] This social justice motif — the Jewish equivalent of the Protestant Social Gospel — became ever more influential within Reform circles over the ensuing decades and provided an alternative road back to Judaism for those whose interests focused less on faith than on religiously inspired work. [72]

The late nineteenth-century American Jewish Awakening outlined here was thus a broad-based and multifaceted movement of religious renewal, parallel to the awakening taking place at the same time within American Protestantism. Of course, many Jews remained unaffected — such is always the case with movements of religious revitalization. Those who did fall under its spell, however, included traditionalists and reformers, women as well as men, and Jews living in all regions of the country. There was no clear focus to this movement, no central leader, and no listing of agreed-upon principles. What did unite the various participants was a shared sense of cultural crisis and personal stress, a palpable loss of faith in the norms, institutions, authorities, and goals of an earlier era, and an optimistic belief, particularly on the part of young people, that through their personal efforts American Judaism as a whole could be saved.

As a consequence of the awakening, a massive long-term paradigm shift took place within the American Jewish community: a shift over time toward greater particularism as opposed to the earlier universalism, toward a heightened sense of Jewish peoplehood as opposed to the former stress on Judaism as a faith, toward a new emphasis on the spiritual and emotional aspects of Judaism as opposed to the former emphasis on rationalism, and toward the goal of a Jewish homeland as opposed to the diaspora-glorifying ideology of mission that was formerly predominant. The transformation of women's roles, the revival of Chanukah and other Jewish ceremonies, the shift back to traditional Jewish terminology, the new emphasis on Jewish education and culture, the rise of the Conservative movement, the Zionist movement, the Social Justice movement, and, of course, many individual "conversions" of assimilated Jews back to their faith — all testify to the magnitude of the transformation that ultimately took place. Meanwhile, massive East European Jewish immigration heightened the sense of urgency that underlay the work of revival and resulted in parallel efforts to revitalize the Judaism of the ghetto. [73] The result, only discernible in retrospect, was a new American Judaism — the Judaism of the twentieth century. [74]

Notes

1. Leon Jick, *The Americanization of the Synagogue, 1820–1870* (Hanover, N.H.: University Press of New England, 1976), 193.

2. *American Hebrew*, Apr. 7, 1911, p. 667; on Schindler, see Arthur Mann, ed., *Growth and Achievement: Temple Israel, 1854–1954* (Boston: Congregation Adath Israel, 1954), 45–62; Arthur Mann, *Yankee Reformers in the Urban Age: Social Reform in Boston 1880–1900* (New York: Harper Torchbooks, 1954), 52–72.

3. Nathan Glazer, *American Judaism* (Chicago: University of Chicago Press, 1972), 53, 60 (quoted); Henry Feingold, *Zion in America* (New York: Hippocrene Books, 1974), 112.

4. *Jewish Advance*, Dec. 12, 1879, p. 4.

5. Max Cohen to Solomon Solis-Cohen, Nov. 10, 1879, Solomon Solis-Cohen Archives, Collection of Helen Solis-Cohen Sax and Hays Solis-Cohen Jr., Philadelphia; Philip Cowen, *Memories of an American Jew* (New York: International Press, 1932), 50.

6. See Jonathan D. Sarna, "The Making of an American Jewish Culture," in *When Philadelphia Was the Capital of Jewish America*, ed. Murray Friedman (Philadelphia: Balch Institute Press, 1993), 148–50.

7. Benjamin Rabinowitz, *The Young Men's Hebrew Associations (1854–1913)* (New York: National Jewish Welfare Board, 1948) [largely reprinted from *Publications of the American Jewish Historical Society* 37 (1947)]; Jonathan D. Sarna, *JPS: The Americanization of Jewish Culture* (Philadelphia: Jewish Publication Society, 1989), 15–16.

8. Sarna, *JPS*, 13–27; Nathan M. Kaganoff, "AJHS at 90: Reflections on the History of the Oldest Ethnic Historical Society in America," *American Jewish History* 71 (June 1982): 466–85; Mitchell E. Panzer, "Gratz College: A Community's Involvement in Jewish Education," in *Gratz College Anniversary Volume*, ed. Isidore D. Passow and Samuel T. Lachs (Philadelphia: Gratz College, 1971), 1–9; Peggy K. Pearstein, "Understanding Through Education: One Hundred Years of the Jewish Chautauqua Society 1893–1993" (Ph.D. diss., George Washington University, 1993), 1–68; Faith Rogow, *Gone to Another Meeting: The National Council of Jewish Women, 1893–1993* (Tuscaloosa: University of Alabama Press, 1993), 9–85; Shuly Rubin Schwartz, *The Emergence of Jewish Scholarship in America: The Publication of the Jewish Encyclopedia* (Cincinnati: Hebrew Union College Press, 1991), 1–36.

9. *Jewish Chronicle* (London), Mar. 11, 1887, p. 13; *American Hebrew*, Nov. 9, 1894, p. 22; Dec. 14, 1894, p. 181; *American Jewish Year Book* 3 (1901–2): 216; 6 (1904–5): 388; see also "What Renascence Means," *Maccabean* 4 (May 1903): 288.

10. Evyatar Friesel comes closest to the mark in his "The Age of Optimism in American Judaism, 1900–1920," in *A Bicentennial Festschrift for Jacob Rader Marcus*, ed. Bertram W. Korn (New York: Ktav, 1976), 131–55, but he sees the idea of "optimism" as the motivating force behind developments in this period, while to my mind this optimism is not a cause but a result.

11. For a review of recent research, see Steven M. Cohen, *American Assimilation or Jewish Revival* (Bloomington: Indiana University Press, 1988), 43–57. Cohen properly observes (43) that "generational change has long occupied a central place in research on Jewish identification in the United States." I have critiqued "generational determinism" in American Jewish historical writing elsewhere; see *Modern Judaism* 10 (Oct. 1990): 353; and *Judaism* 34 (Spring 1985): 246–47.

12. Glazer, writing in 1957, titled his final chapter in *American Judaism*, covering the period 1945–1956, "The Jewish Revival." For more recent developments see, for example, M. Herbert Danzger, *Returning to Tradition: The Contemporary Revival of Orthodox Judaism* (New Haven, Conn.: Yale University Press, 1989).

13. Compare William G. McLoughlin, *Revivals, Awakenings, and Reform* (Chicago: University of Chicago Press, 1978), 2: "Until the present generation . . . periods of cultural readjustment have been associated almost wholly with the Protestant churches."

14. William G. McLoughlin, "Timepieces and Butterflies. A Note on the Great Awakening-Construct and Its Critics, " *Sociological Analysis* 44 (1983): 108; the entire "Symposium on Religious Awakenings," with articles by R.C. Gordon-McCutchan, Timothy Smith, William McLoughlin, John Hammond, and John Wilson may be found in *Sociological Analysis* 44 (1983): 81–122. See also the follow-up by Michael Barkun, "The

Awakening-Cycle Controversy," *Sociological Analysis* 46 (1985): 425–43. The essays that sparked this controversy include McLoughlin, *Revivals, Awakenings, and Reform*; and Jon Butler, "Enthusiasm Described and Decried: The Great Awakening as Interpretive Fiction," *Journal of American History* 69 (1982): 305–25. For a parallel analysis to McLoughlin's that I have found helpful, see Vytautas Kavolis, *History on Art's Side: Social Dynamics in Artistic Efflorescences* (Ithaca, N.Y.: Cornell University Press, 1972).

15. McLoughlin, *Revivals, Awakenings, and Reform*, xiii.

16. Isidor Kalisch, "Ancient and Modern Judaism," in *Studies in Ancient and Modern Judaism*, ed. Samuel Kalisch (New York: George Dobsevage, 1928), 61. For a statistical picture of Jews in this period, see *Statistics of the Jews of the United States* (Philadelphia: Union of American Hebrew Congregations, 1880). See also Benny Kraut, "Judaism Triumphant: Isaac Mayer Wise on Unitarianism and Liberal Christianity," *AJS Review* 7–8 (1982–83): 179–230.

17. Naomi W. Cohen, "American Jewish Reactions to Anti-Semitism in Western Europe, 1875–1900," *Proceedings of the American Academy of Jewish Research* 45 (1978): 29–65 (quote p. 31); Michael A. Meyer, "German-Jewish Identity in Nineteenth-Century America," in *Toward Modernity: The European Jewish Model*, ed. Jacob Katz (New Brunswick, N.J.: Transaction Books, 1987), 247–67; idem, "The Great Debate on Antisemitism: Jewish Reactions to New Hostility in Germany, 1879–1881," *Leo Baeck Institute Year Book* 11 (1966): 137–70; Hans L. Trefousse, "The German-American Immigrants and the Newly Founded Reich," in *America and the Germans: An Assessment of a Three-Hundred-Year History*, ed. Frank Tommler and Joseph McVeigh (Philadelphia: University of Pennsylvania Press, 1985), 160–75.

18. Leonard Dinnerstein, *Anti-Semitism in America* (New York: Oxford University Press, 1994), 39–41; Stephen Birmingham, *Our Crowd* (New York: Dell, 1967), 169–80; *Coney Island and the Jews* (New York: G.W. Carleton and Company, 1879).

19. Hermann Baar, *Addresses on Homely and Religious Subjects Delivered Before the Children of the Hebrew Orphan Asylum* (New York: H.O.A. Industrial School, 1880), 238.

20. *American Hebrew*, Dec. 10, 1897, p. 163. For developments in this period see Naomi W. Cohen, "Anti-Semitism in the Gilded Age: The Jewish View," *Jewish Social Studies* 41 (1979): 187–210; and John Higham, *Send These To Me* (New York: Atheneum, 1975), 116–95.

21. Paul A. Carter, *The Spiritual Crisis of the Gilded Age* (Dekalb: University of Illinois Press, 1971); Naomi W. Cohen, "The Challenges of Darwinism and Biblical Criticism to American Judaism," *Modern Judaism* 4 (May 1984): 121–57; Kraut, "Judaism Triumphant," 202–25; Benny Kraut, "The Ambivalent Relations of American Reform Judaism with Unitarianism in the Last Third of the Nineteenth Century," *Journal of Ecumenical Studies* 23 (Winter 1986): 58–68.

22. David Stern to Bernhard Felsenthal, Apr. 24, 1884, Felsenthal Papers, American Jewish Historical Society (AJHS).

23. *American Israelite* (May 1881) as quoted in Dena Wilansky, *Sinai to Cincinnati* (New York: Renaissance Book Company, 1937), 101. Although not noticed by recent biographers, a contemporary, Henry Iliowizi, believed that a "remarkable change" came over Wise in the 1880s and he became more conservative. See Henry Iliowizi, *Through Morocco to Minnesota: Sketches of Life in Three Continents* (n.p., 1888), 87.

24. The leadership role played by Philadelphia Jews during this critical period in American Jewish history was first pointed to by Maxwell Whiteman, "The Philadelphia Group," in *Jewish Life in Philadelphia, 1830–1940*, ed. Murray Friedman (Philadelphia:

ISHI Publications, 1983), 163–78, and is further analyzed in Friedman, *When Philadelphia Was the Capital of Jewish America.*

25. David G. Dalin, "The Patriarch: The Life and Legacy of Mayer Sulzberger," in Friedman, *When Philadelphia Was the Capital of Jewish America*, 58–74; Philip Rosen, "Dr. Solomon Solis-Cohen and the Philadelphia Group," in Friedman, *When Philadelphia Was the Capital of Jewish America*, 106–25; Sarna, "Making of an American Jewish Culture," 145–55; Jonathan D. Sarna, "Is Judaism Compatible with American Civil Religion? The Problem of Christmas and the 'National Faith,'" in *Religion and the Life of the Nation: American Recoveries*, ed. Rowland A. Sherrill (Urbana: University of Illinois Press, 1990), 162–63; Sarna, *JPS*, 14–15. The quote is contained in a letter from Max Cohen to Solomon Solis-Cohen, Dec. 22, 1879, Solomon Solis-Cohen Papers, National Museum of American Jewish History, Philadelphia. I am grateful to Helen Solis-Cohen Sax, Solomon Solis-Cohen's granddaughter, for permitting me access to these papers.

26. Max Cohen to Solomon Solis-Cohen, Oct. 14, 1879; Max Cohen to Solomon Solis-Cohen, Nov. 10, 1879, Solomon Solis-Cohen Papers.

27. Cyrus L. Sulzberger to Solomon Solis-Cohen, Oct. 5, 1880, Solomon Solis-Cohen Papers. The letter is signed with Cyrus's Hebrew name, "Yitzhak Aryeh."

28. *American Hebrew*, Nov. 21, 1879, p. 3, reprinted in Cowen, *Memories of an American Jew*, 55; see also p. 49 of Cowen, and Max Cohen to Solomon Solis-Cohen, Nov. 10, 1879, Solis-Cohen Papers.

29. Cowen, *Memories of an American Jew*, 40–111, esp. pp. 42, 50; Charles Wyszkowski, *A Community in Conflict: American Jewry During the Great European Immigration* (New York: University Press of America, 1991), xiii-xvii.

30. *American Hebrew*, Nov. 21, 1879, 4, as quoted in Wyszkowski, *Community in Conflict*, 101; Max Cohen, "Some Memories of Alexander Kohut," in *The Ethics of the Fathers*, by Alexander Kohut, edited and revised by Barnett A. Elzas (New York: privately printed, 1920), xcviii.

31. For a somewhat different analysis of the relationship between the "Historical School" and Conservative Judaism, see Moshe Davis, *The Emergence of Conservative Judaism: The Historical School in Nineteenth Century America* (Philadelphia: Jewish Publication Society, 1965), 169–70.

32. Donald G. Mathews, "The Second Great Awakening as an Organizing Process," *American Quarterly* 21 (1969): 23–43. Some measure of the organizational revolution within the American Jewish community of that time may be discerned from the fact that fully thirteen of the nineteen national Jewish organizations listed in the first volume of the *American Jewish Year Book* (1899) had been founded after 1879.

33. Naomi W. Cohen, introduction to *Cyrus Adler: Selected Letters*, ed. Ira Robinson (Philadelphia: Jewish Publication Society, 1985), 1:xxx.

34. Cf. Sarna, *JPS*, 13–20, and "Making of an American Jewish Culture," 149–50, where portions of this argument first appeared.

35. On this point, see Sarna, "Making of an American Jewish Culture," 151.

36. Dianne Ashton, "Rebecca Gratz and the Domestication of American Judaism" (Ph.D. diss., Temple University, 1986); Evelyn Bodek, "'Making Do': Jewish Women and Philanthropy," in Friedman, *Jewish Life in Philadelphia*, 143–62.

37. Panzer, "Gratz College," 1–6. According to Panzer's footnote, three of the college's first four graduates were women (6 n. 12).

38. Jonathan D. Sarna, "The Debate over Mixed Seating in the American Synagogue," in *The American Synagogue: A Sanctuary Transformed*, ed. Jack Wertheimer (New York: Cambridge University Press, 1987), 366–79.

39. John Higham, "The Transformation of the Statue of Liberty," *Send These to Me: Immigrants in Urban America* (Baltimore: Johns Hopkins University Press, 1984), 71–80.

40. A large literature seeks to explain Lazarus's "conversion"; for an analysis of this literature see Joe Rooks Rapport, "The Lazarus Sisters: A Family Portrait" (Ph.D. diss., Washington University, 1988), 12–108. Quotes are from the centennial edition of Emma Lazarus, *An Epistle to the Hebrews,* with an introduction and notes by Morris U. Schappes (New York: Jewish Historical Society of New York, 1987), 64, 73.

41. Emma Lazarus, *Selections from her Poetry and Prose,* ed. Morris U. Schappes (New York: Emma Lazarus Federation of Jewish Women's Clubs, 1978), 35–37.

42. Lazarus, *Epistle to the Hebrews,* 8.

43. Ibid., 34–35, 80; Arthur Zieger, "Emma Lazarus and Pre-Herzlian Zionism," in *Early History of Zionism in America,* ed., I.S. Meyer (New York: American Jewish Historical Society, 1958), 77–108. Emma's older sister, Josephine Lazarus (1846–1910), also came to adopt Zionism as her religion, although she also sought a universal religion and dabbled with Unitarianism. Her *The Spirit of Judaism* (New York: Dodd, Mead, 1895) documents in part American Judaism's spiritual crisis. For her Zionism, see Josephine Lazarus, "Zionism," *American Hebrew,* Dec. 10, 1897, pp. 198–204. No full-length study of Josephine Lazarus exists, but useful information can be found in Rapport, "Lazarus Sisters," 109–54.

44. Cowen, *Memories of an American Jew,* 344.

45. Ray Frank's year of birth is a matter of dispute. I follow Reva Clar and William M. Kramer, "The Girl Rabbi of the Golden West," *Western States Jewish History* 18 (Jan. 1986): 99, who used 1870 United States census records. The standard date, supplied by her husband (who expressed some uncertainty about it) is 1864 or 1865; see Simon Litman, *Ray Frank Litman: A Memoir* (New York: American Jewish Historical Society, 1957), 4. Faith Rogow in *Gone to Another Meeting,* 228, cites unnamed records dating her birth to April 10, 1866. Might she have sought to conceal her date of birth when she married her much younger husband, Simon Litman, who was born in 1873?

46. *Jewish Messenger,* May 23, 1990, reprinted in Jacob R. Marcus, *The American Jewish Woman: A Documentary History* (New York: Ktav, 1981), 380; see also Litman, *Ray Frank Litman,* 12–13. A month later she replied to a question from the *Jewish Times and Observer* on "What would you do if you were a *rebbitzen* [rabbi's wife]." Her reply is reprinted in Litman, *Ray Frank Litman,* 14.

47. Excerpts from her Yom Kippur sermon (1890), where this quote appears, may be found reprinted in Ellen M. Umansky and Dianne Ashton, *Four Centuries of Jewish Women's Spirituality: A Sourcebook* (Boston: Beacon, 1992), 128–29.

48. Litman, *Ray Frank Litman,* 8–9; see also Clar and Kramer, "Girl Rabbi of the Golden West," 104–5, 108.

49. Litman, *Ray Frank Litman,* 68.

50. Quoted in ibid., 15.

51. Ibid., 43–45.

52. Ibid., 55–57.

53. *San Francisco Chronicle,* Aug. 18, 1895, quoted in ibid., 50.

54. *Papers of the Jewish Women's Congress* (Philadelphia: Jewish Publication Society of America, 1894), 8, cf. 52–65; *Reform Advocate,* Aug. 7, 1897, p. 412 as cited in Clar and Kramer, "Girl Rabbi of the Golden West," 231.

55. For her subsequent career and her contributions to the founding of Hillel, see Litman, *Ray Frank Litman,* 143–202; and Winston U. Solberg, "The Early Years of the Jewish Presence at the University of Illinois," *Religion and American Culture* 2 (Summer 1992): 215–45.

56. Reva Clar and William M. Kramer, "Girl Rabbi of the Golden West," 345–51, discount Frank's religious motivations and credit her success to her agent, Samuel H. Friedlander, whom they believe both managed her affairs and kept her name before the press. It would seem more likely that Frank hired Friedlander as a consequence of her success. Only *after* she demonstrated that she had something to promote did it make sense for her to have a promoter. Even Clar and Kramer agree that she was a woman of "multiple and formidable talents."

57. Rogow, *Gone to Another Meeting*, 43–78; Karla Goldman, "The Ambivalence of Reform Judaism: Kaufmann Kohler and the Ideal Jewish Woman," *American Jewish History* 79 (Summer 1990): 477–99.

58. Rogow, *Gone to Another Meeting*, 23. Note that immigrant aid, later so important a part of the council's work, went unmentioned in this resolution.

59. Ibid., 53, 76.

60. No full-scale history of synagogue sisterhoods has yet appeared. I base this sketch on Jenna Weissman Joselit, "The Special Sphere of the Middle-Class American Jewish Woman: The Synagogue Sisterhood, 1890–1940," in Wertheimer, *American Synagogue*, esp. 208–10; Richard Gottheil, *The Life of Gustav Gottheil* (Williamsport, Pa.: Bayard Press, 1936), 179–81; Hannah B. Einstein, "Sisterhoods of Personal Service," *Jewish Encyclopedia* (New York: Wagnells, 1906), 11:398; and David de Sola Pool, *An Old Faith in the New World* (New York: Columbia University, 1955), 369–70. In response to the demand for professional social workers, sisterhoods later transformed their activities and forgot their origins, as Gottheil and Joselit indicate. For the development of the National Federation of Temple Sisterhoods (1913), see Michael A. Meyer, *Response to Modernity: A History of the Reform Movement in Judaism* (New York: Oxford University Press, 1988), 285–86.

61. The most recent full-length biography is Joan Dash, *Summoned to Jerusalem: The Life of Henrietta Szold* (New York: Harper and Row, 1979); for Szold's early life and work see Alexandra Lee Levin, *The Szolds of Lombard Street* (Philadelphia: Jewish Publication Society, 1960); and Sarna, *JPS*, 23–135.

62. *American Jewish Year Book* 16 (1914–15): 284.

63. William R. Hutchison, *Errand to the World: American Protestant Thought and Foreign Missions* (Chicago: University of Chicago Press, 1987), 111; cf. Patricia Hill, *The World Their Household* (Ann Arbor: University of Michigan Press, 1984).

64. Carol B. Kutscher, "Hadassah," in *Jewish American Voluntary Organizations*, ed. Michael N. Dobkowski (New York: Greenwood, 1986), 151–52; idem, "The Early Years of Hadassah, 1912–1922" (Ph.D. diss., Brandeis University, 1976); Henrietta Szold to Alice L. Seligsberg, Oct. 10, 1913, in Marvin Lowenthal, *Henrietta Szold: Life and Letters* (New York: Viking, 1942), 82.

65. On the anti-Reform animus of Mayer Sulzberger, Cyrus Adler, Moses Dropsie, and other Philadelphia Jewish leaders caught up in the spirit of religious renewal, see Sarna, "Making of an American Jewish Culture," 150–51.

66. "Authentic Report of the Proceedings of the Rabbinical Conference Held at Pittsburgh, Nov. 16, 17, 18, 1885," reprinted in Walter Jacob, ed., *The Changing World of Reform Judaism: The Pittsburgh Platform in Retrospect* (Pittsburgh: Rodef Shalom Congregation, 1985), 92–93; Meyer, *Response to Modernity*, 264 70; Jonathan D. Sarna, "New Light on the Pittsburgh Platform of 1885," *American Jewish History* 76 (Mar. 1987): 358–68.

67. Sarna, "New Light on the Pittsburgh Platform," 364; cf. Davis, *Emergence of Conservative Judaism*, 222–28.

68. "Authentic Report," 92–102, 109. The Platform is conveniently reprinted in Meyer, *Response to Modernity*, 387–88.

69. Meyer, *Response to Modernity*, 264–95, covers this period; for the movement away from "Hebrew" and "Israelite," see, inter alia, Kaufmann Kohler, "Arise and Give Light, or Judaism and the Jewish Pulpit," in *The American Jewish Pulpit: A Collection of Sermons* (Cincinnati: Bloch, 1881), 9; the diary of David Philipson, Sept. 11, 1890, in Box 3, David Philipson Papers, American Jewish Archives, Cincinnati; and Benjamin Rabinowitz, "The Young Men's Hebrew Association (1854–1913)," *Publications of the American Jewish Historical Society* 37 (1947): 302, 307. How Judaism in this period gradually ceased to be described in Christian terms and began to be described in its own terms requires a separate treatment.

70. Professor Ellen Umansky properly observes that by this time "many middle and upper middle class Jewish women had already come to identify social service as a spiritual path and didn't need the Reform movement" for this purpose. Instead, she suggests, what Reform Judaism may have done for many Jewish women is to validate as religious "activities in which they were already engaged." (Letter to the author, May 18, 1994; see also Umansky and Ashton, *Four Centuries of Jewish Women's Spirituality*, 15–17.)

71. "Authentic Report," 102, 109, 119–20.

72. On various aspects of the Social Justice movement and its relationship to the Social Gospel, see Egal Feldman, "The Social Gospel and the Jews," *American Jewish Historical Quarterly* 58 (Mar. 1969): 308–22; Leonard J. Mervis, "The Social Justice Movement and the American Reform Rabbi," *American Jewish Archives* 7 (1955): 171–230; Bernard Martin, "The Social Philosophy of Emil G. Hirsch," *American Jewish Archives* 6 (June 1954): 151–66; John F. Sutherland, "Rabbi Joseph Krauskopf of Philadelphia: The Urban Reformer Returns to the Land," *American Jewish History* 67 (June 1978): 342–62; and Jonathan D. Sarna, "Seating and the American Synagogue," in *Belief and Behavior: Essays in the New Religious History*, ed. Philip R. Vandermeer and Robert P. Swierenga (New Brunswick, N.J.: Rutgers University Press, 1991), esp. 195–202.

73. See, for example, Jeffrey Gurock's account of the Jewish Endeavor Society in Dobkowski, *Jewish-American Voluntary Organizations*, 228–31.

74. I am greatly indebted to Professors Ewa Morawska, Lance Sussman, and Ellen Umansky for their helpful and detailed comments on an earlier draft of this essay. Versions of this paper were delivered at Brown University, Brandeis University, and the Council on Initiatives for Jewish Education, and I have benefited from the suggestions made on all three occasions. Errors that remain, of course, are my own responsibility.

The Search for an American Catholicism, 1780–1820

JAY P. DOLAN

Ever since the late nineteenth century when John Gilmary Shea began to study the history of Catholics in the United States, historians of American Catholicism have shaped their understanding of the past according to specific interpretive paradigms. The first dominant model focused on the relationship between Catholics and Protestants and clearly evidenced the influence of the Counter Reformation era. This was a time when Catholics were very much on the defensive and the writing of history had become a form of apologetics. Rightly done it would prove that Roman Catholicism was the one true church. A major representative of this style of history was Peter Guilday (1884–1947), a professor of church history at Catholic University and the most prominent historian of American Catholicism in the first half of the twentieth century. In the Guilday era many historians of American Catholicism concentrated on the theme of anti-Catholicism and sought to show how Catholics were the victims of prejudice and discrimination throughout the course of American history. The publication of Ray Allen Billington's study, *The Protestant Crusade, 1800–1860: A Study of the Origins of American Nativism,* in 1938 was a powerful endorsement of this interpretive paradigm. Given this interpretive model, the Catholic strategy for survival was understood in terms of its struggle with the dominant Protestant culture. For this reason emphasis was placed on self-defense, on the part of both individuals and the institution; apologetics became the trademark of theology, and separatism the chosen posture in the American religious environment. Because of the dominance of the Counter Reform mentality and the power of this interpretive paradigm, all of American Catholic history was filtered through this lens. No other reading of the past seemed plausible.

The writing of American Catholic history began to change after World War II. The war had a decisive influence on the shaping of the American mind. "Indeed," as Philip Gleason wrote, "it would be difficult to exaggerate the importance of the war as the central event in shaping Americans' understanding of their national identity for the next generation."[1] Historians of American Catholicism now began to concentrate on the theme of Americanization, and it was not long before it became the second dominant interpretive paradigm. A key figure in this era was John Tracy Ellis (1905–1992). Ellis succeeded Guilday at Catholic University and became the best-known historian of American Catholicism in the postwar era. In much of his writing he stressed the compatibility of Catholicism and American culture and emphasized what a good job the church had done in Americanizing the immigrants. The debate over Americanism, a controversy in the late nineteenth century, became the focal point for numerous historical studies. Thomas McAvoy, another major interpreter of the American Catholic experience, published a major study of the Americanism episode in 1957, *The Great Crisis in American Catholic History, 1895–1900*, and this book encouraged other studies of Americanism. Biographies of such prelates as James Gibbons and John Ireland underscored in a very positive manner their endorsement of the Americanization concept. John Carroll, the first American bishop, was also portrayed in this manner, as a man comfortable with the American political revolution.

The emphasis on Americanization brought the issue of immigration to center stage, and many scholars began to study various immigrant groups. Philip Gleason, a student of McAvoy at Notre Dame, became a major interpreter of the Americanization theme. His numerous writings on this issue helped to confirm the position of this interpretive paradigm as "the grand theme" in American Catholic history. Anti-Catholicism was still noticeable in American society during this era, and historians did not completely ignore this dimension of the past, but the theme of Americanization replaced anti-Catholicism as the dominant interpretive paradigm. The election of John F. Kennedy as president of the United States in 1960 served to strengthen this view of the past. Kennedy became the symbol as well as the embodiment of the Americanization motif. The grandson of Irish Catholic immigrants, his election symbolized the arrival of Catholics in the United States and their national acceptance both as Catholics and Americans.

Just as changes in the nation shifted attention to the theme of national identity and Americanization, changes within Catholicism and within American society as well began to direct attention to the possibility of a "new theology," or a new understanding of Catholicism. This development began to take shape in the post–World War I period in Europe; it reached a high point in the 1950s as a new generation of scholars, mostly French and German, began to emerge. Their works, translated into English, became best-sellers among American Catholic intellectuals. The Second Vatican Council (1962–65) gave its stamp of approval to many of these ideas. The council also made it clear that the Counter Reformation era was coming to an end; at the Council church leaders were attempting to forge a new agenda that would not only renew the church but also establish a new relationship between Catholicism and the modern world. In the years that followed the Council new advances were made in many areas of Catholic thought; a whole new field of bible studies opened up; a new understanding of church law developed along with a new code of laws; the way Catholics worshiped changed dramatically; and a new history also evolved. The history of the people became more important than the history of institutions and the biographies of prelates. The emergence of social history reinforced this tendency as "religious history" replaced "church history." As historians of American Catholicism began to focus on the religion of the people, an entirely new understanding of the past emerged. Coupled with the emergence of a social history of religion was the widespread acceptance of the concept of historical consciousness or historical-mindedness in theology. The classicist worldview that it replaced emphasized permanence and the unchanging nature of theology whereas historical-mindedness stressed the historical nature of theology and its development over time. In this intellectual climate a renewed interest in the relationship between religion and culture has evolved.

What I would like to argue is that the emergence of a new "church history" and the emphasis on historical-mindedness has opened the door to a third interpretive paradigm for American Catholic history. This model focuses on religion and accepts the principle that religion is and was culturally conditioned; thus, the religion of Mexican immigrants has been shaped by their history in much the same manner that the religious world of Irish immigrants was shaped by their past. Even though they are both Catholic, their religious worlds are vastly different because their histories and cultures are so diverse. Another way of putting this is to say that the culture of the eighteenth century had a decisive influence on the shape of religion in that era, and the same would be true in other historical epochs. In other words, religion is not immune to cultural influence and indeed has been shaped by such forces throughout the ages.

This interpretive model is different from the Americanization paradigm insofar as it asks different questions of the past. The Americanization paradigm focuses on the issue of foreign-born immigrants becoming American. It is concerned with the ethnic identity of individuals and the process over time by which these individuals lose their foreign qualities and "adopt the cultural norms of American society, become fully integrated into American life, and come to think of themselves simply as Americans."[2] It is also concerned with the institutions that the immigrants established and how these institutions have changed over time in the process of adapting to American society.

The Americanization paradigm focuses on the struggle to maintain ethnic identity. Such issues as language retention in the schools, congregations, and other institutions are central to any study operating out of this paradigm. The culture wars that took place over these issues provide much of the drama in a history written from this perspective. For historians of American Catholicism such an interpretive theory makes a lot of sense given the immigrant nature of the community throughout the nineteenth century. The usefulness of this model carries over into the twentieth century as well since the immigrant quality of Catholicism in the United States remained fairly strong right up to the 1940s; the influx of new immigrants in the post-1965 period has kept this issue of American-ization very much in the forefront of discussion and study. Using the American-ization model, historians had a key to open up the past, and much of the histori-cal writing done in the post–World War II period has sought to explain various aspects of American Catholic history from this perspective. What I want to argue is that another interpretive model is available, one that will offer historians an additional interpretive lens through which to view the American Catholic past.

The questions this third interpretive model asks are different from those of the Americanization model. It focuses on the religion of Catholics and seeks to dis-cover their beliefs. How did they understand the concept of God? of sin? of church? How did they pray? What rituals shaped their beliefs? A second major aspect of this model will seek to discover how these beliefs shaped their lives. In all of this the influence of culture on religion is paramount as is the influence of religion on the way people lived.

It is clear to me that these two models or paradigms of interpretation are differ-ent. The religion and culture model is an extension or expansion of the Ameri-canization model. Though it is clearly concerned with the influence of American culture on Catholicism it has a different focus of concern. Its focus is not ethnic identity or ethnic persistence at the group or individual level. Rather its focus is the belief system of Catholics, their religion, and how this was affected by Ameri-can culture. Though in many respects they are related, the term "American" and the term "modern" are not the same, and I want to avoid the use of the term "modern" since it raises so many problems of definition. What I am concerned with is how American culture, the American way of life, has influenced the reli-gious beliefs of Catholics. It clearly is a question that is related to the larger issue of how modernity has shaped Catholicism, but I want to examine this issue in the American context and from a historical perspective.

Using William McLoughlin's idea of an awakening as "a period of fundamen-tal social and intellectual reorientation of the American belief-value system, be-havior patterns and institutional structure,"[3] I want to argue that for Catholics there were three such times of transition; they correspond to the democratic revo-lution of the late eighteenth and early nineteenth centuries, the transition that took place in the late nineteenth century, and the more recent changes in the post–World War II period. These would correspond to McLoughlin's second, third, and fourth great awakenings. In each of these cultural awakenings the be-lief system of Catholics underwent important changes. In this essay I would like to examine the first of these moments of transition and see how an age of Enlight-enment and democratic revolution affected the religion of Catholics.

In the past historians have viewed this era differently. Those who followed the first interpretive paradigm viewed this period as an era of good feelings when Protestants and Catholics got along together rather well. From the perspective of the Americanization paradigm this was a time when Catholics stressed the com-patibility between their religious traditions and the American culture. From the perspective of the religion and culture paradigm I would argue that the way

Catholics thought about their God and their church changed noticeably in this era. More than just compatibility was at issue. Influenced by the American cultural environment, Catholics began to change the way they expressed their beliefs and practiced their religion. What follows is an analysis of the republican era of American Catholicism that reflects this interpretive theory.

On the seventh day of September 1784 the ship, *America*, set sail from Dublin bound for Philadelphia. Hiding on board was a young man disguised "in female dress" who was fleeing Ireland and the likely prospect of "a heavy fine and imprisonment" because of his political activism against the British government. His name was Mathew Carey. After eight weeks of sailing the North Atlantic sea, the *America* finally arrived in Philadelphia on the first day of November. When Carey landed, he only had twelve guineas in his pocket and no friends or family to greet him.[4] Nonetheless, this twenty-four-year-old immigrant had ambition and intelligence, and these gifts would eventually propel him to the highest echelons of Philadelphia society. Indeed, his fame and influence reached beyond Philadelphia as he developed into the foremost publisher in the new nation. When he died in 1839, Carey's funeral was one of the largest that the people of Philadelphia had ever seen.

Carey was not the only Irish emigrant crossing the Atlantic in 1784. Emigration from Ireland was commonplace in the eighteenth century, and in 1784 close to 10,000 Irish men and women emigrated to the United States. By the time of the first national census in 1790 an estimated 400,000 people of Irish descent were living in the new nation. A major center for this immigrant community was Philadelphia, which had become "the center of Irish-American trade on the North American mainland" during the eighteenth century. The Irish merchant community played a leading role in Philadelphia commerce and helped to shape the identity of the Irish community. In fact, one of the first fraternal societies in North America was the Society of the Friendly Sons of St. Patrick, organized in 1771 by prominent Philadelphia Irish merchants. Since commerce closely linked Philadelphia and Ireland, news about Irish affairs was commonplace in the city's newspapers. In fact, the people of Philadelphia had read about the political activities of Mathew Carey in the local newspaper. Since he was somewhat known in the city, Carey decided to move to Philadelphia rather than New York or Baltimore. As he put it, his "case was known," in Philadelphia and he hoped that this "would probably make me friends there."[5]

Mathew Carey was representative of the educated Irish Catholic immigrant in the late eighteenth century. Born and raised in an upper-class home in Dublin, he was educated at a school run by a noted Jesuit educator. His parents were involved in the intellectual and cultural life of Dublin, and they encouraged Mathew's education. In such an environment Carey acquired a love for books that he nourished for the rest of his life. He also gained a taste for politics.

In the late 1770s and 1780s Dublin was a political beehive. Enlivened by the American Revolution and Enlightenment political thought, Irish politicians dreamed of an Ireland free from British control. The young Carey shared these dreams. A radical republican and an ardent patriot, he was highly critical of the English government, so critical in fact that his father shipped him off to Paris so that young Mathew could avoid arrest. A year in Paris did not dampen his radicalism. He returned to Dublin as republican as ever, and like many of his contemporaries he advocated a total reform of Ireland's parliamentary system. It was not long before his politics got him in trouble once again and he was sent to jail in the spring of 1784. In September the authorities were ready to jail him again. Such a prospect persuaded Carey that it was time to leave Ireland.

It did not take long for Carey to make his mark in Philadelphia. Within three months he published a newspaper; then he launched a magazine, the *American Museum*, that reached out to a national audience. In 1790 he published the first Catholic bible in the United States and ten years later a family edition of the King James Bible. A bookseller as well as a publisher, he developed his bookstore into one of the largest in the country. He also became one of the leading citizens of Philadelphia and worked on behalf of many charitable causes. In addition to all these activities Carey was heavily involved in the local Catholic community and became one of the most prominent Catholics in the United States. He was a trustee of his parish, a recognized leader of Philadelphia Catholicism, and a publisher and promoter of the Catholic bible as well as an apologist for Catholicism. In order to understand what Catholicism was like in these years it would be helpful to examine the religion of Mathew Carey.

A few years after his arrival in Philadelphia, Carey began to keep a diary. He wrote his first entry on January 1, 1787: "Began the new year with a solemn invocation of the divine being and a supplication to shield me from the manifold misfortunes that have hitherto pursued me." In referring to God as "the divine being" Mathew Carey was using the language of the eighteenth-century Enlightenment. When he wrote his autobiography, he prefaced it with a famous quote from the classical writer Terence: "Homo sum. Et humani a me nil alienum puto." [I am a man. And nothing human is alien from me.] This was Carey's motto, and he proudly wrote that it "animated me through life." Such attachment to the classical period, its writers, and their humanism was characteristic of the Enlightenment. In other places in his autobiography he quoted from such classical authors as Virgil and Horace and acknowledged that their wisdom inspired him throughout his life. While growing up in Dublin he had read widely in the literature of the French Enlightenment. His personal library included the works of Locke, Voltaire, Rousseau, and Montaigne as well as the humanists Fenelon and Erasmus.[6]

Another trait of the Enlightenment era was enthusiasm for learning, and Carey, the publisher, sought to promote learning in various ways. He published a magazine, the *American Museum*, with the hope that it would foster an American literature; he published the writings of American authors and disseminated these throughout Europe. In Philadelphia he was one of the founders of a Sunday School where poor children could receive instruction in reading, writing, and ethics.

Carey was a strong advocate of the "spirit of toleration," which he wrote, "distinguishes this enlightened age." When he was involved in founding free Sunday Schools, he urged that they avoid "Party, Religious Bigotry, intolerance and superstition."[7] Another characteristic of the age that shaped the mental world of Carey was a concern for moral values. Several times in his diary he reflected on his life, past and future. In these meditative pauses he confessed that he always wanted "to do good," an "overwhelming passion" in his life that, he wrote, "I cannot resist." He wrote that "I have never seen distress without commiseration," and he always sought to provide "relief, as far as my circumstances permit." Terence's dictum that "nothing human is alien from me" was Carey's life motto, and he quoted it often. His generosity was known throughout the city, and later in life, as a result of his kindness to the needy, he ran out of money and had to rely on his son for additional income. When he died, the newspaper described him as an "esteemed philanthropist" and noted that "the cry of the poor, the widow, and the orphan, was never in vain at his door."[8]

This passion to do good inspired Carey to become involved in many benevolent causes. In addition to being one of the founders of the Sunday School, he was a founder of the Philadelphia Society for Alleviating the Miseries in Public Prisons. He was also the guiding force behind the organization of the Hibernian Society for the Relief of Emigrants from Ireland, and he wrote its constitution. An inveterate pamphlet writer he wrote essays defending the poor and the need for public charity; one of his special concerns was poor working women.

In many respects Carey was no different from Benjamin Franklin and Benjamin Rush, two distinguished citizens of Philadelphia with whom he worked on various civic causes. Like Franklin, Rush, and many other individuals influenced by Enlightenment thought, he believed in the perfectibility of humankind, the moral need to reform society, and the value of voluntary organizations to attain this goal. But Enlightenment thought was not the only influence on Carey's mental world; Catholicism also shaped his thought and actions.

In his pamphlets he would quote, in addition to the classics, the Bible. Though he had a very republican view of authority, he upheld the rights of the clergy in the spiritual arena. As a trustee of St. Mary's parish, he was intensely involved in the trustee controversy that divided the parish in the 1820s. In one pamphlet that he wrote concerning this controversy he described what he believed were the basic beliefs of Roman Catholicism. His understanding centered on the sacraments of the church, especially penance and the eucharist, and he believed that if a Catholic did not make a confession and receive the eucharist within a year, he or she should be "debarred of divine service."[9]

An apologist for Catholicism in both Ireland and the United States, in 1826 Carey formed a society named "Vindicators of the Catholic Religion from Calumny and Abuse." Included in his plan to flood the United States with books was the publication of religious works for Catholics who "because of lack of books . . . are ignorant of their religion and some even embrace other religious persuasions whose books they read."[10] After reading the pamphlets that he wrote and often signed with the title, "A Catholic Layman," it becomes clear that he was well read in church history. In his diary he frequently mentions his attendance at Sunday Mass and occasionally comments on the sermons he heard. A strong advocate of education, he served as vice president of the Roman Catholic Sunday School Society in 1816 and 1817.

Mathew Carey was an exemplar of the Enlightenment Catholic of the late eighteenth and early nineteenth centuries. His religion had a strong personalist quality to it, together with a heavy dose of moralism. A humanist, he found inspiration in the classical writers, in what he called their "genuine Roman or Grecian spirit." [11] He also found nurture in the ritual and sacraments of Catholicism and respected the authority of the clergy. Like so many people of his time who sought "to adapt their belief in God to modern ideas," Carey integrated the doctrine of Catholicism with the demands of reason that were so central to Enlightenment thinking.[12] He was able to reconcile moralism and spirituality, faith and reason, nature and the supernatural. In this manner he integrated his religion with the culture of the age so that his Catholicism blended with the Enlightenment culture prevalent in the United States in those years. He was Catholic to the core, but a child of the Enlightenment as well.

Carey never suggested that there was any incompatibility between his Catholicism and his devotion to Enlightenment principles. At one moment he could praise the humanism and moralism of the classical writers; then in the next paragraph he could describe how he and his wife rode to church in their carriage. In his mental world the two realms were not repugnant. In some ways Carey's religious world was similar to that of his contemporary Benjamin Rush, who was "a fervent evangelical Christian" of the Calvinist school as well as an enthusiastic republican who supported Enlightenment causes.[13] In the 1780s and 1790s many people, like Rush and Carey, reconciled apparently incompatible doctrines such as faith and reason, nature and the supernatural, and felt comfortable in doing this. The end result was a new way of believing, an Enlightenment version of Christianity.

Carey's religious world was not unique. Catholicism had taken many shapes over the centuries, and in the late eighteenth century an Enlightenment style of Catholicism was fairly widespread. It attracted followers in England and Ireland as well as in Europe. In the United States it also had its representatives in people like Mathew Carey.

How representative of American Catholics was the religious world of Mathew Carey? That is a difficult question to answer. Everything suggests that he was very representative of the educated, upper class. The spirit of the Enlightenment permeated Philadelphia in the 1790s when it was the leading city in the nation. Henry May, who has written the most detailed study of the Enlightenment in America, concluded that the city's elite were "Enlightened in a thoroughly eighteenth-century manner." Carey certainly fit this description, and most likely so did many of the Catholic upper crust such as the city's Irish merchant class.[14]

Charles Carroll of Carrollton provides another example of how the culture of the Enlightenment shaped the Catholicism of the people. Carroll was the most distinguished and indeed the wealthiest Catholic in Maryland. Active in politics, he was a delegate from Maryland to the Continental Congress and was a signer of the Declaration of Independence. Like many children of the Maryland Catholic gentry Carroll was sent to Europe at a young age to acquire an education. He remained there for sixteen years and received the best education that money could buy. He studied with the Jesuits in France and afterwards studied law in London. He read the writings of Locke, Newton, and Montesquieu, and when he finally returned to his Maryland home in 1765, he was a product of an eighteenth-century Catholic Enlightenment education. Until his death in 1826 Carroll remained a devoted Catholic and an Enlightened aristocrat.

The correspondence between Charles and his father, Charles Carroll of Annapolis, clearly reveals a family shaped by the thought and culture of the eighteenth-century Enlightenment. In urging his son not to omit his daily prayers the father wrote that "Prayer does not Consist in a set form of Words; it is the Heart the Will the Attention & intention that accompanies them that carries them like a pure sacrifice to the Throne of the Almighty." In reply to his father's advice, Charley, the name his father gave him, revealed something of his own religious inclinations. "A good conscience & a virtuous life," he wrote, "are certainly the greatest blessings we can enjoy on earth. I dont aim nor never did at cannonization; I detest scrued up devotion, distorted faces, & grimace. I equally abhor those, who laugh at all devotion, look upon our religion as a fiction, & its holy misteries as the greatest absurdities." For Charley's father, faith and reason were the foundation blocks of his religion, and he saw no contradiction between Catholicism and the rationalism of the Enlightenment. As he noted in a letter to his son, "Whatever a man may grant, whatever Rules he may lay down, whatever Doctrines he may profess, if they be inconsistent with reason and Contrary to Morality, Justice, & Religion they are in themselves void & can have no ill Effect."

In addition to endorsing the reasonableness of religion, Charley also put a high value on toleration. He described himself as a "warm friend to Toleration" and disapproved of what he called "the intollerating spirit of the Church of Rome, and of other Churches." Reflecting on his signing of the Declaration of Independence, he said that he "had in view not only our independence of England but the toleration of all sects professing the Christian religion and communicating to them all equal rights." There is no question that he, like the rest of his family that went before him, had "an unwavering, though sorely tested, commitment to freedom of conscience." This was an integral part of the colonial Catholic tradition and certainly fit in with the spirit of toleration endorsed by the Enlightenment.[15]

Throughout his life Charles Carroll of Carrollton stressed the personal experience of religion, the reasonableness of religion, and the spirit of toleration. These were all characteristics of Enlightenment Christianity, and clearly he did not find such qualities incompatible with his Catholicism. Like Mathew Carey he was able to reconcile faith and reason, nature and the supernatural, moralism and the spiritual. Another example of this style of Catholicism can be found in the first bishop of Baltimore, John Carroll.

Like his cousin Charles Carroll, John Carroll was sent to Europe for his education. After studying with the Jesuits at St. Omer in Flanders he decided to enter the Jesuit order. He was ordained a priest in 1769. When the pope suppressed the Jesuit order in 1773, Carroll returned to Maryland to work as a missionary priest. Then in 1789 he was named the Bishop of Baltimore. From the 1780s until his death in 1815 Carroll was the leading Catholic churchman in the United States.

John Carroll was an eighteenth-century bishop. Educated during the age of the Enlightenment, he was especially influenced by the French humanist tradition and the English Catholic Enlightenment. Because he was a bishop he had an extensive correspondence, and fortunately this was preserved along with his numerous sermons and pastoral letters. This body of material clearly reveals the personality of an individual who came of age during the Enlightenment era.

John Carroll was a strong believer in religious toleration. He supported the American Revolution and believed that religion had "undergone a revolution, if possible, more extraordinary, than our political one." This religious revolution introduced a new spirit of toleration in the states, and "publick protection & encouragement," he wrote, "are extended alike to all denominations & R.C. are members of Congress, assemblies, & hold civil & military posts as well as others." Carroll viewed this new situation as "a blessing and advantage." In accepting the principle of religious toleration Carroll was endorsing the new American way of the separation between church and state. A key corollary of this was the primacy of reason and persuasion over coercion, which for so long had been the norm in Europe where church and state were closely tied together. As he put it in one of his sermons, "in matters of faith everything must be free & voluntary." [16]

Carroll spoke of an "enlightened faith." For him reason was an important element in the shaping of a person's religion. But it was not enough. Although Carroll emphasized the importance of reason and the value of persuasion, he also wanted to add the element of what he called "revelation," that is, grace or the supernatural. In this respect he was typical of many people in the Enlightenment era who had a positive view of human nature and saw the need to integrate it with the supernatural. Another integral part of Carroll's mental world was the Enlightenment language of "rights." He spoke about the "rights of conscience," "the common rights of nature," "the common rights of mankind." Using this language to speak of religious toleration, Carroll clearly considered toleration a natural right and not a political concession. [17]

As a citizen of the Enlightenment John Carroll was very involved in civic causes and joined with ministers and people of other religious traditions to promote the commonweal of Baltimore. Though he could not match Mathew Carey's reputation for philanthropy, Carroll was involved in benevolent enterprises. He had "a leading role in the founding of the Library Company of Baltimore in 1795, the Baltimore Female Humane Association, the first charity school of the city in 1798, the Maryland Society for Promoting Useful Knowledge in 1800, the Humane Impartial Society for the relief of indigent women and the Baltimore General Dispensary in 1802, and others." He also served as a trustee of Baltimore College and St. John's College in Annapolis. [18]

Carey and the Carrolls were not alone in their thinking. The writings of apologists of the English Catholic Enlightenment were well known and read in the United States, and the ideas of the French Enlightenment also circulated through the states. Moreover, John Carroll was a popular bishop, elected to the office by the clergy and widely revered by the people. It is hard to imagine that his views were completely out of step with the rest of the Catholic community.[19] Nonetheless, an equally revealing indicator of the religious worldview of Catholics at this time is the type of religion they practiced.

Joseph Chinnici argues rather persuasively for an Enlightenment Catholic piety during this era. The eighteenth century was a time when Baroque devotionalism was riding high. As Chinnici notes, this style of piety emphasized "relics, indulgences, pious practices and saints' lives" and accepted "a penitential system which stressed the sinfulness of the human condition."[20] The excesses of Baroque devotionalism led to its demise as the century progressed, setting the stage for the development of a different, more personal style of piety that was rooted in the Christian humanist tradition. A very telling indication of this shift away from the Baroque tradition was the design of the new Catholic cathedral in Baltimore, which was to be the premier church in the nation, the showcase of Catholicism.

When Bishop Carroll and the cathedral trustees sought an architect for the new church, they did not turn to Europe and the Baroque tradition of the eighteenth century. They looked to the nation's capital, but a few miles away, and chose the architect of the capitol building, Benjamin Latrobe, as the person to design the cathedral. Wanting something that would fit in with the times, they selected the nation's premier architect to design and build the cathedral. The design Latrobe and the trustees settled on was in the classical Roman tradition, a style "compatible with the ideals of the Enlightenment: order, harmony, discipline, reason, quiet dignity." As Chinnici rightly observed, the cathedral still stands in downtown Baltimore "as a fitting symbol of the spiritual life characteristic of the Catholic community during Carroll's era."[21]

In getting beyond the symbol and uncovering the religion of the people in this era, Chinnici examined prayer books, sermons, catechisms, and popular apologetical treatises. These sources presented a positive view of human nature in contrast to the Baroque view of a sinful, weakened human nature. Catechisms as well as theological manuals described religion as a personal experience with an emphasis on the interiority of religion as opposed to an emphasis on external acts of piety. An English Catholic writer, John Fletcher, in his book *Reflections on the Spirit of Religious Controversy*, which was widely circulated throughout the United States, defined religion as "a system of piety and humility; and it is in holy communication with God, by prayer and meditation, that he speaks most plainly, to the heart, and unfolds the truth and beauty of his law." A widely circulated catechism touched on the same interior and personal dimension of religion. It stated that "men owe to God an inward worship, because this is the only worship which is suited to the nature of God, who being a spirit, desires to be worshipped in spirit and truth. . . . Exterior, without inward, worship would be a mere farce and mockery." Such a view of religion did not focus on the differences between Catholics and Protestants. It was an irenic understanding of religion that blended in well with the environment of religious pluralism and toleration that was prevalent in these years. In his sermons John Carroll emphasized this commonality of Christianity by referring to Catholics as "Christians," or "Catholic Christians," and referring to the church as the "Christian Catholic church." It should be noted that such a view of religion did not do away with devotional practices that were so much a part of the Catholic tradition. Indeed, such practices were encouraged, but the emphasis was always on the personal relation with Jesus and the interior disposition of the individual.[22]

This type of piety was not something new to American Catholicism. It was very much in harmony with the tradition of colonial Catholicism, which manifested the same qualities of a personal, interior style of religion. Moreover, this type of religion blended well with the social situation of Catholics during the republican era. This was a time when priests were scarce and churches were few and far between. To a large extent it was an age of do-it-yourself religion. Moreover, continual interaction with the dominant Protestant society often included worshiping with Protestants, marrying their sons and daughters, and being buried in their cemeteries. The irenic nature of Enlightenment Catholicism was well suited for such interaction between Catholics and Protestants.

For many people the Enlightenment evokes ideas of anti-Christianity or anti-Catholicism. This is not entirely true. Indeed, some Enlightenment figures would fit the description of anti-Christian, but the Enlightenment with its emphasis on reason, nature, and the human was not always the enemy of Christianity, and indeed Catholicism was not always an enemy of the Enlightenment. The Enlightenment was, as the historian Owen Chadwick has written, "new learning, and as such affected Catholic colleges, professors, and bishops."[23] It was a *new way of believing*, in which people sought to adapt their religion to the modern world. It touched Catholics as well as Protestants and Jews, and it substantially altered the way that people thought about their God and the human community in which they lived. In the United States an Enlightenment Catholicism was very evident, and it clearly stamped Catholicism with a distinctive style of religion — a fact that is not as widely recognized as it should be. Catholicism in the republican era was not the same as Catholicism in the 1840s or the 1980s. The culture of the Enlightenment had reshaped the Catholicism of the Baroque era and fashioned what some contemporaries called an "enlightened piety."[24] Enlightenment Catholicism was the Catholic answer to modernity in the republican era. It was one way in which Catholics adapted their religion to the modern world and to the American environment. Indeed, it was an important moment in the ongoing search for an American Catholicism that has been so much a part of the Catholic experience in the United States.

A second major cultural influence on Catholicism at this time was the spirit of democracy that emerged from the democratic revolution that swept through the Western world in the late eighteenth century. The Enlightenment was linked to this political revolution through its emphasis on "the rights of man" and human progress. In terms of religion the Enlightenment influenced the way people thought about God and moral values, while the passion for democracy was most evident in the way people refashioned religious authority. Intimately bound together, these two forces, the Enlightenment and the rise of democracy, produced a cultural revolution that ushered in a new age, an age that most people refer to as the modern era. Historians like to date this transitional period somewhere between 1770 and 1830. In 1770 the dictates of reason and nature were becoming more recognized, and pleas for equality in the political arena were beginning to be heard. In time reason and nature became cultural goddesses while political democracy became a popular slogan. By 1830 the Enlightenment era had passed into history, and "enlightened" religion had been found wanting. Political democracy had more staying power, however, and it had become a permanent feature of the Western world by 1830.

In America the key event in this transition was the Revolution. On one side of 1776 was an age of privilege and deference. The aristocratic values of English society with its kings and lords were visible throughout all the colonies, but most especially in the South. In Virginia the greater ruled over the lesser. The well-to-do planter lived in the great house, a home distinguished not only by its size but also by its elaborate ornaments and orderly design. The aristocratic dress of the privileged set them apart, and English soldiers paraded about in colorful, tailored uniforms. Even the churches reflected the values of old England. Built of brick they were imposing structures, fitting for the established Church of England, which enjoyed the support and protection of the local government. The design of the church mirrored this ordered society. People sat according to their rank in society, and the pulpit, the clergyman's perch, towered above all. A formal liturgy "read in the midst of a community ranged in order of precedence, continuously evoked postures of deference and submission. Liturgy and church plan thus readily combined to offer a powerful representation of a structured, hierarchical community." [25]

Then came the Revolution. It was a revolution of mind as well as a war for independence. The world was turned upside down and a new nation appeared. Privilege and deference were cast aside. Freedom, independence, and equality became cherished values of the new republic. Shunning the type of dress worn by English soldiers, patriots donned hunting shirts and took up arms to fight against the king. Deference vanished, and the prerogatives of privilege did not count for much. The will of the people became supreme, and the people's choice occupied the seats of power. Rank in society counted for little in the new evangelical churches that appeared during this period, as plain tables set in the midst of the congregation replaced ornamented and elevated pulpits. People sensed that a "new order of the ages" had arrived, and this Latin phrase (*novus ordo saeclorum*) became part of the nation's seal. A new type of person had stepped onto the world stage, a republican, one who had inherited "a revolutionary legacy in a world" once ruled by aristocrats and kings. [26]

This transitional age transformed American Christianity in the same manner that it changed American political life. In religion as in politics the people's choice became determinative. People sought to gain control over their own destiny, spiritual as well as political. Thus, they cast aside any monopoly that sought to control their eternal life; in Virginia this meant an end to the established church and the beginning of religious freedom for all people. Heaven was democratized and salvation now became a possibility for all of God's children, not just the Calvinist elect. In such an atmosphere people "wanted their leaders unpretentious, their doctrines self-evident and down-to-earth, their music lively and singable, their churches in local hands. It was this upsurge of democratic hope," wrote historian Nathan Hatch, "that characterised so many religious cultures in the early republic and brought Baptists, Methodists, Disciples and a host of other insurgent groups to the fore. The rise of evangelical Christianity in the early republic is, in some measure, a story of the success of common people in shaping the culture after their own priorities rather than those outlined by gentlemen such as the Founding Fathers." [27] This democratic spirit influenced people everywhere and altered the landscape of American religion. It created a spirit of populism, as the people's choice, not the preacher's prerogative, became determinative.

This new populist spirit in religion affected all denominations. It was the driving force behind the growth and expansion of Methodism; it gave birth to the Disciples of Christ and was a major reason for the popularity of Joseph Smith and the founding of the Mormon church. It shaped the organization of Jewish synagogues as Jews sought to declare their rights and privileges. This passion for democracy also permeated the Catholic community. Where this was most visible was in the government of the local parish.

Before examining the democratic nature of parish life at this time, it would be useful to provide an institutional profile of Catholicism during this era.

At the time of the American Revolution very few Catholics lived in the colonies. Though no one knew for certain, they probably numbered no more than twenty-five thousand, with the bulk of them being concentrated in Maryland and with a few thousand living in Pennsylvania in and around the Philadelphia area. In the years following the war for independence the number of Catholics began to increase and spread beyond Maryland and Pennsylvania. Large numbers of Catholics settled in Kentucky; others chose New York and still others headed south to Virginia and the Carolinas. As the population spread out and multiplied, the institutional church began to take shape. The first development in this regard was the appointment of John Carroll as Bishop of Baltimore in 1789. Carroll was elected by the clergy, and the Pope went along with their decision. At this time there were probably twenty-two priests in the entire country. Carroll remained the only bishop in the United States until 1808, when Rome appointed bishops to newly established dioceses in New York, Philadelphia, Boston, and Bardstown, Kentucky. By this time the only major institutional development had been the establishment of a seminary in Baltimore, St. Mary's, and a men's college, Georgetown, in Washington, D.C.

In 1820 at the end of this republican era the Catholic population numbered around 160,000, and half of them lived in the Baltimore diocese. The only other denominations with more members were the Methodists and Baptists. There were now three seminaries for young men who wanted to become priests, four men's colleges, and ten academies for women. In addition, five communities of women religious had been founded, and about 208 sisters were working in the United States. The number of dioceses had grown to nine, and the clergy numbered around 122 with the vast majority of them, 88, being diocesan priests; the rest belonged to such religious orders as the Jesuits, Sulpicians, Dominicans, Vincentians, and Augustinians, all of whom had come from Europe to work as missionaries in the United States. Clearly the Catholic Church had expanded substantially during the republican era. In 1780 it was a small, poorly organized denomination; by 1820 it was fairly well organized, had a number of promising educational institutions, had a decent number of priests and women religious, and was rivaling such denominations as the Methodists and Baptists in size, if not in prestige.[28]

The vital element in the development of American Catholicism was the parish. Between 1780 and 1820 many parish communities were organized across Catholic America. Perhaps as many as 124 Catholic churches dotted the landscape in 1820, and each one represented a community of Catholics.[29] In the vast majority of these communities laymen were very involved in the government of the parish as members of a board of trustees. The principal reason for such a trustee system was the new spirit of democracy that was rising across the land. In France and Ireland as well as the United States, people were redefining the meaning of authority and coming up with a much more democratic understanding of how authority should be exercised in society. Such questioning ushered in the democratic age. Much like the civil rights movement of the 1950s and 1960s this democratic awakening touched people everywhere, in Paris, France, as well as Bardstown, Kentucky. It changed the lives of kings as well as farmers. In Catholic communities it meant that laypeople wanted to have more control over their parish churches.

In emphasizing the influence of the democratic spirit on the Catholic parish it is well to remember that tradition played a very important role in this development. When they sought to fashion a democratic design for parish government, American Catholics were attempting to blend the old with the new, the past with the present. The establishment of a trustee system was not a break with the past, as they understood it, but a continuation of past practices adapted to a new environment. Lay participation in church government was an accepted practice in France and Germany; English and Irish lay Catholics were also becoming more involved in parish government. Thus, when they were forced to defend their actions against opponents of the lay trustee system, Catholic trustees appealed to tradition and long-standing precedents for such involvement. This blending of the old with the new captured the meaning of the Catholic heritage and enabled the people to adapt an ancient tradition to the circumstances of an emerging, new society.

The American legal system that supported the separation of church and state encouraged the development of the trustee system by classifying churches as voluntary associations or corporations; such corporations could have their own constitutions and be incorporated in the name of lay trustees who would be responsible for the corporation's legal and financial affairs. By their very nature some American Protestant denominations endorsed the participation of the laity in congregational government, and the democratic surge that took place in the republican era served to enhance this tendency. When it came time for Catholics to think about organizing their own congregations, the Protestant example and the American legal system clearly suggested a model in which laypeople would have a prominent role.

The first step in establishing a lay trustee type of parish government was to select the trustees. This took place in a very American manner, by election. Elections would take place each year to select the board of trustees. Only those people who rented pews in the church were eligible to vote; this meant that white males over the age of twenty-one and of some financial means were the only people that voted. Though the trustee system could vary from parish to parish, two types were popular prior to 1820. In one type laymen were in control and the clergy were looked upon as hired servants of the parish. The clergy worked for the board and were subject to the trustees' wishes. The trustees hired them and the trustees could also fire them. This system in which lay trustees had exclusive control over parish affairs was in operation in such cities as New Orleans, Philadelphia, Buffalo, New York, and Norfolk, Virginia. The other model explicitly provided for the participation of the clergy on the board of trustees and made them ex officio members of the board. This type of arrangement was found in parishes in Philadelphia, Baltimore, Boston, and Detroit.

The responsibilities of these trustees were rather mundane. They were engaged in what they described as "temporal concerns." In other words, they were the parish business managers, and their major concern was financial: collection of pew rents, purchasing an organ, selling gravesites in the parish cemetery, determining the salary of the priest, and paying off debts. They also supervised the work of those who worked for the parish such as the organist and the priest. When the priest and the trustees did not agree on some issue, be it salary or the quality of preaching, then conflict did occur and it could be very bitter and prolonged. But as Patrick Carey, the recognized authority on this issue, noted, such conflict took place in relatively few Catholic parishes. In the vast majority of the one hundred or more parishes in the country at this time the trustee system worked well and remained the people's choice for local church government.[30]

While it is true that there were European precedents for lay involvement in parish government, and American law favored a trustee system of parish government, a key influence in the adoption of the trustee system was the democratic spirit that was surging through the nation at this time.

Roman Catholicism was a religion of the old world. Many Catholic immigrants as well as those born and raised in the land that was to become the United

States recognized the contrast between the European tradition of Catholicism and the American style of independence and freedom. Moreover, they realized that there was a need for the Roman Catholic Church to adapt itself to the American situation. They were not talking about Catholic dogma or religious beliefs but about the way the church operated through its bishops and clergy.

Mathew Carey recognized the need of the Irish clergy to adapt to American culture. In Ireland, he wrote, "too frequently the relations between the pastor and his flock partake of the nature of extravagantly high toned authority on the one side and servile submission on the other." Americans, Carey suggested, "never will submit to the regime in civil or ecclesiastical affairs that prevails in Europe." In his opinion "a different order . . . prevails in this country. . . . The extreme freedom of our civil institutions has produced a corresponding independent spirit respecting church affairs, to which sound sense will never fail to pay attention, and which it would be a manifest impropriety to despise or attempt to control by harsh or violent measures. The opinions and wishes of the people require to be consulted to a degree unknown in Europe." As regards bishops, he observed that "an overweening idea of the extent of episcopal authority is not suited to this meridian." [31] In Europe the monarchical tradition had left an indelible imprint on both church and state. In Carey's opinion this feudal tradition was not compatible with the American political and cultural environment. Catholics in New Orleans made the same point when they petitioned the state legislature to enact a law that would force the bishop "to govern the Catholic church here in accordance with the spirit of our national customs and political institutions." [32] This need for adaptation was paramount in the minds of Catholics across the country.

In desiring to have the church adapt to American culture Catholics wanted Roman Catholicism to be more in step with the times and to breathe in some of the democratic spirit that was blowing across the landscape. In doing so they believed that they would be establishing "a National American Church with liberties consonant to the spirit of government under which they live." The way that this could happen would be for the church to adopt what they called "republican" principles in the government of the local church. [33] In his study of trusteeism Patrick Carey has documented the link between trusteeism and republican ideology. The trustees, who often described themselves as "American Republicans," endorsed four major principles of the American democratic experience — the sovereignty of the people, popular elections, religious freedom, and a written constitution. [34]

In the old country the will of the monarch was sovereign; in the new world the will of the people was supreme. One of the more popular slogans of the day was "the voice of the people is the voice of God." Catholic trustees appropriated this maxim and applied it to the church. "Is it wise," asked a Philadelphia Catholic, "is it prudent, that those whose voice is law in everything else, should be made to feel, that in that very thing, in which they are most deeply interested they have no voice at all." [35] The way that the voice of the people would be heard would be through elections. Popular elections were considered a natural right and a natural consequence of popular sovereignty. In advocating elections in the church, trust-ees included not just election of trustees but also the election of pastors and bish-ops. Mathew Carey felt so strongly about this that he wanted to call "a convention of the Roman Catholics throughout the Union" to consider the subject of the election of bishops and eventually send an agent to Rome to negotiate this issue.[36]

Freedom or what was often described as "the spirit of independence" was an-other principle advocated by Catholics. As Mathew Carey noted, the freedom exercised in the civil realm "has produced a corresponding independent spirit respecting our church affairs."[37] What this meant was that the European style of absolutism and the arbitrary exercise of authority were not suited to the American scene. Independent as Americans, they wanted to be independent as Catholics. This did not mean casting off "the spiritual supremacy of the Apostolic See," but keeping it as a bond of union, "not as the yoke of a servile dependency."[38]

The final republican principle was the need for a written constitution. Consti-tution writing had a long heritage in the Anglo-Saxon tradition and was very much in vogue in the republican era. From the federal level to the local level people engaged in the process of writing a constitution. In Scott County, Ken-tucky, a group of Catholics organized themselves into a religious society in 1806 and, as one of their first steps, drew up a constitution. Described as a "Republican Constitution," it had a preamble and a set of articles by which they sought to regulate and define the government of the local church in Scott County.[39] Such a constitution was to serve as a protection against the arbitrary use of authority by incorporating certain checks and balances into the government of the local church. By establishing a balance of power, the likelihood of conflict would be diminished. Moreover, the constitution spelled out the areas of responsibility for both clergy and laity.

These four principles — the sovereignty of the people, popular elections, reli-gious freedom, and a written constitution — provided the rationale for the trustee system in the American Catholic community. Very American and clearly repub-lican, they showed how much democratic thought had permeated the Catholic community. Numerous examples of such republican Catholicism exist from Scott County, Kentucky, to Philadelphia, Pennsylvania, but the most ambitious and comprehensive example took place in the southern regions of Georgia and the Carolinas. Led by their Irish-born bishop, John England, Catholics in this region fashioned an elaborate system of church government that was inspired by the spirit of republicanism.

John England was appointed the bishop of Charleston, South Carolina, in 1820. While in Ireland he was involved in the political and religious reform move-ments of the early nineteenth century, and this experience formed him into a liberal Catholic sympathetic to the democratic spirit of the age. When he came to Charleston, he entered a Catholic community that was bitterly riddled with dissension over the issue of authority in the local congregation. England brought peace to the community by fashioning a republican style of church government in which clergy and laity worked together. As he put it, he wanted to fashion a church in which "the laity are empowered to cooperate but not to dominate." The centerpiece of this was a written constitution that England presented to the clergy and laity in September of 1823; after some discussion the assembly of people voted to accept it. The constitution endorsed the election of parish lay trustees and annual conventions of clergy and laity to discuss the needs of the church as well as lay representatives chosen to participate in these meetings. These conventions met annually from 1823 until England's death in 1842.

The constitution reflected England's belief in republicanism and the need to instill some of its qualities in the church so that the people would be more involved in the decision-making process. For England the constitution was a conscious effort to adapt Catholicism to the American republican environment. He sought to create something new in the Catholic world; his critics in the hierarchy realized this and derisively labeled him a "republican," disapproving of what they called his "republican notions."[40] No other bishop adopted England's vision of church government, and when he died in 1842, republican Catholicism lost its most powerful advocate.

The obvious question is why republican Catholicism with its democratic tendencies and its Enlightenment impulses never endured through the nineteenth century? There are several reasons for this, but a key one is that another understanding of Catholicism prevalent in the United States during the age of John Carroll eventually became the dominant model of Catholicism. It was a more traditional model of the church that emphasized the weakness of human nature, the prevalence of sin, and the need for the church and its clergy to help people overcome this worldly environment. It stressed the authority of the hierarchy and the subordinate role of the laity; its model of government was the medieval monarchy and not the modern republic. Historians have labeled this model of Catholicism Tridentine Catholicism after the Council of Trent because this sixteenth-century church council promoted the reformation of Catholicism by endorsing this style of religion. It was prevalent in eighteenth-century Europe, and after a brief interlude of adaptation to modern thought and culture, this model was revived and restored to prominence by the middle of the nineteenth century. A fine exemplar of this school of thought was John England's contemporary, Ambrose Marechal.

Born in France, Marechal joined the Sulpicians, a society of diocesan priests, and was ordained a priest in 1792 in Paris. Because of the turmoil of the French Revolution, he fled Paris, not even taking time to celebrate his first Mass as a priest. He headed for the United States where he worked mostly as a missionary in Pennsylvania and Maryland; he also taught some courses at St. Mary's Seminary in Baltimore. When the Revolution cooled down, he returned to France for a few years and then was sent back to Baltimore to teach at St. Mary's, a seminary operated by the Sulpicians. In 1817 he was appointed the archbishop of Baltimore.

As the archbishop of Baltimore, Marechal strongly opposed John England's desire to promote a republican model of Catholicism beyond the borders of the

Carolinas. He disparaged the innovations that England promoted in Charleston and pejoratively labeled his diocesan constitution a "democratic constitution."[41] Marechal endorsed the idea of religious liberty, but he wanted no part of democracy in the church. As far as he was concerned the spirit of democracy was the root cause for many of the church's problems in the new nation. Americans loved "the civil liberty which they enjoy," he wrote; as he put it, "the principle of civil liberty is paramount with them," and even the lowest magistrate is elected by the vote of the people. Such principles govern Protestant churches, and in his opinion Catholics "are exposed to the danger of admitting the same principles of ecclesiastical government." He strongly opposed this tendency and sought to establish the supreme authority of the clergy and weaken the power of the lay trustee system.[42] Marechal's model of the church was very French and very monarchical. Moreover, it was the model of church that was gaining ascendancy in France after the downfall of Napoleon in 1814.

Like Marechal, many other French clergy fled to the United States during the revolution, and most of them included in their cultural baggage a very traditional understanding of Catholicism. Their presence was especially influential in Kentucky.

The Kentucky Catholic community was founded in the 1780s by transplanted Marylanders who had abandoned the Chesapeake region for the more promising territory west of the Alleghenies. Though the majority of Kentucky Catholics were native-born Americans, there was only one American-born priest in Kentucky in 1815; the rest were Europeans, with Frenchmen being the most numerous.

The pioneer priest of Kentucky was Stephen Badin. Born in Orleans, France, he came to the United States in 1792 to escape the turmoil of the French Revolution. A year later Bishop John Carroll ordained him to the priesthood and sent him to the Kentucky frontier where he worked for many years. A contemporary of Badin was Charles Nerinckx, who emigrated from Belgium in 1805. Both Nerinckx and Badin would have a decisive influence on the development of Kentucky Catholicism. The first bishop of Kentucky was another émigré priest, Benedict Flaget. Two other bishops appointed to assist Flaget in Kentucky, John B. David and Guy I. Chabrat, were also French. In fact, of the twenty-three bishops appointed to work in the West during the first half of the nineteenth century, eleven were French.

The French influence was very evident in the area of piety. Enlightenment Catholicism encouraged a personal and plain style of religion that stressed the positive side of human nature, toleration, and the reasonableness of religion. Badin and Nerinckx, together with many other French clergy in the United States, promoted a stern code of morality that discouraged dancing and theatergoing. Their moralism was rooted in a negative view of human nature and the need to curb its evil tendencies. Their severity in the confessional was well known, and people complained continuously about both of them. Nerinckx told people to rise at 4 A.M. and forbade them to dance; Badin would impose such penances as holding a hot coal while reciting the Our Father and the Hail Mary or digging a shallow grave and lying in it a brief time each day for a week. Eccentric in their understanding of the spiritual life, they shared a fundamentally pessimistic view of human nature that was characteristic of European Catholicism at this time. Many Kentucky Catholics did not approve of this style of piety, and their resistance suggests that they were attuned to a more moderate and positive type of spirituality.[43]

Bishop Flaget was more balanced in his spirituality, but he too emphasized the enormity of sin and found personal strength in a spirituality centered in the crucifixion of Jesus.[44] As was traditional with priests of the Sulpician society, Flaget put great emphasis on the sacrament of penance and viewed the administration of this sacrament as the most important work of the priest. Such an understanding of the priesthood underscored the pervasive nature of sin, the weakness of human nature, and the need for the priest to provide "divine kindness" to the people through the sacrament of penance. Parish missions, the Catholic counterpart to Protestant revivals, were common along the Kentucky frontier, and they too promoted this understanding of Catholicism in which sin and fear were the foundation on which religion rested. It was clear that these French missionaries were bringing their own style of Catholicism to the new nation, and any idea of adapting the traditional French style of Catholicism to the United States was totally foreign to them.

Kentucky was also the setting for clashes between the monarchical and republican models of Catholicism. Kentucky Catholics were known as ardent Jeffersonians and supported a republican view of government in both the civic and religious arena. The absence of clergy encouraged lay leadership in the church, and most congregations organized themselves into a religious society and wrote republican constitutions that supported the idea of lay trustees. Badin resisted what he called such "extravagant pretensions of Republicanism" and continually opposed any manifestation of lay independence. Flaget also had to deal with such independence and acknowledged that the people were indeed "good republicans."[45] The contrast between the two opposing views of the church was captured very clearly in a letter written by the French-born bishop of New Orleans to a Vatican official:

> It is scarcely possible to realize how contagious even to the clergy and to men otherwise well disposed, are the principles of freedom and independence imbibed by all the pores in these United States. Hence I have always been convinced that practically all the good to be hoped for must come from the Congregations or religious Orders among which flourish strict discipline.[46]

In a hierarchical church discipline was essential, while independence and freedom were counterproductive to the goals of an organization based on authority and the chain of command.

Given the strong presence of these two conflicting views of Catholicism, why did one eventually prevail over the other? The answer is complex. Essentially it can be attributed to three historical developments — the decline of the Enlightenment, the revival and restoration of Catholicism after the demise of the French Revolution, and massive immigration to the United States.

Henry May has written on the decline of the Enlightenment in the United States, and he attributes this mainly to two developments — the rise of evangelical Protestantism and the expansion of democracy. In the early years of the nineteenth century the rational religion of the Enlightenment was overwhelmed by a religious revival that reshaped the landscape of American Protestantism. "The deepest loyalties of the Enlightened," May wrote, "were affronted by the teaching that divine grace, arbitrarily bestowed by an unscrutable God, was more important than any kind of earthly achievement. They were revolted by statements that most of mankind were and always must be miserable sinners. Those who tried hardest to formulate a modern, rational, Enlightened Christianity were continually at war with preachers who insisted that saving knowledge came only through a change of heart."[47] Nonetheless, the Enlightened were in the minority in the nineteenth century, and most American Protestants believed that a change of heart grounded in the affections was more important than a change of opinion rooted in the rational faculties, that the sinfulness of the human person was more believable than the goodness of people and the progress of the human race. By 1840 most American Protestants had opted for the warmth and emotion of evangelical religion rather than the cold logic of rational religion. A rational Christianity did endure, chiefly among Unitarians and mainly in the Boston region, but it never influenced the culture the way evangelicalism did.

The expansion of democracy challenged the elitism of the Enlightenment head on. The Enlightenment was incompatible with the egalitarian ideology of democracy. As May put it, "The theory that man's reason must be protected against his passions, the axiom that numbers must be balanced against property, still more the suggestion that wisdom was likely to lie with the smaller part, could not be used to appeal to a mass electorate."[48] The election of Andrew Jackson in 1828 and the triumph of Jacksonian democracy confirmed what had been developing since the turn of the century. The elite republicanism of the revolutionary period had given way to political democracy. This was a major cultural transformation that continues to shape American society.

Given this demise of Enlightenment thought in the United States, together with its corresponding decline in Europe, it was not unexpected that an Enlightenment-inspired style of Catholicism never developed much beyond the era of John Carroll. It was out of step with the times.

As American culture changed and the age of the Enlightenment passed, Catholicism was forced to adapt once again. This time it turned to Europe, where the church was undergoing an unexpected renewal after the tribulations provoked by the French Revolution and the Napoleonic era. In the eighteenth century the church had reached "a nadir of its prestige and influence."[49] Then along came the French Revolution, and as Owen Chadwick wrote, "The Revolution did to the Roman Catholic Church what the Reformation failed to do. It appeared to have destroyed its structure if not its being." [50] For a time the church in France ceased to function as monasteries were closed, churches destroyed, and priests executed. Under the command of Napoleon, French troops kidnapped the Pope, Pius VI, and he died a prisoner in exile. Then Napoleon kidnapped Pius's successor, Pius VII, and kept him a prisoner for nearly six years. When Napoleon met defeat in 1814, the fortunes of the church changed and a new era began for Europe and the Catholic Church. Within the next generation Catholicism underwent a remarkable revival.

The central feature in this restoration was the strengthening of the papacy and the increasing centralization of the church in Rome. Under Pope Gregory XVI and most especially during the long pontificate of his successor, Pius IX (1846–78), the papacy was able to regain much of the prestige and power that it had lost during the Napoleonic era. More and more Catholics believed that a strong papacy was the only salvation of the church in the nineteenth century. This mentality became known as ultramontanism, a belief that Catholicism must be Rome-centered and all authority should rest in the papacy; it reached its zenith at the First Vatican Council in 1870 with the declaration of papal infallibility. As the pope's authority increased, the likelihood of the continuation of an American style of Catholicism politically independent of the Vatican diminished. A hierarchical model of church with power and authority concentrated in the office of the papacy was antithetical to the republican model that encouraged democracy in the local church.

More was at work in these years than just the restoration of papal authority. The traditional religion of Catholicism, Tridentine Catholicism, was also revived. This style of Catholicism emphasized the primacy of revelation over reason; it favored a spirit of intolerance toward other religions rather than tolerance; and it endorsed a pastoral strategy based on sin and fear rather than one that viewed human nature in a positive, optimistic manner. Moreover, it was very similar to the ethos of evangelical Protestantism that was on the rise in the United States. This emphasis on sin and conversion became so dominant a feature of both Catholicism and Protestantism in the nineteenth century that it simply overwhelmed an Enlightened Christianity.

A final reason for the demise of republican Catholicism was the massive immigration of the nineteenth century. Immigration brought a new class of Catholics to the United States in very large numbers. These newcomers were not like the educated, middle-class Catholics of the republican period. They were unskilled workers who provided the muscle and brawn that fueled the industrial revolution. The religion of republican Catholicism was not suited to the masses; it was a religion of the elite that emphasized an "enlightened piety" whereas the traditional religion of Tridentine Catholicism with its emphasis on such emotion-laden themes as sin and fear was more suited to an evangelization program targeted at the masses. This is precisely what occurred with the revival of the parish mission and evangelical Catholicism in both Europe and the United States. In addition, the immigrants were coming at a time when the traditional model of Catholicism was undergoing a revival in Europe and so the religion that nurtured them in their youth and the religion they carried with them to the United States was antithetical to the religion of the Carroll era. One would have to yield to the other, and the numbers were on the side of Marechal and Badin, not Carey and Carroll.

Republican Catholicism did not entirely disappear. The attraction of democracy never subsided throughout the nineteenth century. Each immigrant group sought in some way to incorporate this ethos into the government of the local church and they succeeded to a degree. The "enlightened piety" of the Carroll era had its counterparts in the form of a romantic Catholicism that emerged in the middle of the century and later as an Americanist spirituality that surfaced toward the end of the century. Each of these models of Catholicism was an effort on the part of Catholics to adapt their religion to the American environment. They constitute another chapter in the search for an American Catholicism that has continually captured the interests of people.

Notes

I would like to thank the Lilly Endowment for the support that enabled me to do the research associated with this essay.

1. Philip Gleason, "American Identity and Americanization," in *Concepts of Ethnicity*, ed. William Petersen, Michael Novak, and Philip Gleason (Cambridge, Mass.: Harvard University Press, 1982), 111.

2. Philip Gleason, *Keeping the Faith: American Catholicism Past and Present* (Notre Dame: University of Notre Dame Press, 1987), 60.

3. William G. McLoughlin, *Revivals, Awakenings, and Reform* (Chicago: University of Chicago Press, 1978), 10.

4. Mathew Carey, *Autobiography* (New York, 1942), 9–10.

5. Ibid.; also Kerby A. Miller, *Emigrants and Exiles: Ireland and the Irish Exodus to North America* (New York: Oxford University Press, 1985), 171; and Thomas M. Truxes, *Irish-American Trade, 1660–1783* (Cambridge: Cambridge University Press, 1988), 118.

6. Archives, Historical Society of Pennsylvania, Diary of Mathew Carey, Jan. 1, 1787; Carey, *Autobiography*, 1; see also another diary of Carey for frequent references to classical authors, Rare Book Room, University of Pennsylvania, Diary of Mathew Carey, Nov. 2, 1825, et passim; Edward C. Carter II, "The Political Activities of Mathew Carey, Nationalist, 1760–1814" (Ph.D. diss., Bryn Mawr College, 1962), 7; *Catalogue of the Library of Mathew Carey* (Philadelphia: Joseph R. A. Skerrett, 1822).

7. Carter, "Political Activities of Mathew Carey," 25, 116.

8. Rare Book Room, University of Pennsylvania, Carey Diary, Dec. 1, 1824; Nov. 2, 1825; and Nov. 15, 1825; *Niles National Register*, 5th Series, No. 4, Vol. 7, Baltimore, Sept. 21, 1839; David Kaser, "The Retirement Income of Mathew Carey," *Pennsylvania Magazine of History and Biography* 80, no. 4 (Oct. 1956): 410–15.

9. Mathew Carey, *An Address to the Roman Catholics of the United States by a Layman of St. Mary's Congregation* (Philadelphia, 1821), 7.

10. Mathew Carey, *Plan for the Publication of Religious Books* (Philadelphia, 1791).

11. Rare Book Room, University of Pennsylvania, Carey Diary, Dec. 1, 1824.

12. See James Turner, *Without God, Without Creed: The Origins of Unbelief in America* (Baltimore: Johns Hopkins University Press, 1985), 35ff.

13. Henry F. May, *The Enlightenment in America* (New York: Oxford University Press, 1976), 210.

14. Ibid., 197–98; in his study of trusteeism Patrick W. Carey notes that many Catholic trustees evidenced an Enlightenment style of religion: *People, Priests, and Prelates: Ecclesiastical Democracy and the Tensions of Trusteeism* (Notre Dame: University of Notre Dame Press, 1987), 148–49.

15. Ronald Hoffman, "A Worthy Heir: The Role of Religion in the Development of Charles Carroll of Carrollton, 1748–1764," Cushwa Center for the Study of American Catholicism, Working Paper Series, Fall 1982, pp. 2, 42–44, and 60.

16. Thomas O'Brien Hanley, ed., *The John Carroll Papers* (Notre Dame: University of Notre Dame Press, 1976), 1:53 and 81; Robert Emmett Curran, S.J., ed., *American Jesuit Spirituality: The Maryland Tradition, 1634–1900* (New York: Paulist Press, 1988), 133.

17. Joseph P. Chinnici, "American Catholics and Religious Pluralism, 1775–1820," *Journal of Ecumenical Studies* 16 (Fall 1979): 733–36; Joseph P. Chinnici, *Living Stones: The History and Structure of Catholic Spiritual Life in the United States* (New York: Macmillan, 1989), 13; Curran, *American Jesuit Spirituality,* 16–18.

18. Thomas W. Spalding, *The Premier See: A History of the Archdiocese of Baltimore, 1789–1989* (Baltimore: Johns Hopkins University Press, 1989), 59–60.

19. See Chinnici, "American Catholics and Religious Pluralism," 736.

20. Joseph P. Chinnici, "Politics and Theology: From Enlightenment Catholicism to the Condemnation of Americanism," Cushwa Center for the Study of American Catholicism, Working Paper Series 9, No. 3 (Spring 1981), p. 22; see also Owen Chadwick, *The Popes and European Revolution* (Oxford: Clarendon, 1981), 3–95.

21. Chinnici, *Living Stones,* 2.

22. Chinnici, "Politics and Theology," 24–25; Chinnici, *Living Stones,* 6; Curran, *American Jesuit Spirituality,* 136.

23. Chadwick, *Popes and European Revolution,* 406.

24. See Joseph P. Chinnici, O.F.M., *The English Catholic Enlightenment, John Lingard and the Cisalpine Movement, 1780–1850* (Shepherdstown, W.V.: Patmos, 1980), 173–74.

25. Rhys Isaacs, *The Transformation of Virginia, 1740–1790* (Chapel Hill: University of North Carolina Press, 1982), 64.

26. Sean Wilentz, *Chants Democratic: New York City and the Rise of the American Working Class, 1788–1850* (New York: Oxford University Press, 1984), 61.

27. Nathan O. Hatch, *The Democratization of American Christianity* (New Haven, Conn.: Yale University Press, 1989), 9.

28. This data was taken from Ronin John Murtha, "The Life of the Most Reverend Ambrose Marechal Third Archbishop of Baltimore, 1768–1828," (Ph.D. diss., Catholic University of America, 1965), 97–99; see also Gerald Shaugnessy, *Has the Immigrant Kept the Faith?* (New York: Macmillan, 1925), 69–73, for a different set of population figures.

29. Edwin Scott Gaustad, *Historical Atlas of Religion in America* (New York: Harper and Row, 1962), 43, for the number of churches.

30. Carey, *People, Priests, and Prelates,* 108; I have relied on Carey for the history of the trustee system in the United States.

31. M. Carey, *Address to the Rt Rev Bishop Conwell and the Members of St Mary's*

Congregation (Philadelphia, 1821), 3–4; *Address to the Right Rev. The Bishop of Pennsylvania and the Members of St. Mary's Congregation, Philadelphia* (Philadelphia, 1820), 3; *Address to the Rt Rev Bishop of Pennsylvania, The Catholic Clergy of Philadelphia and the Congregation of St. Mary in this City by a Catholic Layman* (Philadelphia: H.C. Carey and I. Lea, 1822), v.

32. Quoted in Patrick W. Carey, "Republicanism Within American Catholicism, 1785–1860," *Journal of the Early Republic* 3, no. 4 (Winter 1983): 416.

33. Quoted in ibid., 417.

34. The phrase "American Republicans" appears in the *Documents Relative to the Present Distressed State of the Roman Catholic Church in the City of Charleston, State of South Carolina*, Charleston, S.C., 1818, p. 5; this document was found in the collection at the Library Company of Philadelphia.

35. Quoted in Carey, *People, Priests, and Prelates*, 165.

36. *Address to the Right Reverend The Bishop of Philadelphia, The Catholic Clergy of Philadelphia and the Congregation of St. Mary's in this City By a Catholic Layman* (Philadelphia, 1822), 30–31.

37. Quoted in Carey, *People, Priests, and Prelates*, 161.

38. Ibid., 163.

39. Sr. Mary Ramona Mattingly, *The Catholic Church on the Kentucky Frontier, 1795–1812* (Washington, D.C.: Catholic University of America Press, 1936), 139.

40. Quoted in Thomas T. McAvoy, *A History of the Catholic Church in the United States* (Notre Dame: University of Notre Dame Press, 1969), 130.

41. Spalding, *Premier See*, 93.

42. "Archbishop Marechal's Report to Propaganda, October 16, 1818," in John Tracy Ellis, ed., *Documents of American Catholic History* (Chicago: Henry Regnery Company, 1967), 1:214.

43. Clyde F. Crews, *An American Holy Land: A History of the Archdiocese of Louisville* (Wilmington, Del.: Michael Glazier, 1987), 64.

44. Ibid., 73–75.

45. Ibid., 102; Jay P. Dolan, *The American Catholic Experience: A History From Colonial Times to the Present* (New York: Doubleday, 1985), 119–20.

46. Ibid., 121.

47. Henry F. May, *The Divided Heart: Essays on Protestantism and the Enlightenment in America* (New York: Oxford University Press, 1991), 167.

48. May, *Enlightenment in America*, 314.

49. Thomas Bokenkotter, *A Concise History of the Catholic Church* (Garden City, N.Y.: Image Books, 1979), 285.

50. Chadwick, *Popes and European Revolution*, 481.

Retelling Carter Woodson's Story: Archival Sources for Afro-American Church History

ALBERT J. RABOTEAU AND DAVID W. WILLS, WITH RANDALL K. BURKETT, WILL B. GRAVELY, AND JAMES MELVIN WASHINGTON

For a survey history of the Afro-American churches in the United States, one will still not do better than Carter G. Woodson's *The History of the Negro Church* — a three-hundred-page study first published nearly seventy years ago.[1] Given the extraordinary increase during the last quarter century in scholarly attention to black religious life, it may seem surprising that there has not appeared a modern study capable of supplanting Woodson's classic but dated work. It is, however, in part the very increase in the scholarly literature on the black churches that has deterred would-be synthesizers from attempting a comprehensive survey. Where Woodson confronted his sources more or less unaided — and undetained — by a significant body of contemporary scholarship, the modern scholar faces a thickening array of articles, books, and dissertations.[2]

The contemporary student of Afro-American religious life also finds it far harder to focus his or her attention on the ecclesiastical history of black Christianity than Woodson did. *The History of the Negro Church* is not troubled by any deep concern with the possible African sources of Afro-American religious belief and practice. Neither does it inquire about the relationship between black religious life as it emerged on the North American mainland and the religious patterns evident among Caribbean slaves, nor worry very much about what was going on religiously among mainland blacks themselves before 1750. Instead, it moves briskly toward the history of black evangelicalism. Baptists and Methodists abound in Woodson's pages; they are mostly male and usually clergy, and they are generally busy building institutions, conducting educational and social service enterprises, and fighting the good fight politically. One reads little there about the missionary societies of black women or the special performance styles of black preaching and worship. One also learns nothing from Woodson about the more or less continuous thread of Islam in Afro-American religious life. The concluding chapter, "New Temples for Strange Prophets," added for the 1945 edition, has only the most perfunctory discussion of the Holiness and Pentecostal churches, the Father Divine Peace Mission Movement, and the Nation of Islam. Of course, there is also nothing in Woodson's book about those African-based religious movements from the Caribbean that are such a fascinating part of the contemporary scene — Haitian vodun and Cuban santería. Yet it is precisely an interest in all those things not found in *The History of the Negro Church* that has animated much of the best recent work on Afro-American religion — and with good reason.

The study of the religious history of the United States has been for too long an examination of the institutional and intellectual development of American Protestantism — especially in the Northeast — and it is not the least contribution of much recent work in Afro-American religious history that it has helped break this mold. Students of American religious history generally are slowly but, one hopes, surely coming to see that Africans were as much a part of the earliest history of the Atlantic world as Europeans were, that the American story begins as much in the South as in New England or the Middle Colonies, and that throughout that history the encounter of blacks and whites has been as central a part of the American religious problematic as the heritage of Puritanism or the diversity of Euro-American religions.[3] Historians of religion in the United States have also come even more clearly to embrace a concern for popular as well as elite forms of religion, to make regular use of nonliterary as well as literary resources in their research and teaching, and to pay due attention to that part of the American religious spectrum that lies at the edge of or altogether beyond the Christian and Jewish traditions. Obviously all these changes in the study of American religious history have occurred in relation to deep and pervasive changes, not only among historians and within the academy but in the culture generally. Yet the study of Afro-American religious history has certainly been an integral part of these developments and has contributed importantly to them.

There may, however, be a certain irony in this, for it is possible that these changed directions in the study of American religion have helped keep the institutional (and intellectual) study of black American Christianity under a shadow of neglect. When many scholars who had previously considered themselves "church historians" abandoned that label in the 1960s to become "historians of American religion," they left behind library shelves well stocked with volumes devoted to the history of Euro-American Christianity in the United States, above all to the denominational history of Euro-American Protestantism. There existed no comparable body of modern scholarly literature on the black denominations. The ability of the black churches to generate histories from their own resources, though considerable in the nineteenth century, has seemingly diminished for most of the twentieth.[4] Meanwhile, outsiders attracted to the study of black religious life between World War I and the civil rights era seem more often to have been anthropologists interested in rural folkways or sociologists attracted by urban "sects and cults" than historians curious about the institutional history of the black churches. Important work that was done — especially work concerning the twentieth-century black churches — never made its way into print, it being a long-standing pattern, for example, that dissertations about Father Divine or the Black Muslims rapidly find a publisher while dissertations on major black urban congregations and pastors do not. In the last two decades increased attention to Afro-American religious history has produced significant advances, and the scholarly literature on the black churches is beginning to grow, especially for the nineteenth century. But in a time when church history generally and denominational history in particular are out of fashion, progress has been painfully slow. So Woodson's *The History of the Negro Church* remains the most adequate overall survey of its subject.

In our view the time has come for a major effort to retell the story of the black Christian churches in the United States. We do not put this goal ahead of the other major goals being pursued by scholars of Afro-American religious history, but we do put it alongside them. We think it is tremendously important, for example, to fill out the story of all those decades that Woodson so quickly glides over at the beginning of his work — or never really gets to at the end. But we also think it is equally important to retell the tale that *The History of the Negro Church* was mostly concerned to tell, the story of the emergence of the black churches, primarily out of the matrix of the eighteenth-century evangelical revivals, their development through the nineteenth century, and their changing experience in the twentieth. The story is one that includes both men and women, both eminent leaders and ordinary folk, both forceful assertions of black autonomy and doggedly determined efforts to make biracial collaboration work. The sources for this story are manifold and to a significant degree still untapped. But they are also widely dispersed, difficult of access, and often unrecognized or even unknown. What follows is a survey and assessment of some of the most important resources.

A major initial problem confronting scholars concerned to locate manuscript and archival sources for the history of the black churches is the lack of any current or comprehensive guide to such materials. Walter Schatz's *Directory of Afro-American Resources* remains a useful survey of a vast array of black history collections in cities and towns across the United States, and its index provides some help in identifying collections especially pertinent to black church history. But it is now twenty years out-of-date. The more recent *Howard University Bibliography of African and Afro-American Religious Studies* is enormously useful for hard-to-find printed materials, but it has only a few pages on manuscripts. For current and continuously updated information on manuscript and archival sources for Afro-American religious history, researchers should therefore turn to the *Newsletter of the Afro-American Religious History Group*. Published semiannually at the W.E.B. Du Bois Institute for Afro-American Research, Harvard University, the newsletter has, since its beginning in 1976, regularly carried specialized bibliographies, reports by scholars and librarians about recently processed manuscripts, notes about finding aids, and research queries.[5]

An extremely valuable base line of data on the history and development of the black churches is to be found in the massive body of material gathered by the Historical Records Survey, under the auspices of the Works Projects Administration in the years 1935–1942. Surveys of church records at the congregation level were conducted in each state, and the survey files for thirty-eight states and the District of Columbia survive. Those files make available in standardized form information about the founding and development of individual congregations and the availability of their minute books, membership registers, and other records. Some files also include news clippings and both unpublished and published historical sketches. A useful guide compiled by Loretta L. Hefner, *The WPA Historical Records Survey*, provides a state-by-state analysis of the location and scope of extant church records surveys.[6]

A second general resource relevant to a wide range of topics in black church history is a group of clipping and vertical files that provide ready access to invaluable material in the black press. The black press, from its beginning in 1827, has published substantial information on churches, clergy, and denominational meetings at local, state, and national levels. Because complete texts of these papers often do not survive, they are sometimes accessible only through such clippings files.

Two collections stand out for the scope of their coverage. The first is the Clipping File of the Schomburg Center for Research in Black Culture, New York Public Library. Monumental in scope, with over ten thousand subject headings, it contains in addition to clippings, numerous broadsides, pamphlets, programs, book reviews, and ephemera. Information on religion is organized by individual congregation, geography, individual biography, and denomination, but relevant material will be found under other headings as well, such as bishops, race relations, spirituals, preaching, and religious education. The second is the Tuskegee Institute News Clipping File, which focuses on the period 1910–66 and contains 352 linear feet of mounted clippings, plus a few unmounted clippings, reports, and letters. Categories to consult for information on the black church include biography, carnivals, church and religion, civil rights, education, "missions, foreign," temperance, "women's work," and "YMCA" and "YWCA."[7]

Two other clipping files deserve special mention. The Hampton University Newspaper Clipping File, assembled between 1900 and 1925, contains fifty-five thousand clippings from black and religious newspapers. A substantial number of files are biographical, while others focus on education, women, voluntary associations, and religion. The Gumby Collection of American Negro Scrapbooks, covering the years 1910–50, is held by the Rare Book and Manuscript Library, Columbia University. Compiled by L. S. Alexander Gumby, individual scrapbooks deal with Catholics, Ethiopia, Marcus Garvey, Harlem, "Jewish-Prophet-Others," the Negro in Africa, Negro religions, Protestantism, and Father Divine, among other topics.[8]

Research on the history of the major independent black churches is complicated by the wide dispersal of relevant material for each denomination. This is true for both the most recent and the earliest periods, but it holds in a special way for the late eighteenth and early nineteenth centuries. The written records, published and unpublished, of the rise and early history of the African churches (as they were originally designated) are in widely scattered locations. Consulting all the pertinent denominational archives cited below would not locate more than a fraction of the relevant materials. Some valuable items seem to have been lost. Some pamphlets, church minutes, and private diaries that were available to nineteenth-century black denominational historians have subsequently disappeared. The personal journal of Joseph Cox, influential African Methodist Episcopal (AME) preacher and brother of black Shaker visionary Rebecca Cox Jackson, was, for example, a century ago in the possession of AME historiographer Daniel A. Payne. Today it can no longer be located.[9] Happily, state archives and historical societies have preserved some manuscript minutes for a number of early and important local congregations, but scholars are more likely to find their way to some of these than to others. That the Historical Society of Pennsylvania's holdings include some records of the earliest African Baptist and African Presbyterian congregations in Philadelphia is not surprising, but researchers may easily miss the minutes of the Abyssinian Church of Portland in the Maine Historical Society, Portland. They may also overlook unexpected items in familiar places, such as the record book (1827–48) of the Trenton, New Jersey, circuit of the AME church at the Library of Congress.[10] Similar examples could be given for the later stages of black church history. Research in the history of any of the denominational groupings of Afro-American Christians is then of necessity a multiarchival undertaking. It may well begin with whatever repositories are sponsored by the churches themselves but must also extend over a diverse range of public and private, familiar and unfamiliar archives.

For the black Baptist churches, there are no major archival centers associated with denominational schools, historical societies, or administrative headquarters that currently provide researchers with centralized access to the minutes, correspondence, and other records of major church bodies or the papers of notable church leaders. The National Baptist Convention, U.S.A., Inc., the largest of the black denominations throughout the twentieth century, has recently opened the Baptist World Center in Nashville, Tennessee. It holds important uncataloged materials, including the records of some denominational boards and agencies and the minutes of some state conventions and local associations. The best access to the records of the twentieth-century black Baptist denominations — and their nineteenth-century precursors — is provided by the microfilm collection of the Historical Commission of the Southern Baptist Convention (HCSBC), Nashville, Tennessee. The commission has filmed material from many repositories relevant to various Baptist denominations, both black and predominantly white. It has, for example, filmed minutes of the American Baptist Missionary Convention (1842–72); the National Baptist Convention (1897–1915); the National Baptist Convention, U.S.A., Inc.; and the National Baptist Convention of America. It has also filmed National Baptist Publication Board materials, the *Mission Herald*, the *National Baptist Union-Review*, the *National Baptist Voice*, and the catalogs of Roger Williams University.[11]

The most complete collection of nineteenth-century materials dealing with black Baptist history is to be found at the American Baptist Historical Society (ABHS) in Rochester, New York. Included here is the single largest set of minutes and journals of black state conventions and local associations — some of it material not included in the HCSBC microfilm project. The ABHS also holds a virtually complete run of the *National Baptist Magazine* (1894–1901), the first denominational journal of the National Baptist Convention.[12] Broken runs of William Jefferson White's *Georgia Baptist*, the oldest black southern periodical in continuous publication (1880 to the present), are available at the ABHS and at the Atlanta University Center's Woodruff Library, Atlanta, Georgia.[13] Some of the records of the American Baptist Home Missionary Society are also to be found at the latter location, but for much of the critically important correspondence between this agency and black Baptist leaders, one must consult the holdings of the national headquarters of the American Baptist Churches in the U.S.A., in Valley Forge, Pennsylvania. Material relevant to the history of black Baptists, in a state especially important for both their early history and their eventual development into independent denominations, is also to be found in the Virginia State Archives and the Virginia Baptist Historical Society, both in Richmond.

Very substantial black Baptist material (though sometimes it is not identified as such) is also to be found in most of the major repositories familiar to students of Afro-American history. Especially notable here are the personal papers of some of the most influential Baptist leaders of the twentieth century. The Library of Congress, for example, holds the papers of Nannie H. Burroughs, longtime leader of the Woman's Convention of the National Baptist Convention, U.S.A., Inc., and nationally known political activist. Most of the papers of churchman and educator Benjamin Mays are now being cataloged at the Moorland-Spingarn Research Center of Howard University, Washington, D.C. His Morehouse College presidential papers, as yet entirely uncataloged, are held by the Woodruff Library of the Atlanta University Center. Most papers of Martin Luther King Jr. for the years 1945–62 are currently located at the Mugar Library of Boston University, while those for the period 1962–68 are in the archives of the Martin Luther King Jr. Center for Non-violent Social Change in Atlanta.[14] Researchers should also be aware of significant manuscript collections for lesser-known but nonetheless important black Baptist figures — for example, the papers of Tennessee Reconstruction legislator David Foote Rivers at the Tennessee State Library and Archives, Nashville; those of twentieth-century Cleveland preacher Wade Hampton McKinney at the Western Reserve Historical Society, Cleveland, Ohio; and those of Nashville civil rights leader Kelly Miller Smith at the library of Vanderbilt University Divinity School in Nashville.

The major black Methodist bodies, whose histories reach much further back into the nineteenth century than any of the contemporary black Baptist denominations, have a slightly more established pattern of central archival collecting.[15] Wilberforce University in Wilberforce, Ohio, the oldest black church-related college in the United States, has long served as a major center for the collection of materials concerning the African Methodist Episcopal church (founded in 1816).

Its holdings include the largest (but still quite incomplete) runs of general and annual conference minutes, an extensive collection of the published reports of church departments and organizations, a large but incomplete set of the denomination's quarterly, the *AME Church Review* (1884 to the present), and substantial manuscript materials relating to influential bishops Daniel A. Payne and Reverdy C. Ransom — as well as very substantial printed and manuscript materials related to the university and its faculty. These holdings are supplemented by the much smaller but parallel collections of nearby Payne Theological Seminary. The collections do not, however, include the records and papers of the denomination's major boards and agencies. The most important collection of these is held by the AME Financial Department in Washington, D.C. These holdings include not only the records of that department but also some material related to various other AME agencies. The records of the AME Department of Home and Foreign Missions for the years 1912 to 1960 have recently been acquired by the Schomburg Center. The Schomburg Center also holds an important collection of general conference minutes and a scattering of annual conference minutes for the late nineteenth and early twentieth centuries, and an extensive run of the *AME Church Review*, which is complete through the early 1920s and available on microfilm for the years 1884–1910. Significant though scattered holdings of annual conference minutes are also held by a number of state and local historical societies, such as the Library Company of Philadelphia and the Historical Society of Pennsylvania.[16]

The "Mother Church" of the denomination, Bethel AME in Philadelphia, has also played an important role in documenting African Methodist history from its earliest beginnings. In collaboration with the Historical Society of Pennsylvania, the congregation's Historical Commission has made available on microfilm both Bethel's own records from its founding until 1972 and its nearly complete run of the denomination's *Christian Recorder*, the oldest continuously published black newspaper in America, for the years 1854–1902. Another extensive collection of the *Christian Recorder*, from 1880 to 1917 and from 1941 to the present, housed at Drew University, Madison, New Jersey, nicely complements the microfilm run (1913–36) produced by the American Theological Library Association.[17] Drew also holds a partial run of the *Southern Christian Recorder* for the years 1890, 1896–97, and 1901–4. Copies of the short-lived antebellum AME periodicals, the *African Methodist Episcopal Church Magazine* (1840–48) and the *Repository of Religion and Literature, Science and Art* (1858–64), are not available on film. Fisk University Library in Nashville, Tennessee, holds a complete set of the former, while runs of the latter may be found at the Indiana State Library, Indianapolis (1858–61), and the Houghton Library, Harvard University (1862–63), Cambridge, Massachusetts.

Collections — usually small — of the personal papers of important AME church leaders can be found in a wide variety of archives. The Moorland-Spingarn Research Center holds the 1856 and 1877–78 journals of Daniel A. Payne and a collection of material on AME bishop and black nationalist leader Henry

McNeal Turner. An intermittent series of personal diaries (1851–69) and other papers belonging to AME theologian, editor, and bishop Benjamin Tucker Tanner are located at the Library of Congress. A very substantial collection of the diaries, correspondence, and other papers of another late nineteenth-century theologian, Theophilus Gould Steward, are held by the Schomburg Center, as are the papers of Bishop John Albert Johnson. Duke University in Durham, North Carolina, has the papers of Alabama presiding elder Winfield Henry Mixon, which consist primarily of an incomplete series of personal journals running from 1895 to 1915. The miscellaneous papers of Bishop Charles Spencer Smith (four linear feet) are available at the Bentley Historical Library at the University of Michigan, Ann Arbor, while a collection (five and a half linear feet) of the papers of pastor and presiding elder Charles Henry Boone are held by the Tennessee State Library and Archives. These two collections also contain, respectively, the papers of Christine Shoecraft Smith and Willie Boone, which bear in part on women's work in the AME church.

Livingstone College and Hood Theological Seminary in Salisbury, North Carolina, have the most important collections on the AME Zion church (founded in 1822).[18] They contain extensive though incomplete runs of general and annual conference minutes, as well as manuscript material of some of the denomination's bishops and other leaders, including Joseph Charles Price, John Bryan Small, and John Dancy Sr. Records of the early history of Mother Zion Church in New York are located both at the historic John Street United Methodist Church and also in the New York Public Library. Various partial series of AME Zion conference minutes, together covering much of the nineteenth century, may be found at Boston University (Mugar Library), Wilberforce University, the John Carter Brown Library, and the Rhode Island Historical Society, the latter two in Providence. Of early denominational newspapers, only the *Star of Zion* is known to be extant. Drew University's holdings begin in 1884, and the microfilm run produced by the American Theological Library Association extends from 1896 to 1970. The papers (six linear feet) of Stephen Gill Spottswood, AME Zion bishop and longtime chairman of the national board of the National Association for the Advancement of Colored People (NAACP), are located at the Amistad Research Center at Tulane University in New Orleans.

The last organized (1870) of the major Afro-Methodist denominations, the Colored Methodist Episcopal (since 1954 the Christian Methodist Episcopal) church, has collected its church records, the papers of denominational leaders, and a long run of the *Christian Index*, a church weekly, at the CME Publishing House in Memphis, Tennessee. Drew University also holds a nearly complete set of the *Christian Index* from 1891 to the present. A sizable though as yet uncataloged collection of the papers of retired CME bishop Henry C. Bunton is to be found at the Schomburg Center.

Because the major independent black Methodist denominations emerged as secessions from the Methodist Episcopal Church and the Methodist Episcopal Church, South (the major predecessor bodies to the United Methodist Church), the archival record of black Methodism is in many places bound up with archival records of Methodism generally in the United States. This is especially true for the late eighteenth and early nineteenth centuries, when early records of the Methodist Episcopal (ME) societies along the Atlantic seaboard vividly demonstrate an African presence. The United Methodist Historical Society at the Lovely Lane Museum in Baltimore contains class lists of that area's biracial Methodist societies for the period before a black secession created Baltimore's Bethel AME. Similar documentation is at the Maryland Hall of Records, Annapolis, for black Methodists in Annapolis and for their coreligionists in Richmond and Petersburg at the Virginia State Archives, Richmond.

Because many blacks, despite racial schisms, remained within the ME church throughout its history, the United Methodist Church today has more Afro-American members than any other predominantly white Protestant denomination. The most important body of material on their history is held by the United Methodist archive at Drew University. It has collected minutes of the black annual conferences of the ME Church and of the Central Jurisdiction of the Methodist Church (1939–68). It also holds the correspondence of the Freedmen's Aid Society of the ME Church, which was crucially involved in black education in the post–Civil War South, and microfilm copies of the *Southwestern Christian Advocate* (1876–1929), the *Christian Advocate: Southwestern Edition* (1929–40), and the *Central Christian Advocate* (1941–68), which successively gave voice to the denomination's black constituency. Some papers (three linear feet) of Robert E. Jones, one of the first black Methodist Episcopal bishops elected to serve in the United States rather than in Africa, are at the Amistad Center.

Blacks have also held membership in many other predominantly white Protestant denominations in the United States besides those of the United Methodist tradition. Information concerning them is generally to be found at the major archival centers that most of those churches sponsor. The number of such groups is too large for us to discuss all of them.[19] We will comment, by way of illustration, on only one, the Episcopal church, which has a small but important black membership whose history reaches back into the prerevolutionary missionary efforts of the Church of England.

The starting point for research on black Episcopalians is the denominational archives. The Archives and Historical Collections of the Episcopal Church are located on the campus of the Episcopal Theological Seminary of the Southwest, in Austin, Texas. The extensive records of the Domestic and Foreign Missionary Society there include the especially important Liberian Records, 1822–1952, and the Haitian Records, 1855–1939. Indexes and collection descriptions are available. Among many other valuable collections are those of the American Church Institute for Negroes organized in 1905 to secure funds for eleven Episcopal schools and hospitals for Afro-Americans throughout the South. For information about specific regions, parishes, or clergy, one must also consult the local diocesan archives. One such, the Maryland Diocesan Archives, located at the Maryland Historical Society in Baltimore, deserves special mention. Its more than sixty thousand items, chiefly manuscripts, include important materials dealing with slavery, emancipation, colonization, and the condition of blacks, as well as church work by them and on their behalf. Many items have been indexed by author and recipient, subject, and names of individuals mentioned in correspondence, which greatly facilitates their efficient and effective use.[20] Among seminary libraries, none is more important than that of General Theological Seminary in New York City. Its holdings include bound volumes of George F. Bragg's *Church Advocate* (1913?–40), officially the parish monthly of Baltimore's St. James First African Episcopal Church. The paper also served for many years as the voice of the Conference of Church Workers among Colored People, a caucus of black Episcopal clergy organized in the late nineteenth century. The seminary also holds the papers of prominent Episcopal clergyman, Tollie L. Caution Sr. The papers of individual priests are widely scattered. For example, the bulk of the papers of nineteenth-century intellectual Alexander Crummell are found at the Schomburg Center (though his papers as a whole are to be found in libraries on four continents), while the papers of Pauli Murray, the first female ordained in the Episcopal Church and a major twentieth-century black religious activist, have recently been deposited at the Schlesinger Library, Radcliffe College, Cambridge, Massachusetts.

Until the 1930s, the number of black Roman Catholics was small. Steady growth in the last half century has, however, made black Catholics today the largest constituency of Afro-American Christians belonging to a predominantly white church. Major resources for their history are contained in the archives of religious orders and organizations dedicated to a special mission to African Americans and in the archives of dioceses and archdioceses that have included significant numbers of black communicants. The Josephites, who began their work in the 1870s, have developed the most extensive archive of black Catholic history. Housed at the Josephite headquarters in Baltimore, it includes detailed records of numerous Josephite parishes scattered throughout the South; the letter books of Josephite superior John R. Slattery, an early advocate of the ordination of black priests; biographical files on black Catholic priests; runs of periodicals devoted to the "Negro Apostolate"; and a continuous clipping file of items concerning twentieth-century black Catholics. The archives of the Oblate Sisters of Providence, also located in Baltimore, contain the annual journals of the earliest community of black women religious, founded in 1829. The records of the Sisters of the Blessed Sacrament, founded by Katherine Drexel in 1891 to serve "Colored and Indian" missions, are available to researchers at the community's motherhouse in Philadelphia. They contain important information on Mother Katherine's extensive financial support (based on her inheritance of the Drexel fortune) of missions, parishes, and schools, including Xavier University in New Orleans, the only black Catholic university in the nation. The archives of the Archdiocese of Boston include papers dealing with the career of James A. Healy, the first Afro-American ordained to the priesthood. At the Archdiocese of Chicago archives, the development of black Catholic parishes and issues of black Catholic concern can be chronicled through chancery correspondence. The Msgr. Daniel Cantwell Papers at the Chicago Historical Society contain a wealth of information about the Catholic Interracial Council and other mid-twentieth-century Catholic efforts to improve race relations in that city. An incomplete run of the late nineteenth-century black Catholic newspaper, the *American Catholic Tribune*, edited by Dan Rudd, a layman who organized five black Catholic congresses between 1889 and 1894, is available on microfilm from the American Theological Library Association. The records of the Commission for Catholic Missions among the Colored People and the Indians, located at Marquette University, Milwaukee, Wisconsin, include reports (some detailing conditions) and requests for financial assistance from local parishes and missions from the 1920s.

Special problems arise concerning the rapidly growing Church of God in Christ (COGIC), reportedly now the second largest of all the black denominations, and, indeed, for the other black Pentecostal — and the black Holiness — denominations as well. Charles Edwin Jones, in *Black Holiness*, provides a useful orientation to the organizations, leadership, and literature of these increasingly prominent and influential churches, but does not list manuscript holdings.[21] Efforts are under way at the Historical/Cultural Museum at COGIC headquarters in Memphis, Tennessee, to organize that denomination's archives. Some materials have already been assembled and cataloged, but a large body of minutes, records, and other material remains widely scattered and largely inaccessible, especially for the period before 1956. Difficult to locate too are the papers of major church leaders. The most readily accessible body of unpublished material on Charles H. Mason, the denomination's founder, may be the file assembled by the Federal Bureau of Investigation (FBI). A substantial run of the COGIC periodical *Whole Truth* (1907 to the present) was reportedly held by the late Pentecostal historian, James Tinney. Tinney's papers, currently in private hands, may represent the most significant new material on black Pentecostalism likely to become available for research in the 1990s. The most extensive collection of black Pentecostal and Holiness material currently available is that assembled by Sherry Sherrod DuPree at the Institute of Black Culture of the University of Florida in Gainesville. It contains more than eight thousand items, including minutes, yearbooks, pamphlets, clippings, and a small body of manuscripts. An important uncataloged collection of material on these churches, formerly held by the library of the Interdenominational Theological Center in Atlanta, is unfortunately now in storage at the Woodruff Library of the Atlanta University Center and therefore unavailable to researchers.

While careful attention to denominational loyalties and structures is a necessary and important feature of the study of black church history generally, most scholars will not confine their interests to a single denomination or denominational family. They are likely instead to give their investigations a chronological or thematic definition. Myriad specific research possibilities and problems will naturally be suggested by the specific period or topic chosen. We can do no more here than hint at some of the resources pertinent to such work.

Scholars particularly interested in the mid-nineteenth century will find at the Amistad Center a critically important resource: the extensive correspondence and reports of the American Home Missionary Society and the American Missionary Association, which together include some 550 linear feet of material. Especially important for the years surrounding the Civil War, these collections — like much else in the center's rich holdings — also illuminate black religious life in the twentieth century. For the Civil War and Reconstruction era, extensive if widely scattered materials are also to be found in the War Department records in the National Archives, particularly in the records of the Bureau of Refugees, Freedmen, and Abandoned Lands (Record Group 105). Especially rich are the records of the bureau's assistant commissioners for the different states, most of which are available on microfilm. The records of the Office of the Chief of Chaplains (Record Group 247) and of the Adjutant General's Office (Record Group 407) provide important information on the War Department's dealings with a range of black religious organizations over the first half of the twentieth century.[22] For the period from the 1920s until the early 1960s, researchers will find much of interest in the Claude A. Barnett Papers at the Chicago Historical Society. Founder and director of the Associated Negro Press (ANP), Barnett carried on a voluminous correspondence, thirteen boxes of which are directly cataloged under the heading "religion." Included as well are hundreds of ANP press releases, many concerning the black churches.[23] Important also for the mid-twentieth century are the holdings of the National Archives for Black Women's History and Mary McLeod Bethune Memorial Museum in Washington, D.C., which document the activities not only of Bethune (a Methodist activist) but also of many churchwomen's groups.[24]

For scholars taking a thematic more than a chronological or denominational approach to the study of the black church, one major focus has been — and is likely to remain — the churches' engagement in social reform movements and in electoral politics. The Black Abolitionist Papers project (in addition to publishing documents in what will be a five-volume edition) has microfilmed the correspondence and contributions to newspapers of three hundred Afro-Americans, and the minutes of religious and reform organizations connected with their careers. Since most of these persons were religiously active, this collection sheds important light on church-related participation in the abolitionist movement. The papers of white "carpetbagger" and social reformer Albion Tourgée, at the Chautauqua County Historical Museum, Westfield, New York, contain correspondence from important late nineteenth-century church-based black leaders such as Henry McNeal Turner and Joseph F. Charles Price.[25] The Amistad Center holds a small collection of the papers of Henry H. Proctor, an important black social gospeler. The Booker T. Washington Papers at the Library of Congress are rich in detailed information about the relation of the Tuskegee Machine to the black churches, while patronage-related correspondence involving politically active black clergy is to be found in the papers of every American president since Reconstruction. Certain to cast important new light on the role of the church in twentieth-century black politics, especially during the interwar period, are the papers of Washington's nephew and black Republican power broker Roscoe Conkling Simmons, recently acquired by the Harvard College Library. Consisting of twelve linear feet of correspondence, eight feet of speeches, twelve feet of newspapers, clippings, and political ephemera, and eight feet of photographs, this important new collection is currently being cataloged and should be open for use in 1991. Material pertinent to the activities of twentieth-century church-based reformers, both clerical and lay, is also to be found in the enormous body of archival resources documenting the struggle for civil rights from the founding of the NAACP and the Urban League to the present.[26]

As important as it is to track the churches' role in public life, it is equally important that scholars continue to explore the rich religious life that these institutions have sheltered and nourished for more than two centuries. The distinctive style of worship of black Christians, especially musical performance, has attracted the notice of observers since the eighteenth century. Historians, influenced by anthropologists and folklorists, have of late wisely begun to turn to religious performance, sermons, prayers, and hymns to get at the beliefs and attitudes of the "people in the pew," whose views might otherwise remain inaccessible. To document this crucial aspect of black church life, photographs, recordings, films, and videotapes are increasingly important resources.[27] The single most important collection providing photographic documentation of rural and urban black churches and religious services, though only for the depression era, is the Farm Security Administration Collection in the Prints and Photographs Division of the Library of Congress. Exceptionally rich visual documentation is also sometimes available for specific locations. The Center for Southern Folklore in Memphis, Tennessee, holds a collection of five hundred photographic prints and thirty thousand feet of raw film footage of black church life in and around Memphis from the 1920s through the 1950s.[28] For the study of black religious music, as for black music generally, an important resource is the *Black Music Research Bulletin* (published semiannually by the Center for Black Music Research, Columbia College, Chicago), which carries information about research collections in its field. Another helpful publication is *Rejoice!* the gospel music magazine of the Center for Southern Culture at the University of Mississippi. John Michael Spencer's *As the Black School Sings* provides a guide to the archival collections of ten historically black universities, which include printed, manuscript, recorded, and photographic materials important for the study of Afro-American religious music.[29] The Archive of Folk Music of the Library of Congress contains extensive field recordings of black religious music, some of them never issued. Beginning in the 1920s, recordings of black preachers and gospel singers were produced by many of the major record companies specifically for black audiences.[30] Over seventy of the sermons of the Reverend C.L. Franklin, a master of the art of chanted preaching (and the father of Aretha Franklin), were recorded, primarily under the Jewel and Chess labels.[31] A complete set may be found at the Music Library and Sound Recordings Archives of Bowling Green State University, Bowling Green, Ohio, which also holds an extensive collection of commercially released recordings of popular music, including black gospel music. The holdings of the Center for Popular Music at Middle Tennessee State University in Murfreesboro include a significant number of commercially released recordings of black gospel singers and some field recordings of the black sacred harp tradition. The DuPree collection on the Holiness and Pentecostal traditions includes some 650 audio and 50 video tapes of meetings, personal interviews, and worship services, mostly from Williams Temple (COGIC) in Gainesville, Florida.

Only when such sources as these are fully integrated with the more traditional sources detailed above will an adequate retelling of Carter Woodson's story be possible. And only with the retelling of Woodson's story will it be possible adequately to retell the religious history of the United States in its entirety.

Notes

This essay concerns only one aspect of a larger project, *Afro-American Religion: A Documentary History Project,* funded by the Lilly Endowment. The goal of the project is a three-volume narrative and documentary history of Afro-American religion from its origins in the early development of the Atlantic world until the contemporary period. Correspondence concerning either this essay or the documentary project may be addressed to Professors Raboteau and Wills, c/o Afro-American Religion: A Documentary History Project, 522 Seventy-Nine Hall, Princeton University, Princeton, NJ 08544.

1. Carter G. Woodson, *The History of the Negro Church* (Washington: Associated Publishers, 1921). A second revised edition was published in 1945 and reissued as a third edition in 1972. The most important overviews of black church history since Woodson are E. Franklin Frazier, *Negro Church in America* (New York: Schocken Books, 1964); and Gayraud S. Wilmore, *Black Religion and Black Radicalism* (1972; rpt., Maryknoll: Orbis Books, 1983). The former is a very brief and often unpersuasive sociological essay, while the latter focuses on the relationship of black religion to protest and political activities, so neither is an adequate replacement for Woodson.

2. No edition of Woodson, *History of the Negro Church,* contains footnotes or bibliography, so it is impossible to know clearly and precisely what sources its author used. For important scholarly work of the 1970s and 1980s, focusing wholly or significantly on the institutional history of Afro-American Christianity, see Carol V.R. George, *Segregated Sabbaths: Richard Allen and the Rise of the Independent Black Churches* (New York: Oxford University Press, 1973); Milton Sernett, *Black Religion and American Evangelicalism: White Protestantism, Plantation Missions and the Flowering of Negro Christianity, 1787–1865* (Metuchen, N.J.: Scarecrow Press, 1975); Albert J. Raboteau, *Slave Religion: The "Invisible Institution" in the Antebellum South* (New York: Oxford University Press, 1978); Randall K. Burkett and Richard Newman, eds., *Black Apostles: Afro-American Clergy Confront the Twentieth Century* (Boston: G.K. Hall, 1978); Randall K. Burkett, *Garveyism as a Religious Movement: The Institutionalization of a Black Civil Religion* (Metuchen, N.J.: Scarecrow Press, 1978); Mechal Sobel, *Trabelin' On: The Slave Journey to an Afro-Baptist Faith* (Westport, Conn.: Greenwood Press, 1979); William B. Gravely, "The Social, Polit-

ical and Religious Significance of the Foundation of the Colored Methodist Episcopal Church (1870)," *Methodist History* 18 (Oct. 1979): 3–25; Jualynne Dodsonn, "Nineteenth Century AME Preaching Women: Cutting Edge of Women's Inclusion in Church Polity," in *Women in New Worlds*, ed. Hilah F. Thomas and Rosemary Skinner Keller (Nashville: Abingdon, 1981); David W. Wills and Richard Newman, *Black Apostles at Home and Abroad: Afro-Americans and the Christian Mission from the Revolution to Reconstruction* (Boston: G.K. Hall, 1982); Clarence E. Walker, *A Rock in a Weary Land: The African Methodist Episcopal Church during the Civil War and Reconstruction* (Baton Rouge: Louisiana State University Press, 1982); Walter E. Williams, *Black Americans and the Evangelization of Africa, 1877–1900* (Madison: University of Wisconsin Press, 1982); Evelyn Brooks, "The Feminist Theology of the Black Baptist Church, 1880–1900," in *Class, Sex and Race: The Dynamics of Control*, ed. Amy Swerdlow and Hanna Lessinger (Boston: G.K. Hall, 1983); Will B. Gravely, "The Rise of African Churches in America (1786–1822): Re-Examining the Contexts," *Journal of Religious Thought* 41 (Spring/Summer 1984): 58–73; Aldon D. Morris, *The Origins of the Civil Rights Movement: Black Communities Organizing for Change* (New York: Free Press, 1984); Cheryl Townsend Gilkes, "'Together and in Harness': Women's Traditions in the Sanctified Church," *Signs* 10 (Summer 1985): 678–99; James Melvin Washington, *Frustrated Fellowship: The Black Baptist Quest for Social Power* (Macon: Mercer University Press, 1986); special issue "The Black Catholic Experience," *U.S. Catholic Historian* 5 (1986); Mechal Sobel, *The World They Made Together: Black and White Values in Eighteenth-Century Virginia* (Princeton: Princeton University Press, 1987); Margaret Washington Creel, *"A Peculiar People": Slave Religion and Community Culture among the Gullahs* (New York: New York University Press, 1988); special issue "The Black Catholic Community, 1880–1987," *U.S. Catholic Historian* 7 (Spring/Summer 1988); Taylor Branch, *Parting the Waters: America in the King Years, 1954–63* (New York: Simon and Schuster, 1988); David E. Swift, *Black Prophets of Justice: Activist Clergy before the Civil War* (Baton Rouge: Louisiana State University Press, 1989); David W. Wills, "An Enduring Distance: Black Americans and the Establishment," in *Between the Times: The Travail of the Protestant Establishment in America, 1900–1960*, ed. William R. Hutchison (New York: Cambridge University Press, 1989), 168–92; and Albert J. Raboteau, "The Black Church: Continuity within Change," in *Altered Landscapes: Christianity in America, 1935–1985*, ed. David W. Lotz, Donald W. Shriver Jr., and John F. Wilson (Grand Rapids, Mich.: Eerdmans Publishers, 1989), 77–91.

3. On the encounter of blacks and whites as a major religious theme in American history, see David W. Wills, "The Central Themes of American Religious History: Pluralism, Puritanism, and the Encounter of Black and White," *Religion and Intellectual Life* 5 (Fall 1987): 30–41.

4. Nineteenth-century black denominational histories written from within include, for the African Methodist Episcopal (AME) church, Daniel A. Payne, *The Semi-Centenary and the Retrospection of the African Methodist Episcopal Church in the United States of America* (1866; rpt., Freeport, N.Y.: Books for Libraries Press, 1972); idem, *History of the African Methodist Episcopal Church* (1891; rpt., New York: Arno Press, 1969); and N.C.W. Cannon, *History of the African Methodist Episcopal Church* (Rochester, 1842). For the AME Zion tradition, see Christopher Rush, *Short Account of the Rise and Progress of the African Methodist Episcopal [Zion] Church* (New York: Privately published, 1843); John J. Moore, *History of the A.M.E. Zion Church* (York: Teachers' Journal Office, 1884); and James W. Hood, *One Hundred Years of the African Methodist Episcopal Zion Church* (New

York: A.M.E. Zion Book Concern, 1895). For the Colored, later Christian, Methodist Episcopal (CME) church, see Fayette M. Hamilton, *Conversation on the Colored Methodist Episcopal Church* (Nashville, 1884); and Fayette M. Hamilton, *Plain Account of the Colored Methodist Episcopal Church* (Nashville, 1887). More comprehensive is Charles H. Phillips, *The History of the Colored Methodist Episcopal Church* (1898; rpt., New York: CME Publishing House, 1972). An expanded version of the same volume, called a second edition and bringing the story into the early twentieth century, was published in 1925. Important for their preservation of sources and of the story of blacks in biracial, but predominantly white, denominations are George F. Bragg Jr., *History of the Afro-American Group of the Episcopal Church* (1922; rpt., New York: Church Advocate Press, 1968); Matthew Anderson, *Presbyterianism: Its Relation to the Negro* (Philadelphia: J.M. White, 1897); L.Y. Cox, *Pioneer Foot Steps* (Cape May, N.J.: Star and Ware Press, 1917); and L.M. Hagood, *Colored Man in the Methodist Episcopal Church* (Cincinnati: Cranston and Stowe, 1890). Notable twentieth-century efforts in black denominational history include Charles S. Smith, *History of the African Methodist Episcopal Church* (Philadelphia: Book Concern of the A.M.E. Church, 1922); George A. Singleton, *Romance of African Methodism* (New York: Exposition Press, 1952); Howard D. Gregg, *History of the African Methodist Episcopal Church: The Black Church in Action* (Nashville: African Methodist Episcopal Church, 1980); David H. Bradley, *History of the A.M.E Zion Church* (2 vols., Nashville: Parthenon Press, 1956–70): William J. Walls, *African Methodist Episcopal Zion Church: Reality of the Black Church* (Charlotte: A.M.E. Zion Publishing House, 1974): Othal H. Lakey, *History of the C.M.E. Church* (Memphis: CME Publishing House, 1985); Lewis G. Jordan, *Negro Baptist History, U.S.A., 1750–1930* (Nashville: Publishing Board, Negro Baptist Church, 1930); Leroy Fitts, *History of Black Baptists* (Nashville: Broadman, 1985); and Andrew E. Murray, *Presbyterians and the Negro: A History* (Philadelphia: Presbyterian Historical Society, 1966). Interest within the black churches in documenting and writing their history has recently increased.

5. Walter Schatz, ed., *Directory of Afro-American Resources* (New York: R.R. Bowker, 1970); Ethel L. Williams and Clifton E. Brown, comps., *Howard University Bibliography of African and Afro-American Religious Studies: With Locations in American Libraries* (Wilmington: Scholarly Resources, 1977). For information on the *Newsletter*, address inquiries to the Editor, *Newsletter*, Du Bois Institute, Canaday Hall-B, Harvard University, Cambridge, MA 02138. Annual subscription is $5 (payable to the Afro-American Religious History Group). A reprint edition of previously published newsletters is planned.

6. Loretta L. Hefner, *The WPA Historical Records Survey: A Guide to the Unpublished Inventories, Indexes, and Transcripts* (Chicago: Society of American Archivists, 1980). The Schomburg Center for Research in Black Culture, New York Public Library, is currently engaged in a nationwide effort, supported by the Lilly Endowment, to identify and gather documentary material on Afro-American religious history. One of its projects is to assemble in a single file copies of all Works Projects Administration (WPA) black church records surveys, which should greatly facilitate their use.

7. The Clipping File of the Schomburg Center is available from Chadwyck-Healey: *Schomburg Clipping File, Part 1, 1924–1975* (microfiche, 9500 cards, Alexandria, Va., 1988). For a guide, see *Index to the Schomburg Clipping File* (Teaneck, N.J.: Chadwyck-Healey, 1985). A second series of the Schomburg Clipping Files, for 1975–88, is being filmed. The Tuskegee Institute News Clipping File was organized by Monroe N. Work, who used it to provide data for *Negro Yearbooks* published at Tuskegee beginning in 1912. The comprehensive microfilm edition — *The Tuskegee Institute Clipping File, 1899–1966*

(microfilm, 252 reels, Ann Arbor, 1978), available from University Microfilms International — includes the texts of all published volumes of the *Negro Yearbooks* (1912–52). See John W. Kitchens, ed., *Guide to the Microfilm Edition of the Tuskegee Institute News Clipping File* (Tuskegee: Carver Research Foundation, 1978).

8. *The Hampton University Newspaper Clipping File* (microfiche, 826 cards, Teaneck, N.J., 1987) is available from Chadwyck-Healey. The Gumby Collection of American Negro Scrapbooks (Rare Book and Manuscript Library, Columbia University, New York, N.Y.) has been filmed and is available for interlibrary loan or purchase from Kenneth A. Lohf, Rare Book and Manuscript Library, Butler Library, 6th Floor, 535 West 114th Street, Columbia University Libraries, New York, NY 10027.

9. On this document, see Payne, *History of the African Methodist Episcopal Church*, v. That lost or little-known manuscripts can still be recovered and given new life by researchers is evident from Jean McMahon Humez, ed., *Gifts of Power: The Writings of Rebecca Jackson: Black Visionary, Shaker Eldress* (Amherst: University of Massachusetts Press, 1981). See also William L. Andrews, ed., *Sisters of the Spirit: Three Black Women's Autobiographies of the Nineteenth Century* (Bloomington: Indiana University Press, 1986).

10. This item is in the Carter G. Woodson Papers (Manuscript Division, Library of Congress), one of the most important multidenominational black church manuscript collections.

11. Historical Commission of the Southern Baptist Convention, 901 Commerce Street, Suite 400, Nashville, TN 37203.

12. For an index to *National Baptist Magazine*, see Lester B. Scherer, comp., *Newsletter of the Afro-American Religious History Group* 6 (Spring 1982): 4–9. See also Lester B. Scherer, comp., *Afro-American Baptists: A Guide to Materials in the American Baptist Historical Society* (Rochester, N.Y.: American Baptist Historical Society, 1985), a useful (though not definitive) guide to the Afro-American material of the American Baptist Historical Society, Rochester, N.Y.

13. The American Baptist Historical Society run, which covers the years 1898 to 1949 (with many breaks), is available on microfilm from the American Baptist Historical Society, 1106 S. Goodman Street, Rochester, NY 14620. The authors are indebted to Ralph E. Luker, associate editor, Martin Luther King Jr. Papers, for information about the *Georgia Baptist* and other items cited in this article.

14. The Martin Luther King Jr. Papers Project, which plans to publish a twelve-volume edition beginning in 1991, is drawing on these 2 major collections and 150 additional collections in dozens of archives and in private hands. Inquiries about this project should be directed to Professor Clayborne Carson, Editor, The Martin Luther King Jr. Papers, Cyprus Hall-D, Stanford University, CA 94305-4146.

15. For the most important of the smaller black Methodist bodies, see Lewis V. Baldwin, *"Invisible" Strands in African Methodism: A History of the African Union Methodist Protestant and Union American Methodist Episcopal Churches, 1805–1980* (Metuchen, N.J.: Scarecrow Press, 1983). See also Will B. Gravely, "African Methodisms and the Rise of Black Denominationalism," in *Rethinking Methodist History: A Bicentennial Historical Consultation*, ed. Russell E. Richey and Kenneth E. Rowe (Nashville: United Methodist Publishing House, 1985), 111–24.

16. For information on the holdings of the AME Financial Department and on other points, the authors are indebted to Professor Dennis C. Dickerson of Williams College. Elected AME church historiographer in 1988, Dickerson is exploring the possibility of establishing a central denominational repository. He has produced a pamphlet guide to

research in AME materials: Dennis C. Dickerson, *The Past Is in Your Hands: Writing Local AME Church History* (n.p., 1989), available from Dennis C. Dickerson, P.O. Box 301, Williamstown, MA 01267. *AME Church Review* (microfilm, 4 reels, Millwood, n.d.) is available from Kraus International Publications.

17. Inquiries concerning *Christian Recorder* (1854–1902) microfilm (12 reels) and *The Records of Mother Bethel AME Church, 1760–1972* (24 reels, Historical Commission, Mother Bethel AME Church, Philadelphia) should be addressed to the Historical Society of Pennsylvania, 1300 Locust Street, Philadelphia, PA 19107, and Historical Commission, Mother Bethel AME Church, 419 South Sixth Street, Philadelphia, PA 19147. Inquiries concerning *Christian Recorder* (1913–36) microfilm may be addressed to Preservation Board, American Theological Library Association, 820 Church Street, 3rd Floor, Evanston, IL 60201.

18. The William J. Walls Heritage Center, on the campus of Livingstone College and Hood Theological Seminary, Salisbury, N.C., was intended as the major denominational archive, but it is currently unstaffed and therefore not open to researchers.

19. For blacks in the Presbyterian churches, the researcher is advised to begin at the Presbyterian Historical Society, Philadelphia. For blacks in the Congregational tradition, an especially important collection is that of the Amistad Research Center, Tulane University, New Orleans. On the relevant holdings of the Disciples of Christ Historical Society in Nashville, Tennessee, see *Preliminary Guide to Black Materials in the Disciples of Christ Historical Society* (Nashville: Disciples of Christ Historical Society, 1971).

20. This detailed index was compiled over a lifetime by diocesan historiographer F. Garner Ranney.

21. Charles Edwin Jones, *Black Holiness: A Guide to the Study of Black Participation in Wesleyan Perfectionist and Glossolalic Pentecostal Movements* (Metuchen, N.J.: Scarecrow Press, 1987). For information concerning archival materials on the black Holiness and Pentecostal churches, the authors are indebted to Professor Hans Baer of the University of Arkansas at Little Rock; Professor David Daniels of McCormick Theological Seminary; Professor Robert Franklin of the Candler School of Theology, Emory University; Professor Cheryl Townsend Gilkes of Colby College; Albert G. Miller, doctoral student at Princeton University; and Richard Newman of the New York Public Library.

22. The American Home Missionary Society and American Missionary Association collections have been filmed and are available for purchase or interlibrary loan through the Amistad Research Center, Tilton Hall, Tulane University, New Orleans, LA 70118. Records of the Bureau of Refugees, Freedmen, and Abandoned Lands, RG 105 (National Archives), are available on microfilm from the National Archives Trust Fund Board, National Archives, Washington, DC 20408. *Black Studies: A Select Catalog of National Archives Microform Publications* (Washington, 1984), which includes a detailed description of this and other related microfilm collections, is available for $5 (including postage and handling) from the National Archives Trust Fund, P.O. Box 100793, Atlanta, GA 30384. For information on materials in the War Department records in the National Archives, we are indebted to the Military Reference Branch, National Archives and Records Administration, Washington. A more extensive description of these and related materials is forthcoming in the *Newsletter of the Afro-American Religious History Group.*

23. The Claude A. Barnett Papers (Chicago Historical Society, Chicago) are available on microfilm from University Publications of America: *The Claude A. Barnett Papers: The Associated Negro Press* (microfilm, 198 reels, Frederick, Md., 1985–86).

24. On this and related collections, see Deborah Gray White, "Mining the Forgotten:

Manuscript Sources for Black Women's History," *Journal of American History* 74 (June 1987): 237–42.

25. On the black church in American politics, see David W. Wills, "Beyond Commonality and Plurality: Persistent Racial Polarity in American Religion and Politics," in *Religion and American Politics: From the Colonial Period to the 1980s*, ed. Mark A. Noll (New York: Oxford University Press, 1990), 199–224. On the Black Abolitionist Papers, see George E. Carter and C. Peter Ripley, eds., *Black Abolitionist Papers, 1830–1865* (microfilm, 17 reels, Ann Arbor: University Microfilms International, 1981); and George E. Carter and C. Peter Ripley, eds., *Black Abolitionist Papers, 1830–1865: A Guide to the Microfilm Edition* (New York: Microfilming Corporation of America, 1981). The papers of Albion Tourgée are available on microfilm from University Microfilms International: *The Albion W. Tourgée Papers* (microfilm, 60 reels, Ann Arbor: University Microfilms International, 1965).

26. See Robert L. Zangrando, "Manuscript Sources for Twentieth-Century Civil Rights Research," *Journal of American History* 74 (June 1987): 243–51.

27. Exhibitions can also supply important documentation. See, for example, Edward D. Smith, *Climbing Jacob's Ladder: The Rise of Black Churches in Eastern American Cities, 1740–1877* (Washington: Smithsonian Institution Press, 1988), published in connection with a major exhibition at the Anacostia Museum of the Smithsonian Institution. The exhibition "Climbing Jacob's Ladder" began a three-year tour of thirty-six American cities in the spring of 1990. In each locality, the exhibition will include manuscripts and artifacts newly gathered from congregations in that area; it will therefore augment, as well as display, the literary and material documentation of early black church history.

28. This collection is the work of one person, the Reverend L.O. Taylor. A documentary film on Taylor's life and work, "Sermons and Sacred Pictures," is available from the Center for Southern Folklore, 1216 Peabody Avenue, P.O. Box 40105, Memphis, TN 38104. The center has also published a two-volume catalog useful for locating films and videotapes relevant to the study of black churches (the catalog includes the addresses of distributors): *American Folklore Films and Videotapes: An Index* (Memphis: Center for Southern Folklore, 1976), and *American Folklore Films and Videotapes: A Catalogue*, vol. 2 (New York: R.R. Bowker, 1982). Three films deserve special mention. "Say Amen, Somebody," a commercially released film now on videotape, highlights the careers of gospel singer Willie Mae Ford Smith and gospel composer Thomas A. Dorsey. "Fannie Bell Chapman: Gospel Singer," a film depicting the ministry of a Mississippi gospel singer and faith healer, illustrates the importance of healing in Afro-American religious practice. "The Performed Word," a documentary film now on videotape, examines continuity and change in black preaching through a comparison of bishop Elmer E. Cleveland, Ephesians Church of God in Christ, Berkeley, California, and his daughter, Ernestine Cleveland Reems, pastor of the Center of Hope, Oakland, California. The film is especially effective in presenting the sequential development and congregational response to the chanted sermon. Its producer has analyzed Bishop Cleveland's preaching—and that of other black preachers—in Gerald L. Davis, *I Got the Word in Me and I Can Sing It, You Know: A Study of the Performed African-American Sermon* (Philadelphia: University of Illinois Press, 1985). See also Bruce A. Rosenberg, *Can These Bones Live? The Art of the American Folk Preacher* (Urbana: University of Illinois Press, 1988); and Albert J. Raboteau, "The Afro-American Traditions," in *Caring and Curing: Health and Medicine in Western Religious Traditions*, ed. Ronald L. Numbers and Darrel W. Amundsen (New York: Macmillan, 1986), 539–62.

29. Inquiries concerning *Black Music Research Bulletin* may be addressed to Center for Black Music Research, Columbia College, Chicago, 600 S. Michigan Avenue, Chicago, IL 60605. The authors are indebted to Richard Newman for calling this periodical and related material to their attention. Jon Michael Spencer, *As the Black School Sings: Black Music Collections at Black Universities and Colleges, with a Union List of Book Holdings* (New York: Greenwood Press, 1987).

30. A collection of such "race records" is Paul Oliver, comp., *Songsters and Saints* (Matchbox Records MSEX 2001/2002 and MSEX 2003/2004, 2 vols., 4 disks).

31. C.L. Franklin's recorded sermons have largely gone out of print. Among the places where those still available can be ordered — and other hard-to-find recordings of black religious music and sermons obtained — is Down Home Records, 10341 San Pablo Avenue, El Cerrito, CA 94530. Information about a reissue of "classic recordings of C.L. Franklin" can be obtained from Stan Lewis, Jewel Records, P.O. Box 1125, Shreveport, LA 71163-1125. See also C.L. Franklin, *Give Me This Mountain: Life History and Selected Sermons*, ed. Jeff Todd Titon (Urbana: University of Illinois Press, 1989), which contains texts of several of the recorded sermons.

Religion and the South: Authenticity and Purity—Pulling Us Together, Tearing Us Apart

DONALD G. MATHEWS

For students of American religion(s), the South remains strange and uncharted territory. For students of the American South, religion remains so familiar that its meaning, functions, and expressions are frequently reduced to stereotype. The conviction of Walter Hines Page, who practiced his devotion to Dixie in the North, that progress in the South was largely impeded by preachers is repeated by a contemporary writer who complained that religion betrayed thousands in the late nineteenth century by turning their attention away from real, that is, political, goals, and toward unreal, that is, religious, things.[1] Religion is too much concerned with the transcendent, or "other" world: this is familiar fare. "Otherworldliness" can explain the emotional outbursts of revival as well as defeat of the Confederacy;[2] it had frustrated an ambivalent Benjamin Mays, who thought African-American preachers' focus on heaven and hereafter had been an opiate.[3] And the response is certainly understandable given the political and economic needs of Mays's people. But actions by black preachers during Reconstruction — and even in southern cities of the "nadir" — suggest anything but "otherworldliness." And political action in the 1980s and 1990s by self-styled "Christian" and essentially conservative activists — people every bit as conscious of the divine as their religious predecessors — suggests that the religious understanding of southerners is worldly indeed. Neither of these examples is an aberration.

The entire history of religion in the South is the history of social action and solidarity. To be sure, the narrative does not always reveal the kind of action or communal identity that historians for ideological reasons may value, but it is not "otherworldly" in that it postpones the human search for the authentic beyond death in "another world." It is immediate and immediately gratifying; and it is within the power of the individual to achieve without the possibility of failure that plagues those who rely on elections or force to achieve their goals. The religious history of southerners is about how people living in that wide and diverse region that stretches from the Baltimore suburbs to Irving, Texas, have thought about the meaning of their lives in confrontation with mortality, chaos, pain, and ignorance. It is about how they have thought of the sacred and transcendent and how they have tried to authenticate their connection with, their understanding of, and their obedience to the sacred and transcendent — and to order their lives accordingly. This ordering of individual and collective life is anything but "otherworldly," and to say that people yield to discipline merely in anticipation of heaven and in wariness of hell is to betray a lack of familiarity with the fear of death and the nature of religious devotion, insight, and discipline that is surprising and disappointing to say the very least. The worldly encounter of religion in southern culture has been obvious in the fact that it has been studied primarily in institutional life, although there are studies of southern life and culture that reveal the imaginative life of men and women apart from institutions.[4]

A self-conscious and dedicated search for authenticity is one of the persistent and generative themes of southern religious history. This search has been part of a dialectical process in which religion brings people together even as it pulls them apart. The creative social processes of southern religious history are not to be understood as "declension" — as in the ambiguous jeremiadic New England tradition, or even as "pluralism" — as in the experience of people living between Greenwich, Connecticut, and Cape May, New Jersey, with their extended hinterlands. Rather, the dialectic has been between forces that created an evangelical hegemony among the religious in conflict either with the self-consciously religious who resisted the evangelical style and ambience, or with those who avoided religious identity altogether. The social impact of this process was to create an identity suggested in the first-person plural in the title of this paper, an "us-ness" that seems awkward in an academic exercise but is nonetheless apt. The South may, to be sure, be objectified for purposes of historical, sociological, or cultural analysis, but to understand the compelling power of religion in the South, both insiders and outsiders must feel — if only for a fleeting moment — the "us-ness" of southern culture and religion. Persistent and pervasive is a sensibility that concedes no possibility of being "them"; and to the extent that reference to "us" conveys exclusion of the observer, it conveys the internal dialectic of this fascinating section of the United States and its religious praxis.

The beginnings of a peculiarly southern configuration of religion lay in evangelical revival, that is to say, with the preaching of New Side Presbyterian ministers and New Light Baptists. Samuel Davies helped establish an evangelical Presbyterian presence in Virginia during the 1740s, and New Light Baptists in North Carolina and Virginia during the 1750s and 1760s joined him in bringing what Rhys Isaac has called a counterculture that transformed Virginia.[5] To be sure, Christianity had already come from England under the aegis of the Bishop of London, the Society for the Propagation of the Gospel in Foreign Parts, and vestry acts passed by assemblies in the southern colonies. And with an invasion of Scots, Germans, Welsh, and Protestant Irish together with dissenting Englishmen, the Anglican communion seemed to be challenged by a process that could create an incipient pluralism. They came as Presbyterians, Baptists, Pietists, Lutherans, and Reformers, each celebrating the trajectory of life in religious faith and practice, bonded by public ritual associated with birth, marriage, death, and hope. Religious bonding within community brought people together, but it also separated them from the structure and assumptions of the vestry acts. This fractured religious landscape yielded not to establishment but to the mood and style of Davies, Separate Baptists, and the contagion of Wesleyan societies planted and connected by a plastic and aggressive Methodism in the personae of eager, determined, ubiquitous, and evocative young lay circuit riders.[6] The purpose of each was the purpose of all. They wanted an authentic Christianity based on a sensible practical faith that bespoke personal salvation and collective identity based on their various interpretations of what constituted an authentic — a pure — Christianity. Methodists explained themselves in John Wesley's words that they were a people having the *form* but seeking the *power* of religion. Separates, as children of the Awakening in New England, entered the South devoted to exercising apostolic gifts in bringing together Christians whose experience of the New Birth was neither metaphorical nor rational, but real and transforming as expressed in testimony to a community covenanted in Christ. Davies explained it as a gracious change that brought "holiness of practice," a "conscientious observance of every known duty, and an honest, zealous resistance of every known sin."[7]

They all preached what George Whitefield had called a "felt Christ." The drama of redemption was to be literally experienced in each individual believer, which resulted in an assurance that Christ had indeed died for *me* — the awareness of self was supposed to have been overwhelmed only by the awareness of Christ. Such assurance was offensive to traditionalists, rationalists, and non-Protestant believers because it seemed arrogant and pretentious, especially among those of such low estate, but its triumphalism carried over into the broader culture and brought a new way of pulling people together. The traditional, "worldly" way had been through patterns of deference on the part of persons without much land or standing in the community to those who possessed both. Deference on the part of social inferiors to superiors was reinforced by social distance, education, apparel, manners, and polite conversation. That is, according to the ordinary rules of the world, people were bonded by knowing their place (estate) and keeping their distance, whereas the evangelical ethos provided spaces and times where the ordinary rules did not apply, where people could embrace, sing, and preach a kinetic celebration of rebirth. They seemed to delight in breaking worldly order; even slaves, to the disgust of some, could give evangelical testimony in meeting.[8] This new way provided a new language of acceptable social intercourse: a language of self-discovery (confession of sin), personal transformation (discipline), and piety (holiness). The new way, too, created a forum within which individuals conceded to others the obligation to inquire into the personal behavior and social relationships of their peers as to whether or not they walked in the way of the Lord. This surveillance of private life and attitude eroded boundaries created by distance, education, and wealth and helped create an attitude toward authority that was republican in its implications: everyone could be called to account for action that emulated social elites: fighting, gambling, horseracing, drinking, dancing, gossiping, wearing a "superfluity of apparel." These were not attacks on elites for the political power they wielded — but on everything that elites valued and much of what they did. The social display through which elites exercised influence was repudiated by people who, for the present at least, challenged the mimesis that secured elite hegemony. Thus changing the motivation for behavior from pleasure and risk to self-discipline and godly service, evangelical revival provided a seriousness that gave life order, direction, and meaning. The better sort may have believed that evangelical Baptists, Methodists, and Presbyterians were tearing the fabric of society apart, but from within each communion the achievement of a Christianity authenticated by experience seemed to be pulling people together.

Religion helped to pull black people together in resisting the logic of slavery and creating visible institutions. In the earliest days of enslavement, peoples from different African nations were brought together in ways that confounded a communal celebration of unalloyed African religion in America. Africans resisted Christianity as long as it emphasized the distance between Africans and Europeans. To be sure, a few Africans were converted and socialized into Christianity before the 1740s, but when evangelical preaching evoked responses from Africans that suggested resonance between the religious sensibilities of both races, Africans began to join Presbyterian, Baptist, and Methodist churches and societies. Antiphonal responses to chanted sermons, celebration of the spirit in song and prayer, and the apparent concession by whites to blacks that they inhabited the same moral universe seemed to pull individuals from each race together with the other. The apparent concession by blacks to whites that they experienced the same presence of the spirit helped to create common rituals of community and worship. The shared experience of charismatic worship especially among Separate Baptists and Methodists in the post-Revolutionary generation helped authenticate the evangelical gospel for each people. And some Africans came to believe that being Christian could be a way of being free even if the religion were similar to that of whites. Africans discovered that slave and master when thought of as "sinners" occupied the same position before God; both stood in need of the same salvation, both belonged in fellowship contrary to the ordinary rules of the world. Both could be called to account before the church. This possibility conceded a moral economy in which mutual obligation was implicitly acknowledged and could be as subversive of the masters' claims to authority as it was supportive of the slaves' understanding of themselves as "chosen" when they embraced the Hebrew memory of Exodus as if it were their own.[9]

Christianity was not a discrete body of doctrine and was only partially a concrete moral code. It was also a way of perceiving the divine, receiving power, and ordering life through various conversations about the Christian way. That this conversation was part of a process of acculturation is obvious, but if it did not create a consensus between black and white or among blacks, it did nonetheless concede institutional integrity to African Americans. If the latter created an "invisible" institution from a fusion of African cultural artifacts and Christian myth, they also created a *visible* institution in independent black churches, in black congregations of biracial churches, and in segregated balconies of white churches. This concession of authenticity — sacralized by time, practice, and evangelical mission — allowed blacks to create the basis of public identity. Slowly, erratically, uncertainly, and painfully, slaves and free people of color negotiated space, time, and obligation in establishing the privilege of public worship as a right. To be sure, masters could understand their cooperation and support as an extension of paternalistic self-interest, but it was also in the interests of their slaves who authenticated the whites' religion ironically in authenticating their own.

If both races experienced conversion as receiving welcome coherence out of chaos and discovering purpose within confusion, there was nonetheless a difference between the two peoples besides their station and race. Both races could struggle through private pilgrimage into wilderness, wrestling with Satan or seeking illumination,[10] but whereas traditional Christian cosmology prepared the unified self to die in Christ and to be reborn with him, African cosmology prepared the seeker to discover the real person (*little me*) — in opposition to the outer shell of self — who would be guided through vision and trance into freedom. The difference between the African whose real self is set free in an experience of divine presence and the Briton whose real self deserves death but escapes through the grace of the divine is obvious. This difference, together with the resonance between the two ways of dying and discovering could allow both European and African sensibilities, values, and insights to be expressed in terms of Christian love, forgiveness, assurance, and awe, a fact that enabled slaves to embrace Christian language as their own. They discovered in the Old Testament stories a history of their own redemption; in the gospel they heard justification and hope; in the Revelation of Saint John they anticipated apocalypse and judgment.[11] If assumptions of a shared Christianity could lead whites to use religion as a means of control, they could also justify Africans' resistance and nurturance of a view of life alternative to that of masters.[12] Thus religion that rested on the authenticity of a subjective and internal but sensible experience such as that celebrated in the New Birth, could pull people together in a kind of negotiated settlement that also kept them apart, a paradox valued by both races for different reasons.

Over the course of the generations between Revolution and Civil War, an evangelical ethos came to dominate southern religion. To be sure, there was pervasive and persistent resistance. Not all Baptist churches could succumb to the aggressive institution building that seemed to dilute Calvinist theology; some wished to retain a Primitive and apostolic purity unencumbered with supporting societies and conventions and unaffected by an Arminianizing tendency. Later Landmark Baptists refused to cooperate with or defer to a kind of evangelical ecumenism that conceded Presbyterian, Methodist, Episcopal, Moravian, and Lutheran denominations to be true Christian churches. The few Episcopalians in the South expressed a religious spectrum from rationalism to evangelicalism to high church experimentation, and some Presbyterians and Lutherans were cool to and suspicious of evangelical tendencies even as they conceded to the latter some standing to the experience of grace.[13] Roman Catholics in Baltimore, New Orleans, Mobile, and Kentucky were never present in sufficient numbers in the South to sustain a broad commitment to pluralism in the culture. If they with Quakers provided an obvious religious alternative to evangelical dominations, their locations together with those of various German faith communities by contrast with the surrounding evangelical churches provided a "foreign presence" that could help define evangelical style, mood, and society. As long as such differences were within a consensually normative Protestantism, they were not dangerous to southern solidarity, but rationalists and those who disdained religion were under constant pressure to make a profession of faith as if they were strange if they did not do so.

The long history of Jews in the South is, as evangelicals would have said, "instructive." Before secession, southern Jews had tried to be as invisible as possible, although the Jewish communities in Charleston, Georgetown, Savannah, and New Orleans were as hallowed by time and presence as Episcopalians. Yet, as Jacob Mordecai of Richmond, Virginia, and Warrenton, North Carolina, discovered, the surrounding evangelical culture was so well prepared by theological commitment to seduce or argue Jews into converting, and personal relationships between Jews and Christians so frequently compelling during times of personal distress, that children could embrace Christianity as a necessary fulfillment of their Judaism.[14] Suspicion of difference and pressures for conformity in a society beleaguered by outsiders could allow a festering antisemitism to erupt into scapegoating "blasphemous Jews" during the Civil War and later during the economic crises of the 1890s. A generation later, the same suspicion and demand for conformity in religion could lead an Atlanta mob to lynch Leo Frank for rape and murder, crimes that no historian believes he committed. The Frank case was but the most violent expression of a pervasive suspicion of religious nonconformists that newcomers to the South — Jew or Gentile — felt well into the twentieth century. Jews are favored targets for evangelical proselytizers; their role in Christians' understanding of the New Testament was as the people necessarily antecedent to the Christian church, those who prepared the way for the Messiah and who should have accepted Jesus as the expected one and confessed him as Lord. The evangelical ethos would not necessarily have sustained the epithet "Christ-killer!" but it did reserve Jews for preferred notice among aggressive evangelical activists. "Be especially careful of the *goyim*," young Eli Evans was warned by elders of the synagogue in Durham, North Carolina. "Converting a Jew is a special blessing for them." Of Southern Baptists polled in the 1960s 90 percent believed that the Jews should be converted to Christianity presumably because such an achievement would have been the fulfillment of Christian history.[15]

To be an authentic Christian, according to such southerners, evangelical self-consciousness almost demanded the conversion of Jews. Moreover, there has been among southerners of all religious persuasions an insistent curiosity about other people's faith — "Where do you go to church?" — which can sometimes convey a more assertive scrutiny than is intended. Confrontation on the playground could be more intimidating. A child's query as to "why don't you believe in Jesus" can evoke immediate defensiveness and a feeling of being different; it implies a strangeness that one must explain. All "normal" people believe in Jesus, the inquisitor assumes, and if *you* don't, there is something wrong with you. Such challenges — much more sophisticated but no less intimidating — among adults suggest that religious convention is part of the medium of citizenship and social acceptability. Implied here, as in all discourse in which evangelical vision of a converted world is expressed, is a definition of personal and collective authenticity that both pulls people together and tears them apart. The inclusiveness invites everyone to share in the psychic assurance and personal satisfaction to be had from "a clear sense of personal identity," as one writer calls it, associated with religious commitment.[16] Southern evangelicalism, he writes, is characterized by a self-confident certainty and a "high degree of personal intensity" and assertiveness that may provide the impetus for all kinds of good works which in the evangelical ideology includes a missionary commitment. If most believers are potential missionaries, all others are potential converts — not exactly a pleasant experience because of the implication that acceptability and authenticity are restricted to those sharing the faith.

In the antebellum South, however, evangelical assertiveness and institutional creativity brought ever more black and white people together in church membership. The religious mood and discipline that once had repudiated and scandalized elites now claimed them. The transformation was reflected in part by the changing discourse about slavery. At first — among Davies's Presbyterians, North Carolina's Separate Baptists, and South Carolina's Awakened Independents — the offer of New Birth heedless of race and rank brought slaves and masters both into fellowship with little thought given on the part of one party at least to challenging the status of either. With Quaker scrutiny of slaveholding after 1750, and republican debate about equality and liberty, Methodist circuit riders raised questions about slaveholding that evoked widespread but scarcely popular discussion over whether or not slaveholding was a disciplinable offense. Newly converted slaveholders adamantly insisted that it was not, and the experiment of antislavery piety was aborted, although a debate over the issue continued sporadically throughout the culture until the 1820s.[17] The impulse came to be remembered as misplaced idealism that had failed to be true to the primary evangelical commitment of converting people to Christ, a commitment that by the late 1820s could be channeled into missions to plantation slaves not already incorporated into Christian fellowship.[18] The argument, made most emphatically by Charles Colcock Jones Sr., a wealthy minister-planter of Liberty County, Georgia, explained the danger for the morals and physical safety of whites living among a class of people whose culture was subversive of and potentially hostile to their own. Insisting that only a religiously articulated relationship based on a common Christianity of masters and slaves could create a safe and defensible society, Jones was joined by many others in making the case for Christian slaveholding. In these and similar efforts, apologists were attempting to broaden and intensify claims for Christian faith and practice among both slave children and slaveholding patriarchs. Dismayed at the large numbers of elites and slaves still beyond Christian fellowship, evangelical publicists sought to make Christian commitment a public responsibility as well as a private privilege. They hoped to pull blacks and whites, elites and yeomen, women and men together during a time when antislavery action in the 1830s seemed potentially capable of tearing the Union apart.

Southern Christian apologists required little inventiveness to move from a defense of Mission to a defense of slavery — but one always qualified by the goals of *apologia* and conversion. When northern abolitionists condemned slaveholding Christianity as illegitimate for breaking the Golden Rule and betraying the spirit of Christian brotherhood, they demanded excommunication of all who owned slaves. This demand, together with controversies ignited among national organizations of Presbyterians, Methodists, and Baptists over variations of the same theme, led to the creation of the Southern Baptist convention in 1845 and the Methodist Episcopal Church, South, between 1844 and 1846. The South now seemed to have its own religion. Accusations against northern denominations as having embraced a political religion based on red republican, jacobin, and human ideals rather than the pure truths and specific verses of sacred text reflected the claim among southern religious publicists that their religion was authentic for being based on the clear word of scripture rather than the sentimental and dangerous romanticism of people who had in effect repudiated God. Much southern apologetic rested on a patriarchal model of family life crafted from the Old Testament and resting on a hermeneutic that made ancient Hebrews and modern southerners contemporaries and surrendered the metaphorical power of being "in Christ" to simplistic and absolute commands. The nuanced elevation of Christian brotherhood above Roman servitude in the Book of Philemon, for example, yielded to the strained interpretation of the Epistle as justification for the Fugitive Slave Act of 1850.[19] By arguing that southerners could justify slavery only by Christianizing it, evangelical publicists belied their own claims for a strict "spirituality" of the church and labored to make their culture as well as their religion defensible by reference to appropriate biblical texts. The process helped to secure a hermeneutic that easily fed the fundamentalism of a later day.

In the political process that made the South an idea as well as a place and allowed evangelical preachers to insist upon the importance of religion to that idea, evangelical institutions were becoming essential to southern society. Camp meetings and revivals set aside sacred time and space for seasonal renewal. Singing schools and shape-note hymnals and songbooks provided an oral ecumenism that suffused popular culture and elicited emotional attachment to a fusion of family, kinship, and religion that surpassed in importance both sectarian differences and theological conceits.[20] Academies, institutes, and colleges evolved as the spiritual heirs of those who had pilloried a learned clergy and taunted over-educated parsons now confirmed the sons and daughters of elites in the "refined and enlightened" ways of religion.[21] Missions to slaves were offered as the Christian and southern alternative to atheistic and Yankee abolitionism. And a wide range of periodicals directed to the laity became educational tools to help create a sacred solidarity. Even as editors railed at the dangers of worldliness and declension, they expressed a guarded optimism at the ever increasing possibility (it was to be hoped) that denominational institutions would birth an evangelized public that could eventually provide the leaven to Christianize society.

This goal became increasingly urgent as southerners encountered war, defeat, and Reconstruction. In responding to these traumatic shocks, a generation of ambivalent publicists wrestled to commend their faith as the means of pulling southerners together even as they remained aware of the persistent conflict between church and world. This polarity was not between living in this world and anticipating the "other," although Confederate officers — sharing the same bias as some historians — at first believed that it was. The officers at least changed their minds as they came to realize what evangelical Protestants throughout the South had known since the early days of revival when they committed vast amounts of time to investigating, evaluating, and punishing behavior — a more "this-worldly" enterprise can scarcely be imagined. The conflict between church and world was between competing standards for behavior: that of the church valued restraint, self-denial, effort, obedience, respect for others — as attested by church books throughout the South. That of the world valued independence, pride, indulgence, irreverence, and heedlessness of others — as attested by the same moral ledgers.[22] The difference between the two modes of behaving rests of course on the way in which young men thought about the meaning of their lives and their own personal destinies. The gospel message was of repentance and salvation, one act that could be interpreted as an act of will and the other as an act of Grace. Both provided a sense of self-control in a threatening and potentially fatal environment. As Drew Faust points out, the Christian paradigm of conversion — in which the death of auditors is so essential to understanding the threat of sin, the joy of forgiveness, and the relief of salvation — forced men to relive the terror and horror of battle, thus to relieve the tension, and thus at last to believe that in reaffirming or choosing Christ they could achieve a sense of control and "the ability once again to cope."[23] Faust's demonstration of the morale-inducing function of religion in the ranks raises serious doubts about the presumably dysfunctional characteristics of a theoretically "individualistic" southern faith.

Indeed, it is obvious that the religious life in southern armies breached sectarian differences to become a means of enhancing social solidarity. Even more broadly than in antebellum camp meetings, believers were thrown together heedless of sectarian differences; the religious military press that developed after 1863 preached an evangelical ecumenism that probably transformed even those suspicious of revival and expressiveness in worship into celebrants of a common faith. Certainly there was no division between evangelicals and other Protestants on the importance of discipline and service or the desirability of "religious conversation." Reflecting on such things, young men on their own or with the help of colporteurs and missionaries had already begun to organize prayer groups and Bible study cadres throughout the armies. All became subject to the entrepreneurial marketing of the religious press and the revivals that broke out in southern armies after the fall of 1862.[24] The press produced tracts reassuring soldiers that the war, because it was defensive, was just, and that they should be confident in doing what Christian men should be expected to do under such circumstances[25] and assume a dual mission. "Every motive of justice, love of truth, and of right, and of humanity, which animates the soldier in taking up arms now, urges you to become a soldier of Christ."[26] In a traditional sense, this homily implied the familiar responsibility of each evangelical Christian to live a self-consciously exemplary life so as to demonstrate the reality of Grace and the special status of one who does not live according to the ordinary rules of the world. Each Christian soldier was supposed to be a missionary. Eventually, some sanguine ministers came to believe that the conversion of Confederate armies could be the means eventually of converting the entire South. They could become a "righteous remnant."[27]

The language of encouragement, reassurance, and social solidarity could lend itself to an abortive nationalism. A generation who believed in the Providence of God confidently heard the Word through the words of Jeremiah (1:14, 16, 19b KJV), who warned the southerners of his own day that *"Out of the North an evil shall break forth upon the inhabitants of the land . . . And I will utter my judgments against them touching all their wickedness, who have forsaken me and have burned incense unto other gods, and worshipped the works of their own hands. . . . but they shall not prevail against thee; for I am with thee."* A generation familiar with the Bible could find meaning in such texts and possibly even identify them with the Confederacy when political leaders called for fast days or preachers justified battlefield losses by appeal to "the Cross of Christ and the purity of Christianity."[28] And a recent author can state that "the most fundamental source of legitimation for the Confederacy was Christianity. Religion provided a transcendent framework for southern nationalism."[29] But in reflective moments "source" and "framework" could never produce the kind of corporate identity required to sustain "Confederate nationalism"; southern clergymen considered the "source" and "framework" to be conditional. That is, the war was an opportunity to make the South Christian but only *if* southerners as a people repented and yielded to godly discipline. And this, evangelical Christians knew, their fellow Confederates never did. Even so patriotic a churchman as Bishop George Foster Pierce of the Methodist Episcopal Church, South, knew that there was not a national covenant between God and the Confederacy. Addressing the Georgia state assembly during the war, Pierce observed that achieving the covenant would have required much more than what he called the "Deism" of the Confederate constitution. God would have to have been "acknowledged in his being, perfections, providence and empire" as the Trinitarian God of the Bible. Southerners would have to have Christianized "the African race," reformed "the abuses of slavery," honored the sabbath, repented of rampant greed, lust, and profanity, and "set [their] faces against all injustice, oppression, and wrong."[30] The expectations were high — but Pierce was, after all, a Wesleyan; he believed that the Lord demanded perfection and that Christians were always at odds with the world.

Then came defeat and theodicy. Anger and pain demanded, "Why?!" "Why all these four years of suffering — of separation — of horror — of havoc — of awful bereavement?"[31] The answer came slowly and tentatively at first and then more assuredly and defiantly as southerners attempted to transform themselves into a "righteous remnant" for the nation and American Christianity by insisting that their cause had been just, motives for secession pure, the religion of atonement triumphant. Religion sustained its authenticating function as ministers and laity alike sacralized Confederate history, canonized Confederate leaders, and sanctified Confederate defeat. Defense of homeland and hearth, pure religion and constitutional principles were remembered as motivations for secession and war; generals in gray were remembered for their valor and Christian commitment; defeat was explained as "the discipline which trains," wrote a Presbyterian cleric, "the truly heroic soul to further and better endeavors."[32] If the cause for the South had been lost, it was but a paradigm for life, wise men could agree; life itself was a lost cause as a long preparation for death. The lesson, then, was that "integrity," not prosperity, was God's blessing, and moral grandeur was to be preferred to military victory. God was acting in southern history as he had in the history of Israel: that was the theme as defeat became virtuous. "Reproach, persecution, misrepresentation and poverty," wrote a minister, "have often been the fate of those who have suffered the loss of all for the right and true." And true evangelical insight informed the belief of thousands of southern white Christians that the disciplinary ordeal meant that southern churches had been chosen by God to foil the political religion of Yankees and win America for Christ.[33]

All these sentiments were of course mixed with the mundane, the petty, the anxious affairs of life where such transcendent flights of imagination could easily fail. Recurrent anniversaries of personal loss could evoke recurrent questions as to "why" and the insufficiency of any answer could somehow be transcended by a renewed determination to look ahead. For over a generation, southerners would tell each other these things, and raise monuments and begin to feel that "the South" was indeed more pure, more virtuous, and more religious than the victors. This belief was reinforced by sectional warfare between coreligionists North and South for over a generation and sustained by public rituals, memorial days and less grand reminders that the South was an especially orthodox people.[34] This religious celebration of the South betokened a processual change in the ways religion brought people together. That change has still to be documented and explained to scholarly satisfaction, but there are certain things that have to be taken into account. Before the war, public religion was expressed through ceremonies in seasonal revivals or meetings in which one sect would in effect offer itself to the "public." And this of course continued after the war, as did the familiar phenomenon of conversions occurring within the sponsorship of one sect that fed members into another — a functional ecumenicity that reflected cooperation in other venues as well. But "the South" was not celebrated. To be sure, sectional conflict had divided Methodists and Baptists, and proslavery writers had certainly attempted to define a Christian social ethic specifically for white southerners — most of whom were not slaveholders; but the South was not celebrated as it was after the war. That celebration was drenched in blood and loss and defeat that could be explained in the dramatic paradigm for salvation that was also drenched in blood and seemed to lend its credibility to those touched by its power and seeking its solace. Change also came as the war recruited men into the army of Christ in vast numbers — recruited men in ways they had never been recruited before or since. It sent men into the ministry who had commanded on the battle-field and changed the profession for a generation although we do not know exactly how or how much. Religion now held an honored place in public life — or at least more honored than before; and it seemed to hold the South together at least in ephemeral if public moments when southern memory was honored by crowds at prayer.

But the moments of hallowed memory and sacred solidarity were indeed ephemeral. Resistance to the gravitational pull of "lost cause" religion lay not only in the increasingly class nature of memorial celebrations[35] or the fact that not every southern soldier had fought for the Confederacy or a persistent suspicion among many southern believers that public piety was not as authentic as it should have been. More significant were the facts that 1) issues of religious authenticity expressed a growing complexity in southern life that reflected economic and political developments; and that 2) relations between the races came to be characterized by commitment to segregation — tearing people apart — which, through symbol, sensibility, and taboo became a sacred expression of purity and danger.

Debates about religious authenticity had afflicted the popular denominations (Methodists, Baptists, Presbyterians) in various ways before the Civil War — each faith community had had its family squabbles. After the war these accelerated. The children and grandchildren of "shouting Methodists," for example, wanted less noise and more music; from the pulpit they wanted fewer chants and better diction; in relations among believers, they wanted less intense interaction and more refinement and didacticism — Sunday schools. They called it progress; but Bishop George Pierce called it something else: "We are beginning to deify talent," he said, "and talk too much about the 'age' and 'progress,' and the demands of the times, for the simplicity of the faith, or the safety of the church." He feared that Methodists were becoming less distinctive a people than they had been.[36] Others noted similar changes among Baptists. Congregations in both denominations were raising fine buildings, savoring choirs, and judging the quality of sermons rather than responding in brokenhearted submission to evocative preaching. Denominational boards revised hymnbooks and, some believed, theology. Thousands agreed that much of value was being lost. In response, Baptist churches throughout the South insisted on the keeping the purity of faith by turning inward and repudiating the Christian authenticity of people not agreeing with themselves.[37] Among Methodists there was a similar search for purity and authenticity by emphasizing entire sanctification as a second, instantaneous blessing after that of justification. Holiness preachers of both sexes repudiated an "indulgent, accommodating, mammonized" Christianity; and some more specifically renounced pork, coffee, "doctors, drugs, and devils." After a full cycle of religious insurgency, the search for the authentic experience, the quintessentially charismatic demonstration of religious purity came in Pentecostal revival so that by the 1920s there was a "bewildering array" of such groups insisting on original evangelical renunciation of dances, circuses, fairs — and "corruption."[38] That the economic and political revolt of the People's Party should have been expressed in evangelical figures and moods is not surprising. When Tom Watson, the Georgia Populist Party leader, observed that "religion in the great cities is trying . . . to abolish the simple ways and brotherly teachings of Christ," he spoke for many who believed that religion had lost its power — its authenticity: at least among the bourgeoisie.[39]

Authenticity lay in a surge for purity: the pure and unadulterated church, the pure and holy life, the pure religious experience. The loss of orientation and place with changes in work and production that came with a new, industrializing South seemed to require that the religion of experience be purified just at the time when those in charge of denominations seemed to be replacing that experience with a more objective criterion of purification — the temperance reformation. Since the eighteenth century, southern churches and conferences had disciplined members for drinking too much and cast out habitual offenders from amongst themselves; and by the 1840s temperance reformers among Baptists began to petition for the same suspicion of beverage alcohol that had agitated Methodists from the beginning — theoretically.[40] Antebellum reformers also tried to distance the pollution of public drinking from one to five miles beyond sacred space, and by the 1880s could begin a region-wide assault on King Alcohol that ended with virtual prohibition in the South by 1912. This was part of the national movement, to be sure, which was complex enough in its origins, motivations, and goals, although in both region and nation reformers pushed an agenda that imposed a Protestant approach to social and personal purity upon everyone. Substance and spousal abuse — to use the words of a later day — were linked by activist women who thought of the assault on drinking as an assault on poverty, domestic violence, and husbandly irresponsibility; and, for a while at least, both black and white middle-class people could unite in a common goal. Eventually, however, the white racist politics of the late 1890s and the clever manipulation of "pure" white women as victims to the "Rum-Crazed Negro"[41] helped focus a pervasive sense of danger in such a way as to leave no doubt as to the need for order and safety in southern society.[42] The process was inherently religious in itself not because it was supported by "religious" people and institutions who were responding to the "supernatural" but because it attributed danger to a contagion (drink) that polluted the body. And the body, not surprisingly, represented the social body[43] in such a way that prohibition campaigns became societal rituals of purification.

That southern society should impose a clear definition between pollution and purity by rejecting the ambiguity inherent in the concept of temperance for a stark, outright ban — prohibition — is not surprising. The complexities, ambiguities, contradictions, and confusion of southern society demanded order and authenticity. The search for the pure church had separated "true" Christians from those whose beliefs and actions seemed ambiguous and who, therefore, possibly — one could not be quite sure — had become less than authentic. The search for a clear and unassailably true religious experience reflected the same suspicion of ambiguous expressions that, to be sure, could be interpreted as traditional and therefore authentic, perhaps, but also lacking in total conviction; again, one could not be sure. Thus, profession of faith was not sufficient as it had once been to be accepted by the community; an *un*ambiguous second testimony (of holiness) was required and then an even more pure and authenticating experience.

The same demand for assurance through clarity and purity was taking place in race relations, and the result was segregation. Distancing of the races in some fashion had been an American institution long before the abolition of slavery, but with that act and the industrialization of the South, the racist myth that blacks were incapable of using machinery justified making the new industrial workforce white and reserving agricultural and unskilled labor for blacks. Draconian laws consigned blacks to dependent and even coercible labor, creating a clear economic segmentation of black and white workers.[44] But changes in economic production, although associated with segregation, did not cause it. Rather, the system was crafted from the chaos of industrialization and the orderliness of ethnic prejudice by a "capitalist power elite." This elite consolidated power in the Democratic party by inflaming the racism that pervaded all levels of society and disfranchising blacks.[45] The artificers did their work amidst economic upheaval, fear of federal intervention in elections, and anxiety at a younger generation of black men seemingly beyond control. Whites were becoming increasingly distressed at miscegenation and what they interpreted to be the moral deterioration of African-American life. This they imagined in the vivid and threatening form of the black rapist; hence the danger of the "Rum-Crazed Negro." This distress at African-American decline came during a time when middle-class blacks, ironically enough, were demonstrating an improved economic status and buying, among other things, first-class accommodations on railway cars — space occupied also by white women. In that attempted entry lay abundant and dangerous symbolic power; that the implication was sexual made it especially dangerous. Indeed, places where people of both genders were likely to come into contact and which could be linked with intimacy — schoolrooms, hotels, restaurants, darkened theaters, railway cars — were likely to be the first places to be segregated by race.[46]

Suffused through the anxiety, fear, and anger lay an insistence that there be no anomalous people—people who were not clearly defined, who were placeless, or out of place. The middle-class black man who was well spoken and elegantly and tastefully dressed in space shared with white women was especially anomalous. And if his complexion confused classification, perplexity and discomfort was even greater. Segregation was designed to end confusion (anomaly), establish barriers, clarify form, distance opposites, reinforce margins. To be sure, it was created by powerful people to achieve political ends; but it also relied on intersubjective meanings that in another language can be understood as spiritual powers inherent in the social system. As Mary Douglas points out, "This means that the power of the universe is ultimately hitched to society." Here therefore, there are "pollution powers which inhere in the structure of ideas itself and which punish a symbolic breaking of that which should be joined or joining that which should be separate." The lines of segregation came to be ever more clearly drawn, thus making the danger attributed to pollution ever the greater.[47] Over time, the fact that legal segregation was an innovation crafted by specific men in a specific time under specific if widespread conditions was forgotten, and white southerners came to believe that their racial system was a "given," something so utterly right and "natural" that it seemed inexorable.[48] This sense of inexorability—together with the process that made of racial etiquette a moral code with pollution powers that were truly compelling—transformed segregation into a religious system.

Religion is what concerns us ultimately, and that concern elicits from believers a commitment to meet obligations considered holy. Clifford Geertz's celebrated discussion of religion as a cultural system helps demonstrate the religious character of what one scholar has called the "highest stage of white supremacy."[49] By merging Geertz's outline of a religious system with further elaboration based on the historical record, the "religious" properties of the segregation became clear. Segregation developed after the Civil War into *a system of symbols* confirmed by law, custom, and practice, that *establish[ed] powerful, pervasive, and long-lasting moods and motivations* expressed in taboo, distance, revulsion, and danger. These were fixed upon people by *formulating conceptions of a general order of existence* in which stark distinctions between kind and race came to be embraced as the will of God. These distinctions were treated as sacred and reinforced by sexual taboo and public distancing, which, when fused created a tension that implied violence if the barriers were breached. The sacred connotations of everyday life *clothed these conceptions with such an aura of facticity that the moods and motivations seemed uniquely realistic* and absolutely compelling.[50] The fact that segregation insisted on people being in their appropriate place put such clear emphasis on boundaries, distance, and conformity to type—that is, that black men be black, not white (with all the symbolic freight associated)—reminds us of the draconian ritual that became symbolic of a system breached and of pollution ascribed, that is, *lynching*.

Lynching punished men for violating in either a symbolic or actual way a broad range of racial (distancing) regulations. Violation need not have been intended for ambiguous acts of black men to be interpreted first as anomalous and then as challenging to white supremacy. Breaking taboo could be as dangerous as desecrating the holy through rape in a society where the bodies of white women fulfilled rich symbolic expectations. That most men who were lynched had not in fact desecrated white women but were interpreted in public apologia and folklore as if they had suggested the nature and meaning of the pollution. Because sexuality was so restrained in the South, and because the taboo against interracial sex was so strict and clear, and because any perceived breach of the social barrier — *even if only inferred by a tortured exposition* — was treated as "dangerous pollution," radical cleansing could be demanded. Lynching was that cleansing because it rid society of "dirt" that is "matter out of place" — in this case a man out of place. The cleansing purged perpetrators of guilt for having allowed pollution to occur and removed the pollution to restore equilibrium to the system. The achievement of purity was the achievement of holiness because the latter, writes Mary Douglas, means "keeping distinct the categories of creation. It therefore involves correct definition, discrimination and order. Under this head all the rules of sexual morality exemplify the holy." In a culture seeking the holy in a complex variety of ways, lynching was one way to find it.[51]

The *sensibility* of stark lines, unsurpassable distance, and elemental distinctiveness could never be perfectly institutionalized, of course. There were private as well as ritualized ways to transcend lines. Once boundary, barrier, and distance became clear, a few whites did attempt to reach across them — always within the concession that that clarity be maintained.[52] That public space became segregated by race was, as we have seen, partially because there were more white women in it, and this, writes Ted Ownby, in part explains changes in the way men behaved in other ways as well — all the way from cursing to drinking and hunting.[53] As women and men moved closer together in space outside the home, women could reshape it by seeing their values accepted in a broader range of public action. Sometimes women tried to transform concession to themselves of responsibility for nurturance and moral influence into "Christian" service as public school teachers[54] and sometimes in an enlarged sphere of action within the churches as social workers and missionaries. Eventually, a very few went beyond both negotiated areas to subvert the logic of segregation in moments of interracial cooperation along gendered lines and concerted action with men such as those of the Commission on Interracial Cooperation. Eventually, from within the small but growing community of dissenters from racial fundamentalism, a group of white women scattered across the South gave birth to the Association of Southern Women for the Prevention of Lynching. As white women they attempted to disenchant important religious elements of segregation, to demystify the "myth" of pollution (rape), and thus to discredit lynching as a defensible act.[55] Activists attempted to authenticate such acts as religious commitments in service to Christian fraternity and sorority; and sometimes religious experience could transcend class and race to bring people together. At a meeting of black and white women in 1920 after speeches about the realities of life in the South had evoked anguish, confusion, and discomfort, participants found themselves singing hymns in audible profession of a common faith shared across racial lines.[56] The feeling could not last; it was fleeting for the same reason that it was dangerous; it was subversive of order, clarity, and the rules of separation.

In keeping people apart, religion also kept people together. The religion that could give metaphor and understanding to the Lost Cause, could — in the tradition of exodus and apocalypse: liberation and judgment — bring black people together in elaborating the meaning of Emancipation. While white southerners sanctified suffering after the Civil War, blacks celebrated Jubilee. Now reversed for the races were the polarities of life: sorrow and joy, submission and freedom, despair and hope. Only blacks could sing,

> Slavery chain done broke at last!
> Gonna praise God til I die.

During the generation of emancipation, former slaves began to transform what it meant to be Christian in a South whose leaders remained reluctant to surrender the assumptions of slaveholding. The institutions that had once been the subject of white suspicion and surveillance now became independent, aggressive, self-determining, and (almost) free. With money, advice, and education from black and white Yankees, former slave preachers and missionaries gathered churches from among their fellow Christians. As leaders and spokesmen for the entire community of freedpeople, preachers went beyond the bounds of religion into a broad range of political activities, so long as federal troops and Republican commitment permitted them to do so. Churches represented the corporate desire not only for worship but also for expression, cooperation, and solidarity. The last was sustained not merely by revivals, evangelists, associations, and elaborate funereal commemorations but also by charitable contributions to the sick, the dying, the needy, the orphaned, the elderly: those bereft in many ways. Churches became relief agencies, community centers, employment bureaus, music schools, and entertainment facilities. As buildings they were monuments to the race, sometimes extravagant expressions of community aspirations in brick and mortar that far surpassed the ability to maintain without the help of whites. Even the simple, drafty, unpainted country churches represented the institutional presence of African Americans, the objective facticity of community — which is probably why so many were burned in the 1890s. To these *places*, the community came in dynamic celebration. They symbolized community through eliciting memory of ritual acts once observed there — worship shared, selves realized, hopes elicited, promises made and the narrative of Exodus, Jubilee, Apocalypse (Judgment), and Heaven dramatized. Styles, of course, varied by denomination, locale, class, and taste; but black churches in all their rich variety after Emancipation provided the gravitational core of African-American life.[57]

By 1890 the South was covered by a variety of African-American denominations. In the same process of institution building, northern philanthropy and Af-

rican-American energy and ingenuity combined to create the networks of regional institutions — schools, academies, colleges, a press — that helped to create
an African-American presence beyond aggregate demography and local place.
The gravitational attraction that had drawn the freedpeople to federal camps and
Freedmen's schools drew people also to Hampton Institute, Fisk, and Howard, to
the schools that would become Shaw, Dillard, St. Augustine's, and Johnson C.
Smith, and to schools that would serve their purpose and die. Removed from
local churches but similar to them in the functions they served for the broader
community beyond community, these institutions attracted young people who
left and returned to their neighborhoods transformed and ready to transform in
return. The process of attraction and return, together with the knowledge that
renewed, perhaps "reborn" people brought with them, helped create webs of
meaning and aspiration attached to concrete places that could in turn help create
an imagined and therefore a real "nation." By being essential parts of both
church life and providential history, such institutions became sacred representations of a chosen people, which, in contrast with the draconian purifiers of white
society, seemed radically if ironically inclusive in their emphasis on human
equality and dignity.[58] Where this community beyond communities fit into
broader American life was problematic, as segregation implied; a few northern
black leaders had despaired of achieving equality in the United States before the
Civil War and had sought black nationality through emigration and colonization. When black people's momentary hope for equality after emancipation
was dashed, a new generation of emigrationists was born in the agricultural
South between 1890 and 1915. Simultaneously and not surprisingly, an interest in
Christianizing Africa expressed the importance of that continent in the self-
consciousness of black Americans so that when plans for colonization failed, the
importance of Africa remained, and the local institutions of African-American
nationality remained, too, in local churches as well as the African-American
church.[59] Religion kept a people together in ways peculiar to their history as well
as to their faith(s).

Inherent in those many ways was a dialectical process that pervaded African-
American life so thoroughly that the polarities within it were sometimes lost to
view even as they sustained the tension that drove the process on. The complexity
is suggested first of all in the polarity between black and white that segregationists
attempted so insistently to maintain, and which according to the purifying distance between the races should have been easy to do — but indeed was not. When
black and white were in one person as in the North Carolina novelist, Charles
Chestnutt, she or he could feel drawn in two possible directions, either black
or white — not human — and resolve the tension according to the will of God,
which in the case of brother and sister of equal complexion could be in either
of two directions.[60] The complexity of dialectic is suggested, too, by the para-
digmatic conflict between the political strategy hammered out by Booker T.
Washington in the forge of southern racism and the discursive and critical
strategy of W.E. Burghardt Du Bois that proceeded from a brilliant, analytical

mind into African-Americans' public consciousness primarily (at first) in the North. Washington attempted a strategy of ambiguous ingratiation, calculated "cooperation," and mystifying rhetoric in trying to extract more than whites would otherwise have been willing to concede. Du Bois insisted on stating in clear but not inflammatory language that disfranchisement, segregation, and an education designed merely to provide a southern workforce were simply wrong. Followers of both men agreed, however, that African Americans must use all the tools at their command to fabricate institutions and habits of mind to strengthen black communities from within and protect them from without. This resolution, too, like the ambiguous presence of ancestral miscegenation reminded African Americans of their "twoness" — as Du Bois wrote at the beginning of the twentieth century. The complexity of the dialectic lay in the self as well as in the community, then. "One ever feels his twoness — an American, a Negro"; Du Bois said, "two souls, two thoughts, two unreconciled strivings; two warring ideals in one dark body, whose dogged strength alone keeps it from being torn asunder."[61]

This dialectic — in which the external world so intensely penetrated the internal — characterized the African-American churches of the South in the first half of the twentieth century. The "spiritual striving" of his people Du Bois could dramatize in the epigraph to the second chapter of his *Souls of Black Folk*, which borrowed words from James Russell Lowell:[62]

> Truth forever on the scaffold,
> Wrong forever on the throne;
> Yet that scaffold sways the future,
> And behind the dim unknown
> Standeth God within the shadow
> Keeping watch above His own.

Du Bois's understanding of the African-American dialectic and the conflicts in which African Americans had engaged helps clarify the tension within African-American religion between this world and the next. Benjamin Mays, who wrote about *The Negro's God as Reflected in His Literature*, confessed ambivalence at the "otherworldliness" of the religious world into which he had been initiated as a boy because it had been an opiate. Yet Mays could not leave the matter there; he had to add that he believed opiates were sometimes required to deaden the pain; and then he felt compelled further to qualify the comment about opiates to remind himself and his readers that religion had also fortified him as it had fortified so many others through the passage to freedom.[63] In another place, while discussing Booker T. Washington's public discourse about the "economy of God," Mays reminded his readers that this economy in Washington's view assumed racial equality and made great demands on African Americans to be "one with God," sharing his qualities "in our poor human way" not to be absorbed in Being through mystical fusion, but rather to maintain "the proper relationship with men," as Mays points out. Washington was contemptuous of what he called the "otherworldly aspects of Christianity." "Sentimental Christianity which banks everything on the future and nothing on the present, is the curse of the race."[64] Such statements are characteristic of a constant dialectic within an African-American faith that transcended sectarian conflicts. This was the dialectic between the easily understood flight to God as refuge and service to Him in serving His people. The dialectic demanded theodicy: why did God stand remorselessly in "the shadow?" Did He indeed the watch keep above his own? Envisioning ultimate victory in the midst of despair became possible within a world of worship in which transcendence was authenticated: it pervaded African-American culture. Such a vision could indeed bemuse people who saw no means to act and who experienced the terror, antipathy, condescension, and hypocrisy around them as defeating. Despair is an authentic human feeling; but so is hope. Washington could encourage his people to believe that "progress is the law of God, and under Him it is going to be the Negro's guiding star in this country."[65] And Du Bois could use Lowell's words to inspire those on the scaffold to dignity and assertion. The dialectic persisted; it has still not been resolved. It is a historical process that sustained hope and belied the twin canard that southern religion was merely "otherworldly" and merely white.

This was the message of Martin Luther King Jr. From the fecund social base that had sustained African-American community after imposition of distance, pollution, and danger came a voice of deliverance. As befitted the culture of black southerners, the voice was that of a preacher; but this did not mean that one man led a single movement for black liberation in the 1950s and 1960s. The movements that became The Movement came from African Americans who sensed that their time — the sacred time when promises would be fulfilled and prophecies realized — was at hand. The collective solidarity effected from without by segregation and from within by African-American institutions and culture made possible independent and seemingly spontaneous resistance to white power in such widely scattered places as Topeka, Kansas; Baton Rouge, Louisiana; Tallahassee, Florida; and Montgomery, Alabama, even as legal briefs were being prepared to attack segregation in the courts.[66] The civil rights movements were the explosive conjunction of various efforts by black people throughout the country to end segregation in the United States and begin the assault on institutionalized racism. Women and men from across the South fashioned the movement that was to find in Martin Luther King Jr. its most compelling personification. If the movement made King, so did his ministerial and familial predecessors. He was made possible not only by the calling he shared with his father and his mother's father but also by Atlanta's black community: its colleges, its neighborhood centers, its memory of oppression and sorrow, its history of resistance and protest — its expectation that Du Bois and James Russell Lowell wrote not poetry but prophecy.[67]

King was made possible, too, by a division within white society, one that led him to seek momentary alliance with Billy Graham, the white evangelist who had elicited a positive response among African Americans when he quietly resisted segregationist dogma in his revivalistic crusades. King's vision of interracial crusades, however, had to be surrendered when Graham confessed that he could not address the "worldly [sic] aspects" of race.[68] King's strategy nonetheless continued to be based on the assumption — usually more fictive and rhetorical than concrete — that a body of "good" white people could be counted on to respond positively to the reasonable expectations of black people. The historical roots of this assumption were of course the Mission to slaves with its agenda for converting both black and white, and the small but widespread networks of whites across the South who had attempted to reach across the barriers of segregation to support African-American agendas of education, self-help, and justice.[69] That the children of these people could be found in the civil rights movements in the 1960s[70] suggested that the white audience was there. That there were white ministers who could try to be the audience that King wanted it to be[71] suggests social support for his assumption that religion could pull people together in the midst of a social system that tore them apart. If from the sermonic tradition of African-American preachers, King could fashion evocative and familiar images, figures, and symbols to fuse sacred history with history about to be fulfilled for blacks he could do the same for whites. Or almost the same. The identification of black auditors with sacred experiences shared in African-American community made of his preaching a social bond in much the same way as that of his predecessors with whom he shared the call. He placed his black hearers so expertly within the story of redemption and the story so thoroughly within their own situations and in the political vision yet to be attained that his voice could be lost in the immediate authority of what he was saying. The response of willing white people was not the evocation of shared experiences but the recognition that familiar images of sacrifice, atonement, redemption, judgment, repentance, and millennium could now be renewed in racial reconciliation; at least that should have been the appropriate response postulated by the ideal behind King's public discourse. That ideal rested on the acceptance and sharing of a Christian Mission that white idealists had once envisioned as a gift from them to blacks; in King's ministry it was a gift from blacks to whites, if the latter could accept it.

King's ministry to the South was thus complex and regenerative. His power lay in his language, but it was a language expressed in events as well as words. He structured those events on a model of the evangelical conversion experience, as is obvious from a reading of his "Letter from a Birmingham Jail." When King and the Southern Christian Leadership Conference targeted a town, they did so not only as a political act but as a religious duty: to consecrate space through a civic ritual of tension, release, and transformation. Antecedents in the Presbyterian communion season, Methodist conference, Baptist protracted meeting, and evangelical camp were distant, to be sure, but real because they were the cultural predecessors of Graham's crusades that prefigured King's own. The language of moral renewal was compelling to whites when confronted by the ghastly meaning of the violence that the logic of segregation demanded. If Eugene "Bull" Connor turned hoses and dogs on innocent blacks, many whites in seeing themselves implicated turned away their gaze. It could have telling implications. "I knew it was over," a southern white student told his professor in 1966, "when my mother started humming 'We Shall Overcome' in the kitchen."[72] The language of moral renewal was not individualistic: personal salvation was not its goal. It was biblical but not by text (white) so much as by typology (black); it was compelling because it linked the tension of social confrontation with familiar, shared feelings evoked by the ways in which white as well as black southerners learned their moral lessons — from their mother. Obvious though the interface was between movement and the familiar words and formulae of the white southern ethos, (white) evangelicalism was not the medium. King's appeal to whites was as effective as it was because he merged the homiletic style of his people's background with that of white religious liberals.[73] Both could understand and be moved. It is true that he despaired of white *racial* liberals who counseled "time," "peace," and "patience," but he used the language of *religious* liberals to challenge "prevailing opinion" and to become "creatively maladjusted." The reference was not biblical text but psychology; the goal was not to be "saved" but to "Christianize the social order,"[74] not to rage against worldly things but to transform them in a great concert of moral action.[75]

If the movement to bring people together through a shared religious mood faltered in the desert of racism, the movement to separate us by appeal to pollution and danger has gained momentum in the past decade with the growth of the "new Christian" right. Its leaders learned to model their arguments, justify their agendas, and defend their goals through community action analogous to that of African-American churches in the sixties. They defended themselves at times as an embattled minority defending their values from destruction by a voracious and secular state and, at other times, as a "moral majority." Essential to their collective identity has been their schools, through which they hope to guarantee that their children will share their values, a goal not especially peculiar to themselves. Replication of parental values in the young was challenged by the racial desegregation of public schools in the South after 1954 and especially after 1970. One response to desegregation came in the form of "Christian" academies that became so popular throughout the South that the federal government began to challenge their tax-exempt status in the early seventies. This threat aligned segregationist academies with other, less compromised Christian schools outside the South to create a broad coalition in resistance to the contagion of secularism. When in the early sixties the Supreme Court had struck down devotional reading of the Bible and public prayer in the schools for violating the establishment clause of the first amendment, religious academies earned great legitimacy among certain conservative Christians. As the Internal Revenue Service sustained its interest in such institutions, a self-consciously "Christian" public interest seemed to be endangered. Academies were defended not for their whiteness but for principles defined as characteristically Christian: work, chastity, and patriotism. Equally important was the repudiation of the "sixties" counterculture; academies would brook no dashikis (such as those worn by black "militants"), no "demonstrations," no longhaired boys or shorthaired girls. Fear of pollution by ambiguous gender identity and danger through collective resistance to authority seemed to make such schools into Christian boot camps. It is not surprising that they should have rejected "moral relativity" and the Darwinian hypothesis of natural selection.[76]

Resisting secularization and racial integration were not the only matters targeted by conservative activists in the 1970s. Changes in gender roles were freighted with pollution and danger to become the focus of conservative wrath in a "pro-family" movement. Funded by right-wing political action committees, activists exploited President Jimmy Carter's White House Conferences on Families as a threat to summon counterconferences on *the* family. By condemning planned parenthood, abortion rights, the equal rights amendment, and homosexuality, these meetings suggested the salience of gendered issues to conservatives styling themselves "Christian." In such issues political activists hoped to use the Bible Belt of the South and Midwest to supply a geographical base for future action. That the Moral Majority, Religious Roundtable, and Christian Broadcast Network could be so thoroughly identified with southerners, and that North Carolina's ultraconservative Senator Jesse Helms should be so prominent in establishing the authenticity of the pro-family movement suggest the importance of southern culture to the Christian Right.[77] Certainly, traditionalism on gender issues, so necessary to conservative Christians, was consistent with traditional southern values: Tennessee had been the only southern state to ratify the woman suffrage amendment; Texas had been the only southern state to sustain its ratification of the equal rights amendment. Accusations by opponents that the equal rights amendment would confuse gender roles and do irreparable damage to women and culture were consistent with the need to maintain boundaries, exaggerate differences, and separate opposites very much as had the artisans of segregation a century earlier. Themes associated with gender were linked with those associated with race even in indirect but nonetheless compelling ways. The Christian Right defended the "white man's burden" by opposing the Panama Canal Treaty and economic sanctions against the white government of Rhodesia as if to support segregation abroad after it had been lost at home. These issues were tied to those once essential to resisting racial integration, such as local control of educational policy. That these motifs were linked with the politics of sexuality is scarcely surprising to historians of the South. Jesse Helms of North Carolina has used the politics of sexuality in much the same way as he once did the politics of race:[78] to evoke anxiety about boundaries and identity; to avoid ambiguity, anomaly, and confusion; to achieve purity by avoiding pollution and danger — that is, to realize "holiness."

It is not insignificant that Helms was firmly identified with the fundamentalist party that took control of the Southern Baptist Convention (SBC). Conflict over Christian authenticity in the SBC is a parable of religion in the South today. The issue of authenticity — always important to evangelicals — became even more important with the encroachment of modern science upon the popular mind in the late nineteenth century. In response came a vituperative fundamentalism that offended SBC leaders also uncomfortable with "modernist" redefinitions of faith; they attempted to wend their way between the two poles through ambiguous language that mystified differences by appealing to matters that could keep Baptists together instead of tearing them apart.[79] Suspicion of college professors, seminary faculties, and denominational bureaucrats lay beneath a public affability and surfaced when divisive issues shook southern society during the 1950s and 1960s. Then, a few SBC bureaucrats seemed to deviate from traditional caution by applauding the U.S. Supreme Court in its decision on *Brown v. Board of Education* (1954) or supporting student opposition to the war in Viet Nam or supporting racial equality. They printed books that reflected the influence of biblical higher criticism and held conferences that offended — the appearance of a *Playboy* editor at one of these was especially galling. When a new church member training program bore the same name as a feminine hygiene deodorant (Quest), the coincidence seemed almost satanic. By the early 1970s, conservatives were planning an offensive to rescue the SBC for authentic Christianity. They wanted purity: nothing but the clear word of God proclaimed from a Bible believed by the expositor to be inerrant in all things. This also meant conservatism on race, gender, sex, and abortion. Purists developed a constituency that enabled them to take over the presidency of the SBC in 1979 and purge denominational seminaries, commissions, and boards by 1988. Surveys suggest that people supporting this change tended to be less likely than opponents to believe that they could learn anything they would want to know from people unlike themselves and that they certainly did not want their children to do so. The diversity and heterogeneity of a rapidly differentiating world was threatening. They seemed to want, writes Nancy Ammerman, to "re-create inside the religious world what was no longer available in the world outside."[80] Restricting the range of authenticity and insisting on purity had torn the SBC apart.

Encounter between faith and world will continue in the South as it has for two hundred years. As long as it continues to rest its authority on the foundation of personal experience and biblical exposition, the dominant religious mood of the South will undoubtedly continue to be articulated between two "types": that represented by the inclusiveness and creativity of African-American religious life modeled in the civil rights movements and the punitiveness and demand for purity modeled in the new "Christian" Right. This is not to deny elements of restraint and discipline among African Americans or elements of fellowship and inclusiveness among whites; the search for authentic experience and community birthed antislavery radicalism and racial liberalism as well as a demand for purity and the ascription of danger. Moreover, many from within the black National Baptist Convention opposed Martin Luther King Jr. But the "types" remain indelible in consciousness because their vivid and political action dramatizes the search for authentic community in such starkly different ways. For those who remain suspicious of recognizably political action, religion has not meant the contemplative ambience suggested by the description, "otherworldliness," but rather a socially creative way to maintain and affirm one's humanity in the encounter with all the forces of the world that deny it—the collective demonstration of what Paul Tillich called *The Courage to Be*. In the face of slavery, poverty, isolation, and "modernity," this collective refusal to be defined by either the ideology of ruling elites or the seemingly "irreligious" quality of denominational leadership could birth religious moods that affirmed an authentic piety and a communal identity that brought many of "us" together. Historians who by profession are not included in such usage of the first-person plural should nonetheless concede that confirmation of the Transcendent in social life is a legitimate because an authentic historical act. That religion in social action can punish as well as liberate should not conceal that fact.

Notes

1. Burton J. Hendrick, *The Life and Letters of Walter Hines Page* (Garden City, N.Y.: Doubleday, Page, 1923), 1:76; George M. Fredrickson, "The Old New Order," *New York Review of Books*, Mar. 11, 1993, pp. 40–42. I have used this opportunity to rethink, reformulate, and develop ideas originally expressed in the essay "'Christianizing' the South—Sketching a Synthesis," which appeared in *New Directions in American Religious History*, ed. Harry S. Stout and Darryl G. Hart (New York: Oxford University Press, 1977). The narrative here emphasizes recurring demands for authenticity and purity as essential to the "this-worldly" character of religion in the South.

2. Richard E. Beringer, Herman Hattaway, and William N. Still, *Why the South Lost the Civil War* (Athens: University of Georgia, 1986); Gardiner H. Shattuck Jr., *A Shield and A Hiding Place: The Religious Life of Civil War Armies* (Macon, Ga.: Mercer University Press, 1987); and John B. Boles, *The Great Revival: The Origins of the Southern Evangelical Mind* (Lexington: University Press of Kentucky, 1972).

3. Benjamin E. Mays, *Born to Rebel: An Autobiography*, with a foreword by Orville Vernon Burton (1971; rpt., Athens: University of Georgia Press, 1987), 16.

4. Drew Gilpin Faust, *The Creation of Confederate Nationalism: Ideology and Identity in the Civil War South* (Baton Rouge: Louisiana State University Press, 1988); Elizabeth Fox Genovese, *Within the Plantation Household: Black and White Women of the Old South* (Chapel Hill: University of North Carolina Press, 1988); Steven M. Stowe, *Intimacy and Power in the Old South: Ritual in the Lives of the Planters* (Baltimore: Johns Hopkins University Press, 1987), to name but a few.

5. Rhys Isaac, *The Transformation of Virginia* (Chapel Hill: University of North Carolina Press, 1980); Donald G. Mathews, *Religion in the Old South* (Chicago: University of Chicago Press, 1977).

6. Mathews, *Religion in the Old South*, 1–38.

7. Samuel Davies, *Sermons on Important Subjects* (Boston: Lincoln and Edmands, [1811]), 2:343.

8. For a discussion of early African participation in a common religious life, see Harvey H. Jackson, "Hugh Bryan and the Evangelical Movement in South Carolina," *William and Mary Quarterly* 43 (Oct. 1986): 594–614; see also John B. Boles, ed., *Masters and Slaves in the House of the Lord* (Lexington: University Press of Kentucky, 1988).

9. See Margaret Washington Creel, *"A Peculiar People": Slave Religion and Community Culture Among the Gullahs* (New York: New York University Press, 1988); Charles Joyner, *Down by the Riverside: A South Carolina Slave Community* (Urbana: University of Illinois Press, 1984); Mechal Sobel, *"Trabelin' On": The Slave Journey to an Afro-Baptist Faith* (Westport, Conn: Greenwood, 1979); Albert J. Raboteau, *Slave Religion: The Invisible Institution in the Ante-bellum South* (New York: Oxford University Press, 1978).

10. See for example Ezekiel Cooper, Journal, 1:2–30, Manuscript in Ezekiel Cooper Papers, Ezekiel Cooper Collection, Garrett Evangelical Seminary, Northwestern University.

11. Theophus Smith, *Conjuring Culture: Biblical Formations of Black America* (New York: Oxford University Press, 1994), 222–48; also Raboteau, *Slave Religion*, 290–318.

12. For a classic discussion of culture and the many nuanced ways in which both resistance and power are expressed, see Raymond Williams, *Marxism and Literature* (London: Oxford University Press, 1977).

13. See David Edwin Harrell Jr., "The Evolution of Plain-Folk Religion in the South, 1835–1920," in *Varieties of Southern Religious Experience*, ed. Samuel S. Hill (Baton Rouge: Louisiana State University Press, 1988), 24–51; Richard Rankin, *Ambivalent Churchmen and Evangelical Churchwomen: The Religion of the Episcopal Elite in North Carolina, 1800–1860* (Columbia: University of South Carolina Press, 1993). There was theological agreement, too, structured on the Scottish Common Sense Philosophy and common reformed antecedents. See E. Brooks Holifield, *The Gentlemen Theologians: American Theology in Southern Culture, 1795–1860* (Durham: Duke University Press, 1978).

14. Emily Bingham's work on the family of Jacob Mordecai and Rachel Mordecai Lazarus is currently in process and has been instrumental, together with that of Leah Hagedorn, in helping me understand the place of Judaism in southern culture. See Leonard Dinnerstein and Mary Dale Palsson, eds., *Jews in the South* (Baton Rouge: Louisiana State University Press, 1973), and Samuel Proctor and Louis Schmier with Malcolm Stern, eds., *Jews of the South: Selected Essays from the Southern Jewish Historical Society* (Macon, Ga.: Mercer University Press, 1984).

15. Eli N. Evans, *The Provincials: A Personal History of Jews in the South* (New York: Atheneum, 1976), esp. 120–39 and 211–26; see also Howard N. Rabinowitz, "Nativism, Bigotry, and Anti-Semitism in the South," *American Jewish History* 77 (Mar. 1988); see also the negative reference to Jews in Erskine Caldwell, *Deep South: Memory and Observation*, with an introduction by Guy Owen (Athens: University of Georgia Press, 1980), 148–49.

16. Samuel S. Hill, "The Shape and Shapes of Popular Southern Piety," in *Varieties of Southern Evangelicalism*, ed. David Edwin Harrell Jr. (Macon, Ga.: Mercer University Press, 1981), 89–114, esp. 96–99.

17. James D. Essig, *The Bonds of Wickedness: American Evangelicals Against Slavery, 1770–1808* (Philadelphia: Temple University Press, 1982); Donald G. Mathews, *Slavery and Methodism: A Chapter in American Morality* (Princeton: Princeton University Press, 1965).

18. Mathews, *Slavery and Methodism*, 62–87; Mathews, *Religion in the Old South*, 136–84.

19. See Augustus Baldwin Longstreet, *Letters on the Epistle of Paul to Philemon; or, The Connection of Apostolic Christianity and Slavery* (Charleston: B. Jenkins, 1845), 37–45 and throughout; Mathews, *Religion in the Old South*, 136–84; Drew Gilpin Faust, ed., *The*

Proslavery Argument (Baton Rouge: Louisiana State University Press, 1981). See also Dale B. Martin, *Slavery as Salvation: The Metaphor of Slavery in Pauline Christianity* (New Haven, Conn.: Yale University Press, 1990), esp. xiii-xxii and 42–49.

20. See George Pullen Jackson, *White Spirituals in the Southern Uplands* (Chapel Hill: University of North Carolina Press, 1933), esp. 242–302.

21. Mathews, *Religion in the Old South*, 81–135; Stowe, *Intimacy and Power*, 250–54.

22. Drew Gilpin Faust, "Christian Soldiers: The Meaning of Revivalism in the Confederate Army," *Journal of Southern History* 53 (Feb. 1987): 63–90, esp. 70–75.

23. Ibid., 86.

24. See Harrison Daniel, *Southern Protestantism in the Confederacy* (Bedford, Va: Print Shop, 1989); Shattuck, *Shield and a Hiding Place*, 35–72; Pamela Robinson-Durso, "Chaplains in the Confederate Army," *Journal of Church and State* 33 (Autumn 1991): 747–63; G. Clinton Prim Jr., "Interdenominationalism in the Civil War: Army Churches," *Journal of Mississippi History* 51 (Feb. 1989): 17–29. For army life see Reid Mitchell, *Civil War Soldiers* (New York: Viking Penguin, 1988). Also William W. Bennett, *A Narrative of the Great Revival Which Prevailed in the Southern Armies* (Philadelphia: Claxton, Remsen and Haffelfinger, 1877), and John William Jones, *Christ in the Camp; or, Religion in Lee's Army* (Richmond: B.F. Johnson, 1887).

25. [Jeremiah Bell Jeter], "A Mother's Parting Words to Her Soldier Boy," (n.p.: n.d.) in Southern Pamphlet Collection, Louis Round Wilson Library, University of North Carolina. Courtesy of Timothy A. Long.

26. From "I Am a Soldier," introduction to *The New Testament of Our Lord and Savior Jesus Christ* (Nashville: Graves, Marks and Company, 1861), 6.

27. The phrase is that of Kurt O. Berends, who kindly allowed me to read part of his manuscript on the religious military press in the southern armies. See Kurt O. Berends, "Wholesome Reading Purifies and Elevates the Man: The Religious Military Press in the Confederate States of America" (manuscript in possession of the author, 1995).

28. *Daily Richmond Enquirer*, Sept. 27, 1861, quoted by Harry S. Stout in "The Life and Death of the Confederate Jeremiad," Manuscript of James A. Gray Lectures, Duke University Divinity School, Lecture 1, p. 29, in possession of the author. Stout lists ten fast days for the war in note 13 of Lecture 1.

29. Faust, *Creation of Confederate Nationalism*, 24–25.

30. George G. Smith, *The Life and Times of George Foster Pierce, D.D., LL.D., Bishop of the Methodist Episcopal Church, South* (Sparta, Ga.: Hancock, 1888), 468–69, also 470–77.

31. Francis Butler Simkins and James Welch Patton, *The Women of the Confederacy* (Richmond: Garrett and Massie, 1938), 246.

32. Charles Reagan Wilson, *Baptized in Blood: The Religion of the Lost Cause, 1865–1920* (Athens: University of Georgia Press, 1980), 20, quoting Moses Drury Hoge.

33. Ibid., 68–76.

34. Gaines M. Foster, *Ghosts of the Confederacy: Defeat, the Lost Cause, and the Emergence of the New South, 1865 to 1913* (New York: Oxford University Press, 1987); Ralph E. Morrow, *Northern Methodism and Reconstruction* (East Lansing: Michigan State University Press, 1956).

35. Foster, *Ghosts of the Confederacy*, 178.

36. Smith, *Life and Times of Pierce*, 560; see also 495, 505, 508, 530, 536, 545, 558–61, 578–80.

37. Bill J. Leonard, *God's Last and Only Hope: The Fragmentations of the Southern*

Baptist Convention (Grand Rapids, Mich.: William E. Eerdmans, 1990), 34–35; Nancy Tatom Ammerman, *Baptist Battles: Social Change and Religious Conflict in the Southern Baptist Convention* (New Brunswick, N.J.: Rutgers University Press, 1990), 33–34.

38. David Edwin Harrell Jr., "Religious Pluralism: Catholics, Jews, and Sectarians," in *Religion in the South*, ed. Charles Reagan Wilson (Jackson: University Press of Mississippi, 1985), 68–69, 77; Louis Keith Harper, "Old Landmarkism: A Historiographical Appraisal," *Baptist History and Heritage* 25 (Apr. 1990): 31–39; Jackson, *White Spirituals in the Southern Uplands*, 303–15; George Pullen Jackson, *White and Negro Spirituals: Their Life Span and Kinship* (New York: J.J. Augustin, 1943), 133–37; Vincent Synan, *The Pentecostal Holiness Movement in the United States* (Grand Rapids, Mich.: William B. Eerdmans, 1971).

39. Bruce Palmer, *"Man Over Money": The Southern Populist Critique of American Capitalism* (Chapel Hill: University of North Carolina Press, 1980), 201.

40. See Anne C. Loveland, *Southern Evangelicals and the Social Order, 1800–1860* (Baton Rouge: Louisiana State University Press, 1980), 130–58.

41. *Raleigh (N.C.) News and Observer*, Feb. 22, 1903.

42. For a few studies of prohibition in the South, see: Mrs. J.J. Ansley, *History of the Georgia Women's Christian Temperance Union from its Organization 1883 to 1907* (Columbus, Ga.: Gilbert Printing, 1914); John Evans Eubanks, *Ben Tillman's Baby: The Dispensary System of South Carolina* (Augusta, Ga.: n.p., 1950); Joseph Gusfield, *Symbolic Crusade* (Urbana: University of Illinois Press, 1963); Nancy Hardesty, "'The Best Temperance Organization in the Land': Southern Methodists and the W.C.T.U. in Georgia," *Methodist History* 28 (Apr. 1990): 187–94; Paul Isaac, *Prohibition and Politics: Turbulent Decades in Tennessee, 1885–1920* (Knoxville: University of Tennessee Press, 1963); James Benson Sellers, *The Prohibition Movement in Alabama, 1702 to 1943* (Chapel Hill: University of North Carolina Press, 1943); James H. Timberlake, *Prohibition and the Progressive Movement, 1900–1920* (Cambridge, Mass.: Harvard University Press, 1963); Ian Tyrell, "Drink and Temperance in the Antebellum South: An Overview and Interpretation," *Journal of Southern History* 48 (Nov. 1982): 485–510; Daniel Jay Whitener, *Prohibition in North Carolina* (Chapel Hill: University of North Carolina Press, 1946).

43. Mary Douglas, *Purity and Danger: An Analysis of Concepts of Pollution and Taboo* (1966; rpt., Baltimore: Penguin, 1970), 137–38, also 14, 15, and 17–40.

44. George M. Fredrickson, *White Supremacy: A Comparative Study in American and South African History* (New York: Oxford University Press, 1981), 209–15.

45. John. W. Cell, *The Highest Stage of White Supremacy: The Origins of Segregation in South Africa and the American South* (Cambridge: Cambridge University Press, 1982), 131–70.

46. Edward L. Ayers, *The Promise of the New South: Life After Reconstruction* (New York: Oxford University Press, 1992), 67–68, 136–46; Joel Williamson, *The Crucible of Race: Black-White Relations in the American South Since Emancipation* (New York: Oxford University Press, 1984), 111–223; idem, *New People: Miscegenation and Mulattoes in the United States* (1980; rpt., New York: New York University Press, 1984), 94–100.

47. Douglas, *Purity and Danger*, 136.

48. Peter L. Berger, *The Sacred Canopy: Elements of Sociological Theory of Religion* (1966; rpt., Garden City, N.Y.: Doubleday [Anchor Books], 1967), 85–101.

49. Cell, *Highest Stage of White Supremacy*. See note 45 above.

50. Clifford Geertz, *The Interpretation of Cultures* (New York: Basic Books, 1973), 90–123.

51. Douglas, *Purity and Danger*, 17–72, esp. 67 and also 165.

52. Cell, *Highest Stage of White Supremacy*, 171–91.

53. Ted Ownby, *Subduing Satan: Religion, Recreation, and Manhood in the Rural South, 1865–1920* (Chapel Hill: University of North Carolina Press, 1990).

54. A[mory] D[wight] Mayo, *Southern Women in the Recent Educational Movement in the South*, edited by Dan T. Carter and Amy Friedlander (1892; rpt., Baton Rouge: Louisiana State University Press, 1978), 59–70, 120–29, 150, 160.

55. John Patrick McDowell, *The Social Gospel Movement in the South: The Woman's Home Mission Movement in the Methodist Episcopal Church, South, 1886–1939* (Baton Rouge: Louisiana State University Press, 1982); Wilma Dykeman and James Stokely, *Seeds of Southern Change: The Life of Will Alexander* (Chicago: University of Chicago Press, 1962); Jacquelyn Dowd Hall, *Revolt Against Chivalry: Jessie Daniel Ames and the Women's Campaign Against Lynching* (New York: Columbia University Press, 1979). See also Arthur Raper, *The Tragedy of Lynching* (Chapel Hill: University of North Carolina Press, 1933).

56. Dykeman and Stokely, *Seeds of Southern Change*, 95, and 57–95; Hall, *Revolt Against Chivalry*, 58–106.

57. William E. Montgomery, *Under Their Own Vine and Fig Tree: The African American Church in the South, 1865–1900* (Baton Rouge: Louisiana State University Press, 1993), 97–141, 283–306.

58. See James D. Anderson, *The Education of Blacks in the South, 1860–1935* (Chapel Hill: University of North Carolina Press, 1988); see also W.E. Burghardt Du Bois, ed., *The Negro Church* [Atlanta University Publications, No. 8] (Atlanta: Atlanta University Press, 1903); W.E. Burghardt Du Bois, ed., *Efforts for Social Betterment among Negro Americans* [Atlanta University Publications, No. 14] (Atlanta: Atlanta University Press, 1909); W.E. Burghardt Du Bois, ed., *The College-Bred Negro American* [Atlanta University Publications, No. 15] (Atlanta: Atlanta University Press, 1910).

59. Montgomery, *Under Their Own Vine and Fig Tree*, 203–52. Also Floyd J. Miller, *The Search for a Black Nationality: Black Colonization and Emigration, 1787–1863* (Urbana: University of Illinois Press, 1975); Edwin S. Redkey, *Black Exodus: Black Nationalist and Back-to-Africa Movements, 1890–1910* (New Haven, Conn.: Yale University Press, 1969).

60. Benjamin E. Mays, *The Negro's God as Reflected in His Literature*, with a preface by Vincent Harding [Studies in American Life Reprint Series] (1938; rpt., New York: Atheneum Press, 1968), 149–52.

61. W.E. Burghardt Du Bois, *Souls of Black Folk: Essays and Sketches*, with introduction by Saunders Redding (1903; rpt., Greenwich, Conn: Fawcett, 1961), 17. Also David Levering Lewis, *W.E.B. Du Bois: Biography of a Race 1868–1919* (New York: Henry Holt and Company, 1993), 265–96. See also Louis R. Harlan, "Booker T. Washington and the Politics of Accommodation," in *Black Leaders of the Twentieth Century*, ed. John Hope Franklin and August Meier (Urbana: University of Illinois Press, 1982), 1–18.

62. Du Bois, *Souls of Black Folk*, 23.

63. Mays, *Born to Rebel*, 15–16.

64. Mays, *Negro's God*, 146 (quoting Washington's *Black Belt Diamonds* [New York: Fortune and Scott, 1898], 34); see also 142–47.

65. Ibid., 146, quoting Washington's *Black Belt Diamonds*, 115.

66. Taylor Branch, *Parting the Waters: America in the King Years, 1954–1963* (New York: Simon and Schuster, 1988), 1–205; Adam Fairclough, *To Redeem the Soul of America: The*

Southern Christian Leadership Conference and Martin Luther King Jr. (Athens: University of Georgia Press, 1987), 13–35.

67. The most complete biography is David J. Garrow, *Bearing the Cross: Martin Luther King, Jr., and the Southern Christian Leadership Conference* (New York: Random House, 1986).

68. Branch, *Parting the Waters*, 227–28.

69. Ralph E. Luker, *The Social Gospel in Black and White: American Racial Reform, 1885–1912* (Chapel Hill: University of North Carolina Press, 1991), 1–88; Dykeman and Stokely, *Seeds of Southern Change*; Hall, *Revolt Against Chivalry*.

70. See Sara Evans, *Personal Politics: The Roots of Women's Liberation in the Civil Rights Movement and the New Left* (New York: Knopf, 1979).

71. See for example, Donald W. Shriver Jr., *The Unsilent South: Prophetic Preaching in Racial Crisis* (Richmond: John Knox Press, 1965).

72. One Southern Baptist minister active in the interracial movement of the twenties and thirties wrote something that whites had possibly repressed in the fifties but that this woman's response suggests was still operative. He commented on the subtle ways in which African Americans' mood and sensibility could affect whites. See Edwin McNeill Poteat, "Religion in the South," in *Culture in the South*, ed. William Couch (Chapel Hill: University of North Carolina Press, 1935), 251.

73. Keith D. Miller, *Voice of Deliverance: The Language of Martin Luther King, Jr., and Its Sources* (New York: Free Press, 1992).

74. The phrase is typical of the social gospel liberals whose works so inspired King in seminary; it is similar to the language of a social gospel book used by white Southern Methodists in the leadership training classes. See John W. Shackford, *The Program of the Christian Religion* (Nashville: Cokesbury Press, 1917). See also Miller, *Voice of Deliverance*, 86–141.

75. Miller, *Voice of Deliverance*, 107–11; Martin Luther King Jr., "Letter from a Birmingham Jail," in *I Have a Dream: Writings and Speeches that Changed the World*, by Martin Luther King Jr., ed. James M. Washington (1986; rpt., San Francisco: Harper Collins, 1992), 91.

76. See Peter Skerry, "Christian Schools versus the I.R.S.," *Public Interest* 61 (Fall 1980): 14–41; also Michael Lienesch, *Redeeming America: Piety and Politics in the New Christian Right* (Chapel Hill: University of North Carolina Press, 1993); also Samuel S. Hill and Dennis E. Owen, *The New Religious Political Right in America* (Nashville: Parthenon Press, 1982).

77. Ernest B. Furgurson, *Hard Right: The Rise of Jesse Helms* (New York: Norton, 1986).

78. Ibid., 69–91; and personal observation of television commercials in Helms's run for reelection in the 1984 senatorial campaign.

79. See Leonard, *God's Last and Only Hope*, 128.

80. Ammerman, *Baptist Battles*, 44–125, 80–167; Leonard, *God's Last and Only Hope*, 135–72.

"When the Subject Is Female":
The Impact of Gender on Revisioning
American Religious History

ROSEMARY SKINNER KELLER

Each age writes the history of the past anew with reference to the conditions uppermost in its own time. . . . The aim of history, then, is to know the elements of the present by understanding what came into the present from the past. For the present is simply the developing past, the past the undeveloped present. . . . The antiquarian strives to bring back the past for the sake of the past; the historian strives to show the present to itself by revealing its origin from the past. The goal of the antiquarian is the dead past; the goal of the historian is the living present.

Frederick Jackson Turner wrote these words in 1891, just over one hundred years ago and immediately preceding the publication of his now classic essay, "The Significance of the Frontier in American History." The disappearance of all continental frontiers in the United States marked the close of a movement begun in 1607 and the beginning of a new age in American history. There is no more pivotal statement of revisionism in American history than the "Turner Thesis," positing the question at the turn-of-the-century: with nothing left to conquer, civilize, and settle within the country's physical boundaries, what is to become of the "American spirit?"[1]

Turner, at thirty-two years of age, unleashed new directions in American history, as scholars soon began to envision emerging frontiers in urban, immigration, and other areas of "the developing past" that were right before their eyes but that they had failed to see. His understanding of the purpose of historical scholarship, to write "the history of the past anew with reference to the conditions uppermost in its own time," is as relevant to revisionist research today as it was a century ago.

Sydney Ahlstrom highlighted virtually the same purpose in charting a significant new direction in American religious history more than eighty years later, in 1972, in the publication of *A Religious History of the American People*. Ahlstrom's book, which became my first real textbook on the subject, caught the spirit of the day. As the final quarter of the twentieth century began, he wrote that "social and intellectual developments of the last decade have profoundly altered our interpretation of the entire course of American history. The terrible moral dilemmas that began to intensify during the sixties have had an especially rude impact on long-accepted views of the country's religious development."[2]

Ahlstrom's very title, *A Religious History of the American People*, as well as the methodology of his book, grew out of his two major premises. First, as Turner had stated, to revise history meant to be responsible to the contemporary context in which the historian lived. The story of the past could never again be told in the same way that it was written before the social revolutions of the 1960s, either in terms of what was included in history or how the story was interpreted.

Second, American religious history needed to be interpreted as a part of the wider world of American culture. Denominational and institutional church history had marginalized, even isolated, religious studies. Within this larger cultural context, denominational and institutional religious changes were still Ahlstrom's primary concern, but he also sought to introduce into his chapters the idea of racial, ethnic, and gender inclusiveness and the presence of new religious movements in the final quarter of the twentieth century.

As a result of the social revolutions of the 1960s and the "New Social History" following upon their heels, a host of subcultures surfaced in the study of American history in the 1970s, among these the histories of women, African Americans, race and ethnicity, class, urban and local communities. If the term "American culture" seemed to infer one predominant, defining middle-class mainstream, historians now acknowledged that they had been blinded to the reality that many cultures, not one, had created the American experience.

We finally recognized that we lived in a culturally diverse and cross-cultural world in which American history no longer could be defined almost exclusively in terms of the public leadership of white men in government and the military. No longer could American religious history be interpreted exclusively or even primarily as the world of ordained white male bishops, preachers, and pastoral leaders. Some scholars in American religious history sought to put aside entirely, or at least to marginalize drastically, the hierarchical world of institutional Christianity. But whether they hoped to reform or reject it, all students recognized that in the future institutional Christianity could represent only one of many cultural religious worlds that interacted with each other daily.

The history of women, as a new direction in social history, had its origin at the same time that the field of religion and American culture became increasingly prominent in the 1960s and 1970s. Ahlstrom's book was something of a marker for women and religion, too. He acknowledged the presence of more women in American religious history than previous writers had done by including the names of more women in his text. Along with the famous threesome of Anne

Hutchinson, Frances Willard, and Jane Addams, Ahlstrom had a total of 43 names of women and women's organizations, out of approximately 1,300 entrants altogether, listed in his thirty-four-page index—even though the list of women included the names of Mary, Queen of Scots, and Rebecca of Sunnybrook Farm!

Today, almost twenty-five years since the publication of Ahlstrom's *Religious History of the American People*, is a fitting time to assess new directions in American religious history from the perspective of the history of women and religion. This essay seeks to make an evaluation in two ways. My first question is: what is the current state of revisionism as it relates the history of women to the religious history of the American people? To put it another way, what has been done in the last twenty-five years and what needs to be done now to reconceive American religious history in light of the presence of women as subjects within it?

Second: how does a part of "an age" come to life in a different way through the experience of women? Or, how does a woman's experience become a different prism or mirror for interpreting the history of a period than does a man's experience? That question frames a case study of Georgia Harkness, the first professional female theologian in the United States, to which a major part of this essay is devoted.

I

First, to point out the obvious: historiography, as it demonstrates the inclusion of women and the difference that their presence makes in interpreting the history of religious institutions as well as the interaction of religion and American culture, has not come as far in the last twenty-five years as feminist scholars of women and religion would have hoped. Reference to four highly creditable surveys of church and religious histories, written in the 1980s and 1990s, defines the current state of the relationship of the history of women and religion in America to the writing of survey accounts. These include Catherine Albanese, *America: Religions and Religion* (1981; second edition 1992); Martin E. Marty, *Pilgrims in Their Own Land* (1984); Peter W. Williams, *America's Religions: Traditions and Cultures* (1990); and Mark A. Noll, *A History of Christianity in the United States and Canada* (1992).

All of these surveys give more space to women and accounts of their contributions than any previous overviews of American religious history have done. However, these volumes do not demonstrate any reconceptualization of themes or different ways of analyzing church and religious history growing out of efforts to include women in their texts. To blame the authors is far too simplistic and a distorted response to their work. The reviewer cannot simply say that they lack sensitivity to women's presence and contribution. The question becomes: what is *possible* at this stage in the process of developing a new direction in American religious history based upon the leadership and participation of both men and women?

The state of revisionism is this: we haven't come far enough, we are still in the early stages of doing substantial revision of church and religious history. The serious work of acknowledging and developing the study of women and religion as a field of religious history is hardly two decades old, even when dated most generously from Ahlstrom's work in 1972. To keep the subject in perspective, it is sobering to acknowledge that the present state of writing of religious history, with its focus primarily on white men, has been in process two or three centuries, depending upon how one dates the beginning of scholarly church history.

Substantial revision in the rewriting of history is a several-step process that is well illustrated in the recovery of the history of women and religion as a part of the "new social history" being written over the past twenty-five years. The cycle of revising history begins when the mainline consensus regarding the essential content of historical inquiry is seriously challenged. Regarding women and religion, something so basic was at stake as *who* are the subjects of the historical field? Social events of the 1960s caused secular historians to realize that the long-held emphasis on military and governmental history was inadequate. Similarly, as Ahlstrom's work attests, religious historians began to recognize that their focus upon leadership of white men, primarily in Protestant Christianity, was narrow, oversimplified, and insufficient.

The second step in revising history relates closely to the first. Historians begin to research primary sources that previously were not recognized as of historical worth. Established and budding scholars, who became interested in women and religion in the 1960s, began to read private papers such as diaries, autobiographies, and personal letters. They discovered a religious worldview of women that had not been known before, a world of women whose lives had long been restricted to the domestic sphere. Such neglected sources, which soon became important historical documents, were often found in corners of attics of a home in which several generations of one family had lived, in unopened boxes handed down to a daughter at the death of her mother or grandmother, and in uncataloged areas of library archives, given no attention because professional archivists did not know what to do with such gifts. Another type of archival holding, obscure until the recovery of women's history came into prominence, are denominational women's missionary society journals, newly significant because they document over a century of Christian missionary work and contact with other religions throughout the world. Of course, these "new" sources had always been there. But, because they had never been valued or used, the work of delving into them in the 1960s and 1970s was disparate and fragmented.

Sydney Ahlstrom's words pointed to the reality that a host of subcultures became visible in the light of the social revolutions of the 1960s. A third step was taken in revising the tradition: new fields of history emerged as historians recognized the significance of their disparate sources against the backdrop of the "terrible moral dilemmas that began to intensify during the sixties" and that have accelerated since then. Women's history, feminist history, and gender studies were among the several subcultures, along with studies of African Americans, race and ethnicity, class, urban and local communities, youth and aging, that emerged in the 1970s and 1980s.

New interest in religion as it was a part of American culture became a focus within religious studies. Suddenly, primary sources were put together into documentary histories, dissertations were written, and monographs were published, signifying that a field of women and American religious history had been constituted. Among American religious historians, acknowledgment also was being made that the pluralism of faiths no longer could be marginalized.

A fourth step in revisionism constitutes recognition of the larger unity of these subcultures into a "New Social History" and new directions in American religious history. By the 1980s and 1990s, women and religion was recognized to be essential to revisioning both the new social and religious histories. The voices of feminist historians within Roman Catholicism and Judaism, as well as Protestantism, created this awareness that the story of Christianity was distorted without the contributions of women. Similarly, within the interreligious worlds of Native American spirituality, Hinduism, Buddhism, Islam, lesbian options, New Age spirituality, and Goddess religion, feminist scholars have been at the forefront in visioning and revisioning American religious history.[3]

While the steps need to be delineated, the reality is that all of them are being taken at the same time in the mid-1990s. It is not possible rigidly to separate the steps in practice. To try to do so would curb the creativity of the revisionist process. Social events and the presence of women and racial and ethnic individuals and communities in mainstream public life continue to confront historians with the necessity to understand the complexity of the present day by interpreting the fullness of the past. Disparate sources are still being brought to light. Through documentary histories and monographs, scholars are bringing these sources together and interpreting them. Women's and feminist history, gender studies, and the new social history are becoming increasingly fruitful fields in terms of the amount of material being retrieved and the ways of revisioning the past that are being conceived.

A new consensus is emerging in religious historiography, the fifth and final step in the cycle. The essential place of women within the overview of American religious history is established. But this inclusivity still takes place in survey texts only at the level of adding more names and telling more stories of women who were leaders within movements and institutions. Reconception of themes and new ways to tell the story of American religious history, which do honor and justice to the greater inclusivity of women, as well as to persons of different races and religious faith, has not yet taken place in the writing of American religious history.

Sara Alpher, Joyce Antler, Elizabeth Israels Perry, and Ingrid Winther Scobie, editors of The Challenge of Feminist Biography, make the point that "when the subject is female, gender moves to the center of analysis."[4] Further, when both men and women are included in the history of religious institutions in the United States, the writers must consider the socially conditioned roles that have defined the functions of both sexes in these institutions if they are to analyze how the lives of institutions, as well as the experience of women and men themselves, have changed.

When only men were the subjects of church and religious history, their functions and roles were implicitly defined as universal, the experience of all persons within the movements and institutions studies. Or, at least, the implication was that they were the only persons who mattered in determining the course of American religious history.

Biography is *one* notable lens for telling the story and stories of history. An essay written by a woman, Barbara Tuchman, sums up succinctly the purpose and significance of "Biography as a Prism of History" as she saw it in 1979 and as has been widely interpreted in modern times. She begins her essay, "In so far as I have used biography in my work, it has been less for the sake of the individual subject than as a vehicle for exhibiting an age." As a prism of history, biography "encompasses the universal in the particular. It is a focus that allows both the writer to narrow his or her field to manageable dimensions and the reader to more easily comprehend the subject."

Tuchman emphasizes the writer's responsibility to communicate effectively to potential readers. Biography engages the reader directly and immediately, enabling one who becomes involved in the life story to relate and identify with the subject personally. The reader cannot connect so intimately with history when it is presented simply as a panorama of events or abstract ideas. "The reader is the essential other half of the writer," Tuchman continues. "I never feel my writing is born or has an independent existence until it is read. It is like a cake whose only *raison d'etre* is to be eaten. Ergo, first catch your reader." [5]

Tuchman's essay was written just over fifteen years ago, and it is now a classic piece in the writing of biography. It is ironic that a woman, who is distinguished as one of the great biographers of the modern age, wrote the essay. The irony intensifies when we realize how recently she described the purpose of biography in this way. By 1979, the feminist consciousness in United States society was strong, and women's studies, women's history, and biographies of women were being published in considerable numbers. Gender analysis underlay the work being done by feminist scholars at this time, though not stated as explicitly as in the 1980s and 1990s.

However, Tuchman wrote only the biographies of men. She believed that she was encompassing universal experience in the particular story of a man. Apparently it did not occur to her that the story of an age might unfold differently through a woman's experience. Nor did she consider that women might not "relate and identify with the subject personally" when the male studied is a military or political leader or an ecclesiastical official. We now realize that many dimensions of the history of an age emerge and people identify in a host of different ways depending upon whether the prism is gender, class, race, or ethnicity.

This essay relates gender to biography as a prism of history through the life story of Georgia Harkness (1891–1974), the first professional woman theologian in the United States. More modest than claiming to be a "vehicle for exhibiting an [entire] age," it focuses on her rise to leadership within institutions of higher education and in religious institutions of the seminary and the church. Further, Harkness was white, middle-class, and Protestant. The essay claims to address only a limited part of universal experience! However, I believe that its implications are wider, and invite readers to identify them.

The underlying questions addressed are: what happens when we look at the rise of a woman's leadership in religious institutions through the lens of gender? When the life of this particular woman is studied, is her vocational journey significantly different from that of a man's? And does this woman's experience portray a side of an institution's life that is not contained in a man's story?

II

Georgia Harkness was arguably the first professional woman theologian in the United States. She wrote almost forty books on theology, ministry of the laity, spiritual life, and the responsibility of the church to combat war and discrimination against women and ethnic persons. The first female theologian to teach in Protestant seminaries in the United States, she served on the faculties of Garrett Biblical Institute and the Pacific School of Religion during the 1940s and 1950s. Throughout the twenty years prior to seminary teaching, she taught at two colleges for women, Elmira College and Mt. Holyoke College, both of which claim distinctions as pioneers in the education of women. Issues of gender were crucial at every point in her vocational journey; they were the focus of the defining moments in her early years of childhood and family experience, through her educational training and teaching career. In turn, the gender hurdles Harkness confronted in her own life also created defining moments in advancing the rights of women in church and in higher education.

Harkness was born in the tiny village of Harkness in upstate New York on April 21, 1891, and died eighty-three years later in Claremont, California, on August 21, 1974. Nestled in a picturesque valley in the Adirondacks, the family farm, on which she lived from birth through her high school, was located fifteen miles south of Plattsburgh and one hundred miles south of the Canadian border.[6]

Growing up during a time when the functions of men and women were strictly demarcated between the public and private spheres, it is not surprising that a woman, who would pioneer in the profession of higher education, would find her primary role models in the males of her family line. Georgia's father, J. Warren, and her grandfather, Nehemiah, were builders of the community and servants of the church. On the local level, they provided the examples that she would emulate on the national and international scenes. Only later did the value she placed upon her mother increase.

Nehemiah Harkness used his influence and physical energy to have a branch of the railroad being built from Albany to Montreal run through the community, an area containing rich deposits of iron ore. His granddaughter wrote in her autobiographical statement, when she was sixty years old, that "unable to get men who would work in the hot sun to drive their oxen to pull stumps for making the road-bed, and determined that the railroad should go through at all costs, he did it himself." Overworked by the strenuous task of supervision and physical labor,

Nehemiah died the following year. The grateful community honored its "favorite son" by changing the name of the hamlet from AuSable to Harkness, in his honor.[7]

Nehemiah also passed on a vision of peace and racial justice to his grand-daughter, who would become a pacifist and a passionate prophet for racial equality. In a letter that Georgia kept all of her life, her grandfather brooded over the impending doom of a civil war, fearing that "much blood will be shed between the North and the South." He hoped that the old Democratic Party would be "annihilated and a Republican party established in lieu of it." Although he dreaded the possibility of an overcentralized national government, his greater fear was the curse of slavery. "I for one am willing to come under a Monarchy for the sake of getting rid of Slavery," he wrote in a personal letter, "for I think it is a great National evil and had ought to be done away with."[8]

The tie between religious faith and social responsibility was at the core of Georgia's father's identity, and she pointed to him as the most influential person in her life. A prosperous farmer and land surveyor by occupation, he taught Sunday school in the Harkness Methodist Episcopal Church almost continuously from the time he was sixteen years old until he died in his eighties. Like his own father, Warren introduced the advantages of modern secular life to the rural community: he was the leader in bringing the Normal School to nearby Plattsburgh and founded the county Grange, as well as gaining rural mail delivery and telephone service for the area. And he laid the telephone lines himself![9]

However, Warren Harkness never gained his personal vocational dream. He attended Oswego State Normal School after graduation from high school, "and he longed to be a teacher," his daughter wrote. "When his father died, about the time of his graduation, he surrendered his ambitions to come home, look after his mother and sisters, and run the farm. Though he taught country school in the winter term for many years when the farm work was slack, he remained a farmer all his days."[10]

Georgia was the youngest of four children. Her one sister, Hattie, was twelve when she was born, and her brothers, Everett and Charles, were eight and six respectively. Their parents recognized when the children were young that their father's intellectual curiosity and abilities had been inherited by the daughters. They concluded that the girls had greater educational potential than their sons and would have college educations, not a typical decision for parents of the day. When Hattie was seventeen and a senior in high school, she anticipated entering Plattsburgh Normal School to gain a teaching degree. Tragedy struck the family and Hattie died of diphtheria only a few months before her high school graduation.[11]

Only five when her sister died, Georgia grew up on the adage "to be as smart as Hattie Harkness." The mantle of both Warren and Hattie fell upon the younger daughter. Reflecting back upon her vocational journey later in life, Harkness wrote that "as far back as I can remember, I expected when I grew up to be a teacher. No other vocational possibility ever crossed my mind." She undoubtedly anticipated becoming a high school teacher in a nearby rural school or perhaps in one of the major cities of New York State. This was one of the few career options open to women of her day, and it perfectly suited her aptitude and interest.

The realistic possibility for any young woman of northeastern New York who sought teacher training was to attend Plattsburgh Normal School, relatively inexpensive and located only fifteen miles from the Harkness farm. This was her expectation, too, and she took pride in the fact that her father had a guiding hand in founding the school. But Warren and Lillie Harkness wanted their youngest and smartest child to receive the best education available from one of the distinguished institutions of the nation.

"It was a great day, therefore, when my father told me that if I wanted to go to college he thought he could manage it, particularly if I could win a Cornell scholarship. One per county was awarded by competitive examination, and I straightway began to prepare for it. It was still an all-day examination, preceded by a 3-hour ride to Plattsburg behind a horse, and I thought I had failed it." In due time she received her official notification. Returning home after picking blueberries in their pasture one day, Georgia found a letter that announced that she "stood Number One. That settled the matter."

Georgia Harkness always stood number one, or very close to the top in her academic work. This was the pattern beginning in elementary and high school, continuing throughout her undergraduate experience at Cornell University, and culminating in her master's and doctoral work at Boston University.

Cornell University was one of the earliest coeducational institutions of higher education in the United States. It opened in 1868 as an all-male university, with 412 men, the largest entering class of any contemporary American college. Four years later, it became coeducational, in large part because of the radical vision of its male founders. Ezra Cornell stated his expansive vision to his daughter, Eunice, in 1867: "I want to have girls educated in the university as well as boys, so that they may have the same opportunity to become wise and useful to society that boys have." [12]

Despite the advocacy of its founders, the unwritten law issued by male students resulted in a highly oppressive atmosphere for their female peers. Women students were discouraged from participating in campus organizations and excluded from social activities of fraternities. A classroom photograph taken in 1910 portrays the academic atmosphere in terms of male-female relationships during Harkness's years. About sixty men dressed in suits and ties are pictured in a large lecture hall, with three women seated in the first three desks in the right-hand corner of the first row. Sexual segregation was the order of the day. [13]

Harkness was among the second generation of college women who entered from 1890 until 1920. Widespread popular perception held that female students were more interested in marriage than scholarship and wanted a social, rather than an academic, degree. Women students of this generation were depicted traditionally as "frivolous and socially preoccupied," contrasting "unfavorably with the serious and dedicated pioneer generation of 1865 through 1890." [14]

First-generation university women students customarily have been considered the pioneers for women's rights in education and professions; they were committed to careers and rarely talked of combining careers and marriage. However, recent revisionist studies demonstrate that the large number of women students of Harkness's generation were not seeking marriage rather than careers but that they hoped to combine the two. Lynn Gordon, in her *Gender and Higher Education in the Progressive Era*, contends that "what truly distinguished the second generation from its predecessor (and its successors) was the linking of gender consciousness to campus life and to post graduate plans for social activism, a growing commitment to egalitarian rather than separatist feminism, and a simultaneous interest in marriage." [15]

Georgia Harkness probably hoped to combine marriage with a public career. Though she dated young men during her twenties and thirties, no relationship ever led to marriage. In fact, she felt like something of a social misfit at Cornell and the pain of her extracurricular experience in college left a deep mark on her. Looking back, Harkness described herself as "shy, green and countrified, and when I left for college I had never been more than twenty miles away from home. . . . My clothes were queer; I had no social graces. . . . I never, in my four years, held a campus office. In fact, I was the utter antithesis of a Big Shot on the Campus." [16] Her extracurricular experience fit the pattern of large numbers of women students of the day.

Equality of opportunity appears to have prevailed in the classrooms of Cornell, even though not reflected in seating arrangements. Women earned high academic status because of their superior performance. Male faculty members may have been dismayed by the high calibre of work by women students. In 1895, for instance, only 14 percent of the students were women, but half of the most recently elected Phi Beta Kappas were female. [17]

Georgia was among the Phi Beta Kappas selected from her class. She probably tended to downplay her accomplishments, like many marginalized persons of her day. She stated it in these words: I "accepted my inferior social status as being in the natural course of events." Harkness also described herself as getting "middling good grades," clustered in the high 80s to the mid-and-upper 90s. Evaluating her transcripts in 1990, a member of the Cornell Registrar's staff described Harkness as an exceptional student in a day when professors graded much more rigorously than in the late twentieth century. [18]

The Student Christian Association and the Student Volunteer Band provided both the social and religious grounding for Harkness throughout her college years. In high school she had thought of being a missionary but told no one. In college, however, like thousands of other students, she signed the Student Volunteer Movement's pledge, "It is my purpose, if God's permits, to become a foreign missionary." [19] The SVM sought to supply missionary boards of church denominations in the United States and Canada with volunteers to meet the demands of foreign mission work in the twentieth century.[20] Single women now were being commissioned in their own right as missionaries, while in earlier years only women married to male missionaries could enter this national and foreign missionary service. Their husbands received the official commission. The requirement and the assumption was that "he was appointed, they served."[21]

Harkness, like countless other male and female students who signed the pledge, did not become a foreign missionary. After college, she felt her parents, and particularly her mother because of ill health, needed her to remain closer to home. The SVM did not lose heart over such people but believed that their commitment would make them stronger lay and clergy persons in ministries within the United States.

This proved to be the case for Georgia Harkness. Immediately after college, she became a high school teacher for two years, following the most natural occupation open to women and the one she had thought most likely for herself. She taught English and foreign languages in two small towns of Schuylerville and Scotia, New York, close enough to her family home to enable her to see her mother regularly.[22]

During this time, "when I read an article in *The Christian Advocate* about a new profession for women in religious education which was opening up, I decided forthwith that if I could not be a missionary, this was my calling."[23] The "new profession for women" provided a unique stepping-stone for Harkness that would become apparent to her only in retrospect. It enabled her to plan to enter a profession approved for her sex as a director of religious education in a church. In fact, however, the plan led her to Boston University, where her training shifted toward that of teaching in higher education, a profession dominated by males.

While on her master's program, Harkness took courses in the philosophy department of Boston University, where she "fell under the spell of Dr. Edgar Brightman's kindling mind."[24] A scholar and teacher of philosophy, he became Georgia's most significant lifetime mentor and model, second only to her father. Entering the master's program in 1918, she shortly thereafter also began a Ph.D. in philosophy and was Brightman's first Ph.D. candidate.

When Harkness asked Brightman if he would take her as his Ph.D. advisee, he responded that he thought she had the ability but doubted whether she had the "stick-to-it-ness" to complete a dissertation.[25] With that additional impetus, Harkness completed her residency requirements for her Ph.D. in 1921, during the period in which she also finished her master's degree. In the spring of 1922, she was invited to join the faculty of Elmira College, in central New York, as assistant professor of philosophy of religion and religious education. Her dissertation was accepted in the spring of 1923 and her Ph.D. was granted in June.

While men were Harkness's primary models and mentors for public leadership, she came to value her mother more highly during her years at Boston University. Georgia had never wanted to live the restricted, subordinate life as wife and mother that Lydia (Lillie) Harkness embodied. Paradoxically, however, Georgia's mother spoke to her the word of liberation from the traditional social constraints placed on a woman.[26]

Comments that Georgia made in her diary when she was twelve years old leave no doubt that her mother's domestic role was not appealing to her. However, in a time and in a setting in which gender roles were not questioned or challenged, she took it for granted that her mother's life, in relating to her husband and family, should be "centered in him and the children." That her mother should or might have an identity of her own was never a question for Georgia as she was growing up.

When Harkness was in her early sixties, she perceptively described in her autobiographical statement the social constraints put upon Lillie Merrill Harkness. "Having spoken at such length of my father, I should say something of my mother. There is much less to say. Due to a fall and ensuing illness, she did not go to school beyond the eighth grade. She married my father at the age of eighteen and adapted her life to his." In her almost unrestricted praise of her father, Harkness identified only one negative characteristic about him: "I am afraid her husband did not praise her as much as he should have — he took her fidelity for granted." Georgia never remembered hearing scolding and sharp words exchanged between her parents. But, also, she did not recognize until later that such peace may have been achieved by her mother's self-imposed silence.

Georgia recorded three events that occurred during her years at Boston University that demonstrate how she came to value her mother in a new way. Only after coming to young adulthood did she realize "how deeply her [mother's] devotion to her family ran" and how much she had sacrificed in their behalf. These events also indicate that her mother sought for Georgia a different way of life than her own.

One circumstance grew out of Georgia's pressing financial condition as a student. During her second year, she gained her first experience teaching students at the university level, giving an introductory course in Bible to incoming religious education majors at Boston University. "I loved it; apparently they did too; and I hoped to continue." However, despite the positive student evaluations, her invitation was not renewed. "I was told that there was no money; but the money was straightway given to someone else. So, whatever the reason, I was left with no job, and no prospects of one." Left unemployed, she "expected to borrow the money for this third year, but my mother insisted on turning over to me a small inheritance from her parents."

A second event occurred during the Christmas vacation of her first year at Boston University. "I came down with the flu and was ill for six weeks, for half that time very critically. My mother nursed me back to health with night and day attention, though she was never well herself after that."

A final crisis and the most telling of the three for Georgia's identity, grew out of the strains of intergenerational living in the Harkness farmhouse. Through the years, that home was filled beyond capacity many times with members of the extended family, taking a heavy toll on her mother. Much of her mother's life "was made un-happy by having to live, first with her mother-in-law and then with her daughter-in-law, both of whom had sharp tongues." As the youngest child and only surviving daughter, Georgia "wrestled mutually with this problem in the latter instance for over twenty years, often vainly attempting to interpret the viewpoint of each to the other and with my heart torn with sympathy for both."

After Georgia made her vocational decision to pursue a Ph.D. in preparation to teach religion to college students, tension came to a head within the extended family living in the Harkness farmhouse. The problem seemed insoluble, so Georgia offered to stay at home and run the farm to enable her brother Charlie and his wife, Minnie, to go elsewhere. Two considerations prevented such a radical move: "(1) the agreement on the part of everybody that I was incompetent, and (2) the insistence by Mother that I *had my own life to live*, and must not be deflected by it on her account" (italics added).

Undoubtedly Warren strongly concurred with Lillie's unequivocal pronouncement. However, her mother's support, even mandate, that "I had my own life to live," made the difference for Georgia in this family crisis, on which she never elaborated further.

Harkness took her first steps in following her mother's admonition by joining the faculty of Elmira College in 1922. Founded in 1853, Elmira claims distinction as the first women's college in the United States. She remained on the faculty for fifteen years, from 1922 until 1937. During these years, Harkness gained her own voice, not only as a classroom teacher but also as a leader among her faculty colleagues. By 1925, she led a successful faculty fight for a major curriculum revision to raise the academic standards of the institution. Harkness described it as a "complete victory for the forces of reform," in which she stood in direct opposition to the dean. He had "ruled with an absolute monarchy for twenty-five years," she stated, realizing that the dean might fire her if he could. But Harkness grew in confidence with the backing of her president and a large segment of the faculty, and through her belief that this was "the most constructive achievement I ever accomplished. Elmira is on its way, I think, toward becoming a college instead of a boarding school."[27]

During these years, Harkness also became a socially prophetic leader in the ecumenical movement, nationally and internationally, as well as in her own Methodist Episcopal and Methodist churches. Over her lifetime, she wrote countless articles combatting the evils of sexism, racism, militarism, and classism that were published in religious journals. Notably, the first essay she wrote in 1924 was entitled "The Ministry as a Vocation for Women" and was particularly addressed to the delegates attending the Methodist Episcopal Church's 1924 General Conference.[28] This article marked the beginning of advocacy of women in church-related occupations, and reached a high mark thirty-two years later. In 1956, due in large part to her leadership, women were finally granted ordination with the guarantee of full conference membership equal to the rights and responsibilities open to men in the Methodist Church. Harkness's own entrance and rise as a woman in a profession related to the church and dominated by men was tied throughout her life to opening those ranks to a much larger body of women.

She began that drive in her 1924 article in which she set down the argumentation that she would uphold throughout her life. Harkness was not claiming sexual superiority of women over men, but that women had a legitimate sphere outside, as well as inside, the home. Sounding the keynote of the liberal tradition, she contended that both logic and Christian commitment were defied by the strange dispensation that granted men the opportunity to fill the primary paid positions in the church, while women were valued as volunteers, missionaries, deaconesses, and church secretaries. Within the nation's largest Protestant denomination, 27 percent of the ministers had less than a full high school education. Further, a net loss of 613 ministers had been reported in the past four years. Even so, "the Church which would not choose a mediocre man in preference to a superior woman is one among a thousand."

Harkness wrote while counseling a considerable number of women who were considering religious vocations. "I do not advise any of them to prepare for the ministry, though I consider it the highest religious calling." The prospect was futile under present conditions. The time had come for public opinion to be refashioned, and the clergy and the religious press had to take the lead. They had not done all they could to eradicate this "deep-seated relic of medievalism in the attitude of the church at large."

Always addressing the mainstream membership of religious institutions, Harkness reminded her readers that a person does not need to be "an ultra-feminist" to recognize the wrong in this situation. She concluded on this prophetic note, which characterized her entire ministry: "We wonder if the advancement of the Kingdom is not more important than the maintenance of an ancient prejudice."

During her tenure at Elmira, Harkness received several distinctions that were "firsts" for women, evidencing that ancient prejudices that created gender barriers denying women public leadership were beginning to fall. By the late 1930s, *Time* magazine cited her as "famed woman theologian"; she became the first female member admitted to the American Theological Society; she was selected by the *Christian Century* to write an essay in its series by notable religious leaders on "How My Mind Has Changed"; and she became one of the few women delegates to attend the conferences of the International Missionary Council at Oxford in 1937 and at Madras the following year, as well as the Board of Strategy of the Provisional Conference of the World Council of Churches held at Geneva in 1939.[29]

Harkness thrived on her increasing prominence in the public spotlight on the national and international scenes. However, she used these opportunities to preach the gospel as she believed it, which included challenging the church to fulfil its socially prophetic mission. The position of women in the church continued to be a primary cause for her.

After the International Missionary Council at Oxford, Harkness described the personal consequences of it for her. She had made a four-minute speech on the place of women in the church that was cabled under the Atlantic in an Associated Press dispatch. The publicity precipitated so many invitations to speak "that I ran myself ragged in the attempt to keep up my school work and accept even a few of them." [30] (italics added).

Those numerous invitations included a speech delivered at the annual Leadership School at the Methodist Assembly in Lake Junaluska, North Carolina, as well as an article in the *Christian Century* that spelled out in greater detail her arguments made at Oxford attacking the paternalism of the church and the reasons for diversion of women's activity into secular professions. Her basic point was that "it is a paradoxical fact that the Christian gospel has done more than any other agency for the emancipation of women, yet the church itself is *the most impregnable stronghold of male dominance*. It is this fact more than any other which makes women of intelligence and ability restive, and skeptical of the church as the most effective channel for their effort" (italics added).[31]

Harkness's forthrightness in challenging the church to live up to its theological affirmation of oneness and equality in Christ did not alienate her from mainstream Protestantism but increased her credentials to call the church to accountability. One invitation extended to Harkness in January 1939 illustrates the glory, burden, and pressure of the mantle of leadership resting on her shoulders because the subject was female. Edgar Brightman informed her that Duke University was holding a celebration and that the planners were "convinced that you were the speaker that they wanted to represent the leadership of women in the church." [32]

One would wonder whether any man had ever been invited to speak in order to represent all the men of the churches! She continued to run herself ragged because so many of her invitations grew out of her singular female leadership. Brightman, however, supplied a rationale to make it impossible for her to decline the invitation from Duke:

> Your position of leadership among women in America in the field of religious thought is undoubted (of course you have heard of how *Time* christened you "famed woman theologian"), and I am convinced that your acceptance of the invitation will mean a great deal in promoting good feeling between the Church North and the Church South in the unification. As a delegate to the Uniting Conference you will have additional reason for accepting this invitation. . . . I understand that the Committee is fighting hard to have you also invited to preach in the chapel on Sunday. If this invitation does come, I hope you will see it in the light of no mere routine item, but an extraordinary victory for the cause of woman's place in the church, especially in the South.[33]

Georgia Harkness received countless distinctions and invitations simply because she was a female pioneer in the church and in higher education. But the other side, the reality of sexism, also constricted professional opportunities that might have opened to her. While at Elmira, Harkness was bypassed for teaching positions at several major women's colleges, including Smith, Radcliffe, Skidmore, and Mt. Holyoke, some due to overt, and others to more covert, sexism.

The president of Skidmore wrote to Brightman on one occasion asking him to recommend "a good man" for a position in its Department of Religion. When Brightman sent in Harkness's name and credentials, he received no response from the president. On another occasion, William Earnest Hocking was impressed with her work after she had graded papers for him during her sabbatical at Harvard. Hocking pleaded her cause vigorously when a position opened at the sister college, Radcliffe. Tradition prevailed, and the Radcliffe possibility turned out to be a fiasco. When positions opened at Mt. Holyoke and Smith in the early thirties, "the desire to hire a man" again caused her to be eliminated.[34]

The sexism expressed covertly and personally by her friend and colleague, Edgar Brightman, was even more painful for Harkness to receive. In 1928, she asked Brightman to write a recommendation for her for a Sterling Fellowship for a year of postgraduate study at Yale University. He sent Georgia the original copy of his recommendation, with the intent that she would send it on to the Scholarship Committee of the Yale Graduate School with her completed application.[35]

After reading his highly complimentary evaluation of her, Harkness immediately expressed her appreciation for his "many gracious words. However, Georgia also asked Brightman to do two things further regarding the recommendation. First, he should send the statement directly to the Dean of the Graduate School. Second, Harkness asked Brightman to change a phrase in his letter. After his several complimentary statements, Brightman referred to Georgia's "lack of feminine charm." She undoubtedly interpreted his comment as a reference to her large body and her physical awkwardness, as well as her feeling of discomfort and social inferiority in relationships with men. "I know what you mean, and am not offended by it," she stated, though she undoubtedly was offended. "If it would be taken at its face value, as you meant it, no great harm would be done. But . . . I suspect that a committee might be prone to read this as suggesting freakishness, or at least a conspicuous masculinity of dress or manner. And if so, the fellowship would probably go elsewhere." Then she asked him directly, "If something less dangerous could be substituted for this half-line, I should appreciate it: if not, let it go."

Harkness continued to pierce to the heart of the matter by confronting Brightman with the blatant sexism of his reference to her "lack of feminine charm."

In this connection, I wonder whether you realize the extent to which *a woman with a PhD must, among other obstacles, contend against the tradition* that female PhD's are so "intellectual" that they are freakish and sloppy. A degree of queerness that would be overlooked in a man is unforgivable in a woman — when both are contending for the same prize. (italics added)

She might well have taken her position one step further and told Brightman that any reference to "feminine charm," whether positive or negative, was out of order. He would have been horrified to think of anyone raising the issue of a man's "masculine charm" in a letter of recommendation.

Brightman responded, first, as a gentleman, acknowledging that he wronged her by including the phrase. But he missed the point that he had acted in a highly sexist manner: "It was crude of me to put that charm passage in a letter *that you were to read, and I regret it for that reason*" (italics added). After such a cursory apology, he continued by putting up his defenses. Objectively considered, the matter was not so bad as it sounded, he wrote. "A testimonial which contains no frankly unfavorable comment is always under suspicion. On the other hand, women applicants for scholarships are always under suspicion of being candidates for matrimony and using the funds of scholarships as stepping-stones thereto."

Brightman did his best to apologize to Harkness. "I hope that the 'strong personality . . . dignity and poise . . . presence and confidence' will serve to obviate any inferences as to freakishness, masculinity, or sloppiness, which of course are far from the truth. . . . I am very sorry about my thoughtlessness." However, he would not retract his statement. "Chiefly, then, because I don't have another blank form and a corrected one would make a bad matter worse, I think I'd better let it stand."

Did it occur to Edgar Brightman that he might have discarded the recommendation form and simply sent a letter to the scholarship committee, certainly an acceptable alternative in today's academic world? This thought probably did not cross his mind, for the entire incident pointed to the truth in his self-evaluation: "I have to work like sin to get a student's point."

In this particular case, Brightman was incapable of hearing Georgia's emerging voice. She was moving on to a new inner identity, regardless of whether Brightman could discern it.

Harkness received the Sterling Fellowship to Yale University and she forgave Brightman for his inappropriate statement in his letter of recommendation for her. Their relationship continued to be cordial and trusting. But her forgiveness could never erase the hurt she experienced. After Harkness had been dead for over fifteen years, her niece remembered her Aunt Georgia telling her of the experience she had, when she was thirty-seven years old, of "applying for a job or something and whoever had written this recommendation let her see it. One of his statements was that she was completely without sex appeal." [36]

In 1937, Harkness joined the faculty of Mt. Holyoke College. Like Elmira, Mt. Holyoke held rightful honor as a pioneer institution for the education of women. One hundred years before, in 1837, it became the first female seminary to provide young women with training equal to a high school education; and, in 1888, it gained college status. The move enabled Harkness to maintain her commitment to the advancement of women, as well as to be seated officially in theological studies at a distinguished college.

She had been brought to Mt. Holyoke with the strong advocacy of President Mary Woolley. Harkness and Woolley held strong commitments to international peace and pacifism, social and political stands that brought criticism from other faculty members. Harkness remained at Mt. Holyoke only two years. Her time there might have been happier, Harkness said, had Woolley not retired at the same time that she arrived.[37]

The positive reason for Harkness's departure, however, was the opportunity to become professor of applied theology at Garrett Biblical Institute in Evanston. After teaching for seventeen years in undergraduate institutions for women only, she made the major transition to a graduate seminary of the Methodist Church whose major vocation was to prepare men for ordained ministry. Drawing students from a wide range of denominations, it was closely affiliated with the Chicago Training School, which trained women, and a small number of men, to be Christian educators in local churches and deaconesses in home and foreign mission work.

The Chicago period of Georgia Harkness's vocational journey extended for ten years, from 1940 until 1950, between the fiftieth and sixtieth years of her life. She became the first full-time woman professor in theological studies, which included Christian thought, Bible, church history, and ethics, in a Protestant seminary in the United States, and was highly valued by students and colleagues. Of all the institutions at which she taught, Garrett became her "academic home," and she willed her large collection of private and public papers to the seminary.

Harkness never married, but during these years she experienced the entrance of a "significant other" into her life. In 1943, Dr. Ernest Fremont Tittle, Harkness's pastor at the First Methodist Church in Evanston, Illinois, introduced her to Verna Miller, a musician and member of the congregation, believing that they would provide an enriching friendship for each other. They soon decided to share a home together and maintained that relationship for the next thirty years of their lives until Harkness died in 1974. In 1950, they moved together to Berkeley, California, where Georgia taught at the Pacific School of Religion. And in retirement, in the 1960s, they relocated to Claremont, California.[38]

By the late 1940s, Harkness gained her widest national and international distinction and was widely sought after as a lecturer within both the church and the academy. However, she received a particularly hard blow when President Horace Greeley Smith failed to name her to the chair in systematic theology vacated by the retirement of Harris Franklin Rall. Though not promised the position, Harkness felt that President Smith had intimated to her when she was hired that the chair in systematics would be hers upon Rall's retirement.

The title of professor of applied theology was created for Harkness when she was hired at Garrett in 1940. It well defined the application to practical ministry that had characterized her professionally since she began teaching at Elmira in 1922. The term embraced Harkness's work in religious education and her strong advocacy of social justice issues, including women's rights, peace, race relations, and economic justice, which she saw as inseparably connected.

However, in the academic world of religion during Harkness's career, a systematic theologian was the professional of full stature in the field. This person interpreted and interrelated in an ordered and formal manner the basic doctrines of the Christian faith. The movements for social freedom and justice during the 1960s were influential in increasing the stature of "Applied Theology" in seminaries by the last quarter of the twentieth century.

When Harkness came to Garrett, Dr. Rall was almost seventy years old, and administrators and faculty thought that he might retire at the end of that academic year. While she was negotiating her contract with President Horace Greeley Smith during the summer of 1939, she wrote two letters to Edgar Brightman, expressing her belief and anticipation that she would be selected to succeed Rall when he retired. She jubilantly shared with Brightman, in a letter dated July 10, 1939, her first word of the invitation to come in applied theology to Garrett. Then she continued in a confident tone, "Dr. Smith did not say definitely that I would be Dr. Rall's successor but I think this is what it amounts to." [39]

Writing slightly over one month later, on August 17, she again interpreted what she believed to be President Smith's unstated intention. As if to justify her appointment in applied theology to herself as well as Brightman, she wrote, "It wouldn't do to call my field Systematic Theology because then the public would think I was selected to be Dr. Rall's successor." [40]

Harkness made no further comment to Edgar Brightman about the appointment to be made in systematic theology to replace Harris Franklin Rall until May 13, 1944, almost three years after she had previously mentioned it. She was clear by then that the chair in systematic theology would not be offered to her, but she wrote of that reality only indirectly and in the most professional manner. Harkness gave no indication to Brightman of whether she had been considered to receive Rall's chair. She simply stated that "the Trustees wanted someone with a reputation already established, and we on the faculty want somebody who has proved his ability to teach."

Over the next year, Harkness and Brightman discussed possible candidates openly and candidly, with Brightman giving his honest estimate of their strengths and weaknesses. It was a difficult time to fill such a major appointment because, as Georgia put it, "all the people I can think of whom I should like to see here are already so well established in their own institutions that I doubt if they want to leave." Her professional concern was that the best possible person, with whom she would work in very close conjunction, be hired. [41]

Harkness made considerable input into the consultation process and gained significant evaluation from Brightman regarding Gerald McCulloh, the candidate who was selected by early 1946 to replace Rall. McCulloh was a young man who had taught briefly at Hamline University and was then serving as the pastor of a church in St. Paul, Minnesota. He had done work toward his doctorate at Boston University but completed his degree in Scotland because he "was not quite sure of making the grade with us," Brightman wrote on December 10, 1945. Brightman evaluated him as "vivacious, musical, cordial, a good mixer, adaptable to all sorts and kind of people, he is a grand personality. . . . What would need to be looked into closely is his scholarship." After thanking Brightman for his "fine frank statement about McCulloh," Harkness indicated that she would share with President Smith "what you say about his possible academic limitations."[42]

President Smith hired Gerald McCulloh to replace Harris Franklin Rall, and McCulloh assumed the newly established Henry Pfeiffer Chair of Systematic Theology. However, he remained on the faculty only until 1953. McCulloh then moved to the staff of the Methodist Board of Higher Education, where he remained until his retirement in 1977.

Interviews with some of Harkness's closest confidants while she was at Garrett Biblical Institute and in the years to follow demonstrate the centrality of gender issues in piercing to the heart of the problem. A former student of Harkness, Henry Kolbe, stated that Georgia Harkness was clearly overlooked. President Smith saw systematics to be the crown of theology and not appropriate for a woman.[43]

Harkness's faculty colleague, Murray Leiffer, whose office was next to hers, described Smith as "never too sure of his relationship with women." On occasions, he would show extreme deference toward women, and he always believed that men and women played separate roles. Such attitudes defined latter-day Victorian relationships between the sexes. But they were outdated as women pioneered in sharing professional status with men. Leiffer stated the situation succinctly: "It was a lack of clarity of definition of being a woman on an all male or predominantly male faculty."[44]

When Georgia Harkness was fifty-nine years old, she made her final academic move to join the faculty of Pacific School of Religion in Berkeley, California. She negotiated a half-time contract, which she maintained for ten years before retirement. In part, this was her decision to scale down her intense schedule of teaching, writing, speaking, and traveling. Also, it was a reaction against her treatment by President Horace Greeley Smith at Garrett, though her relationships with the faculty there were always highly congenial.

Harkness was well accepted at Pacific School of Religion, and her years as a senior member of the faculty in a mentoring role to younger colleagues were happy ones. Verna and Georgia maintained their home together in Berkeley until the late 1960s when they moved together to Claremont, California, where, in 1974, Georgia preceded Verna in death.

III

Georgia Harkness came of age and began her career as a woman at a time in which seminaries, as well as universities and colleges, had few if any women on their faculties. She pioneered as "a first," and during her years at both Garrett Biblical Institute and Pacific School of Religion from 1940 until 1960 she was the only female theologian on their faculties. Edgar Brightman also summed up her place as a forerunner in opening doors for women in the churches, both as professionals and volunteers, when he prevailed upon Harkness to be a plenary speaker at Duke University in which she was to "represent the women of the church" — all the women!

When biography is understood as a prism of history, as Barbara Tuchman puts it, the significance of a pivotal, catalytic moment of change comes into focus. "A lack of clarity of definition of being a woman on an all male or predominantly male faculty": Murray Leiffer's words can be extended to capture the ambiguous circumstance relating to gender confronting institutions of the family, church, and higher education, as well as those of the society at large, at mid-twentieth century. The functions of women and men within these institutions had been clearly set and demarcated prior to the early twentieth century: men were professors and women played the supportive roles. Prefeminists, such as Georgia Harkness, challenged this demarcation and tested new boundaries. A brief analysis of issues emerging out of her life demonstrates "the lack of clarity of definition of being a woman" as Georgia Harkness experienced it.

First was her relationship to male authority figures. All of her role models, primarily her father, grandfather, and Edgar Brightman, were men. They were the persons whom she emulated and with whom she interacted in determining her own identity. Her grandfather's and father's vision and acts of labor in building the railroad and laying the telephone lines are notable. Harkness did the same type of thing when Brightman challenged her determination to complete her Ph.D. dissertation. Always standing number one academically throughout elementary, high school, and undergraduate university studies, Harkness only needed Brightman's challenge further to motivate her to finish her Ph.D. and to inaugurate a distinguished teaching career. Perseverance and hard work were defining qualities of Georgia Harkness throughout her life.

Brightman's inability to relate to Harkness as a female professional colleague was demonstrated in his statement regarding Harkness's "lack of feminine charm" in his recommendation for her sabbatical leave at Yale. He either could not begin to comprehend the obstacles that a woman faced in contending against the tradition of exclusion of women from academic circles or could not admit that he might have been wrong in writing such words. Harkness's stature of grace was evidenced in her openness to maintain the friendship despite his inexcusable blunder.

Male figures of authority did not know what to do with a woman who gained greater national and international distinction than male members of their faculties. This was true of the dean of Elmira and the president of Garrett Biblical Institute, both of whom had primary roles in hiring her. The issue was much larger than the relationship between a particular woman and man, however. As Murray Leiffer pointed out, President Smith was accustomed to showing deference to women as long as men and women operated in highly separate spheres. When a strong and assertive woman, such as Harkness, challenged that definition, Smith, just as Brightman, was unable to take a more flexible stance and relate in an egalitarian manner.

The lack of definition of what it meant to be a woman arose also in Georgia's relationship with her mother. The notable lack of references to Lillie Merrill in Harkness's letters and diaries is perplexing, until one realizes that as a young person Georgia took for granted the accepted social understanding of her day that a middle-class married woman had no identity outside that of caring for her husband and children. And, as a young woman, Georgia found nothing in her mother to emulate because, in exploring a career in the public world her only role models were men. Only in looking back as an older adult could Harkness empathize with the boundaries of gender definition that tightly constricted her mother's life and her mother's deep desire to release Georgia from those same constraints.

There is no evidence to suggest that Harkness had a wide network of close female friends and confidantes. Because there were few professional women in institutions of higher education and the church, the likelihood is that her friendship and collegiality with other women came in singular and scattered relationships.

Harkness had one extended long-term relationship with another woman, Verna Miller. Little is known about that relationship because Verna and Georgia lived together for more than thirty years and no private letters exist. Verna was never interviewed because she died before research began into Harkness's life. No evidence exists to determine whether theirs was a lesbian partnership in terms of a sexual relationship. However, it is clear that Georgia and Verna were deeply committed, supporting, caring, and nurturing to each other. Friends described their personalities as highly complementary. Verna's spontaneity and lightheartedness balanced Georgia's more serious and reserved nature. Their partnership held qualities that any couple might well emulate.

A brief look into three events in Harkness's older adulthood might provide a fitting conclusion. They demonstrate Harkness's emerging self-understanding and self-assurance as a lone woman in a field dominated by men during this historical period of ambiguity regarding a professional woman's role.

The first relates to her participation as the one woman on the Dun Commission, the Commission of Christian Scholars appointed by the Federal Council of Churches in 1950 to consider the moral implications of obliteration bombing and the use of hydrogen bombs for mass destruction. In a picture of the commission, made after she joined the faculty of Pacific School of Religion, Harkness stands in the front row surrounded by nine men. They include Reinhold Niebuhr, Paul Tillich, and John Bennett of Union Theological Seminary in New York City, Robert Calhoun of Yale Divinity School, and Angus Dun, bishop of the Washington, D.C., Diocese of the Episcopal Church and chair of the commission. Harkness was "appropriately" dressed in her man-tailored suit and "sensible" shoes. She stands out in the picture as the only woman, but she also seems to "fit" among the members. The picture portrays the fundamental reality of Harkness's professional life: she was one woman, well-rooted but standing alone, in a male academic world.

Harkness clearly knew her own mind on the subject confronting the committee. Only two persons took a position of absolute pacifism, Georgia Harkness and Robert Calhoun. Harkness was not swayed by the many distinguished male religious leaders on the commission from her position that under no circumstances should nuclear weapons ever be used.

A second definitive event occurred two years earlier, in 1948, when Harkness confronted Karl Barth, the giant among twentieth-century systematic theologians, at the organizing meeting of the World Council of Churches. As the picture of the Dun Commission tells the previous story so well, Harkness's words demonstrate her clarity and self-confidence in relating to the predominant white male theologian of her day:

> With a few other men, Karl Barth chose to participate in the section on the Life and Work of Women in the Churches. At the beginning of the discussion Sarah Chakko, the Chairman, asked me without warning to state its theological basis. I said briefly that in the O.T. it is stated that both male and female are created in the image of God; in the N.T. Jesus assumed always that men and women were equal before God, and in our Christian faith is the chief foundation of sex equality. Barth claimed the floor; said that this was completely wrong; that the O.T. conception of woman is that she was made from Adam's rib and the N.T. that of Ephesians 5, that as Christ is the head of the Church, so man is the head of woman. Then followed a lively interchange in which I did little but to quote Gal. 3:28, but the room buzzed. Barth convinced nobody, and if I have been told he was trying to have some fun with the women, his joke back-fired. A year later when a friend of mine asked him if he recalled meeting a woman theologian from American, his cryptic reply was, *"Remember me not of that woman!"* [45]

Finally, an event that occurred on Harkness's eighty-first birthday, two and one-half years before her death, well illustrates the paradox of the impact of gender in her own life as it relates to her support of other women. She was elected a delegate to the General Conference of the United Methodist Church held in Atlanta, the sixth and last general conference she would attend. The conference asked her to stand while the delegates rose to sing "Happy Birthday" to her. Georgia replied that "above all the things that have come to me, you touch my heart deeply. This is the greatest." [46]

However, the greatest joy that she experienced that day came later in the vote of the conference to establish the General Commission on the Status and Role of Women (COSROW) in the church. Since its inception at the 1972 General Conference, COSROW has been an advocate, catalyst, and monitor to ensure the full participation and equality of women in the church at the general, regional, and local church levels. Harkness's words to the conference clearly define her, not as a pioneer who sought her own singular stature as a woman but as an advocate and political strategist who over many years helped to open the doors of the church to equality of women with men. Harkness's final statement conveys her understanding of the theological significance of the establishment of the

General Commission on the Status and Role of Women. In traditional language, Harkness the "prefeminist," stated: "With the action taken this morning in regard to the place of women in the church, I can say that I believe *the Kingdom is nearer than when we believed.*"[47]

The particular experience of one woman, Georgia Harkness, carries significance in opening doors to a much larger part of the universal change in gender roles at the end of the twentieth century. That reality brings us full circle to the relevance of Frederick Jackson Turner's statement of one hundred years ago, that "each age writes the history of the past anew with reference to the conditions uppermost in its own time." Only now in the final decade of the twentieth century are institutions of higher education served by faculty that are no longer all male or even predominantly male. Only now are these socially conditioned roles and working relationships of men and women being consciously reconceived as women move into faculty and administrative positions of collegiality and leadership — because a woman such as Georgia Harkness gained clarity about the ambiguity of gender relationships in her circumstances and about who she was in seeking to work within those treacherous currents. Her life, therefore, is significant today in helping us to understand and interpret the history of our very recent past anew for today.

Notes

Epigraph is from Frederick Jackson Turner, quoted in Susan E. Hirsch and Robert I. Goler, *A City Comes of Age: Chicago in the 1890s* (Chicago: Chicago Historical Society, 1990), 2.

1. See George Rogers Taylor, ed., *The Turner Thesis: Concerning the Role of the Frontier in American History*, 3rd ed. (Lexington, Mass.: D.C. Heath, 1972).

2. Sydney E. Ahlstrom, *A Religious History of the American People* (1972; rpt., Garden City, N.Y.: Image Books–Doubleday, 1975), 20, 30.

3. See Rosemary Radford Ruether and Rosemary Skinner Keller, eds., *In Our Own Voices: Four Centuries of American Women's Religious Writings* (San Francisco: Harper-SanFrancisco, 1995).

4. Sara Alpher et al., eds., *The Challenge of Feminist Biography* (Urbana: University of Illinois Press), 7.

5. Barbara Tuchman, "Biography as a Prism of History," in *Biography as High Adventure*, ed. Stephen B. Oates (Amherst: University of Massachusetts Press, 1986), 94.

6. See Rosemary Keller, *Georgia Harkness: For Such a Time as This* (Nashville: Abingdon Press, 1992), for the fuller account of Harkness's life.

7. "Days of My Years," unpublished autobiographical essay of Georgia Harkness written for the Pacific Coast Theological Group during the 1950s, Georgia Harkness Collection: Garrett-Evangelical Theological Seminary, Evanston: Ill., p. 5. Hereafter cited as "Harkness Collection: G-ETS."

8. Newspaper obituary notice of Nehemiah Harkness and letter from Nehemiah Harkness to unidentified recipient, undated, Harkness Family Papers, in possession of Georgia Harkness's niece and her husband, Peg and John Overholt, of Kilmarnock, Virginia. Hereafter cited as "Harkness Family Papers: Overholt."

9. Harkness, "Days of My Years," 5–7; Newspaper Collection, Harkness Family Papers: Overholt; and J. Warren Harkness, "History of Peru," unpublished, Harkness Family Papers: Overholt.

10. Harkness, "Days of My Years," 7.

11. Material from this and the following paragraphs is taken from ibid., 8–15, and from Georgia Harkness, *Grace Abounding* (Nashville: Abingdon Press, 1969), 39–40.

12. Charlotte Williams Conable, *Women at Cornell: The Myth of Equal Education* (Ithaca, N.Y.: Cornell University Press, 1977), 51.

13. Ibid., 117.

14. Lynn D. Gordon, *Gender and Higher Education in the Progressive Era* (New Haven, Conn.: Yale University Press, 1990), 4.

15. Ibid., 5.

16. Harkness, "Days of My Years," 15.

17. Conable, *Women at Cornell*, 80.

18. Harkness, "Days of My Years," 15, 16; a copy of Harkness's official transcript and its evaluation courtesy of Registrar's Office, Cornell University.

19. Ibid., 16.

20. C. Howard Hopkins, *John R. Mott* (Grand Rapids, Mich.: Eerdmans, 1979), 60.

21. Rosa Peffly Motes, "The Pacific Northwest: Changing Roles of the Pastor's Wife Since 1840," in *Women in New Worlds: Historical Perspectives on the Wesleyan Tradition*, vol. 2, ed. Rosemary Keller, Louise L. Queen, and Hilah F. Thomas (Nashville: Abingdon, 1982), 154.

22. Harkness, "Days of My Years," 17.

23. Ibid., 18.

24. Ibid.

25. Ibid.

26. Material from this and the following paragraphs is taken from ibid., 7, and Harkness, *Grace Abounding*, 28.

27. Georgia Harkness to Edgar Brightman, May 2, 1924, Edgar S. Brightman Papers, Mugar Library, Boston University. Collection hereafter cited as Brightman Papers: BU.

28. This and the following paragraphs are based on Georgia Harkness, "The Ministry as a Vocation for Women," *Christian Advocate*, Apr. 10, 1924, pp. 454, 455.

29. Georgia Harkness to Edgar Brightman, Feb. 4, 1939; Georgia Harkness to Edgar Brightman, Mar. 26, 1937, Brightman Papers: BU; *Christian Century*, Mar. 15, 1939, pp. 349, 350.

30. Harkness, "Days of My Years," 24.

31. Georgia Harkness, "Women and the Church," *Christian Century*, June 2, 1937, p. 708.

32. Edgar Brightman to Georgia Harkness, Jan. 13, 1939.

33. Ibid.

34. Georgia Harkness to Edgar Brightman, Dec. 22, 1926; Georgia Harkness to Edgar Brightman, Jan. 22, 1927; Georgia Harkness to Edgar Brightman, Jan. 16, 1935, Brightman Papers: BU.

35. Material for this and following paragraphs is based upon Georgia Harkness to Edgar Brightman, Jan. 27, 1928, and Edgar Brightman to Georgia Harkness, Jan. 29, 1928, Brightman Papers: BU.

36. Interview of Peg Overholt by Rosemary Keller, Apr. 27, 1991.

37. Harkness, "Days of My Years," 24.

38. Interview of Murray and Dorothy Leiffer by Rosemary Keller, Sept. 8, 1989, La Jolla, Calif.

39. Georgia Harkness to Edgar Brightman, July 10, 1930, Brightman Papers: BU.

40. Georgia Harkness to Edgar Brightman, Aug. 17, 1939, Brightman Papers: BU.

41. Georgia Harkness to Edgar Brightman, May 18, 1944; Georgia Harkness to Edgar Brightman, Sept. 26, 1944; Georgia Harkness to Edgar Brightman, Jan. 4, 1945; Georgia Harkness to Edgar Brightman, Dec. 7, 1945, Brightman Papers: BU.

42. Edgar Brightman to Georgia Harkness, Dec. 19, 1945; Edgar Brightman to Georgia Harkness, Dec. 14, 1945, Brightman Papers: BU.

43. Quoted in Martha Lynne Scott, "The Theology and Social Thought of Georgia Harkness" (Ph.D. diss., Garrett-Evangelical Theological Seminary, 1984), 44.

44. Interview with Murray and Dorothy Leiffer by Rosemary Keller, Sept. 8, 1989.

45. Harkness, "Days of My Years," 28.

46. *Daily Christian Advocate* (General Conference of the United Methodist Church), Apr. 22, 1972, p. 334.

47. Ibid., 335.

History, Historians, and the Historiography of Indigenous Sectarian Religious Movements in America

STEPHEN J. STEIN

The passage of thirty years seems like a lifetime — at least when considering the changes that have taken place in the study of indigenous sectarian religious movements in America. No less a distinguished historian of Christianity than Horton Davies, writing in 1965, bewailed the "renewal of heresy and schism" that he associated with the rapid "expansion of sects and cults" in the United States. Writing in a second revised edition of a volume initially entitled *The Challenge of the Sects*, Davies raised the specter of a "menace" that was "perpetuating error, strife and bitterness." The success and strength of movements such as Pentecostalism, Mormonism, Seventh-Day Adventism, the Jehovah's Witnesses, and Christian Science led him to warn that these groups could "no longer be regarded as harmless oddities or eccentric deviations from the historic norms of Christian faith, worship and behavior."[1] Davies's comments reflect both the fear and the disdain that were widespread in the 1960s, attitudes fueled in some measure by the rapidly expanding number of new religious movements during that decade.

Even as late as the 1960s, much of the study of sectarian communities was motivated by the urge to refute their teachings and convert their members. That was an overriding concern in the widely circulated volume by Anthony A. Hoekema, published in 1963, entitled *The Four Major Cults*, which dealt with four of the five groups mentioned above. "Though the task of witnessing to cultists is not an easy one," Hoekema wrote, "we do have a responsibility toward these people, who are so thoroughly enmeshed in error while firmly convinced that they are in the right."[2] Knowledge and understanding were therefore viewed by him as critical for success in the apologetic and evangelistic task. "Know your enemy" might well have been the slogan for those determined to carry on the polemic against sectarian movements.

The contrast twenty years later could not have been more dramatic. In 1985 in a study widely regarded as a landmark in the historiography, Jan Shipps mounted a sustained argument that turned on end longstanding attacks on Mormonism. Utilizing insights from the comparative study of religions, she countered historians and apologists who "argued that Mormonism could not possibly be Christian because the movement rests on a foundation of subterfuge, chicanery, deception, and trickery, and therefore must be defined as fraud." Driven by a desire to understand the success of the Latter-day Saints and a determination to deal with the historical evidence in an evenhanded manner, Shipps came to the conclusion that "Mormonism ought not to be classified as a part of *traditional* Christianity." Rather she made the case that it is "a separate religious tradition" deserving of understanding and respect on its own terms.[3] Written by a religious outsider, not a member of the Mormon tradition, Shipps's work reflects a fundamental shift in the historiography of sectarian communities. By the 1980s the primary motivation behind much of the more important scholarship in the field was the desire to know in order to understand. Curiosity replaced fear, tolerance supplanted disdain, and at times a note of admiration and even celebration sounded among those working in sectarian studies.[4]

The passage of more than another decade since 1985 has witnessed continuing change in the field. Today there exists a greater willingness than ever before to enter the world of sectarian religious traditions, to take them on their own terms, to withhold judgment in an effort to understand the appeal and the inner workings of such movements. In his study of one of the most controversial religious groups in recent decades, David Chidester employs what Ninian Smart has labeled "structured empathy" in his approach to the Peoples Temple and the tragedy at Jonestown. This method, according to Chidester, requires that the historian "temporarily suspend prejudicial biases and value judgments in order to enter imaginatively into the worldviews of others." Using that method he explains how the "evil" at Jonestown "could look good within its own consistent, coherent internal context."[5] Chidester's judgment, however, by no means condones evil; rather it provides the clarity needed for sound interpretation. In her study of spiritualism in America in the nineteenth century, Ann Braude strikes a similar methodological note. Her interest in exploring spiritualism as a religious phenomenon rests on the assumption "that faith is a crucial and little understood element of the social structure . . . [that] provides a window into the complex realm of human motivation." She writes, "I want to know why and how people believe the things they believe and how social, political, and religious beliefs combine to form a comprehensive understanding of reality."[6]

A similar desire drives much of the contemporary scholarly interest in the history of indigenous sectarian movements in America. Assisted by an expanding number of subdisciplines, researchers engaged with the subject are poised to move forward, leaving behind polemical or apologetical agendas, pressing toward an understanding of these communities more useful to students of America's religious life and culture and more consistent with prevailing canons and concerns in the larger field of United States history. In what follows I will describe select historiographical accomplishments of the recent past, evaluate promising developments at the present, and sketch the lines for an expanding program of historical work in the area of American sectarian studies.

Problems with terminology dog the study of sectarian communities in America. Two foundational terms with a history of widespread usage by scholars — "sects" and "cults" — possess overwhelmingly negative connotations for many people, so much so that their unexplained use is nearly prohibited. Sociologists and historians of religion have shaped the scholarly language in this field over several generations, having adopted and adapted Max Weber's distinction between sect-type and church-type religious communities.[7] Ernst Troeltsch's examination of historical expressions of these contrasting religious patterns within the history of Christianity, as well as of more mystical groups he called "cults," has left an equally deep impression on the scholarship.[8] But the ecclesiastical assumptions inherent in their use of these terms has resulted in a negative frame of reference for movements designated as "sects." That problem, however, pales in significance when compared with stereotypes created by ill-informed journalists, aggressive deprogrammers, and religious polemicists who turn these terms, especially "cults," into linguistic weapons trained against those who participate in such religious movements. The media construct screaming headlines to sensationalize and attract attention. Anticult organizations generalize unfairly about a host of divergent groups. Television preachers condemn the beliefs and practices of sectarians who do not share their religious convictions. The categories "sect" and "cult" have become terminological tar babies, soiling whatever they are attached to.[9]

For all of the above reasons, scholars have (perhaps unadvisedly) shied away from the use of these categories, seeking other terminology free of negative associations. In that connection they have created a number of new terms for sectarian communities including marginal religious communities, outsider religious groups, alternative religions, new religious movements (NRMs), new religions, or simply, "religious movements."[10] Among those working in the field, there is no consensus regarding these categories. Each term has advantages and disadvantages. For instance, calling all sectarian groups "new religious movements" has the advantage of using a neutral category, but it is patently an error. Many so-called NRMs are not "new" in any historical sense. In America, for example, some of the most successful *new* religious movements are more than a century *old*.

The problems with terminology will not go away, nor will they be solved by fiat. There are good reasons for retaining the term "sectarian" as a useful way of identifying the diverse group of indigenous religious movements. "Sect," free of negative associations and stereotypes, refers to a religious movement that dissents significantly in one way or another from prevailing cultural and societal norms. The "dissenting" quality of sectarian religious life is its distinctive, defining feature. Dissent is not an end in itself but rather a measure of fundamental disagreement with the values of the host culture. Dissent need not be only negative, nor does it always require condemnation. Prophets dissent, and sometimes they command respect. Reformers protest, and often they motivate substantial numbers of followers. The heart of dissent is drawing distinctions, and the most common manifestation of religious distinctions is the establishment of boundaries. Sectarian communities construct religious boundaries of one kind or another, setting themselves apart from others who do not share the presuppositions of those within the sect. The fundamental argument between the members of the sect and those outside, who are often called the "world," involves disagreement over the prevailing patterns of the society in which they find themselves.

The term "cult" is fraught with even greater difficulties because of popular misunderstandings. It should, in fact, be understood within the same framework as "sect," implying patterns of dissent and boundaries. Typically, "cult" is used to describe a religious movement that carries the principle of dissent and distinction to more radical or extreme positions. One way to distinguish between the two terms is to speak of the difference as a matter of degree, not of essence. Both "sect" and "cult," in my opinion, retain considerable usefulness for students of American religious history. Both are worth redeeming, or at least restoring to a measure of integrity and usefulness.

In the theoretical and methodological realm, the study of indigenous sectarian communities suffers from a different problem, namely, the abundance of diverse disciplinary perspectives in the field, many of which are operating in relative isolation from one another. The result is a surplus of interest that has not produced a well-integrated interdisciplinary approach to these movements. For instance, sociologists engaged in the study of conversion and deconversion often seem unaware of the broader historical contexts shaping the decisions made by members of sectarian groups. In other words, they artificially restrict the field of variables in their explanations. Anthropologists, in their enthusiasm for fieldwork, tend to disparage the use of documentary sources, at the same time often failing to acknowledge the fact that their presence among sectarians in the field is potentially a powerful, distorting influence on their study. Historians researching one or another particular sect frequently are blind to patterns persisting across movements that undermine claims for distinctiveness. Scholars employing psychological or economic theories to unlock the individual or collective biography of sectarians fall into reductionist modes of explanation, failing to grant even a measure of integrity to the religious claims of their subjects. In turn, researchers who focus on the religious dimension of the topic sometimes, unwittingly, privilege religion as a category, thereby neglecting to subject religious phenomena to critical scholarly evaluation. The challenge for historians of American religions working in the field of sectarian studies is to be aware of the methodological and theoretical possibilities represented by different disciplines and at the same time to avoid the pitfalls associated with each of these approaches.

In spite of terminological problems and the plethora of approaches, the historical study of indigenous sectarian groups in America has witnessed substantial advances in recent years. But these scholarly gains have not been uniform across all movements. On the contrary, the diverse impact of the historical profession and of the established canons of contemporary scholarship upon the various sectarian communities is itself highly instructive.

The most striking historical achievements have occurred in the study of the Church of Jesus Christ of Latter-day Saints, a tradition that has prided itself for generations on its historical sensitivities. The Mormon interest in history extends back to its origins and founder, Joseph Smith Jr. Smith's preoccupation with sacred history and his determination to integrate his own experiences into the larger framework of salvation history have left an indelible mark on the community.[11] He was instrumental in creating a distinctive narrative complex that incorporated the Bible, *The Book of Mormon*, events during his lifetime, and an eschatological vision of the future. In that story, history and theology are woven tightly together, both underscoring Mormon distinctiveness.[12] Among the specific theological notions of the Latter-day Saints reinforcing the interest in history is the ordinance of baptism for the dead, based on revelations given to Smith in 1841 and 1842. Described as "a welding link of some kind or other between the fathers and the children,"[13] this temple rite has nurtured widespread interest in family history and genealogical studies as well as in the practice of keeping diaries and journals. Similarly, the saga of the westward trek by the Saints to the Salt Lake Valley has fostered a continuing infatuation with tales of Mormon pioneers who suffered hardship and persecution at the hands of their enemies but who rose above those circumstances to create a prosperous society in the intramountain region of the West. It should come as no surprise to discover that almost all aspects of the Mormon tradition are the object of sustained investigation by both professional and amateur historians. The astonishing number of books and other publications focusing on Mormonism is one measure of the widespread historical interest within the community.[14] The annual meetings of the Mormon History Association further document the fact that this interest spans a wide spectrum within the church, including both trained historians as well as laypersons of all stripes.[15]

Ironically, the success of the historical enterprise and the widespread interest in history has created an intellectual crisis within Mormonism. In the early 1970s the church invested substantial resources in strengthening and professionalizing historical activity within the church. Under the leadership of Leonard Arrington in the office of church historian, archives were opened, monographs commissioned, and the general level of work enhanced. But within a decade or so, the General Authorities in the church became increasingly uneasy with the "new Mormon history." Historians were accused of raising doubts and questions, of undermining the authority of the leadership, and of failing to use history to nurture the faith of the Saints.[16] The conflict stems, in part, from the fact that the Mormon Church does not have a professional clergy, and as a result there is no subset of intellectuals (that is, theologians) who shape the collective reflections on theological topics. The president of the church possesses the power of revelation, but that is a different process than theological reflection. During the second half of the twentieth century, intellectual functions have fallen increasingly into the hands of Mormon historians. As they professionalized and organized, the ecclesiastical hierarchy has become restive and apprehensive. As a result, the General Authorities have taken steps to curtail the power and influence of historians. A generation of professionally trained scholars has been forced to turn away from projects, to alter their public judgments concerning controversial issues, or in some cases to leave the church or church-supported institutions. The LDS hierarchy seems determined to control the use of Mormon history. That objective has been thwarted somewhat by the fact that a few Mormon historians have spoken out against church authorities and an ever-growing number of non-Mormon scholars continue to address attention to all aspects of this most successful of American sects.[17] Despite these problems, Mormon history remains a growth industry.

Two other sectarian communities in which scholarship by professional historians has produced both positive results and internal conflict are Christian Science and Seventh-Day Adventism. In neither case does the scope of the historical enterprise compare with that among the Latter-day Saints; both are much smaller denominations.

In the Church of Christ, Scientist, the fruits of such scholarship have become apparent over the past three decades. Prior to the 1960s historical attention from both insiders and outsiders focused primarily on the figure of Mary Baker Eddy, the founder of Christian Science and an extremely successful yet enigmatic figure. Already during her lifetime, Eddy and her religious ideas attracted widespread public criticism, including vitriolic commentary from no less a literary figure than Mark Twain.[18] The church, in turn, has consistently mounted a vigorous defense of Christian Science, often focusing on the person of the founder. The result has been a protracted biographical battle characterized by sharp division between the detractors and the defenders of Eddy.[19] Even Edwin Franden Dakin's biography, which attempted to mediate between depictions of Eddy as "an earthly archangel and a maniacal fiend"[20] was extremely controversial, so much so that it was rumored to have been systematically purloined from the shelves of public libraries throughout the country. Eddy remains a figure locked in controversy.

Yet the 1960s witnessed a breakthrough in the conflict over the founder and discoverer of Christian Science. In 1966 Robert Peel published the first volume of his three-part biography of Eddy, which set a new standard for thoroughness and for an evenhanded perspective.[21] Peel, a devout Christian Scientist and a historical consultant to the church, expressed sympathy and admiration for Eddy, but he did not skirt or ignore the complex and controversial aspects of her person and career. He took full advantage of materials contained within the archives of the church, documents and resources not universally available to non–Christian Science historians. In other words, Peel made substantial advances and inaugurated a new stage in the examination of the origins of the movement. Equally significant during the next decade was the appearance of Stephen Gottschalk's study situating Christian Science within the larger framework of America's religious and intellectual history. He, too, wrote as an insider, but he applied the established canons of the historical profession to his work. Gottschalk's not-so-hidden objective was to extricate Christian Science from the radical fringe by linking it directly to dominant currents in American life.[22] The effect of his work was to open a new conversation about the place of Christian Science within American religious history.

Peel's and Gottschalk's works remain the most sophisticated accounts of the early period of Christian Science. The work of scholars outside the community, unfortunately, has received at best a lukewarm reception by Christian Scientists.[23] A strong sense of territoriality persists within the church, perhaps shaped in part by the difficulties Eddy experienced during her lifetime. That defensive attitude also is reinforced by the metaphysical and theological position of the church, a view that regards the truly real as spiritual and outward manifestations of the spiritual as ultimately secondary (some might say, illusive). About history, Eddy herself once wrote, "It is well to know, dear reader, that our material, mortal history is but the record of dreams, not of man's real existence, and the dream has no place in the Science of being. It is 'as a tale that is told,' and 'as the shadow when it declineth.'"[24] Perhaps therefore it is not surprising that the church, in general, has responded unenthusiastically to the work of historians in the fields of women's studies and feminism. Even scholars writing about the evolution of medical practices and methods of healing in the United States have not been welcomed readily as colleagues.[25]

There is therefore some irony in the fact that recently Christian Science has been torn apart by a public controversy within its ranks over the historical image of Mary Baker Eddy. The controversy is caught up with other problems the church is experiencing, including new legal challenges to the practice of spiritual healing, declining membership, and financial problems associated with major investments by the church in the world of electronic media. These matters came to a head in 1991 when the church decided to publish a volume by Bliss Knapp entitled *The Destiny of the Mother Church*. Originally copyrighted in 1947, this publication was involved with settlement of the Knapp estates, estimated by one source at $92 million. The book is controversial to some Christian Scientists because it elevates Eddy to the same status as Jesus, declaring one to be God's "original man" and the other God's "original woman," and both "incarnations of Truth."[26] For some Christian Scientists, including Stephen Gottschalk, these are blasphemous and heretical judgments, and the church is compromising itself theologically by its desire to secure the funds from the estate. Gottschalk, perhaps the most prominent living historian associated with Christian Science, has himself been alienated from the Mother Church. He is now calling for a renewal of Christian Science based on the "original sources of the church's strength" rather than on unthinking compliance with decisions made by the organization.[27] History is clearly involved in the firestorm within Christian Science. No founder of an American sect has ever been more successful in establishing and maintaining an unchanging ecclesiastical institution from beyond the grave; yet now that institution is itself threatened by controversy over her image in history.

The situation within Seventh-Day Adventism, an American sectarian community identified preeminently with eschatological concerns, bears a certain resemblance to that in Christian Science. Here again history has aroused controversy as it cast new light on the activities of the founder, Ellen Gould White. In this community, too, recent decades witnessed the professionalization of historians, as more Adventists sought training in advanced centers of graduate education and as those working in the field organized themselves and established the conventional institutions of the profession. Two new journals, one for a popular audience — *Adventist Heritage: A Magazine of Adventist History* — and the other for professionals and academics — *Spectrum* — set out to raise the level of historical understanding within the church. At the same time, Adventist historians dedicated themselves to improving the image of the church among other scholars working in the field of American religious history. As part of the latter task, they reevaluated the Millerite movement and recast the origins of Seventh-Day Adventism in a more favorable light, thereby removing from the former the stigma of being part of a lunatic fringe.[28] Images of enthusiastic Millerites in white robes climbing trees in anticipation of Christ's apocalyptic return in the 1840s had persisted in the popular mind.

One signal evidence of the success of these new historical efforts was Ronald L. Numbers's biographical study of Ellen G. White published in 1976.[29] Only a few years removed from a degree program in the history of medicine, nurtured deeply in the tradition as the son of an Adventist pastor, Numbers set out to make sense of White's career as a health reformer. As part of that undertaking, he explored her writings on a range of issues, including hydropathy, vegetarianism, phrenology, dress reform, and sexual activity. Numbers discovered that White's publications often bore a close resemblance to sources she was reading. That alone would not have been unusual in the nineteenth century, for modern conventions governing citations or curbing plagiarism were not yet uniform. But faithful Adventists regarded her writings as inspired and authoritative. Therefore Numbers's scholarship was potentially damning, and church officials tried to persuade Numbers not to publish his study or, failing in that request, to change his manuscript before publication. Numbers's father also entered this effort. The eventual publication, which proved to be "a shattering experience," led to Numbers's alienation from the church, the loss of his teaching position at Loma Linda University, and a systematic effort to discredit him.[30] Numbers's exodus from the church was followed by that of other scholars whose work was also seen as heretical. But, somewhat surprisingly, despite the intellectual losses sustained by the church through these departures, the conflict over critical scholarship has had a positive effect as the church has become more willing to confront difficulties of interpretation. The last ten years have witnessed a burst of historical activity inside and outside the Adventist community with the result that considerable light has been shed on the place of Adventism in American religious history.[31] And, significantly, an increasing number of studies are moving beyond the formative period to explore subsequent developments within the tradition.

The Jehovah's Witnesses, another highly successful sectarian movement even more preoccupied with an eschatological kerygma, has maintained a very different attitude toward history. Established initially in the 1870s by Charles Taze Russell under the title of the International Bible Students' Association, this organization has proclaimed its message of an imminent end to the present order with a courage and impertinence that has won few friends.[32] Moreover, it has alienated possible allies who share the eschatological concern by its blanket condemnation of all churches. The Jehovah's Witnesses operate a highly touted publishing operation in the Watchtower Bible and Tract Society, but they have managed to keep virtually all members of the historical profession away from the organization. As a result, there is neither a public group of historians inside nor a significant number of professional historians outside directing attention toward the sect.

This antihistory bias of the Jehovah's Witnesses stems in part from the community's eschatological expectations and from its frontal attack on the principal institutions of modern society, including churches, governments, business corporations, and higher education. They see these as allied against Jehovah. As a result, the movement cannot be expected to cultivate historical scholars; nor with its notion of impending apocalypse does backward-looking activity make much sense. History loses significance when compared with the immediate future. Other reasons also exist for the lack of historical concern. The tradition may have reason to fear the results of historical investigation, for this movement has gone through dramatic shifts in its interpretation of biblical texts and in its teachings over the past century. Additionally, in recent decades the publications have downplayed the role of personalities in the leadership and featured the impersonality of the organization.[33] From the perspective of the Witnesses, little is to be gained by close examination of the life of the founder or his successors. There is no room for a personality cult within the Jehovah's Witnesses.

One kind of history has prospered on the edge of this movement, namely, that written by apostates. Former Witnesses, who seek to expose or condemn the organization of which they once were a part, write passionate and moving narratives. But the formulaic quality of their accounts gives cause for caution. Despite claims of fairness and impartiality, ex-Witnesses rarely keep from pronouncing moral or religious condemnation on their former organization. The titles of their publications are sometimes sufficiently revealing to warn of bias, for example, *The Orwellian World of Jehovah's Witnesses*.[34] In other works, as in *Visions of Glory: A History and Memory of Jehovah's Witnesses*, it is more difficult to discern the author's perspective.[35] The point is not to condemn all apostate literature as worthless. On the contrary, it is possible to learn a great deal about sectarian communities from these "insider-out" writings. Rather the point is that the reader must be cautious and alert to the fact that such authors frequently have an ax to grind with their former coreligionists. One should not look to such accounts for evenhanded assessments.

This division in perspective between outsiders and insiders is common in historical literature concerning sectarian movements. The case of Pentecostalism is typical. Robert Mapes Anderson, writing in relative isolation as an outsider, distinguished himself by his collective biography of the early leaders in the movement.[36] The application of deprivation theory and a Marxist perspective set his work apart from scholarship being carried out simultaneously within the tradition, epitomized by Vinson Synan's volume dealing with the holiness/Pentecostal family of churches.[37] The contrast between the two perspectives could not be greater. One explains the ecstasy and charismatic gifts of the Pentecostals in social scientific terms, and the other affirms the reality of the Holy Spirit's presence within the community. Both, however, acknowledge the importance of historical investigation because of the rising strength of this "Third Force in Christendom."[38]

One subset of sectarian historiography has focused on communal societies in America, many of which are indigenous, others of which are imported, and some of which are virtually indigenous because their history has been concentrated largely in America. The Oneida Perfectionists were a truly indigenous communal sect, reflecting the religious and social views of their founder and charismatic leader, John Humphrey Noyes. Few more controversial figures graced the American religious scene in the nineteenth century. Noyes, who published in 1870 the pioneering *History of American Socialisms*, has attracted attention from historians especially interested in psychohistory.[39] The economic successes of the Oneida community have also been the subject of investigation.[40] Another fully indigenous communal movement in the twentieth century was the Peoples Temple established by Jim Jones. Homegrown and then exported to Jonestown, Guyana, this movement has been studied almost exclusively in the aftermath of the mass murder/suicide in Guyana. In the quest to understand that tragedy, historians (using tape recordings made at the instigation of Jones himself) have divided sharply on Jonestown, some assailing Jones as demonic, others condemning the entire society on political and religious grounds, and still others attempting an analysis free from recriminations.[41] The more recent tragic conclusion to the standoff between the followers of David Koresh and federal law enforcement personnel has yet to be assessed thoroughly by historians.[42]

Perhaps the most widely studied communal sect in America is the United Society of Believers in Christ's Second Appearing, a virtually indigenous communal movement. The Shakers, technically imports from England, have been active in America for more than two hundred years, although at present the society has been reduced to one site and a handful of Believers.[43] Nonetheless, the historical attention given of late to the Shakers has been disproportionate to their present status. During much of the twentieth century, that is, until recently, the leadership of the United Society seemed content to preside over its own eventual demise, confident that the accomplishments of the past were sufficient reputation. Simultaneously, the public image of the Shakers came to be controlled by outsiders increasingly preoccupied with the Believers' material culture. The multiple publications of Edward Deming Andrews, in particular, shaped the public's perception of the society's history.[44] Andrews focused on antebellum Shakers, depicting them as paragons of virtue, simplicity, industry, and primitive Christian values. But in the 1960s the Shakers at Sabbathday Lake, Maine, refused to accept the closing of the society; and under the leadership of a convert, the late Theodore Johnson, they effected a renaissance of interest in the society's history and its future, manifest in such developments as the inauguration of the *Shaker Quarterly* and the cultivation of a group of professionally trained young scholars outside the community.[45] The resulting wave of historical interest in Shakerism shows no sign of subsiding today.

These select examples of recent sectarian studies demonstrate the power and the potential of historical scholarship as well as the possible reasons for conflict over the control of history. Presumably publications that advance knowledge and understanding of the origin and development of sectarian movements will be welcomed by all religious communities, including especially the subjects of that research. To know oneself is a virtue, and those who assist with the process of self-understanding ought to be commended. But some sectarian groups have reacted negatively to the work of historians, oftentimes even to the scholarship carried out by members of their own community. They view history as a potential threat. That fear is confirmation of the power of a historical narrative, the importance of a positive public image, and the sense of hazard triggered by the processes of research and investigation. Control of their own history is an advantage that sectarian communities are unwilling to surrender. Religious organizations traditionally invest heavily in attempts to tell their own story, witnessed by the fact that denominational historians, also called "church historians," have been an organized profession in America for more than a century.

But important changes in the profession in recent years are affecting attitudes toward the study of sectarian movements. Today historians are more honest about the inevitable bias that enters into all historical writing. The nineteenth-century notion that one could write history "as it really happened" has been destroyed by twentieth-century theorists.[46] And an increasingly large percentage of all religious history is being written by outsiders for whom its meaning is detached from personal conviction or the truth of religious claims. These scholars wish to know in order to understand rather than in order to believe. The historical canons of fairness, accuracy, and correlation with established data are replacing the notion of total objectivity or neutrality.

In this context it is naive to expect all historical scholarship to be free of polemics or other limitations. Attacks published under the guise of the history of sectarianism still appear regularly. Fortunately, the alternative approach that begins with the community itself and seeks to understand it on its own terms is gaining ground. Research conducted with empathy and respect does not require the historian to surrender a critical perspective or the responsibility of evaluation. But neither does it demand moral censure or theological refutation. Both outsiders and insiders stand to profit from open exchange of views and judgments.

Another limitation currently evident in the historiography of sectarianism in America is the inordinate preoccupation by both insiders and outsiders with the founders of sects and cults. Although the focus on early leaders is understandable because of the importance of these figures, this fixation often retards fuller understanding of the movements. Historians must observe both continuity and change. Overemphasis on origins creates an impression of stasis that belies the fact that these groups have experienced astonishing evolution over time. Even continuity requires a diachronic explanation. The point is that the history of successive generations has not received adequate historical attention.

The emphasis on founders also tends to reinforce a hagiographic perspective because of the reverence and affection engendered by these figures. When founders are attacked or maligned, communities feel compelled to defend them. For example, the charges leveled by apostates against Ann Lee, including accounts that she was verbally and physically abusive of her followers, that she engaged in promiscuous activity, and that she was often intoxicated, gave rise to a tradition of Shaker apologetics that emphasized Lee's feminine virtues, a positive image reinforced among the Believers by the standard practice of referring to her as "Mother Ann."[47] Joseph Smith was an extremely controversial figure during his lifetime who made more than his share of enemies, including many among the Latter-day Saints. But the martyrdom of Smith created a different situation and contributed directly to the elevation of "The Prophet" and to the special status which he still enjoys among all branches of Mormonism, including the Reorganized Church of Latter-Day Saints. Concentration on the history of the earliest period of Mormon history keeps Smith's stock very high.[48] Opposition from yellow journalists and criticism by biographers have created a cottage industry within Christian Science devoted to the protection of Eddy's reputation.[49] That widespread defensiveness concerning the founder has, no doubt, made the current controversy within the church all the more fractious.

Another common result of preoccupation with early leaders is a corresponding historical neglect of the membership. Contemporary developments within the larger field of American history make the situation of the latter potentially more accessible than ever before. Social historians have provided a paradigm for discovering answers to questions about race, class, gender, and national origin, to name but the most obvious categories. Unfortunately, too little scholarship is available concerning the demographics of sectarian communities.[50] Even though sociologists of religion have done considerable work in the area, much remains unexamined.

These problems notwithstanding, at present many reasons exist to be encouraged concerning the historical study of indigenous sectarian communities. The most promising developments are taking their cue from wider trends in the study of American history. One such development rests on the recognition that outsider groups are drawn into the cultural patterns of the general society, call it "mainstreaming" if you will. Sects, too, move in that direction, toward what Weber categorized as a church-type community, one that provides a positive sanction for cultural values. It is common for sectarian movements to abandon radical dissent with the passage of time and to drift toward a position of increasing accommodation. Some of the earliest students of American sectarianism, including H. Richard Niebuhr, observed this phenomenon.[51] But the processes of change within sectarian communities are not only one-directional. Although many examples exist that reinforce the prevailing pattern of cultural accommodation, it is possible for sects and cults to reverse that process and to heighten their sense of alienation and dissent from the host culture. Three examples of "mainstreaming" will illustrate different outcomes.

Pentecostalism, which emerged among the ranks of disinherited persons at the edge of the social and economic order around the turn of the century, has moved steadily upward on the socioeconomic ladder. A considerable reduction in the tension felt by many Pentecostals within modern society has accompanied this mainstreaming process. Where once Pentecostal preaching pronounced a blanket condemnation of the "world," now it offers a more selective censure. Changes have also occurred in the standards governing clothing, hairstyles, jewelry, entertainment, medicine, education, athletics, and a host of everyday concerns within the community.[52] Pentecostals still draw boundaries, but the contrast with their non-Pentecostal neighbors is much less. Some of these changes are directly attributable to improved economic circumstances. (It is always easier to condemn evil activities when one does not have sufficient financial resources to participate in them.)

During the second half of the twentieth century, no more graphic example of this accommodation process exists than Oral Roberts. His career mirrors the complexity of modern Pentecostalism. From tent preacher and faith healer to television celebrity, founder of Oral Roberts University, and convert to United Methodism, Roberts epitomizes the desire for acceptance and respectability as well as the paradoxical character of contemporary Pentecostalism. His biographer describes him as a man who makes major decisions only after hearing a direct word from God.[53] Miracles and tongues-speaking stand side by side with satellite hookups and multimillion dollar production budgets. Roberts and many other preachers in this tradition no longer represent the dispossessed. On the contrary, they see their faith as the means for rising above oppressive circumstances. It may be this belief that has caused so much difficulty and brought scandal to several nationally prominent Pentecostal televangelists.

The Shakers represent a different outcome of this mainstreaming process. In the 1770s they comprised a small radical sect (or maybe even cult) that first gained public attention by disrupting worship services in the established denominations in England. In America Ann Lee and others were jailed during the War for Independence as possible traitors or British sympathizers because they would not participate in the conflict. Lee was a charismatic in the fullest sense of the term, forbidding her followers to write their beliefs lest the witness of the Spirit be constrained. Only after her death did the Shakers institutionalize her principles and build the society that is today regarded as a symbol of American inventiveness and rural values. By the mid-nineteenth century the Believers lost much of their sectarian edge, and after the Civil War many joined cause with liberals to fight on behalf of women's rights, peace, temperance, health reform, and other pro-gréssive causes.[54] By the mid-to-late twentieth century, the Shakers were idealized and idolized by Americans who saw them as nostalgic reminders of a day gone by. At the present time the remaining Believers advocate ecumenical activity, welcoming to their meetinghouse Christians of all varieties and fellow spiritual travelers, no matter what their religious tradition. One of the most unusual ecu-menical events occurred in 1994 when the widow of Father Divine and some of her followers met with the Shakers in Maine, an occasion reported with great satisfaction by the Believers. The Shakers still draw a few boundaries, but those lines are obviously porous.

The Nation of Islam, or the Black Muslims, as they were formerly known, provides yet a third example of the mainstreaming process. This racially defined sectarian community, which came into existence in the African-American ghet-tos of Detroit and Chicago in the 1930s under the leadership of W.D. Fard and his convert Elijah Muhammad, proclaimed a message of black superiority and of an impending apocalypse for whites.[55] Following the death of Elijah Muham-mad in 1975, the Nation of Islam experienced a deliberate transformation under the leadership of his son and successor, Wallace Deen Muhammad, who at-tempted to move the sect within the boundaries of orthodox Islam. Wallace Deen Muhammad abandoned his father's racial and political views, changed the name of the organization twice, opened its membership to nonblacks, and began to cooperate with the federal government on a variety of programs. But not all members of the community followed willingly. One prominent leader, Louis Farrakhan, dissented from this mainstreaming and called for a return to the sepa-ratist principles that characterized the movement in earlier decades. By the end of the 1980s Farrakhan had emerged in the public eye as the leading voice for the Nation of Islam.[56] In this instance, sectarian dissent was followed by accommo-dation, which gave way in rapid fashion to a reassertion of sectarian principles. Farrakhan's recent involvement in political and economic initiatives makes pre-dicting the future of this movement a high-risk activity.

Sectarian studies have profited in other ways from trends in the larger field of American history. Millennialism is a theme that has occupied American histori-ans for more than twenty-five years. It has also been a useful focus for the study of dissenting religion. Millennialism is part of a larger complex of eschatological issues that comprises a rich vein for research and scholarship. Colonial settlers from Europe, especially from England, brought with them a consuming interest in eschatology. What they planted in the wilderness flourished in subsequent generations, providing a narrative for interpretation of the revolutionary struggle, the birth of the new nation, its westward expansion, and the internecine conflict that subsequently tore it apart. Millennialism proved highly malleable and there-fore attractive to nearly all religious parties in America. It provided a way to un-derstand the past and to anticipate the future. The book of Revelation was the central text for this tradition. It became a kind of Rorschach blot for Americans who saw in its pages what they wanted to see. Religious leaders and theologians in the major denominations spent long hours deciphering apocalyptic images. Sectarians, too, frequently turned to eschatology.[57]

Millennial calculations figure prominently in the history of sectarian religion in early America. By the eighteenth century individual charismatic leaders used apocalyptic to attract followers because the knowledge of these matters was so widespread. The Shakers may be the most prominent of the millennial movements to emerge at this time, but they were hardly the only sectarian group interested in these issues. Johann Kelpius came to America and founded the short-lived Society of the Woman in the Wilderness in Pennsylvania in anticipation of the beginning of the millennium.[58] Jemima Wilkinson, known as the Public Universal Friend, presented herself as reborn to a life of prophecy that included directions for a communal settlement called Jerusalem.[59] Shadrach Ireland, many of whose followers in Harvard, Massachusetts, eventually joined cause with the Shakers, declared himself immortal and announced that the return of Christ was near.[60] Members of the Ephrata Cloister founded by Conrad Beissel, also in Pennsylvania, structured aspects of their monastic life in ways that were informed by apocalyptic beliefs.[61] In the nineteenth century, the Mormons, the Millerites, the Perfectionists at Oneida, the Harmonists or followers of the German sectarian George Rapp,[62] the Amana Inspirationists,[63] and other groups, too, wove eschatological teachings into the core of their beliefs. There was no consensus on particulars; nearly every issue involved with millennialism was hotly debated, including the chronological timetable, the identification of Antichrist and of the beasts of the Revelation, and the course of future events. The followers of William Miller triggered the most celebrated eschatological episodes of the nineteenth century. Events surrounding the Great Disappointment of 1843–44 continue to be the object of sustained and conflicting historical interpretation.[64]

The twentieth century has not dampened the appetite for apocalyptic calculations. Millennialists find confirmation for their views in local and international happenings. Sectarians use eschatology to position themselves on the pages of history. Frank Weston Sandford, for example, thought that his effort to build Shiloh in Durham, Maine, would prepare the world for the second coming of Christ.[65] Jim Jones thought that the socialist principles that he was implementing, first in California and then in Guyana, would lead others into the future. David Koresh, leader of the Branch Davidians in Waco, Texas, spent his last days writing what he regarded as a definitive commentary or interpretation of the seven seals of the book of Revelation. But no sect has capitalized more consistently on apocalyptic than the Jehovah's Witnesses, who have pointed repeatedly to specific impending moments on the eschatological clock — first 1914, most recently, 1975 — and have used these marked years to great religious advantage. They have managed to maintain a higher sense of eschatological tension throughout the century than any of the other groups discussed in this chapter. As the last years of this century and this millennium pass into history, there is every reason to believe that apocalyptic will gain even more advocates among the members of major denominations as well as in sectarian communities.

Primitivism is another theme of general interest to American historians that has been useful for historians of sectarianism, too. Primitivism, or restorationism (another name for the same theme), refers to the normative role of "first times" for measuring ideas and actions.[66] The impulse to make such an appeal was not confined to sectarian groups, but enjoyed widespread acceptance across religious and denominational lines. Theodore D. Bozeman, for example, has argued that primitivism was the driving and defining force in Puritan thought.[67] Tension sometimes occurs between a commitment to the authority of antiquity and an orientation to the future explicit in millennialism.

Several American sectarian communities have managed to live easily with this tension. Early Pentecostalism, intent on restoring the primitive Christian church of the first century, also held strong premillennial views, without apparent cognitive dissonance. Their primitivism led to an exegetical concentration on the biblical book of Acts and its account of Pentecost in the second chapter.[68] The same restorationist impulse within Mormonism supported very different convictions. In the case of the Latter-day Saints, many of the institutions of ancient Israel, including the priesthood, the temple, patriarchal blessings, and the spirit of prophecy, were restored through the revelations received by Joseph Smith.[69] What the Pentecostals, Mormons, and other restorationists share is a commitment to the authority of antiquity, not to the particulars of any one tradition, time, or place in the past.

Gender studies is another area of research in American history that has yielded positive results for sectarian studies. It is one of the fastest growing specialties within the historical profession today. Much of the research in this area may be described more narrowly as women's history. As a result of the Second Women's Movement of the 1960s, historians focused new attention on the place of women in all aspects of American life and culture, including religion. Successive waves of scholarship have explored the doctrine of separate spheres, the cult of domesticity, the suffrage movement, the quest for equal rights, and the rise of feminism. Each has left a mark on sectarian studies.

Nearly every religious movement in this essay has been the object of historical research focusing on gender issues. Many of these communities continue to attract a great deal of attention from scholars interested in women's studies because their founders were women (Shakerism, Christian Science, Seventh-Day Adventism), because they established and publicly defended alternative family arrangements in which women functioned differently from patterns in the larger society (the Oneida community, Mormonism, Shakerism), because they held notions about God that included some feminine element or component (Mormonism, Shakerism, Christian Science), because they were especially concerned with the health and welfare of women (Seventh-Day Adventism, Shakerism,

Christian Science), because they allowed women to exercise leadership positions in their communities (Shakerism, Christian Science, Pentecostalism), or because they are credited with anticipating later feminist concerns (Shakerism, Christian Science). The converse reason for attention also exists in that some groups attract contemporary scholars because they explicitly embody patriarchal values (Mormonism, Pentecostalism) or they exploit women physically or sexually (Jonestown, the Branch Davidians).

This wave of scholarship on women in sectarian religions has sometimes had the effect of creating new complexity where unexamined assumptions had previously prevailed. Two contrasting examples, Mormonism and Shakerism, will illustrate this phenomenon. The institution of plural marriage within Mormonism has attracted considerable historical attention through the years, much of it hostile and ill-informed. Opponents of the Latter-day Saints, relying on nineteenth-century polemical exchanges, have depicted the polygamous family as the equivalent of a harem. Anti-Mormon literature drew on personal narratives and apostate accounts in describing lurid and exploitative sexual circumstances. Now more than a century after the Mormon Church officially brought the practice of polygamy to an end with the Woodruff Manifesto of 1890, historians are describing the situation very differently.[70] Only a relatively small percentage of Mormons lived in polygamous family units. The practice of plural marriage was often attended with extreme hardships, and yet it created close bonds of sisterhood among plural wives. Without offering a brief for the practice, it must be acknowledged that the institution has been badly misrepresented. Some have even argued that polygamy may have been liberating for women on the frontier. Instead of being isolated, burdened by a host of domestic tasks, and endangered with the risks of frequent pregnancies and childbirth, women in polygamous families often found themselves in the company of other women, sharing tasks and responsibilities, and subject to less danger from pregnancy and childbirth. In other words, the impact of polygamy was mixed for women, perhaps for some even an improvement over their previous circumstances.

Historians of Shakerism have often celebrated the celibate situation of female Believers as liberating because of the United Society's public principle of sexual equality. Shaker eldresses exercised authority alongside elders. Women lived separate from men, freeing them from sexual intercourse, childbirth, and childcare. The contrast between the life circumstances of Shaker women and their contemporaries outside the society was striking. But that situation must not be construed as reflecting late twentieth-century principles of equality. On the contrary, the principle of sexual equality within Shakerism was accompanied by the continuing division of labor along traditional lines. In most villages (with some notable exceptions), men continued to exercise primary responsibility, making the decisions regarding politics, economics, and theology. Women were in charge of women's affairs and domestic activities. This situation cannot be represented as sexual equality in any contemporary sense.[71] Only when the number of men within the United Society fell dramatically during the second half of the nineteenth century did Shaker women begin to assume the roles normally filled by men. Shaker principles notwithstanding, larger cultural patterns exercised a strong influence on the United Society.

Closely bound up with the principle of sisterhood that historians have observed operating in both Mormonism and Shakerism is the issue of access to leadership roles for women within these and other sectarian movements. Studies of contemporary Pentecostalism, for instance, have shown how that community, which holds conservative views concerning the role of women, has maintained the principle of subordination at the same time that it has opened the pulpit. Individual women within this tradition have risen to local and even national prominence through their oratorical skills. From female exhorters in small midwestern congregations to Aimee Semple McPherson, a flamboyant revivalist and founder of the International Church of the Foursquare Gospel, the spoken word and the spirit-led performance have empowered women religiously.[72] Yet in Pentecostalism men typically retain control of the ecclesiastical structures. Within Mormonism, the Relief Society—the organizational focus of sisterhood—has been a powerful force for women. But individual women have been effectively silenced by the official voice of the church's male hierarchy when they spoke out in support of the Equal Rights Amendment.[73] In Christian Science, where the role of minister was formally proscribed by Mary Baker Eddy, duly elected readers—both male and female—exercise local leadership.[74] But even in this community, the Board of Directors of the First Church of Christ, Scientist, is largely under the control of men. In other words, some of the sectarian traditions that seemingly have empowered women have done so in ways that still subtly maintain male control and dominance. Even Mother Divine lives with the spiritual presence of Father Divine near at hand.[75] There is less ambiguity for women who are members of the Jehovah's Witnesses or the Nation of Islam where female subordination is the formal position of the organizations.

One additional area that has received attention from historians focusing on women in sectarian communities is the concept of the deity articulated by these groups.[76] Mormon theologians, for example, have speculated about the notion of a Heavenly Mother parallel to the Heavenly Father. In 1909, for example, the First Presidency stated, "All men and women are in the similitude of the universal Father and Mother and are literally the sons and daughters of Deity."[77] In the opening decade of the nineteenth century Shaker theologians, writing in defense of their society, argued that God's nature as Father was revealed in Christ's first appearance in Jesus of Nazareth, the Beloved Son, and that God's nature as Mother was revealed in Christ's second appearance in Ann Lee of Manchester, the Beloved Daughter of God. Later spiritualistic manifestations within the society led to additional clarification and further personification of the dual nature of God, manifest in the Eternal Father and Holy Mother Wisdom.[78] In Christian Science, the concept of God as "Father-Mother" is a central idea, though by no means equated with a physical or personal notion. Rather Father-Mother is the "name for Deity, which indicates His tender relationship to His spiritual creation."[79] The emphasis within Christian Science on the motherhood of God corresponds to the accent on God as Love. These sectarian views of the deity usually accompany an attack on orthodox Trinitarianism. Mormonism's doctrine of God is properly classified as tritheistic, each person of the godhead constituting a separate entity. Shakerism condemns the doctrine of the Trinity as the work of Antichrist, substituting instead the concept of the duality of God. And for Christian Science, "Life, Truth, and Love constitute the triune Person called God, — that is, the triply divine Principle, Love."[80] In all cases, issues of gender intertwine with constructive theology.

The historical developments and trends described in the preceding section of this essay hold considerable promise also for the future. There is, for example, no sign of abatement in gender studies.[81] Graduate students are flocking to this research area, making prospects very favorable. Other equally worthwhile research topics beg for attention, many of which invite comparative historical study.

One such area involves patterns of power and authority within sectarian communities. These movements traditionally face a crisis of authority with the death of the founder at which time they must establish new ways to structure power and make decisions.[82] The charisma of the first leader is rarely replicated in the successor, and as a result different structural arrangements are put in place. Brigham Young, himself a powerful figure, was forced to compete with several others for authority, which he subsequently solidified within the Mormon community, armed with revelation and the power of appointment.[83] Mary Baker Eddy provided for succession in an unusual manner, setting up ecclesiastical structures in the *Church Manual* including a self-perpetuating board of directors. Ann Lee's death forced the Shakers to establish the institutions required for a national communal society, including the creation of a Central Ministry at the head of a network of local villages and a system of uniform "Millennial Laws." "Judge" Joseph F. Rutherford, the second leader of the Jehovah's Witnesses, organized and structured the movement that he inherited from Charles Taze Russell. Mother Divine stepped into the leadership role vacated by the death of Father Divine, even though his memory remains a powerful presence in the community. Within Pentecostalism, charismatic preachers exercise almost unlimited authority within local congregations, linked to one another only by loose consociational alliances. The flight of John Humphrey Noyes from the Oneida community to Canada brought the rapid demise of that movement because there was no successor.[84] The variety of possible solutions to the problem of succession is almost infinite, but every religious movement must make some arrangement for the transfer of power and authority.

Another cluster of potential research topics for future investigation includes the private choices individuals make regarding food and drink, clothing styles and personal appearance, health ways, and sexual activity. Once considered of secondary importance, these topics now command increasing attention from social historians who recognize that matters of lifestyle often typically reflect a person's values.

Food and drink, for example, figure prominently in the self-definition of members of sectarian communities. The Shakers debated among themselves the virtues of the Graham diet in the 1830s and 1840s.[85] During the latter decade, they adopted for a time even more severe dietary restrictions as evidence of their desire to draw sharp boundaries between themselves and the "world." Seventh-Day Adventists promoted vegetarianism as part of a larger concern for healthful living.[86] The temperance cause, which became widespread throughout American society, attracted considerable sectarian support, including both of the above communities at various times. Mormonism's "Word of Wisdom" went beyond the prohibition of liquor to include hot beverages, such as coffee and tea, and, in the twentieth century, caffeinated soft drinks.[87] Prohibitions against alcohol are common in many sects, including the Peace Mission Movement and the Nation of Islam. In the former, Father Divine forbade liquor, but he served sumptuous banquets in the "heavens." Elijah Muhammad proscribed not only alcohol but also foods associated with the slave past of African-Americans, including possum, black-eyed peas, and pork. Shaker foodways, by contrast, have come to be celebrated in recipes and cookbooks, but not for spiritual or religious reasons.

Clothing and personal appearance, like food and drink, usually mark boundaries that separate and distinguish sectarians from the world's people. Patterns of dress and hairstyles are obvious indications of membership within a particular religious community. Early converts to Shakerism were distinguished by the women wearing caps or bonnets and the men cutting their hair in a prescribed manner. Shaker women retained distinctive patterns of dress long after men in the society dressed like their counterparts in the world. Shaker sisters retained rural styles that once had been widespread in an effort to embody simplicity and to eschew worldly fashion.[88] The dress reform movement of the nineteenth century was supported by several sectarian groups including the Oneida Perfectionists and the Seventh-Day Adventists. The former argued for "bloomer-like" apparel for women on grounds of practicality and freedom of movement while the latter looked on these same reforms as promoting the health of women by freeing them from constraining fashions of the day.[89] Pentecostal styles for women have traditionally applied a principle of modesty in order to avoid promiscuity or sexual excitement. Within this same group, hairstyles are a public indication of marital status and of strict adherence to biblical standards.[90] Mormon undergarments, given in temple rites, are a contrast to other sectarian dress patterns; they do not mark public boundaries. Temple garments are an insider's measure of status and a means of confirming the commitment of faithful Latter-day Saints.

Sexual activity among sectarian groups is more difficult to document outside certain obvious items, such as the average size of families and public regulations regarding divorce, masturbation, homosexuality, the use of contraception, and abortion. Historians have studied some of these issues in nineteenth-century groups, but they have paid less attention to more recent history.[91] Theological incentives exist within Mormonism for large families, and practice has followed theology. By contrast, Mary Baker Eddy's remarks in *Science and Health* concerning marriage constitute a not-so-hidden discouragement to frequent sexual relations between husband and wife.[92] Her own difficult life, including three marriages, and a troubled relationship with her only son, may have been the formative influence on her judgments. Similar speculation about the source of Ann Lee's move toward celibacy has abounded in the historical literature, which takes note of the fact that she had an unhappy and unsuccessful marriage and possibly four children, all of whom may have died in infancy. Ellen White, influenced by the ideas of Sylvester Graham and nineteenth-century vitalist theory, publicly attacked masturbation as a major social problem in her day, and she also urged that married couples have sex only infrequently.[93] The contrast with the sexual practices at the heart of Oneida's system of complex marriage could not be more striking.[94] In sum, sectarian groups consistently treated sexuality as powerful, whether they encouraged, discouraged, or forbade its use.

Historians are beginning to chart the range of research possibilities in the area of sectarian health and healing practices.[95] This work is closely associated with wider interests in alternative healing methods, such as Thomsonianism, hydropathy, homeopathy, and other therapies.[96] Both Mormonism and Pentecostalism have held positive views regarding faith healing, the latter having made it a central element in the believer's life.[97] Christian Science espouses spiritual healing, which differs both theologically and practically from faith healing. An immense body of literature, including published testimonies, has been generated by this community, describing and defending its healing practices. Christian Scientists commonly refuse modern medical resources for treating illness.[98] As a result of their refusal, considerable public criticism of this tradition has occurred, including that found in legal records involving charges against parents, practitioners, and the church. In Father Divine's movement, all public evidence of reliance on medicine was strictly forbidden because the logic of the "heavens" allowed no room for illness. The epistemological principle in both Christian Science and the Peace Mission Movement led to the denial of the reality of sickness and ultimately of death itself. The Jehovah's Witnesses, by contrast, prohibit only the acceptance of blood transfusions, a position based on scriptural injunctions against the eating of blood.[99] The health ways of Seventh-Day Adventists, which have been the subject of historical attention by scholars both inside and outside the community, reflect wider social patterns of the late nineteenth century. The Shakers, too, mirrored their times, at one early point resorting to faith healing and forbidding the Believers to consult with the world's physicians, but later allowing a variety of alternative options, including Thomsonianism, the water cure, and even Christian Science. John Humphrey Noyes judged that sexual relations, when ordered according to the principle of "ascending fellowship," not only promoted spiritual well-being but also physical health. In other words, in nearly every case the principle of sectarian dissent has led to distinctive health and healing practices.

Worship activities within sectarian communities constitute another area for possible comparative historical study. Little attention has been paid to these matters, even though these movements have been highly innovative in constructing worship forms and rituals. Here historians may benefit from anthropological approaches and from firsthand observation. But not all sectarian rituals are equally accessible. Mormon temple worship, with its distinctive ordinances, including marriage for time and eternity, baptism for the dead, and sealings, is closed to nonmembers, by contrast with the open, weekly ward activities. The celebration of communion by the Latter-day Saints, which involves the use of cubes of white bread and individual paper cups of water, sets their sacramental practice apart from that of other traditions. Even more distinctive is the annual communion service of the Jehovah's Witnesses in which only those who regard themselves as part of the 144,000 dare to take part. Christian Scientists celebrate communion twice yearly, in accord with directions in the *Church Manual*, following an order of service prescribing "silent Communion" in which no physical elements are involved.[100] The Shakers also reject all material ordinances and sacraments, believing rather in the spiritual presence of Christ. Father Divine's banquets served as both dinner and eucharist. Other aspects of sectarian worship that invite examination include the place of ecstasy; the role of music and musical instruments;[101] the function of the sermon, exhorting, and testimonies; the use of the Bible and other scriptural texts; and standards for proper decorum.

One additional area deserving attention from historians of sectarianism is what might be designated as social issues. This category embraces a range of political concerns including participation in government activities such as voting, military service, and the payment of taxes as well as judgments concerning public schools, welfare programs, and other agencies designed to assist and protect citizens (for example, environmental protection, affirmative action). Attitudes toward race and civil rights are additional indices for measuring the social concern of sectarians as is the willingness of these movements to sponsor and fund hospitals or other institutions of mercy and charity.

America's indigenous sectarian communities greatly enrich the religious situation in the United States by adding variety, texture, and originality. These movements are highly innovative in religious thought and practice. They provide a refuge for persons who do not find the more conventional or established denominations religiously satisfying and a haven for those rejected by other communities. These groups play the role of cultural gadfly, singling out aspects of the dominant society for censure and condemnation. Although these dissenters also, in turn, receive sharp criticism or sometimes harassment and persecution, they are resolute in their convictions. Indifference and lack of commitment are not the standard qualities of sectarians.

One contribution made by sectarian religious movements deserves special comment because it has brought benefits to all citizens of the United States. Dissenting communities have played a major role in the definition of religious liberty. The presence of sectarian groups outside the legally established churches during the colonial period forced the founders of this nation to create a religious settlement more inclusive than was common at the time. The continuing presence of such dissenting groups and, even more, their expansion in numbers during the nineteenth and twentieth centuries, have kept the system honest. During the twentieth century sectarian movements have often turned to the First Amendment to secure protection under the law. Christian Scientists, Jehovah's Witnesses, the Amish — to name but a few — have used the federal courts to seek redress and to protect unique beliefs and practices. In doing so, however, they have expanded the protection afforded religious liberty under the Constitution. Their efforts have resulted in unintended positive consequences for all Americans. Thus sects and cults have contributed toward making this nation a place where people of all religious convictions may exist side by side. The United States is a better place as a result. The history of religion in America is also more interesting because of such movements.

Historians are seeking new models for understanding and explaining America's religious history. To date, the prevailing efforts have not done justice to the contributions of indigenous sectarian communities. This land has been a fertile seedbed for sects and cults. Several periods of American history have been especially productive of such groups. The 1840s spawned a host of innovative religious communities; the 1960s also saw many similar movements flourish for a time. The rapid approach of the end of the millennium seems likely to generate another burst of sectarian activity. In that respect the challenge facing the United States represents in microcosm the same challenge facing the entire planet. As distances shrink and the world rapidly becomes one community, its inhabitants must learn to live side by side in peace. Knowledge and understanding of diversity can contribute to this goal. Historians have a part to play in this process.

Notes

1. *Christian Deviations: The Challenge of the New Spiritual Movements*, rev. ed. (Philadelphia: Westminster, 1965), 11. See also Marcus Bach, *Strange Sects and Curious Cults* (New York: Dodd, Mead and Company, 1961).

2. *The Four Major Cults: Christian Science, Jehovah's Witnesses, Mormonism, Seventh-Day Adventism* (Grand Rapids, Mich.: Eerdmans, 1963), 406. See also Frederick Emanuel Mayer, *The Religious Bodies of America*, 4th ed. (St. Louis: Concordia, 1961).

3. *Mormonism: The Story of a New Religious Tradition* (Urbana: University of Illinois Press, 1985), x.

4. See Karen McCarthy Brown, *Mama Lola: A Vodou Priestess in Brooklyn* (Berkeley and Los Angeles: University of California Press, 1991), for a provocative and instructive example of scholarly empathy and engagement.

5. *Salvation and Suicide: An Interpretation of Jim Jones, the Peoples Temple, and Jonestown* (Bloomington: Indiana University Press, 1988), xiv.

6. *Radical Spirits: Spiritualism and Women's Rights in Nineteenth-Century America* (Boston: Beacon, 1989), 9.

7. See Max Weber, *From Max Weber: Essays in Sociology*, trans. and ed. H.H. Gerth and C. Wright Mills (New York: Oxford University Press, 1958).

8. Ernst Troeltsch, *The Social Teaching of the Christian Churches*, 2 vols. (London: Allen and Unwin, 1931).

9. See Aidan A. Kelly, ed., *The Evangelical Anti-Cult Movement: Christian Counter-Cult Literature* (New York: Garland, 1990); and Anson D. Shupe Jr., David G. Bromley, and Donna L. Oliver, *The Anti-Cult Movement in America: A Bibliography and Historical Survey* (New York: Garland, 1984).

10. Representative titles include Bryan Wilson, *The Social Impact of New Religious Movements* (Barrytown, N.Y.: Unification Theological Seminary, 1981); Rodney Stark, *Religious Movements: Genesis, Exodus, and Numbers* (New York: Paragon House, 1985); Janet Liebman Jacobs, *Divine Disenchantment: Deconverting from New Religions* (Bloomington: Indiana University Press, 1989); R. Laurence Moore, *Religious Outsiders and the Making of Americans* (New York: Oxford University Press, 1986); and Timothy Miller, ed., *America's Alternative Religions* (Albany: State University of New York, 1995).

11. For contrasting biographical approaches to Smith, see Fawn M. Brodie, *No Man Knows My History: The Life of Joseph Smith*, 2nd ed. (New York: Knopf, 1971); and Richard L. Bushman, *Joseph Smith and the Beginnings of Mormonism* (Urbana: University of Illinois Press, 1984).

12. See Shipps, *Mormonism*, 87–108.

13. Section 128 in *The Doctrine and Covenants of the Church of Jesus Christ of Latter-day Saints Containing Revelations Given to Joseph Smith, the Prophet* (Salt Lake City: Church of Jesus Christ of Latter-day Saints, 1967), 234.

14. The most useful general histories of Mormonism are James B. Allen and Glen M. Leonard, *The Story of the Latter-day Saints* (Salt Lake City: Deseret, 1976); and Leonard J. Arrington and Davis Bitton, *The Mormon Experience: A History of the Latter-Day Saints* (New York: Knopf, 1979).

15. See articles in *Journal of Mormon History*, *Dialogue: A Journal of Mormon Thought*, and *Sunstone*.

16. Shipps, *Mormonism*, 106–7.

17. D. Michael Quinn has been one of the most outspoken Mormon historians. See his *Early Mormonism and the Magic World View* (Salt Lake City: Signature Books, 1987); *The New Mormon History: Revisionist Essays on the Past* (Salt Lake City: Signature Books, 1992); and *The Mormon Hierarchy: Origins of Power* (Salt Lake City: Signature Books, 1994). See also George D. Smith, ed., *Faithful History: Essays on Writing Mormon History* (Salt Lake City: Signature Books, 1992).

18. Mark Twain, *Christian Science, with Notes Containing Corrections to Date* (New York: Harper and Brothers, 1907). A new edition of Twain's volume was issued by Prometheus Books (Buffalo, N.Y.) in 1986.

19. See Georgine Milmine, *Mary Baker G. Eddy: The Story of Her Life and the History of Christian Science* (New York: S.S. McClure, 1906–8); Sibyl Wilbur, *The Life of Mary Baker Eddy* (Boston: Christian Science Publishing, 1913); and Lyman P. Powell, *Mary Baker Eddy: A Life Size Portrait* (Boston: Christian Science Publishing, 1930).

20. Edwin Franden Dakin, *Mrs. Eddy: The Biography of a Virginal Mind* (New York: Scribner's, 1970), vii.

21. Robert Peel, *Mary Baker Eddy: The Years of Discovery* (New York: Holt, Rinehart and Winston, 1966); *Mary Baker Eddy: The Years of Trial* (New York: Holt, Rinehart and Winston, 1971); and *Mary Baker Eddy: The Years of Authority* (New York: Holt, Rinehart and Winston, 1977).

22. Stephen Gottschalk, *The Emergence of Christian Science in American Religious Life* (Berkeley and Los Angeles: University of California Press, 1973).

23. For example, Julius Silberger, *Mary Baker Eddy: An Interpretive Biography of the Founder of Christian Science* (Boston: Little, Brown, 1980); and Stuart E. Knee, *Christian Science in the Age of Mary Baker Eddy* (Westport, Conn.: Greenwood, 1994).

24. Eddy, *Retrospection and Introspection* (Boston: Nixon, 1891), 21. See Stephen J. Stein, "*Retrospection and Introspection*: The Gospel According to Mary Baker Eddy," *Harvard Theological Review* 75 (1982): 97–116.

25. Rennie B. Schoepflin, "Christian Science Healing in America," in *Other Healers: Unorthodox Medicine in America*, ed. Norman Gevitz (Baltimore: Johns Hopkins University Press, 1988), 192–214.

26. Bliss Knapp, *The Destiny of the Mother Church* (Boston: Christian Science Publishing, 1991), 187, 213.

27. Stephen Gottschalk, "Honesty, Blasphemy and *The Destiny of the Mother Church*," *Christian Century*, Nov. 6, 1991, pp. 1028–31.

28. See essays in Edwin S. Gaustad, ed., *The Rise of Adventism: Religion and Society in Mid-Nineteenth-Century America* (New York: Harper and Row, 1974); and in Ronald L. Numbers and Jonathan M. Butler, eds., *The Disappointed: Millerism and Millenarianism in the Nineteenth Century* (Bloomington: Indiana University Press, 1987).

29. Ronald L. Numbers, *Prophetess of Health: A Study of Ellen G. White* (New York: Harper and Row, 1976).

30. Jonathan M. Butler, "Introduction: The Historian as Heretic," in *Prophetess of Health: Ellen G. White and the Origins of Seventh-Day Adventist Health Reform*, by Ronald L. Numbers (Knoxville: University of Tennessee Press, 1992), xxv–lxviii.

31. For example, David L. Rowe, *Thunder and Trumpets: Millerites and Dissenting Religion in Upstate New York, 1800–1850* (Chico, Calif.: Scholars Press, 1985); Gary Land, ed., *Adventism in America: A History* (Grand Rapids, Mich.: Eerdmans, 1986); Ruth Alden Doan, *The Miller Heresy, Millennialism, and American Culture* (Philadelphia: Temple University Press, 1987); and Douglas Morgan, *The Remnant and the Republic: The Public Impact of Seventh-Day Adventist Apocalypticism* (Bloomington: Indiana University Press, forthcoming).

32. M. James Penton, *Apocalypse Delayed: The Story of Jehovah's Witnesses* (Toronto: University of Toronto Press, 1985); and Melvin D. Curry, *Jehovah's Witnesses: The Millenarian World of the Watch Tower* (New York: Garland, 1992).

33. James A. Beckford, *The Trumpet of Prophecy: A Sociological Study of Jehovah's Witnesses* (New York: Wiley, 1975).

34. Heather and Gary Botting, *The Orwellian World of Jehovah's Witnesses* (Toronto: University of Toronto Press, 1984).

35. Barbara Grizzuti Harrison, *Visions of Glory: A History and Memory of Jehovah's Witnesses* (New York: Simon and Schuster, 1978).

36. Robert Mapes Anderson, *Vision of the Disinherited: The Making of American Pentecostalism* (New York: Oxford University Press, 1979).

37. Vinson Synan, *The Holiness-Pentecostal Movement in the United States* (Grand Rapids, Mich.: Eerdmans, 1971).

38. Henry P. Van Dusen, "Third Force in Christendom: Gospel-Singing, Doomsday-Preaching Sects," *Life* 44 (June 9, 1958): 113–22.

39. Robert David Thomas, *The Man Who Would Be Perfect: John Humphrey Noyes and the Utopian Impulse* (Philadelphia: University of Pennsylvania Press, 1977).

40. Maren Lockwood Carden, *Oneida: Utopian Community to Modern Corporation* (Baltimore: Johns Hopkins University Press, 1969).

41. James Reston Jr., *Our Father Who Art in Hell* (New York: Times Books, 1981); J. Gordon Melton, ed., *The Peoples Temple and Jim Jones: Broadening Our Perspective* (New York: Garland, 1990); John R. Hall, *Gone From the Promised Land: Jonestown in American Cultural History* (New Brunswick, N.J.: Transaction Books, 1987); and Chidester, *Salvation and Suicide.*

42. "Report on the Events at Waco, Texas, February 28 to April 19, 1993 / United States Department of Justice" (Washington, D.C.: Dept. of Justice, 1993); and James R. Lewis, ed., *From the Ashes: Making Sense of Waco* (Lanham, Md.: Rowman and Littlefield, 1994).

43. For a general history of the Shakers, see Stephen J. Stein, *The Shaker Experience in America: A History of the United Society of Believers* (New Haven, Conn.: Yale University Press, 1992).

44. Edward Deming Andrews, *The Gift to Be Simple: Songs, Dances and Rituals of the American Shakers* (New York: J.J. Augustin, 1940); *The People Called Shakers: A Search for the Perfect Society,* new ed. (New York: Dover, 1963); *Religion in Wood: A Book of Shaker Furniture* (Bloomington: Indiana University Press, 1966); and with Faith Andrews, *Visions of the Heavenly Sphere: A Study in Shaker Religious Art* (Charlottesville: University Press of Virginia, 1969).

45. Two examples of the scholarship affected by this renewal are Michael Brooks Taylor, "Developments in Early Shaker Ethical Thought" (Ph.D. diss., Harvard University, 1976); and Stephen A. Marini, *Radical Sects in Revolutionary New England* (Cambridge, Mass.: Harvard University Press, 1982).

46. See Peter Novick, *That Noble Dream: The "Objectivity Question" and the American Historical Profession* (Cambridge: Cambridge University Press, 1988).

47. For contrasting judgments on the value and interpretation of apostate charges, see Nardi Reeder Campion, *Mother Ann Lee: Morning Star of the Shakers* (Hanover, N.H.: University Press of New England, 1990), 103–11; and Clarke Garrett, *Spirit Possession and Popular Religion: From the Camisards to the Shakers* (Baltimore: Johns Hopkins University Press, 1987), 195–213.

48. See Jan Shipps, "The Prophet Puzzle: Suggestions Leading toward a More Comprehensive Interpretation of Joseph Smith," *Journal of Mormon History* 1 (1974): 3–20.

49. See, for example, "Mary Baker Eddy: Her Influence Upon Theology," in *Christian Science: A Sourcebook of Contemporary Materials* (Boston: Christian Science Publishing, 1990), 94–100.

50. The *Journal for the Scientific Study of Religion* is the principal location where demographic information on sects and cults appears with some regularity. See also Roger Finke and Rodney Stark, *The Churching of America, 1776–1990: Winners and Losers in Our Religious Economy* (New Brunswick, N.J.: Rutgers University Press, 1992), 239–45.

51. H. Richard Niebuhr, *The Social Sources of Denominationalism* (Hamden, Conn.: Shoe String Press, 1954).

52. For a discussion of the process of accommodation within recent Pentecostalism, see Grant Wacker, "Pentecostalism," in *Encyclopedia of the American Religious Experience: Studies of Traditions and Movements,* 3 vols., ed. Charles H. Lippy and Peter W. Williams (New York: Scribner's, 1988), 2:933–45.

53. David Edwin Harrell, *Oral Roberts: An American Life* (Bloomington: Indiana University Press, 1985).

54. See Stein, *Shaker Experience*; and Priscilla J. Brewer, *Shaker Communities, Shaker Lives* (Hanover, N.H.: University Press of New England, 1986).

55. See E.U. Essien-Udom, *Black Nationalism: A Search for Identity in America* (Chicago: University of Chicago Press, 1962); and C. Eric Lincoln, *The Black Muslims in America*, rev. ed. (Boston: Beacon, 1973).

56. See Hans A. Baer and Merrill Singer, *African-American Religion in the Twentieth Century: Varieties of Protest and Accommodation* (Knoxville: University of Tennessee Press, 1992).

57. See Leonard I. Sweet, "Millennialism in America: Recent Studies," *Theological Studies* 40 (1979): 510–31; Charles H. Lippy, "Millennialism and Adventism," in Lippy and Williams, *Encyclopedia*, 2:831–44; and Paul Boyer, *When Time Shall Be No More: Prophecy Belief in Modern American Culture* (Cambridge, Mass.: Harvard University Press, 1992).

58. Robert S. Fogarty, *Dictionary of American Communal and Utopian History* (Westport, Conn.: Greenwood, 1980), 62–63.

59. Herbert A. Wisbey Jr., *Pioneer Prophetess: Jemima Wilkinson, the Publick Universal Friend* (Ithaca: Cornell University Press, 1964).

60. Marini, *Radical Sects*, 50–51.

61. E. Gordon Alderfer, *The Ephrata Commune: An Early American Counterculture* (Pittsburgh: University of Pittsburgh Press, 1985).

62. Karl John Richard Arndt, *George Rapp's Harmony Society, 1785–1847* (Philadelphia: University of Pennsylvania Press, 1965).

63. Diane L. Barthel, *Amana: From Pietist Sect to American Community* (Lincoln: University of Nebraska Press, 1984).

64. See Numbers and Butler, *Disappointed*; and Stephen D. O'Leary, *Arguing the Apocalypse: A Theory of Millennial Rhetoric* (New York: Oxford University Press, 1994).

65. Shirley Nelson, *Fair Clear and Terrible: The Story of Shiloh, Maine* (Latham, N.Y.: British American Publishing, 1989).

66. Richard T. Hughes, ed., *The American Quest for the Primitive Church* (Urbana: University of Illinois Press, 1988); and Hughes and C. Leonard Allen, *Illusions of Innocence: Protestant Primitivism in America, 1630–1875* (Chicago: University of Chicago Press, 1988).

67. Theodore Dwight Bozeman, *To Live Ancient Lives: The Primitivist Dimension in Puritanism* (Chapel Hill: University of North Carolina Press, 1988).

68. See Grant Wacker, "Playing for Keeps: The Primitivist Impulse in Early Pentecostalism," in Hughes, *American Quest*, 196–219.

69. See Jan Shipps, "The Reality of the Restoration and the Restoration Ideal in the Mormon Tradition," in Hughes, *American Quest*, 181–95.

70. See, for example, Richard S. Van Wagoner, *Mormon Polygamy: A History* (Salt Lake City: Signature Books, 1986); and Jessie L. Embry, *Mormon Polygamous Families: Life in the Principle* (Salt Lake City: University of Utah Press, 1987).

71. See Marjorie Procter-Smith, *Women in Shaker Community and Worship: A Feminist Analysis of the Uses of Religious Symbolism* (Lewiston, N.Y.: Edwin Mellen Press, 1985); Sally L. Kitch, *Chaste Liberation: Celibacy and Female Cultural Status* (Urbana: University of Illinois Press, 1989); and Jean M. Humez, ed., *Mother's First-Born Daughters: Early Shaker Writings on Women and Religion* (Bloomington: Indiana University Press, 1993).

72. Elaine J. Lawless, *God's Peculiar People: Women's Voices and Folk Tradition in a*

Pentecostal Church (Lexington: University Press of Kentucky, 1988); idem, *Handmaidens of the Lord: Pentecostal Women Preachers and Traditional Religion* (Philadelphia: University of Pennsylvania Press, 1988); and Edith Waldvogel Blumhofer, *Aimee Semple McPherson: Everybody's Sister* (Grand Rapids, Mich.: Eerdmans, 1993).

73. Maureen Ursenbach Beecher and Lavina Fielding Anderson, eds., *Sisters in Spirit: Mormon Women in Historical and Cultural Perspective* (Urbana: University of Illinois Press, 1987).

74. Mary Baker Eddy, *Manual of The Mother Church: The First Church of Christ, Scientist in Boston, Massachusetts* (Boston: First Church of Christ, Scientist, 1895), 29.

75. Jill Watts, *God, Harlem U.S.A.: The Father Divine Story* (Berkeley and Los Angeles: University of California Press, 1992).

76. The most sophisticated study of comparative sectarian theology is Mary Farrell Bednarowski, *New Religions and the Theological Imagination in America* (Bloomington: Indiana University Press, 1989). See also the pathbreaking work by John L. Brooke, *The Refiner's Fire: The Making of Mormon Cosmology, 1644–1844* (Cambridge, Eng.: Cambridge University Press, 1994).

77. Linda P. Wilcox, "The Mormon Concept of a Mother in Heaven," in Beecher and Anderson, *Sisters in Spirit*, 69.

78. Linda A. Mercadante, *Gender Doctrine and God: The Shakers and Contemporary Theology* (Nashville: Abingdon, 1990).

79. Gottschalk, *Emergence of Christian Science*, 52; and Mary Farrell Bednarowski, "Outside the Mainstream: Women's Religion and Women Religious Leaders in Nineteenth-Century America," *Journal of the American Academy of Religion* 48 (1980): 207–31.

80. Gottschalk, *Emergence of Christian Science*, 53.

81. For example, see Carol A. Kolmerten, *Women in Utopia: The Ideology of Gender in the American Owenite Communities* (Bloomington: Indiana University Press, 1990); Wendy E. Chmielewski, Louis J. Kern, and Marlyn Klee-Hartzell, eds., *Women in Spiritual and Communitarian Societies in the United States* (Syracuse: Syracuse University Press, 1993); Catherine Wessinger, ed., *Women's Leadership in Marginal Religions: Explorations Outside the Mainstream* (Urbana: University of Illinois Press, 1993); and Susan Starr Sered, *Priestess, Mother, Sacred Sister: Religions Dominated by Women* (New York: Oxford University Press, 1994).

82. See Timothy Miller, *When Prophets Die: The Postcharismatic Fate of New Religious Movements* (Albany: State University of New York Press, 1991).

83. Leonard J. Arrington, *Brigham Young: American Moses* (New York: Knopf, 1985).

84. Spencer Klaw, *Without Sin: The Life and Death of the Oneida Community* (New York: Penguin Books, 1993).

85. Stephen Nissenbaum, *Sex, Diet, and Debility in Jacksonian America: Sylvester Graham and Health Reform* (Westport, Conn.: Greenwood, 1980).

86. Richard Schwarz, *John Harvey Kellogg, M.D.* (Nashville: Southern Publishing Association, 1970).

87. Section 89, *Doctrine and Covenants*, 154–55.

88. Beverly Gordon, *Shaker Textile Arts* (Hanover, N.H.: University Press of New England, 1980).

89. Gayle Veronica Fischer, "Who Wears the Pants? Women, Dress Reform, and Power in the Mid-Nineteenth-Century United States" (Ph.D. diss., Indiana University, 1995).

90. For a discussion of hair as a boundary marker, see Elaine J. Lawless, "'Your Hair is Your Glory': Public and Private Symbology of Long Hair for Pentecostal Women," *New York Folklore* 12 (1986): 33–49.

91. See Lawrence Foster, *Religion and Sexuality: Three American Communal Experiments of the Nineteenth Century* (New York: Oxford University Press, 1981); and Louis J. Kern, *An Ordered Love: Sex Roles and Sexuality in Victorian Utopias — the Shakers, the Mormons, and the Oneida Community* (Chapel Hill: University of North Carolina Press, 1981).

92. Mary Baker Eddy, *Science and Health with Key to the Scriptures* (Boston: First Church of Christ, Scientist, 1991), chapter on "Marriage."

93. Numbers, *Prophetess of Health*, 129–59; and Roy E. Graham, *Ellen G. White, Co-Founder of the Seventh-Day Adventist Church* (New York: P. Lang, 1985).

94. See Marlyn Klee-Hartzell, "Family Love, True Womanliness, Motherhood, and the Socialization of Girls in the Oneida Community, 1848–1880," in Chmielewski, Kern, and Klee-Hartzell, *Women in Societies*, 182–200.

95. See, for example, Ronald L. Numbers and Darrel W. Amundsen, eds., *Caring and Curing: Health and Medicine in the Western Religious Traditions* (New York: Macmillan, 1986), as well as a series of volumes focusing on health and medicine in particular religious traditions.

96. See Gevitz, *Other Healers*; and Robert C. Fuller, *Alternative Medicine and American Religious Life* (New York: Oxford University Press, 1989).

97. See David Harrell, *All Things Are Possible: The Healing and Charismatic Revivals in Modern America* (Bloomington: Indiana University Press, 1975); Douglas Reinhardt, "With His Stripes We Are Healed: White Pentecostals and Faith Healing," in *Diversities of Gifts: Field Studies in Southern Religion*, edited by Ruel W. Tyson Jr., James L. Peacock, and Daniel W. Patterson (Urbana: University of Illinois Press, 1988); and Lester E. Bush, *Health and Medicine among the Latter-Day Saints: Science, Sense, and Scripture* (New York: Crossroad, 1993).

98. Robert Peel, *Health and Medicine in the Christian Science Tradition: Principle, Practice, and Challenge* (New York: Crossroad, 1988).

99. Jerry Bergman, *Jehovah's Witnesses and Kindred Groups: A Historical Compendium and Bibliography* (New York: Garland, 1984).

100. Eddy, *Manual*, 61, 125–26.

101. The magisterial study by Daniel W. Patterson, *The Shaker Spiritual* (Princeton: Princeton University Press, 1979), is a model for the work that needs to be done on other traditions.

Dissident History: American Religious Culture and the Emergence of the Metaphysical Tradition

CATHERINE L. ALBANESE

When the English Puritan settlers touched land in what eventually became the state of Massachusetts, they carried in their cultural baggage two traditional accounts of origin and fall. In the first, the Lord God planted Adam and Eve, first man and first woman, in a paradise garden until the pair succumbed to a serpent's promise that, by eating fruit from a forbidden tree, they should be "as gods." Their fall into knowledge earned them divine punishment and eviction from paradise. In the second account, by the time of the biblical Noah the people were long-lived, and "there were giants in the earth," "mighty men" and "men of renown." But there was also pervasive wickedness, and its offense before God became unbearable. So he sent a death-dealing flood to the corrupt and violent earth, sparing only Noah, his family, and male and female representatives of each species in Noah's divinely designed ark. Human culture and animal life, as the New England Puritans had come to know them, originated from flood survivors on the ark.[1]

Less than a century after their first landing on New England's shores, another, self-consciously literary, tale of origins celebrated Puritan sacred themes. In a rhetorical display that emulated the opening lines of Vergil's Latin *Aeneid*, Cotton Mather announced his purpose and plan. "I write the Wonders of the Christian Religion, flying from the depravations of Europe, to the American Strand," he sententiously declared. "And, assisted by the Holy Author of that Religion," he went on to tell, "I . . . report the wonderful displays of His infinite Power, Wisdom, Goodness, and Faithfulness, wherewith His Divine Providence hath irradiated an Indian Wilderness."[2]

But Mather was uneasy in his celebration, and he worried that the tale of origins might end in one of horrendous fall. He was, he confessed, "smitten with a just fear of incroaching and ill-bodied *degeneracies*," and he sought to use his "modest endeavours to prevent the *loss* of a country so signalized for the *profes-*

sion of the purest *Religion*, and for the *protection* of God upon it, in that holy profession." He went on to explain that he would count his "country lost, in the *loss* of the primitive *principles*, and the primitive *practices*, upon which it was first established." And he ventured that "one good way to save that *loss*, would be to do something that the memory of the *great things done for us by our God*, may not be *lost*, and that the story of the circumstances attending the *foundation* and *formation* of this country, and of its *preservation* hitherto, may be impartially handed unto posterity."[3] Indeed, it was to this enterprise that he dedicated himself in his nearly 800-page *Magnalia Christi Americana*.

By the twentieth century, other — very different — voices were carrying Mather's tune and its older echo from Genesis. There was, for salient example, Frederick Spencer Oliver's "channeled" narrative, *A Dweller on Two Planets*. Purportedly the work of "Phylos the Thibetan," a "Theochristian student and Occult Adept" for whom Oliver functioned as "amanuensis," the volume announced in its preface that its manuscript original was "finished in Santa Barbara County, California, A.D. 1886." "Phylos the Thibetan's" book had been published in Los Angeles by 1905, and it enjoyed a modest success, appearing in at least six editions in less than fifty years. With a convoluted plot in which the narrator learned that in a previous incarnation he was Zailm Numinos from Atlantis, the novel lengthily chronicled life on that ancient continent with its society's scientific and technological advances. But the narrative told, too, of the fall of the lost continent. "The seeds of corruption sown in the hearts of men by the Evil One," wrote Oliver, "germinated and throve." So began "a long, steadily downward course which weakened the self-respect, manhood and womanhood of Poseid." This was, wrote the somber author, "a loss revealed in countless ways, culminating in national depravity and ruin."[4]

And so, announced by a "Son of the Solitude," Atlan's "day of destruction" dawned. After "three days of horror, and three nights," with mountains falling "on the plains" and floods sweeping "unrestrained," the end came. "Suddenly it seemed as if the foundations of the world were withdrawn, for by one frightful, universal motion the lands left unflooded began to sink. With never a pause to the hideous, sickening sensation, all things sank, down, down down." Atlantis had sunk beyond rescue into the sea. But still, some life and hope remained. One man, Nepth, on his "vessel of refuge" drifted over the waters and was grounded in Asia. Meanwhile, Europe and America failed to sink under the tidal wave and survived.[5]

I

Narratives of foundation seemed thoroughly intertwined in Puritan consciousness with other narratives of threat and fall. And, as the glimpse, above, of one fairly well-known occult literary production shows, in our own century themes of foundation and fall appear again, in dissimilar contexts but strikingly similar terms. The juxtaposition is a clue — a straw, if you will, in the metaphysical wind. For it is my argument in the pages that follow that the Puritan construal of origin and fall, of grace and its subsequent loss or the perilous threat of the same, organized major strands in American religious culture from seventeenth-century times to our own. It is my argument, as well, that this was manifestly the case in, of all places, the American metaphysical tradition, beginning in the middle years of the nineteenth century and leading on into our own century and into the New Age consciousness of its last decades.

And it is my argument, finally, that evolving narratives of grace and fall, even as they unconsciously expressed consensus with a Puritan past, also became, in metaphysical dress, forms of dissident history.[6] This is to say that American metaphysicians dissented from orthodox Christian and Calvinist narratives as so many religious fixtures from the past. They turned, instead, to newer-seeming narratives that metaphysical authors believed the science and learning of their time authenticated. In fact, dissident history has been so strongly characteristic of the American metaphysical tradition that narratives of dissent function as clear, identifying markers of these religious forms.

Scholarly studies of the American metaphysical tradition have been few, and they have largely gravitated toward its theology of Truth, linking it to practical demonstrations in quests for health and wealth. J. Stillson Judah's *History and Philosophy of the Metaphysical Movements in America*, published in 1967, set the tone for much of what followed. Calling metaphysics "a practical type of philosophy" that was "both scientific and religious," Judah located its origins in a region between Maine and New York in the period from 1840 to 1875. Still more, he construed metaphysics broadly, including in his account not only the obvious movements of New Thought and Christian Science but also, and significantly, spiritualism and theosophy. He tied metaphysical foundations to "the extreme liberalism of American transcendentalism," and — important here — also found them to be indirectly linked to Puritanism. Moreover, he associated metaphysical growth with "becoming a mirror of the hopes, thoughts, and aspirations of a large part of the American people." The metaphysical movements "form one side of our culture's profile," Judah wrote perceptively.[7]

All the same, the long list of identifying characteristics Judah supplied was innocent of history — and in notable ways missed the evidence of the fear of sin that shadowed the movement. He noticed, instead, metaphysical individualism and exaltation of the self as divine. He marked the impersonality of the metaphysical ultimate deity and the quasi-dualism of a matter-mind dichotomy that disappeared in final monism. Judah pointed to metaphysical understandings of Jesus as moral teacher, to repudiations of the concept of sin and denials of the existence of evil, to metaphysical preferences for occult (higher truth) meanings for words and ideas. And Judah touted the optimistic pragmatism of the tradition, its prosperity and mental-healing orientations, its quests for self-realization, and its emphases on the psychology and scientific validity of religious experience.[8]

All that Judah said was there was there. But there was something more and something less — something within the metaphysical tradition that undercut celebratory promulgations of Truth and Well-being with a fear of corruption that gnawed like a worm at the root. Alongside the theology, there were grand narratives of dissident history within the metaphysical tradition, and they told, as in the "rounds" and "root races" of theosophy's Helena Blavatsky, of vast and cosmic beginnings that at first glance seemed appropriate accompaniments for proclamations of unitive Truth. But the narratives were also harried by a fear of failure and fall that made American metaphysics even less purely "transcendental" and more Puritan than Judah thought.

Nor is Judah's the only extant version of metaphysical history and identity. For Robert S. Ellwood and Harry B. Partin, the distant origins of American metaphysics lay — and rightly — outside the United States and in the European centuries. Ellwood and Partin read American metaphysics in terms of the "alternative reality" tradition of the West, and for them "new" religious movements in America were ultimately very old. Significantly, they pointed to an Elizabethan cultural tradition that crossed the Atlantic in the seventeenth century with important results for American metaphysics. This tradition, they argued, was "at the basis of much science and popular belief." It featured a Ptolemaic astronomy with earth at the center, conceptualizations of a "great chain of being" stretching from earth to heaven and of correspondences between the two, expressions of these ideas in a medical theory of "humors" and "airs," and practices of ceremonial magic and witchcraft.[9]

Elements of this world construction remained for American Puritans like Jonathan Edwards and Cotton Mather and for American revolutionaries like Benjamin Franklin. In tension with newer views, the old doggedly held on. And observing the tenacity, Ellwood and Partin cited "the continuing life of what might be called the 'spiritual' perspective underlying the old worldview even as certain of its manifestations dwindled: the idea that consciousness underlies the universe, that its parts are all interrelated and guided by hidden laws and relationships, and that humanity has a central place in its meaning." Backpedaling, even in America, from a theory of Transcendental origination for an alternative-reality tradition, they turned to colonial Freemasonic lodges. These, they said, although "deeply tinctured . . . by Enlightenment Deism and ethical rationalism," still "preserved the idea of an ancient wisdom conveyed by symbols often of occult background, and of initiatory societies dedicated to its inculcation."[10] From here it was a short journey, for them, through nineteenth-century spiritualism to theosophy, New Thought, and Eastern religious imports and then to the new religious manifestations of the 1960s and thereafter.[11]

Ellwood and Partin had identified an ancient lineage giving structure and shape to the diffusive Truth of metaphysics, and they had also astutely recognized a major institutional predecessor for the nineteenth-century tradition in the Freemasonic lodges. Still, beyond the institutional Truth of Freemasonry, there was a dissident history whispered in the lodges' initiatory secrets and, in fact, written large in the lodges' construction and eastward orientation. At once re-erecting the biblical temple of Solomon and building the city of the Sun, the master masons of the lodges attempted, in the midst of Christian culture, to suppress a narrative of sin and the need for salvation with another sort of tale.[12] Throughout their colonial and early national presence in America, they maintained an ambiguous alliance with Christian teaching and practice, absorbing the tensions between Truth and the fall in a synthesis of their own making.

Outside the Freemasonic lodges and before the early national period, other dimensions of American popular and folk religion may be related to the rise of metaphysics. Herbert Leventhal, David D. Hall, and Jon Butler have pursued related scholarly enterprises in teasing these dimensions out, and their results are important. Leventhal, like Ellwood and Partin, saw the centrality of an Elizabethan "world picture" in the early American cultural legacy. He argued persuasively on a variety of fronts — astrology, witchcraft, alchemy, rattlesnake beliefs — that what, in the early eighteenth century, were the shared assumptions and practices of a common culture were, by century's end, disdained by elites. Hall, who devoted his study to seventeenth-century New England, found a common fund of meaning that was shared by ministers and ordinary members of their congregations in a spectrum of beliefs about ghosts and supernatural visitations, about signs and portents and prescient dreams. And Butler, with an eye on colonial libraries from Massachusetts Bay through Pennsylvania to Virginia, noticed the prevalence of occult beliefs and practices in a consensual Anglo-American culture until, in the eighteenth century, magic became "folklorized."[13]

In their agreements and overlaps, the three studies point to early American habits of mind and life that historical hindsight can link to a nineteenth-century American metaphysical tradition. Occult America in its colonial incarnation operated, as later metaphysicians would, out of a version of the ancient theory of correspondence. The doctrine "as above, so below" became, for American colonists, warrant for occult explanation and magical action. Later, for nineteenth-century metaphysicians it would become warrant for Truth above and practice below to achieve the Truth, inscribing it on bodies thereby made healthy and prosperous. But beyond the theology of Truth, again, lay the metaphysical account of origin and fall, and its genesis cannot be fully disclosed in the terms of these studies.

The same is the case for Sydney Ahlstrom's well-known account of "harmonial religion" in his *Religious History of the American People*. There Ahlstrom named what scholars like Judah had called the metaphysical phenomenon with his own term, characterizing it by means of a theological essentialism that he argued it expressed. "Harmonial religion," Ahlstrom wrote, "encompasses those forms of piety and belief in which spiritual composure, physical health, and even economic well-being are understood to flow from a person's rapport with the cosmos." Linking New Thought, Christian Science, and Norman-Vincent-Peale-style "positive thinking" under the harmonial canopy, Ahlstrom distinguished them from theosophy, occultism, and "non-Western religion," all subjects of a later chapter in his history. And treating spiritualism separately, he connected it only minimally to any of these movements.[14]

Ahlstrom's distinction is useful in separating strands in an entangled lineage, but — even when he called "harmonial" and theosophical orientations "parallel streams" — the distinction also deflected attention away from the continuities. Indeed, from the vantage of these continuities, it seems fair to characterize magical practice, spiritualist communication, and mental healing and prosperity seeking as part of a single tradition. More significant here, from the vantage of the continuities, it seems as useful to look for how the tradition has handled history. How and where did the human lineage begin, and from what cosmic dust (or rain) clouds did humanity hail? What had become of the achievements of the ancestors, and where was memory of them preserved and recorded? Why was the past important, and how could it instruct for a (darkly) impending future? To blur the distinction between mental healers and theosophists in the service of uncovering a history of metaphysical answers to these questions seems a trade-off worth the price of barter.

Something like that trade-off has run, with a vengeance, through the more recent foray of gnostic literary critic Harold Bloom into the territory of American religious history and historians. A celebrator of the tradition he would exegete, Bloom has hardly claimed neutrality in his heavily interpretive account. Announcing an experiment with "religious criticism," which he called "a mode of description, analysis, and judgment that seeks to bring us closer to the workings of the religious imagination," Bloom was intent on finding "the irreducibly *spiritual* dimension in religious matters or phenomena of any kind." Bloom's gnostic commitment led him to affirm a divine origin for what he knew as "the American self" — "not the Adam of Genesis" but a "more primordial Adam." This Adam, said Bloom, was "as old as God, older than the Bible, and . . . free of time, unstained by mortality." Translated into a program for social description, the commitment led Bloom to search for the "Orphic and Gnostic abysses of the national self," and he found them in expected but also surprising places. There were five "indelible strands of the American Religion," he declared, and they were Mormonism, Christian Science, Seventh-Day Adventism, the religion of Jehovah's Witnesses, and Pentecostalism. Meanwhile, Bloom announced he had discovered that Mormons and Southern Baptists were remarkably similar.[15]

Over and over, Bloom discovered the essence of the American religion in the theological proclamation that "we are mortal gods, destined to find ourselves again in worlds as yet undiscovered." In this context, God in America could not be a creator deity, and American selves had never endured the radical contingency of being created. The Calvinist God of the Puritans had "remarkably little in common with the versions of God now apprehended by what calls itself Protestantism in the United States." If there was dualism in America, for Bloom, it was hardly dualistic at all, and the nonmonistic traces that remained had to do with devaluing context in favor of a gnostic theory of origins. The clue for Bloom was manifest: for the American religion, "the origin of the occult self, the saved element in one's being, goes back beyond nature to God, beyond the Creation to the Creator."[16]

Bloom was right in what he affirmed when he found an American religion with strongly gnostic leanings. Indeed, American religious historiography has often overvalued the evangelical presence in American religious history by assuming that its massive strength and visibility render other explanatory theses about the nation's religious culture moot. Still, Bloom surely missed the lingering presence of Puritanism, and he failed to come to terms with the cultural power of its early vision. Bloom's mystical declaration of an American myth of origins of the self within the Godhead startles with its tour de force; it also manifestly deflects attention from another sort of narrative. If Bloom recognized a dissident history for the American self, he missed the traces of sin and fall that colored and, in fact, controlled the dissidence.

II

The dissident religious history of the metaphysical tradition in America begins with the Puritans, and it also, even earlier, begins with Plato. Scholarly consensus suggests that when, in his *Timaeus* and his unfinished dialogue *Critias*, the Golden-Age Athenian philosopher recounted the exploits and catastrophes of the island-continent of Atlantis he was producing a work of imagination and not one of history.[17] The tale Plato told was so thoroughly riveting, though, that it captured the Western literary imagination through the European and into the American centuries. In the *Timaeus*, in an account purportedly collected at Sais, in Egypt, by the Athenian lawgiver Solon and transmitted to Critias, the proud island continent ruled its day with its "powerful and remarkable dynasty of kings" until Athens rose to defend the Greeks and others against Atlantean invasion. But later, at a time of "earthquakes and floods of extraordinary violence," Atlantis was "swallowed up by the sea and vanished."[18]

In the *Critias*, a much more extensive treatment of Atlantis formed much of the substance of the dialogue — this in the context of a promised history of Athenian-Atlantean war, the details of which were never recounted. Here Critias told the story learned from Solon: "Atlantis was an island larger than Libya and Asia put together, though it was subsequently overwhelmed by earthquakes and is the source of the impenetrable mud which prevents the free passage of those who sail out of the straits [of Gibraltar] into the open sea." Readers subsequently learned of the natural resources of the island and the origins of its semidivine inhabitants from the god Poseidon and a mortal woman. They learned, too, of how "the inhabitants proceeded to build temples, palaces, harbours and docks, and to organize the country as a whole." All was accomplished far and above the common scale, as Critias related, with buildings and their precious metals amply described. Moreover, as Critias also described, the countryside was etched with irrigation canals, which served as well to transport lumber and produce. There was an impressive form of military service, and there were kings, ten of them, each with "absolute power, in his own region and city, over persons and in general over laws."[19]

But the Atlantean paradise, like the (unrelated) Edenic one, could not endure. In what formed the final part of Solon's story, Critias narrated the devolution and fall of the Atlanteans. "For many generations, so long as the divine element in their nature survived," he declared, the Atlanteans "obeyed the laws and loved the divine to which they were akin." The results were exemplary: "They bore the burden of their wealth and possessions lightly, and did not let their high standard of living intoxicate them or make them lose their self-control." But as in Genesis, so, with its own twist, on Atlantis. "When the divine element in them became weakened by frequent admixture with mortal stock, and their human traits became predominant, they ceased to be able to carry their prosperity with moderation." And so, in almost the final line of the abruptly ended dialogue, Zeus, "the god of gods," made the decision to punish the Atlanteans.[20]

Platonic beginnings joined Puritan beginnings, however, in the dissident history created by the American metaphysical tradition. In an island history of their own, the English brought with them to Massachusetts Bay a mentality that had developed over centuries through their experience in a place far smaller than the hypothetical Atlantis. Separate, intact, cut off from continental Europe (or so the English liked to think), they transported across the ocean their environmental requirement for existence in the separatist mode. Doubly separate as English *Puritans*, the new Atlantic settlers had essentially refused to be members of a cultural coalition that would bring them out of their island selves. They eschewed not only a European continental blending (the Pilgrim immigration, after all, had fled Holland and not England) but also complicity in a form of high-church Anglicanism that brought, they believed, the corruption of papal forms and lackadaisical observance.

Moreover, in their new Atlantic world English Puritans lived out an ideology of wilderness fears and dark forebodings of fusion with native inhabitants. Indeed, we have clear evidence that the major body of Puritan settlers actively feared wilderness even as they were drawn to it.[21] And it does not take much reading between the lines to link their fears and secret attractions to social and psychological forces that were spin-offs of their culture and its transformed circumstance. On the one hand, Puritans, an ocean away from England, were anxious people, haunted by a sense of the fragility of their cultural order, a mode of containment that they understood, in the shadow of the Enlightenment, as a civilization to be contrasted with Indian ways.[22] On the other hand, Puritans had chafed under the fear of religious impurity in their old-world home. Caught between two forms of corruption — the wild American one and the ordered devolution of England — the Puritans expended considerable cultural energy in the project of maintaining purity and warning against the danger of a fall from grace.

As if that were not enough, the intellectual order that prevailed in English Puritan thought and organized Puritan New England knowledge, which — somewhat ironically — was a French gift to English culture, encouraged a separatist stance and a dread of mental slack. The logical system of the sixteenth-century Frenchman Petrus Ramus, which the Puritans had appropriated, stressed disjunction and discontinuity in its approach to naming and organizing the world through the mind. In a mode of presentation that was essentially spatial and visual, the Ramean logic proceeded from dichotomy to dichotomy, dividing and subdividing the world into ever smaller contraries and oppositions.[23] Contemplating Ramean logic as a self-conscious enterprise in a new Atlantic "wilderness" could only enhance Puritan habits of life and thought that worked against ease and comfort. To be rational and right meant, in accord with preferred logic, to separate, to disjoin. The structure of Puritan consciousness, then, built in the fear of a loss of vigilance, of an indiscriminate mixing of categories and its analogue in a careless behavioral slide into degeneracy.

To speak of these cultural currents in Puritan life is, of course, to try to name what was nebulous, to label the miasmas that shifted in and out of the spaces within the Puritan order. Still, the labeling helps explain the special blend of poignancy and terror that lurked in Cotton Mather's grand narrative of Puritan history. And beyond that, with the Ramean label at least, we confront the Platonic world that undergirded much of Puritan intellectual life. For elite and educated Puritans were Christian humanists who knew and used the Greek and Roman classics, quoting Plutarch and Seneca as well as Plato, Cicero, and Aristotle.[24] Puritan comfort with the classical world of the West would point the way for a rising generation of metaphysicians who looked to Plato and read him, in their turn, with a Neoplatonic gloss.

If, as Perry Miller wrote, "certain basic continuities persist in a culture" and the continuities "underlie the successive articulation of 'ideas,'" then — as he also noticed — there was a connection between the Puritan religious awe of Jonathan Edwards and the Transcendental nature mysticism of Ralph Waldo Emerson. What was persistent, Miller argued, was "the Puritan's effort to confront, face to face, the image of a blinding divinity in the physical universe, and to look upon that universe without the intermediacy of ritual, of ceremony, of the Mass and the confessional."[25] But what was persistent, too, was a history of grandeur and fall, and the outlines of the narrative could be found at the heart of the gospel of New England Transcendentalism. "A man is a god in ruins," Emerson's "Orphic poet" announced in *Nature* (1836). "Man is the dwarf of himself. Once he was permeated and dissolved by spirit. He filled nature with his overflowing currents. Out from him sprang the sun and moon; from man, the sun; from woman, the moon. The laws of his mind, the periods of his actions externized [sic] themselves into day and night, into the year and the seasons. But, having made for himself this huge shell, his waters retired; he no longer fills the veins and veinlets; he is shrunk to a drop."[26]

Here was the fall internalized and contracted into the center of the self. But significantly, the canon of the American Renaissance also contained an early image that adumbrated a fall external and spread large, a fall become the demise of a city in the sea and of even an Atlantis. Edgar Allan Poe's poem "The City in the Sea" appeared in one version in 1836, the same year Emerson published *Nature*. The poem was probably, in its original, about the Dead Sea ruins of the city of Gomorrah. Still, for readers with a classical bent, the shadow of Plato's Atlantis must have hovered. "Death," told Poe, had "reared himself a throne, / In a strange city lying alone / Far down within the dim West." What Poe described next could have been taken straightway from the *Critias*. "There shrines and palaces and towers / (Time-eaten towers that tremble not!) / Resemble nothing that is ours. / Around, by lifting winds forgot, / Resignedly beneath the sky / The melancholy waters lie." And there was even, in the final stanza of the poem, a veiled reference to an earthquake sinking the already-ruined city. With "a stir in the air," with "wave" and "ripple," Poe predicted the time "when, amid no earthly moans, / Down, down that town shall settle hence."[27]

To point to the high literary culture of the American Renaissance, however, is to miss, in at least one major way, what was central to the metaphysical tradition as it created its dissident tales of origin and fall. Religious entrepreneurs and self-starters, metaphysical tradition-builders proved their mettle as fit exponents of what might be termed the popular Enlightenment. Historian David Jaffee has called attention, in a related way, to what he names the "Village Enlightenment" in New England. Here Jaffee meant a process in which intertwined aspects of commerce and culture fostered, as he said, "the democratization of knowledge." The Village Enlightenment, in Jaffee's reading, encompassed "the formation of a market for cultural commodities in printed form." It included, too, "erosion of a hierarchical structure of authority, in which cultural controls were held by a clerical or college-trained elite," and it looked to "the emergence of a social organization of knowledge suitable to the requirements of rural folk in the rising republic."[28]

The rising metaphysicians of the nineteenth century conformed in great part to Jaffee's Village Enlightenment checklist. But they tended to be, more and more, urban or urbanizing instead of rural folk. Still more, their nonelite status for religion was more nuanced and inflected than in Jaffee's straightforward account. Often, metaphysical pacesetters were college-educated and professional, to be sure — lawyers, judges, and the like among them. And other times they were widely, even voraciously, read regarding religion and science especially. What they lacked, however, was steady immersion in a sustained and systematic tradition of religious inquiry — or, as important, disciplined and sophisticated knowledge in a field they sought to relate to religion. Under the lingering light of the republican ideology of the American Revolution, these factors hardly gave any would-be metaphysician pause. Like the new generation of young and enthusiastic evangelical leaders that Nathan Hatch wrote about in *The Democratization of American Christianity*, the new metaphysical leaders denied distinctions between the work of theological elites and their own populist efforts. Like the evangelicals, too, they empowered themselves by trusting their ideas and intuitions about the life of the spirit and not waiting for the imprimatur of orthodoxy. And finally, like the evangelicals whom Hatch called "religious outsiders," they worked out of an expansive confidence that included little sense of personal limit.[29]

In fact, the nineteenth-century world that spawned the metaphysicians and their dissident history could hardly be divided, religiously, into neat camps — with orthodox, evangelicals, and metaphysical believers all inhabiting separate quarters. The realities of nineteenth-century lives slid into one another. Distinctions between Christians and meta-Christians, between religious conformists and revolutionaries, between respectable pillars of the church and self-starting creators of new religions became decidedly blurred. If the legacy of the Revolution was an internalized ideology of power to the people, translated into socioreligious terms "power to the people" emerged in a complex religious spectrum in which vernacular dialects were seemingly as numerous as believers. Robert Bellah's well-remembered "Sheilaism" is hardly and merely a function of late twentieth-century religious life.[30]

The mix that brought an army of metaphysical Sheilas to American homes included, it is true, the influence of European leaders and their followers. Writing to English author Thomas Carlyle in 1834, Emerson especially noticed the religious progeny of Emanuel Swedenborg. The Swedenborgians, he thought, were "deeply interesting as a sect which . . . must contribute more than all other sects to the new faith which must arise from out of all."[31] And the Swedenborgians had their own form of dissident history in their founder's expansive accounts of life in the heavenly and hellish realms that, in mystical trance states, he had visited time and again.[32] Meanwhile, disciples of Franz Anton Mesmer spread enthusiastically across the land in the wake of a series of lyceum-hall lecturers who brought to the small towns and cities of America news and practical demonstrations of the mesmerist's art. In fact, it was the itinerant mesmerist, or animal magnetist, J. Stanley Grimes whose lecture-demonstration in Poughkeepsie, New York, started a youthful Andrew Jackson Davis on the dissident journey that transformed him into the leading theologian of nineteenth-century American spiritualism.[33] And even the high literary romanticism that yielded, on the western side of the Atlantic, the American Renaissance, had its popular expression not only in the catalog of pulp novels that David Reynolds has explored but also in a series of sentimental spiritualities. If a goodly number of these were Christian and evangelical, another goodly number were metaphysical.[34]

Not to be outdone by foreign influence, though, Americans early displayed their own resources for the creation of religious cultures that were metaphysically inclined. In this context, one expression of the spiritual productivity of early-to-mid-nineteenth-century western New York commands immediate attention. There, in a region settled by New Englanders that contemporaries called the "burned-over district," Mormonism was born. Important here, its spiritual sources lay, at least in part, within the same popular matrix that gave rise to the metaphysical tradition. Jan Shipps has shown the blurring, in the life of Joseph Smith, between acts of dowsing for material treasure and other acts that led to announcements of buried golden plates, their unearthing, and their eventual decipherment in what became *The Book of Mormon*. Still more, D. Michael Quinn has exhaustively documented the prodigious role that folk magic and a magical "world view" played in its creation. Divining rods, treasure hunting, and seer stones were all part of the religious world that formed Latter-day founder Joseph Smith, and so were ritual magic and astrology as well as visitations by spirits and by mysterious occult animals like salamanders. Local knowledge extended, too, to the mystical transports of Emanuel Swedenborg (with an account published on the first page of Canandaigua, New York's *Western Repository* in 1808). And it included familiarity with the alleged secrets of Freemasonic ritual (exposed in the anti-Masonic movement of the 1820s) that would involve Smith by the 1840s.[35]

Within this setting, Joseph Smith and his creation in the Church of Jesus Christ of Latter-day Saints hardly represented religious anomaly. Instead, they signaled religion-as-usual or religion-as-usual nudged to heightened acts of self- and community-expression. More than that, they signaled the full expression of a dissident history with familiar ties to New England settlement. For *The Book of Mormon* functioned from the first as a sacred narrative of grace and fall. It extended the story of the biblical tribe of Joseph, telling how tribal descendants Lehi and his family, led by the Lord to leave the city of Jerusalem in 600 B.C.E., made their way to an American promised land. There, however, Laman and Lemuel, two of the sons of Lehi, became leaders of a rebellious faction. Violating divine order, they turned on their brother Nephi, were cursed, in heavenly retribution, with dark skin, and so became ancestors of the American Indians. Nor was this the end of the saga of descent and fall. Throughout *The Book of Mormon* a chosen Nephite people hovered at the edge of moral disaster. As Mormon scripture declared, "the Lord saw that his people began to work in darkness, yea, work secret murders and abominations; therefore the Lord said, if they did not repent they should be destroyed from off the face of the earth."[36] The warning of future generations was central to scriptural business; the fall of the past ever reminded of the potential for a fall to come.

Nearly two decades after the appearance of *The Book of Mormon*, New York State saw the beginnings of a more fully metaphysical movement. Midcentury American spiritualism made its appearance as a speculative endeavor in the publication, in 1847, of Andrew Jackson Davis's nearly 800-page *Principles of Nature*.[37] The following year, with the spirit rappings announced by the youthful Kate and Maggie Fox in Hydesville, it made its appearance as a phenomenal practice concerned with contacting spirits of the dead.

Davis's *Principles of Nature*, which purportedly had gone through thirty-four editions by 1881, heralded no new Atlantis in its own version of dissident history. But it clearly celebrated the popular Enlightenment, self-consciously announcing on its title page that "any theory, hypothesis, philosophy, sect, creed, or institution, that fears investigation, openly manifests its own error." "Reason is a flower of the spirit, and its fragrance is liberty and knowledge," It also announced.[38] And although Davis made no secret of his hostility to Christianity, his own account of human origins was a narrative of splendor and fall in a hodge-podge blend of popular lyceum-hall science and traditional Christian teaching.

Davis had produced the book through a series of 157 lectures delivered in New York City in a magnetic (trance) state and recorded by Universalist minister William Fishbough, who apparently did not hesitate to revise them.[39] The lectures themselves traced the origin of all things from liquid fire and propounded an evolutionary model to explain the formation of millions of suns and attendant planets from what the *Principles* called the "Great Centre" and the "great Sun of the '*Univercoelum*.'"[40] The mark of the magnetized Davis was evident in alternate references to the universe's first principle as the Great Positive Mind, and his penchant for otherworld journeys was expressed in his account of life among the inhabitants of a series of planets in our solar system. But when Davis arrived on earth, his lengthy account of the origins of the mineral, vegetable, and animal kingdoms culminating in the emergence of "man" acquired a familiar ring.

The short version of Davis's narrative was that man had been born from "the earth, and Nature, and her laws" and that man was "the ultimate of material perfection." But delight had been all too brief, for "instead of cherishing the incessant and spontaneous inflowings of thought respecting the foundation and magnificent structure of the Universe, and enjoying the steady unfoldings of light and truth," the human mind had "left Nature and Reason." "And thus," Davis lamented, man had "lost sight of the true relation between Nature and science, and science and himself." "So depressed and degraded" had become the world's condition that Davis thought language "inadequate to describe it" and relied instead on "thoughts and feelings."[41]

In his more elaborate rendering of the tale, Davis told of an Asian garden of Eden with "lower and kindred races" that had been "designated by the comprehensive term *Adam*" and an "associate tribe comprehended by the term *Eve*." These first people, according to Davis, began to "advance," and they partook "a little of the fruit of the tree of Knowledge"; so it came about that "they began to conceal their true sentiments, and to clothe them with an arbitrary vocal sound." The rest was history. "The inhabitants became disunited in social affection in consequence of the misconceptions conveyed by those sounds," and "they finally could not enjoy each other's society." "This," Davis explained with Calvinist precision, "has been distinguished in the original history as a state of depravity."[42]

Spiritualist fortunes waxed and waned, enjoying a peak period in the 1850s, declining during the era of the Civil War, and experiencing resurgence in the 1880s. With the growth of an organizational base, however weak, in the postbellum years, spiritualism was poised to enter the twentieth century with prospects of remaining. But what spiritualists contributed most to the dissident history of new Atlantis was already presaged in Davis and his neo-Calvinist discourse of Reason and Science. For by the mid-nineteenth century, the popular Enlightenment had acquired a scientific aura, and spiritualists prided themselves as moderns who engaged in forms of empirical action that the evolving new science of their time could test. "Leading spiritualists held a childlike faith in empirical science as the only approach to knowledge," wrote R. Laurence Moore. "They tried to emulate the scientific method; more important, they copied and helped popularize scientific language. Certainly no others tried so hard to borrow science's prestige, and as a consequence, probably no one else benefited as much as they did from the great interest in science awakened in that [the nineteenth] century."[43]

Take, as an example, spiritualist explanations for the communications and materializations of spirits during their séances. Spirits could do such things, according to Davis and numbers of other spiritualists, because the spirits existed as refined manifestations of matter. And talk of "spirit matter" among the spiritualists was only a mental hair's-breadth away from the explanations of Austrian physician Franz Anton Mesmer and his followers, who spoke of unseen, but real, tides and forces in the universe, the free circulation of which ensured good health. More than that, and in a more orthodox scientific world, "spirit matter" seemed to contemporaries an easy partner for Newtonian postulations of a vague environmental "ether" believed to fill unoccupied space and to conduct, as a medium, electromagnetic waves. "In what way," asked Moore, "did the hazily defined ether, which scientists used to fill space, differ from the spirit matter they [spiritualists] believed in?"[44]

Hence, with all the glamour of their darkened séance rooms, spiritualists adamantly rejected supernatural explanations for their productions. They asserted the primacy of natural law, turning to empirical demonstration to support their claims, and they often actively invited investigation. Above all, spiritualists had faith in progress. With Andrew Jackson Davis — who was more interested in the future than in the ancient fall of the tribes of Adam and Eve — they looked to unending disclosures and revelations of knowledge that would transport them to new horizons and worlds.[45]

III

When, after the Civil War, a spiritualist reform movement took new and organizational direction in the Theosophical Society of Helena P. Blavatsky and Henry Steel Olcott, the same or similar observations could be made.[46] And, as we shall see, Puritanism persisted there, and Plato had a second coming in what became the new Atlantean age. Already in 1877, two years after the Theosophical Society's foundation, Blavatsky in New York City published her huge (over 1,300-page) corpus that she titled Isis Unveiled. The ambitious two-volume edition was subtitled A Master-Key to the Mysteries of Ancient and Modern Science and Theology, and the "science" of the subtitle was intended seriously, with an entire volume of the two devoted to it.

Writing in that scientific volume, Blavatsky noted what she called the "perfect identity of the rites, ceremonies, traditions, and even the names of the deities, among the Mexicans and ancient Babylonians and Egyptians." This, she argued, was "a sufficient proof of South America being peopled by a colony which mysteriously found its way across the Atlantic." Nor was Blavatsky reticent about speculating on how the mysterious passage had been made. "Those who consider that there is no tradition, sanctified by ages, without a certain sediment of truth at the bottom of it," she announced to readers, "believe in the *Atlantis*-legend." Invoking a "handful of thoughtful and solitary students" who studied the "great problems of the physical and spiritual universes" in "secret records," Blavatsky cited, significantly, "the legends and traditions commented upon by the masters of Solon, Pythagoras, and Plato, in the marble halls of Heliopolis and Sais."[47] Then Blavatsky got more specific:

> These men believe the story of the Atlantis to be no fable, but maintain that at different epochs of the past huge islands, and even continents, existed where now there is but a wild waste of waters. In those submerged temples and libraries the archaeologist would find, could he but explore them, the materials for filling all the gaps that now exist in what we imagine is *history*. They say that at a remote epoch a traveller could traverse what is now the Atlantic Ocean, almost the entire distance by land, crossing in boats from one island to another, where narrow straits then existed.[48]

We do not know for certain what provoked the extended reflection from Blavatsky here, but it is not frivolous to suggest that she may have known the work of Jules Verne.[49] Called the inventor or "father" of science fiction for his numerous productions in the genre, Verne, like Blavatsky, was actively concerned with occult-metaphysical themes. Indeed, Michel Lamy has argued at length that Verne encoded secrets of French Masonry and Rosicrucianism in his novels for decipherment by other initiates.[50] Whatever its secrets, the Frenchman's *Twenty Thousand Leagues under the Sea* first appeared in a French magazine serial between 1869 and 1870, and by 1873 an English translation was available and more or less continued to be. Verne's novel introduced the memorable Captain Nemo and his submarine *Nautilus* (named, not inappropriately, for Robert Fulton's "diving boat" of 1800–1801). And with prophetic verve, the Nemo of the novel busily occupied himself in mapping the bottom of the ocean, even as he carried the novel's narrator, Professor Aronnax, and two others on a tour of the world that, at the time, was scarcely believable.

It was in this context that Aronnax recorded the remarkable sequence in which, in heavy diving suit, copper headgear, and lead soles, he climbed a grotesque underwater mountain until he came upon the startling ruins of a classical city or town. Where was he? Aronnax burned to ask. And, as if he understood, Captain Nemo obliged with the answer. "He picked up a piece of chalky stone, walked toward a black basaltic rock, and scrawled just one word: ATLANTIS."[51]

The deeply impressed Aronnax went on to celebrate Atlantis in a rash of "historical" memories about the "now submerged region that had once existed outside Europe, Asia, and Libya, . . . home of those powerful Atlantians against whom the early Greeks had waged their first wars." Plato, he added, had "recorded the lofty deeds of those heroic times."[52] Commenting in the 1950s, L. Sprague de Camp marked the impact Verne had made and counted over fifty novels on the "lost-continent" theme published by his successors. De Camp noticed, too, that they had brought not only Atlantis but also live Atlanteans onto their fictional stages.[53] So it was clear that F.S. Oliver's Zailm Numinos of Atlantis had metaphysical company.

Meanwhile, whether or not Blavatsky directly knew Verne's work, the evidence for her acquaintance with the novels of the Victorian Sir Edward Bulwer-Lytton is incontrovertible. Indeed, S.B. Liljegren has argued that Blavatsky owed the beginnings of theosophy to Bulwer-Lytton, pointing to strong thematic connections and numerous quotations from Bulwer-Lytton, acknowledged and unacknowledged, in *Isis Unveiled*.[54] And in Bulwer-Lytton's *The Coming Race* — which already in 1871, the year of its publication, went through five editions — hints of Atlantis were only thinly veiled. The didactic metaphysical plot told of an American who discovered a subterranean and technologically advanced civilization featuring air-boats and a mysterious, apparently electromagnetic, fluid called the *vril* or *vril*-force. Members of this people belonged, according to the novel, to the great Ana family race. Significantly, the Ana had come to dwell in the underground when once, thousands of years before the biblical Noah, a portion of their former upper world was "subjected to inundations, not rapid, but gradual and uncontrollable, in which all, save a scanty remnant, were submerged and perished."[55]

Prompted perhaps by Verne and certainly by Bulwer-Lytton — who, it is important to notice here, belonged to the occult Golden Dawn — Helena Blavatsky used the emerging science-fiction genre as grist for metaphysical production.[56] But she was manifestly drawn more to what she considered fact than to the fiction. Indeed, the urgent story, for Blavatsky and the metaphysical tradition in general, lay not with make-believe but with what metaphysicians construed as unimpeachable science. Especially, the urgent story lay with a version of science that challenged conventional verities and functioned, with a dissident voice, on the cutting edge of culture.

Enter, then, Ignatius Donnelly. A Philadelphian by birth, son of an Irish immigrant father and a mother of Irish ancestry as well, Donnelly studied and practiced law, worked as a town developer and an editor, became involved in politics, and by 1860, at twenty-eight, became Republican lieutenant governor of Minnesota and then, from 1863 to 1869, a United States congressman. Donnelly championed liberal causes, working in Congress for black education and woman suffrage and introducing a bill for the forestation of public lands. Later, he continued to be a member of the state legislature in Minnesota, and he became identified with third-party movements with liberal and reform intent, helping to found the Granger movement and the Populist Party. Donnelly, in fact, was its vice presidential candidate when he died in 1901.[57]

These were not credentials that could be predicted to bring Donnelly to the notice of metaphysicians. What did assure him of their sustained and enthusiastic notice, though, was his publication, in 1882, of *Atlantis: The Antediluvian World*.[58] Donnelly had been interested in science and in what many would call pseudoscience for years, and, like other Americans, he had been influenced by

Jules Verne's novelistic evocation of Atlantis with Captain Nemo's ocean-bottom journey. Thus, at a time when his political career and personal life were at low ebb, Donnelly turned his considerable energies to producing a manuscript on the "lost continent." He succeeded in selling it to Harper and Brothers in 1881, and when it appeared the following year the positive critical reaction was sweeping and effusive, with the *Chicago Times* calling it "one of the notable books of the century." Already, in 1882, there were seven editions. And meanwhile, in England, William Gladstone, the prime minister, penned a four-page letter to Donnelly filled with warmth and admiration. The following year came a Swedish translation, and by 1890 there had been twenty-three American and twenty-six English editions.[59]

David D. Anderson tells that the book made Donnelly "an international figure, a seriously regarded scientific theorist, and a central figure in an Atlantis-centered cult that continues to the present." "He was probably the most discussed literary figure outside professional and intellectual circles," wrote historian Martin Ridge. "The New Orleans 'Mardi Gras' of 1883 was based on the *Atlantis* theme, as was the Baltimore 'Oriole' pageant of the same year. Thousands of people who normally did not read or hear of current books were exposed to Donnelly's work and many of them bought it." Even further, Donnelly was elected to membership in the American Association for the Advancement of Science, even if Charles Darwin read his *Atlantis* skeptically and other serious scientists did not take the work seriously.[60] Scrutinized even cursorily, in fact, the book emerges as a relentless tour de force, with scientific "facts" amassed indiscriminately from a variety of scholarly and popular science sources and interwoven with a rhetorical voice that suggests a lawyer's skill.

Donnelly found "nothing improbable" in Plato's account of Atlantis and called it a "plain and reasonable history." He cited, as well, biblical references to the lost continent, as in Old Testament allusions to the "islands of the sea." Forthrightly chastising skeptics, Donnelly declared to readers that he failed to see why Atlantean history "should have been contemptuously set aside as a fable by Greeks, Romans, and the modern world." It could only be, he answered his own objection, "because our predecessors, with their limited knowledge of the geological history of the world, did not believe it possible that any large part of the earth's surface could have been thus suddenly swallowed up by the sea." The rest of his work, point by "scientific" point, obligingly corrected their ignorance.[61] To do so, Donnelly used not merely the geological record as he understood it but likewise hypothetical evidence from the oceans, from the distribution of flora and fauna, from ancient deluge legends and other mythologies in widely distributed cultures, and from comparative cultural belief and practice.

Donnelly saw the cataclysmic Lisbon earthquake of 1775 as an aftershock of the earthquake that destroyed Atlantis, and he announced that the Azores Islands were "undoubtedly the peaks of the mountains of Atlantis." He thought that deep-sea soundings proved the Atlantean thesis, and he supported his view with quotations from articles in recent issues of the *Scientific American* and the *Popu-*

lar Science Review. He told readers that the sunken continent was the "pathway which once extended between the New World and the Old, and by means of which the plants and animals of one continent travelled to the other." Not only that, asserted Donnelly, but Atlantis also provided the "avenues" by which "black men found their way . . . from Africa to America, and red men from America to Africa." The testimony of the flora and fauna throughout the world also offered "abundant" proofs that "there must have been at one time uninterrupted land communication between Europe and America." Donnelly quoted an essay from the *Westminster Review* of 1872 for support. "Recent discoveries in the fossil beds of the Red Lands of Nebraska prove that the horse originated in America," he assured readers. Likewise, he told them that "fossil remains of the camel" could be "found in India, Africa, South America, and in Kansas." He cited Asa Gray as he continued to develop his argument, and he also quoted Charles Darwin.[62]

Turning from nature to culture, Donnelly surveyed widely separate deluge legends, which, he argued, all gave testimony to the catastrophic history of Atlantis. "Whether we turn to the Hebrews, the Aryans, the Phoenicians, the Greeks, the Cushites, or the inhabitants of America," he pronounced confidently, "we find everywhere traditions of the Deluge." And, he continued, "all these traditions point unmistakably to the destruction of Atlantis." Reconciling the biblical account of the Flood to Plato and connecting Hebrews to Phoenicians, Donnelly wove a tale of collective memory of Atlantean disaster. Not only that, he reported, but "nearly all the arts essential to civilization" had come to humankind from "the time of Atlantis" and from "that ancient Egyptian civilization which was coeval with, and an outgrowth from, Atlantis." "*In six thousand years the world made no advance on the civilization which it received from Atlantis,*" Donnelly underscored emphatically.[63]

Donnelly had begun his controversial book with a no-nonsense list of thirteen propositions that summarized what he expected to demonstrate in the course of his work. By the time he ended he was satisfied that he had established beyond question that Atlantis existed and that Plato's description of the island-continent was "veritable history." He had celebrated Atlantis as the site of human rise out of "barbarism" and into "civilization" as a "mighty nation" that had peopled, as well, a world catalog of locations ranging from the Gulf of Mexico, the Mississippi, and the Amazon to the Baltic and the Black and Caspian Seas. Donnelly had identified with Atlantis cultural "memories" of an "Antediluvian world," as in traditional accounts of the Garden of Eden and the Gardens of the Hesperides. He had argued for ancient gods and goddesses as "the kings, queens, and heroes" of Atlantis, and he had read their acts — as in the sacred mythologies of ancient Greeks, Phoenicians, and Hindus — as "a confused recollection of real historical events." Similarly, Donnelly had identified Atlantean religion as sun-worship in the tradition of Egypt and Peru, had estimated that Atlantis's oldest colony lay "probably in Egypt," and had credited the Bronze Age implements of Europe and the manufacture of iron to Atlantis. The island-continent, Donnelly said, had provided the original source for Phoenician and Mayan alphabets; it had spawned the Aryan (Indo-European) and Semitic peoples and possibly the

Turanians. With memories of the convulsive sinking of Atlantis into the sea preserved in "the Flood and Deluge legends of the different nations of the old and new worlds," Donnelly had declared, "a few persons escaped in ships and on rafts, and carried to the nations east and west the tidings." [64]

All of this had been so much preparation for Donnelly's bottom line. The good news that his work proclaimed was that the Atlanteans were, "in some respects," a lot like the British. "There were the same, and even greater, race differences in the population," Donnelly confided. There was "the same plantation of colonies in Europe, Asia, and America; the same carrying of civilization to the ends of the earth." Indeed, Donnelly waxed, "England, with a civilization Atlantean in origin, peopled by races from the same source, is repeating in these modern times the empire of Zeus and Chronos." That the United States had separated politically from its own island parent was no obstacle to the grand proclamation of connection, for — as Donnelly told it — the "race characteristics" remained "after the governmental connection had ceased." With England, the modern branch from the Atlantean tree, Donnelly could conclude enthusiastically that "this lost people were our ancestors, their blood flows in our veins; the words we use every day were heard, in their primitive form, in their cities, courts, and temples." Assuredly, Donnelly thought, "every line of race and thought, of blood and belief, leads back to them." [65]

Once, in his classic essay "From Edwards to Emerson," Perry Miller argued memorably that New England Transcendentalism had been a "natural reaction of some descendants of Puritans and Quakers to Unitarian and commercial times." [66] In that context, if we read "Unitarian" as "liberal" and "free-thinking," then Donnelly's Atlantean thesis was an equally natural reaction to Unitarian, commercial, and *scientific* times. Even as he pursued a political career in a populist middle America that feared the onslaught of commerce, Donnelly had poured over the latest pronouncements of the science of his era; his antediluvian report was his view from the open plain to the far horizon. Significantly, though, Donnelly was no Puritan or Quaker. And his Irish Catholic legacy, with its more moderate investment in Edenic sin, was probably implicated — along with a general cultural Arminianism and perfectionism — in the only news that was missing from the Donnelly account. [67] Unlike the tale that Plato told and unlike the accounts that haunted Calvinist Christians and Cotton Mather, Donnelly, quite startlingly, had no fall from grace to report. In all the nearly five hundred pages of his work, the fate of Atlantis emerged as a lamentable natural catastrophe, with no imputation of moral guilt or blame upon the former denizens of the sunken continent.

IV

Meanwhile, in the wake of the sunken land and Donnelly's book, a scientifically minded Helena Blavatsky tooled up to write a second major work. *The Secret Doctrine* appeared in 1888. There, not reticent to compare her new work to what she had previously done, Blavatsky looked back on her earlier *Isis Unveiled* and belittled its contents in comparison with what she would reveal now. "In those days the writer hardly knew the language in which the work was written, and the disclosure of many things, freely spoken about now, was forbidden," she confessed to readers. In contrast, *The Secret Doctrine* was "not a treatise, or a series of vague theories." Rather, it contained "all that can be given out to the world in this century."[68] With its two volumes titled, respectively, "Cosmogenesis" and "Anthropogenesis," Blavatsky's massive work totaled over 1,500 pages. This time around, all that could be given to the world notably included more about Atlantis.

Interwoven in Blavatsky's mix of occult metaphysics and the latest teachings of the scientists, were, in the table of contents to the second volume, at least eight specific references to Atlantis. The separate 1939 index to the original edition of *The Secret Doctrine* listed some ninety references to Atlantis and ninety-eight to Atlanteans, many of them extended over two or more pages. Significantly, the index also recorded ten references to Ignatius Donnelly and, of them, four specifically to his book *Atlantis*.[69]

It was clear, too, that Blavatsky liked what she read in Donnelly and could wax enthusiastic in his behalf. She cited "that wonderful volume of Donnelly's" and approvingly quoted its author for "bravely" announcing that "'the roots of the institutions of today reach back to the Miocene age.'" Even if she explained that Donnelly had not gone back far enough, she admitted that his statement was "an enormous allowance for a modern scholar to make." Elsewhere Blavatsky noted the "rare intuition" with which Donnelly had remarked on the Atlantean origins of modern civilization. And she was astute enough to notice that Donnelly's book had changed the sociology of Gilded Age knowledge. The theory that a giant continent had once united Africa with America, she told readers, "had greater chances than ever of becoming an accepted fact," and this "only quite lately, and after Donnelly's book had been published several years."[70]

Still, ten or so Donnelly references in a work that had spun its thesis in significant part around the Atlantean narrative was perhaps small acknowledgment. And Blavatsky was not above trying to milk her earlier *Isis Unveiled* for a more occult allusion to Atlanteans as historic predecessors than the obvious and straightforward one she had made.[71] Even so, allegations that Blavatsky had plagiarized Donnelly, made in 1895, are overwrought and do not stand to scrutiny.[72] What Blavatsky took from Donnelly she elaborated and transformed in ways that made it markedly her own metaphysical creation. For Blavatsky used the drowned inhabitants of Atlantis as protagonists in a dissident history of root races that finally eventuated in humans as the nineteenth century knew them. Constructed in the shadow not only of Donnelly but also of Charles Darwin, what Helena Blavatsky proposed — or, better, proclaimed — was a counternarrative of evolution that unfolded according to incontrovertible law. This law was the ponderous burden of her "Secret Doctrine." She had absorbed it from South Asian (Hindu) literature, from the occult Buddhism that she and the Theosophical Society's cofounder Colonel Henry Steel Olcott had developed, and from the writings of fellow metaphysical travelers and assorted others.

Again and again she cited, apparently for convenience, the *Esoteric Buddhism* of the Anglo-Indian journalist Arnold P. Sinnett with its evocations of a great lost Atlantean continent and civilization. Produced, as Sinnett himself had explained, partly from materials previously published in the theosophical monthly, the *Theosophist*, Sinnett's book had functioned, as Charles J. Ryan has observed, as a "harbinger" of Blavatsky's work to come. Sinnett's materials, the author himself claimed, were the results of revelations he had received from ancient and perfected adepts whom he, with Blavatsky, called the "Mahatmas." He had not hesitated to quote his "revered Mahatma teacher" on Atlantean themes in his book, and in the reflecting hall of mirrors within the theosophical community Blavatsky in her turn now duly looked to Sinnett.[73]

Synthesizing this material, then, with Donnelly, Darwin, a hodgepodge of contemporary elite and popular scientific literature, and other sources, Blavatsky told readers of an elaborately extended series of "rounds" or world periods and races, cast against a planetary horizon beyond. In the part that is important here, during the present round a first prehistoric root race grew up on a continent called "The Imperishable Sacred Land." After that, Blavatsky declared, came a second root race on the "Hyperborean" continent, a third one on Lemuria, and a fourth on Atlantis. "The famous island of Plato of that name was but a fragment of this great Continent," she divulged as she cited Sinnett's *Esoteric Buddhism*. And Atlantis was, in her view, but marginally prehistoric. "It would be the first historical land, were the traditions of the ancients to receive more attention than they have hitherto," she lectured readers.[74] Meanwhile, the fifth root race of Blavatsky — and the one that flourished in the nineteenth century — was the Aryan race of Europe.

As she told the tale of former worlds, Helena Blavatsky wove together an account of simultaneous human descent and ascent. Mingled in her narrative were archetypal evocations that resembled myths of devolution (like golden ages turned to silver, bronze, and clay), assured declamations of a scientific law of periodicity, and newer, scientific proclamations of evolutionary progress. In this regard, Blavatsky's explanation of the plight of the Atlanteans was especially instructive.

All had not gone well with that former civilization, as Blavatsky recalled a struggle between those whom — with a Noachian echo perhaps made unawares — she called the "'sons of giants,' or the inhabitants and magicians of Atlantis," and the "'sons of God.'" The Atlanteans, according to her report, fell into sin and so begot children and monsters. At first brown-colored, they later became "black with sin," experiencing "degeneracy into magical practices and gross animality." Their evil ways grew more manifest as they approached their historical end, and their trajectory into darkness was lamentable, if predictable. For the Atlanteans had arisen as "the first progeny of *semi-divine* man after his separation into sexes," and they became "the first 'Sacrificers' to the *god of matter*." In fact, they were "the first anthropomorphists who worshipped form and matter," their worship degenerating "very soon into *self-worship*" and then "phallicism."

Blavatsky found all of this to be a "clue to the vexed question of the Origin of Evil"; she underscored her observation that the Atlanteans were "marked with a character of SORCERY"; and she pointedly told that they had lost the use of the "third eye."[75]

Yet, astoundingly, Blavatsky's secret teachings contained a different report on why the Atlanteans had perished — "not," she explained, "on account of their depravity, or because they had become 'black with sin,' but simply because such is the fate of every continent, which — like everything else under our Sun — is born, lives, becomes decrepit, and dies." This was in accord with what she had elsewhere identified as the "absolute universality of that law of periodicity, of flux and reflux, ebb and flow, which physical science has observed and recorded in all departments of nature." Contra periodicity, though, Blavatsky confided that the Atlanteans, as previous root races, had developed "in accordance with evolutionary law." This, too, conformed to the "Secret Doctrine." For Blavatsky also told readers that "the Secret Doctrine teaches the progressive development of everything, worlds as well as atoms; and this stupendous development has neither conceivable beginning nor imaginable end." Indeed, Blavatsky continued, "our 'Universe'" was "only one of an infinite number of Universes, all of them 'Sons of Necessity,' because links in the great Cosmic chain of Universes, each one standing in the relation of an effect as regards its predecessor, and being a cause as regards its successor."[76]

Unitarian, commercial, and scientific times, in short, had provided their gloss on American doctrines of providence and fall. Caught amidst the optimistic perfectionism embodied in Donnelly, the triumphal evolutionism of social Darwinism, the new epistemological world of comparative religions with its South Asian Indian cosmologies of cyclic ebb and flow, and the lingering legacy of a biblical fall, Blavatsky had embraced them all. If the *Secret Doctrine* had a single ultimate message, it was unity.

Blavatsky's journey to unity, however, was an extraordinarily complex and detailed one, and there is more to be said here even than Atlantean unity. If we pursue the message of a fall from grace to Blavatsky's earlier account of a third root race, we set foot on a Lemurian continent that, as a Pacific "land of lemurs," provided an ancestor and double for Atlantis. In the late nineteenth century, significantly, news of Lemuria could be read as perhaps more scientifically credible than Donnelly's reports of Atlantis. Donnelly himself had matter-of-factly acknowledged Lemuria in his famous book. "There can be no question that the Australian Archipelago is simply the mountain-tops of a drowned continent, which once reached from India to South America," he explained to readers. "Science has gone so far as to even give it a name; it is called 'Lemuria,' and here, it is claimed, the human race originated."[77]

"Science" in this case meant the published writings of Philip Lutley Sclater, erstwhile secretary of the Zoological Society of London and fellow of the Royal Society, whose interest in ornithology and, more extensively, the fauna of Central and South America, had led him to wide-ranging inquiries about geographical distribution. Friend of Thomas Huxley and Charles Darwin, Sclater could boast a small army of animals named after him.[78] In turn, he had also not been remiss to name. In keeping with evolutionary theory and his concerns regarding zoological distribution, Sclater took up the theory of a land bridge from Madagascar across southern India to the Malay Peninsula and called the bridge "Lemuria."

"Science" also meant the selectively appropriated theorizing of well-known German evolutionary biologist Ernst Heinrich Haeckel, who had reflected in print (and later changed his mind) on the probability of Sclater's Lemuria being the original habitat of humankind. In his definitive *History of Creation*, with its first published English translations in 1876, Haeckel announced his adherence "for many and weighty reasons" to the "monophyletic hypothesis" that there was "a *single primaeval home* for mankind, where he developed out of a long since extinct anthropoid species of ape."[79] Haeckel argued that neither Australia, America, nor Europe could have served as this first home, and he acknowledged that Southern Asia or Africa, on the other hand, were possible.

"But," he continued forthrightly, there were "a number of circumstances (especially chorological facts)" suggesting "that the primaeval home of man was a continent now sunk below the surface of the Indian Ocean." Supplying the familiar Indo-Madagascan outlines of its location and nodding to Sclater as its namer, Haeckel argued that the Lemurian thesis "greatly facilitate[d] the explanation of the geographical distribution of the human species by migration." Elsewhere in his lengthy work, he also noted that Sclater's Lemuria was "of great importance from being the probable cradle of the human race, which in all likelihood here first developed out of anthropoid apes," and he was not averse to labeling the territory "'Paradise'" with scientifically correct quotation marks around the proper name.[80]

Haeckel had pro forma covered himself with the fig leaf of probability. And in a later edition he would announce that the Lemurian "hypothesis — formerly advocated by me also — has of late years been opposed by such weighty considerations, especially from a geological point of view, that we must for the present give it up."[81] In the 1880s though, Helena Blavatsky and her fellow-travelers had all the science they wanted and needed, and the changing Lemurian mind of Haeckel and the rest of the scientific community lay still ahead.

Blavatsky knew all about Sclater, as her *Secret Doctrine* testified. When she proposed a name for her own third continent, which would be home for the third root-race, Blavatsky owned that the name "Lemuria" was "an invention, or an idea, of Mr. P.L. Sclater, who asserted, between 1850 and 1860, on zoological grounds the actual existence, in prehistoric times, of a Continent which he showed to have extended from Madagascar to Ceylon and Sumatra."[82] And Blavatsky knew, as well, very much about Haeckel, citing his work in various ways at least forty times in her book.[83]

Nor was the German Darwinist chiefly persona grata, despite his Lemurian credentials. He subscribed, after all, to what she called the "'animal' and 'ape' theory,'" and she complained strenuously even as she repeated his news of Lemuria. "It is only later, that reading Haeckel's 'Pedigree of Man,' it was found that the German 'Animalist' had chosen the name for his late continent. He traces, properly enough, the centre of human evolution to 'Lemuria,' but with a slight scientific variation. Speaking of it as that 'cradle of mankind,' he pictures the gradual transformation of the anthropoid mammal into the primeval savage!!"[84] And this was not all that was to Haeckel's discredit. Blavatsky energetically repudiated his theory of a "Moneron" as the origin of all life and expatiated at length against any protoplasmic thesis.[85] There was a "fundamental difference," Blavatsky argued for readers, "between the accepted (or nearly so) conclusions, as enunciated in 'The Pedigree of Man,' viz., that man and ape have a common ancestor; and the teachings of Occultism." For her part, Haeckel was an abomination, whatever his insights about Lemuria, for through him "our divine races" were "shown to be the descendants of Catarrhine apes, and our ancestor, a piece of sea slime." In short, Blavatsky's theory of common origins for all humanity told of "evolution" downward from spirit, not ascent upward from animals.[86]

V

Science marched on, leaving behind Atlantean and Lemurian speculations like so many discarded shards on the shore. But the afterlife of Atlantis and Lemuria in the metaphysical community was extensive. Blavatsky taught the teachers of the late-century, new-century metaphysical tradition, and their American contingent fanned out, attracting followings of their own and embellishing the account of lost continents to solidify a new dissident history. To trace the twists and turns, tracking the English and continental sources that fed and nourished it, would take us here too far afield.[87] But the American who had perhaps the most to do with what would become the late twentieth-century metaphysical and New Age appropriation of a dissident and "scientific" past was Edgar Cayce. The clairvoyant Cayce became renowned among metaphysicians for his trance messages regarding health and reincarnation and for his Virginia Beach Association for Research and Enlightenment. As important for the American metaphysical movement, Cayce gave so many "readings" on Atlantis that together they form a complete volume in the twenty-four-volume Edgar Cayce Library Series published by the association.

Cayce's readings recount a saga of three destructions for Atlantis with the final one foreseen in sufficient time by Atlanteans to allow them to depart. According to Cayce's trance productions, large numbers of them dispersed outward both to the east and to the west. They settled in Egypt, in the Pyrenees, in the area around the Caspian Sea, in Peru, in the Yucatan Peninsula, in other places in South and Central America, and even in the Ohio River Valley in what is now the United States. For Cayce, the technology of Atlantis was mightily advanced, and Atlanteans were particularly adept at manufacturing explosives. "Much of it," lamented Cayce, "brought destruction, hence was not for the glorifying of Him who gave the ability or who made for the activities in a material plane for the influences of the higher forces."[88]

Born in 1877 and reared in the Disciples of Christ tradition, Cayce had been a high school dropout and photographer's apprentice before his discovery of his own apparent clairvoyance in hypnotic states drastically altered his life. The Christian shaping of his life had run deep. From the time he was ten, he reportedly read the Bible entirely through during the course of each calendar year. And he had thought, at one point in his life, that he would like to become a preacher.[89] Hence, as Cayce worked through his trance productions for a seemingly endless stream of clients, there were Christian subtexts to his messages, and among them sin was clearly one.

Most of the Atlantean readings were, in fact, past-life descriptions for those who came to consult Cayce in the present. In case after case, he found a life for the "entity" on Atlantis, and in case after case the entity had fallen there into sin through overreaching pride or sensual, especially sexual, indulgence. The overall moral message was clear. The "Sons of the Creative Force" had looked upon "the daughters of men," and the results were notoriously destructive. "There crept in those pollutions, of polluting themselves with those mixtures that brought contempt, hatred, bloodshed, and those that build for desires of self *without* respects of *others'* freedom, others' wishes — and there began, then, in the latter portion of this period of development, that that brought about those of dissenting and divisions among the peoples in the lands."[90]

Cayce sketched a chronicle of conflict between Atlanteans called the Sons of Belial and others who followed the Law of the One. But he also narrated the fall of adherents to the Law of the One, who were gradually drawn into excess and dissipation. "Spiritual forces" were employed for the satisfaction of "material appetites," and the people brought destruction upon themselves. According to Cayce, there were "convulsive movements which came about in the earth through the destruction of Lemuria, Atlantis, and — in later periods — the flood." Before that eventful time, Atlantis had extended from the Gulf of Mexico to the Mediterranean; and the British West Indies, the Bahamas, and especially Bimini hinted of foregone splendor. Thus for Cayce, when the earth changes he predicted came, the portions of Atlantis close to Bimini would "rise among the first."[91]

The expected reemergence was a prophetic marker for a Caycean confession of sin. As surely as in the Genesis narrative of Adam and Eve in Eden and as clearly as in the Puritan fears of Cotton Mather, Cayce had constructed a history of decline and fall. Natural convulsions could ultimately be traced to moral ones, as Cayce repeatedly insisted. "With the continued disregard of those that were keeping the pure race and the pure peoples, of those that were to bring all these laws as applicable to the Sons of God, man brought in the rule, that combined with those natural resources of the gases, of the electrical forces, made in nature and natural form the first of the eruptions that awoke from the depth of the slow cooling earth." Adam and Eve were real enough, and they were symbolically reordered in the Caycean account to become actors in a metaphysical drama in neotheosophical form. Meanwhile, the biblical flood of Noah was identified with the second destruction of Atlantis.[92]

In short, the technological heights achieved by Atlanteans functioned as a prophetic parable for late twentieth-century America. As J. Gordon Melton summarized, "Atlantis began to function as an equivalent to the Garden of Eden as a
place of moral failure." With more and more invocations of the analogy between
the technological prowess of Atlanteans and that of late-modern Western society,
the implications were clear. Americans, as they neared the end of the twentieth
century, were "faced with the same dangers the ancients faced." [93] It remained for
the New Age movement of the 1970s and after to expand on the doctrine of earth
changes and to find therein a moral fable of its own. Cayce's trance accounts of
his soliciting "entities'" former Atlantean lives paled before a new wave of chan-
neling and past-life memories. And, witnessing to the continuing chronicle, in
1995 the *New Age Journal* could run a feature in which psychic "archeologist"
George McMullen was reported to have seen "the Lost Continent of Atlantis"
along with other remarkable sights. "'It's far out,' he admits," alleged the essay's
author.[94]

New Agers looked across a great ideological divide to the latter-day children of
the Puritans in the late twentieth-century evangelical movement. Yet as surely as
Cayce's Sons of Belial had connections with his followers of the Law of the One,
New Agers in the 1990s consented despite themselves to Puritan culture even as
they promulgated their dissident Atlantean and Lemurian history. Whatever their
protest, they were still connected to the former denizens of Eden, still original
sinners who worried with Cotton Mather about the fall of the saved from New
World grace. Champions, as they saw themselves, of the far-flung margins of new
noetic sciences, they wove them, still, with the thread of the fear of moral declension. In New Age dissident history, change and continuity went hand in hand.[95]

Notes

1. Gen. 2:8; 3:5, 23–24; 6:4, 12–20.
2. Cotton Mather, *Magnalia Christi Americana; or, The Ecclesiastical History of New-
England, from Its First Planting, in the Year 1620, unto the Year of Our Lord 1698*, 3rd ed.
(Hartford, Conn.: Silas Andrus and Son, 1853), 1:25. Italics in original. The *Magnalia* was
first published in a 788-page folio volume in London in 1702.
3. Ibid., 40.
4. Phylos the Thibetan [F.S. Oliver], *A Dweller on Two Planets; or, The Dividing of the
Way* (Los Angeles: Borden, 1940), xi, 417.
5. Ibid., 421, 423–24.
6. I originally became acquainted with the phrase "dissident history" at the annual
winter meeting of the American Society of Church History in 1993, when an audience
member, Brian Brackney, introduced the term as part of the discussion of a scholarly
paper. I do not know exactly how he defined his "dissident history," but the name stuck,
and I own my debt to his usage.
7. J. Stillson Judah, *The History and Philosophy of the Metaphysical Movements in
America* (Philadelphia: Westminster, 1967), 11–12, 22.
8. Ibid., 12–18.

9. Robert S. Ellwood and Harry B. Partin, *Religious and Spiritual Groups in Modern America*, 2nd ed. (Englewood Cliffs, N.J.: Prentice-Hall, 1988), 54. The interpretation is Ellwood's and follows that in his original edition of 1973.

10. Ibid., 55.

11. Ibid., 55–71.

12. For American Freemasonry as a religion of the sun and of nature, see Catherine L. Albanese, *Nature Religion in America: From the Algonkian Indians to the New Age*, Chicago History of American Religion (Chicago: University of Chicago Press, 1990), 55–58.

13. Herbert Leventhal, *In the Shadow of the Enlightenment: Occultism and Renaissance Science in Eighteenth-Century America* (New York: New York University Press, 1976); David D. Hall, *Worlds of Wonder, Days of Judgment: Popular Religious Belief in Early New England* (New York: Knopf, 1989), esp. 71–116; Jon Butler, *Awash in a Sea of Faith: Christianizing the American People* (Cambridge, Mass.: Harvard University Press, 1990), 67–97, 83.

14. Sydney E. Ahlstrom, *A Religious History of the American People* (New Haven, Conn.: Yale University Press, 1972), 1019, 1019–54, 488–90, 1025, 1052.

15. Harold Bloom, *The American Religion: The Emergence of the Post-Christian Nation* (New York: Simon and Schuster, 1992), 21 (emphasis in original), 15–16, 31, 35.

16. Ibid., 103, 259–60.

17. See, for example, H.D.P. Lee, trans., "Appendix on Atlantis," in Plato, *Timaeus and Critias*, trans. H.D.P. Lee (Middlesex, Eng.: Penguin Books, 1971), who called Plato's efforts "the first work of science fiction" (153); James Bramwell, *Lost Atlantis* (London: Cobden-Sanderson, 1937), who concluded that Atlantis was myth; L. Sprague de Camp, *Lost Continents: The Atlantis Theme in History, Science, and Literature* (New York: Dover, 1970), who considered Plato's work on Atlantis a "fascinating fiction" with a "moral and philosophical purpose" (275–76); and Edwin S. Ramage, ed., *Atlantis: Fact or Fiction?* (Bloomington: Indiana University Press, 1978), which argued the latter from literary, mythological, historical, and geological perspectives.

18. Plato *Timaeus* (trans. H.D.P. Lee), 24–25.

19. Plato *Critias* (trans. H.D.P. Lee), 108–9, 113, 115, 116–18, 119.

20. Ibid., 120–21.

21. See the classic study by Peter N. Carroll, *Puritanism and the Wilderness: The Intellectual Significance of the New England Frontier, 1629–1700* (New York: Columbia University Press, 1969).

22. This was perhaps most cogently expressed in Puritan miscegenation fears. See, for example, David D. Smits, "'We Are Not to Grow Wild': Seventeenth-Century New England's Repudiation of Anglo-Indian Intermarriage," *American Indian Culture and Research Journal* 11, no. 4 (1987): 1–31.

23. For a brief but useful overview, see *The Encyclopedia of Philosophy*, ed. Paul Edwards (New York: Macmillan, 1967), s.v. "Ramus, Peter."

24. See the discussion in Perry Miller, *The New England Mind: The Seventeenth Century* (Cambridge, Mass.: Harvard University Press, 1963), 98–99.

25. Perry Miller, *Errand into the Wilderness* (1956; rpt., New York: Harper Torchbooks, 1964), 184–85.

26. Ralph Waldo Emerson, *Nature*, in *Nature, Addresses, and Lectures*, vol. 1 of *The Collected Works of Ralph Waldo Emerson*, ed. Alfred R. Ferguson et al. (Cambridge, Mass.: Belknap Press of Harvard University Press, 1971), 42.

27. Edgar Allan Poe, "The City in the Sea (1831–1845)," in *The Collected Works of*

Edgar Allan Poe, ed. Thomas Ollive Mabbott (Cambridge, Mass.: Belknap Press of Harvard University Press, 1969), 201–2. Mabbott comments in detail on a Dead Sea reading for the poem (197–98).

28. David Jaffee, "The Village Enlightenment in New England, 1760–1820," *William and Mary Quarterly* 47 (July 1990): 327–28.

29. Nathan O. Hatch, *The Democratization of American Christianity* (New Haven, Conn.: Yale University Press, 1989), 9–10.

30. The term "Sheilaism" derives from Robert N. Bellah et al., *Habits of the Heart: Individualism and Commitment in American Life* (Berkeley and Los Angeles: University of California Press, 1985), 221, 235, where it is used to describe a private and individual faith self-consciously created by one of the research subjects.

31. Ralph Waldo Emerson to Thomas Carlyle, Nov. 20, 1834, in Joseph Slater, ed., *The Correspondence of Emerson and Carlyle* (New York: Columbia University Press, 1964), 109.

32. See Emanuel Swedenborg, *Heaven and Its Wonders and Hell, from Things Heard and Seen*, trans. J.C. Ager (1852; rpt., New York: Swedenborg Foundation, 1964).

33. See the account in Robert C. Fuller, *Mesmerism and the American Cure of Souls* (Philadelphia: University of Pennsylvania Press, 1982), esp. 96–99.

34. See David S. Reynolds, *Beneath the American Renaissance: The Subversive Imagination in the Age of Emerson and Melville* (New York: Knopf, 1988).

35. See Jan Shipps, "The Prophet Puzzle: Suggestions Leading toward a More Comprehensive Interpretation of Joseph Smith," *Journal of Mormon History* 1 (1974): 3–20; Jan Shipps, *Mormonism: The Story of a New Religious Tradition* (Urbana: University of Illinois Press, 1985), esp. relevant portions of the chronological appendix (151–53); D. Michael Quinn, *Early Mormonism and the Magic World View* (Salt Lake City: Signature Books, 1987), esp. 27–77, 127–33, 13; Kenneth W. Godfrey, "Joseph Smith and the Masons," *Journal of the Illinois State Historical Society* 64 (Spring 1971): 79–90. For anti-Masonry in New York, see Alice Felt Tyler, *Freedom's Ferment: Phases of American Social History from the Colonial Period to the Outbreak of the Civil War* (1944; rpt., New York: Harper Torchbooks, 1962), 351–57; and for the "burned-over district," see Whitney R. Cross, *The Burned-Over District: The Social and Intellectual History of Enthusiastic Religion in Western New York, 1800–1850* (1950; rpt., New York: Harper Torchbooks, 1965).

36. *Book of Mormon*, Alma 37:22.

37. Andrew Jackson Davis, *The Principles of Nature, Her Divine Revelations, and a Voice to Mankind* (New York: S.S. Lyon and W. Fishbough, 1847).

38. Andrew Jackson Davis, *The Principles of Nature, Her Divine Revelations, and a Voice to Mankind*, 34th ed. (Boston: Colby and Rich, Banner of Light, 1881; rpt., Mokelumne Hill, Calif.: Health Research, 1984), 1:i. I cite this edition in all references that follow.

39. On Fishbough's efforts, see Robert W. Delp, "Andrew Jackson Davis: Prophet of American Spiritualism," *Journal of American History* 54, no. 1 (1967): 44.

40. Davis, *Principles of Nature*, 1:xxiii. Emphasis in original.

41. Ibid., 217.

42. Ibid., 329, 330, 332. Emphasis in original.

43. R. Laurence Moore, *In Search of White Crows: Spiritualism, Parapsychology, and American Culture* (New York: Oxford University Press, 1977), 7.

44. Ibid., 36.

45. The best discussion and summary of these trends in spiritualism may be found in Moore, *In Search of White Crows*, 3–39.

46. For the Theosophical Society as a spiritualist reform movement, see Stephen Prothero, "From Spiritualism to Theosophy: 'Uplifting' a Democratic Tradition," *Religion and American Culture: A Journal of Interpretation* 3, no. 2 (Summer 1993): 197–216.

47. H.P. Blavatsky, *Isis Unveiled: A Master-Key to the Mysteries of Ancient and Modern Science and Theology* (1977; rpt., Los Angeles: Theosophy Company, 1975), 1:557–58. Emphasis in original.

48. Ibid., 558. Emphasis in original.

49. In an essay that originally appeared in the *Theosophist* 3, no. 5 (Feb. 1882): 113–15, Blavatsky cited Jules Verne and his *Voyage round the Moon*, an English-language translation of his *De la Terre a la Lune*. See H.P. Blavatsky, "Spiritualism and Occult Truth," in H.P. Blavatsky, *Collected Writings*, vol. 3, 1881–82 (Wheaton, Ill.: Theosophical Publishing House, 1991), 472. I am indebted to Darryl Caterine for bringing this material to my attention.

50. Michel Lamy, *Jules Verne, Initié et Initiateur: La clé du secret de Rennes-le-Château et le trésor des Rois de France* (Paris: Payot, 1984). I am indebted to Darryl Caterine for bringing this work to my attention.

51. Jules Verne, *Twenty Thousand Leagues under the Sea*, trans. and annotated by Walter James Miller and Frederick Paul Walter (Annapolis, Md.: Naval Institute Press, 1993), 266. See, also, the useful introduction to the volume, vii-xxi.

52. Ibid., 266–67.

53. De Camp, *Lost Continents*, 257.

54. See S.B. Liljegren, *Bulwer-Lytton's Novels and ISIS UNVEILED*, Essays and Studies on English Language and Literature, no. 18 (Upsala: A.-B. Lundequistska Bokhandeln, 1957); and S.B. Liljegren, "Quelques Roman Anglais: Source Partielle d'une Religion Moderne," in *Mélanges d'Histoire Littéraire Générale et Comparée Offerts a Fernand Baldensperger, Tome Deuxième* (Paris: Librairie Ancienne Honoré Champion, 1930), 60–77. I am indebted to Brian Wilson for bringing this material to my attention.

55. The Right Hon. Lord Lytton [Edward Bulwer-Lytton], *The Coming Race* (1871; rpt., London: George Routledge, 1877), 51–52.

56. For Bulwer-Lytton and Golden Dawn, see Lamy, *Jules Verne*, 190–91.

57. For an account of Donnelly's political career, see Martin Ridge, *Ignatius Donnelly: The Portrait of a Politician* (Chicago: University of Chicago Press, 1962), and David D. Anderson, *Ignatius Donnelly* (Boston: Twayne, 1980).

58. Ignatius Donnelly, *Atlantis: The Antediluvian World* (New York: Harper and Brothers, 1882).

59. See the account in Ridge, *Ignatius Donnelly*, 201–2.

60. Anderson, *Ignatius Donnelly*, 34; Ridge, *Ignatius Donnelly*, 202.

61. Ignatius Donnelly, *Atlantis: The Antediluvian World* (1882; rpt., New York: Harper and Brothers, 1910), 22, 28, 30.

62. Ibid., 40, 42, 46, 49–50, 54, 55, 59, 61.

63. Ibid., 65–66, 72, 73, 130 (emphasis in original).

64. Ibid., 1–2.

65. Ibid., 475–76, 479.

66. Miller, *Errand into the Wilderness*, 189.

67. With a mother and five sisters who were devoutly Roman Catholic — one sister, Cecilia Eleanor Donnelly, composed devotional poetry for which she became known — Ignatius Donnelly left Catholicism by the 1850s and never participated in organized religion thereafter. His first wife, though, was a practicing Catholic and his second a practic-

ing Methodist. Significantly, Donnelly had been named for the founder of the Jesuit order, and his full baptismal name was Ignatius Loyola Donnelly. See Anderson, *Ignatius Donnelly*, 21–22.

68. H.P. Blavatsky, *The Secret Doctrine: The Synthesis of Science, Religion, and Philosophy*, 2 vols. (1888; rpt., Los Angeles: Theosophy Company, 1974), xxxviii.

69. [The Theosophy Company, comp.], *Index to* THE SECRET DOCTRINE *By H.P. Blavatsky* (Los Angeles: Theosophy Company, 1939), 14–15, 42.

70. Blavatsky, *Secret Doctrine*, 2:266n, 782n, 791.

71. Blavatsky claimed that in *Isis Unveiled* she had pointed to Atlanteans as predecessors in her allusions to the Book of Job. In it, she said, there were references to dead "giants, or mighty primitive men, from whom 'Evolution' *may one day trace our present race*." See Blavatsky, *Secret Doctrine*, 2:496 (emphasis in original); and, for comparison, see Blavatsky, *Isis Unveiled*, 1:133.

72. William Emmette Coleman argued polemically in a short essay (preceding a promised longer work that was never forthcoming) that "Donnelly's *Atlantis* was largely plagiarized from." He went on to allege that Blavatsky "coolly appropriated" a series of "detailed evidences" of the connections of Eastern with Atlantean civilization without crediting Donnelly. Citing chapter and verse, Coleman wrote that "Vol. ii., pp. 790–793, contains a number of facts, numbered *seriatim*, said to prove this Atlantean derivation [of Eastern civilization]. These facts were almost wholly copied from Donnelly's book, ch. iv., where they are also numbered *seriatim*: but there is no intimation in *Secret Doctrine* that its author was indebted to Donnelly's book for this mass of matter" (William Emmette Coleman, "The Sources of Madame Blavatsky's Writings," Appendix C, in Vsevolod Sergyeevich Solovyoff, *A Modern Priestess of Isis*, trans. Walter Leaf [London: Longmans, Green, 1895], 358). I am indebted to Brian Wilson for locating this material for me.

A comparison of Donnelly's part 3, chapter 4, with Blavatsky's *Secret Doctrine* reveals overall dependence not simply on this Donnelly chapter but, more generally, on all of Donnelly's book. There is no clear verbal dependency that I can locate in the three-page sequence Coleman identifies; the series in Blavatsky is different from the series in Donnelly's chapter; Donnelly is cited twice and, beyond that, quoted at some length once. Blavatsky did quote from original sources that were also quoted in Donnelly's book. She did not, however, acknowledge that she took quoted material from the secondary source that Donnelly's book constituted — a research-and-writing shortcut that it is likely that she did take. In fact, Sylvia Cranston, Blavatsky's recent theosophical biographer, tells that "in *Isis Unveiled*, HPB frequently gave credit to the original author but not to the secondary source." Of Blavatsky's work, in general, Cranston writes: "As was common in books of her day, HPB's works had no bibliographies. However, her secondary sources were often referred to in the text when quoting primary material; thus the reader became aware of the book as a worthy source of information" (Sylvia Cranston, *HPB: The Extraordinary Life and Influence of Helena Blavatsky, Founder of the Modern Theosophical Movement* [New York: G.P. Putnam's Sons, Jeremy P. Tarcher/Putnam Book, 1994], 380–81). Cranston seems essentially correct.

73. Charles J. Ryan, *H.P. Blavatsky and the Theosophical Movement*, 2nd and rev. ed., ed. Grace F. Knoche (Pasadena: Theosophical University Press, 1975), 111; A.P. [Arnold Percy] Sinnett, *Esoteric Buddhism* (Boston: Houghton Mifflin, 1883), x-xi, 55, 44–65. The "Mahatma" Sinnett specifically cited was Master Koot Hoomi, or KH. Sylvia Cranston claims, in her recent biography of Blavatsky, that "some of the metaphysical teachings given Sinnett did not commence with the letters received from KH, but came from HPB

herself" (Cranston, *HPB*, 227). On the probable identities of the Mahatmas, see the revealing short essay by Paul Johnson, "Imaginary Mahatmas," *Gnosis: A Journal of the Western Inner Traditions* 28 (Summer 1993): 24–30, in which Johnson argues that "the Masters were real persons systematically fictionalized in Blavatsky's accounts" (24).

74. Blavatsky, *Secret Doctrine*, 2:6–7, 8.

75. Ibid., 2:223, 227, 785, 272n, 723, 724, 287, 202, 306. Emphasis in original.

76. Ibid., 2:350, 1:17, 2:319, 1:43.

77. Donnelly, *Atlantis*, 32.

78. I count forty-one species in the list provided by G. Brown Goode in the biographical sketch that accompanies *The Published Writings of Philip Lutley Sclater, 1844–1896*, Smithsonian Institution, Bulletin of the United States National Museum, No. 49 (Washington, D.C.: Government Printing Office, 1896), xvi-xvii. The dates in the title refer to Sclater's publications; he was born in 1829. My preceding biographical material on Sclater is also taken from the Goode sketch, vii-xix.

79. Ernst Haeckel, *The History of Creation: Or the Development of the Earth and Its Inhabitants by the Action of Natural Causes*, trans. revised by E. Ray Lankester, 2 vols. (New York: D. Appleton, 1876), 2:325. Emphasis in original. Haeckel's work, intended by the biological scientist and Darwinian disciple, for a mixed and popular audience, first appeared in German in 1868. The earliest English translations — including the one cited here and a second edition published in London by the firm of Henry S. King, also in 1876 — reproduced the fourth German edition of 1873. E. Ray Lankester remarked by way of introduction that he "gladly undertook to revise for the publishers the present translation, which was made by a young lady" (xx).

80. Ibid., 2:325–26; 1:361; 2:325, 399.

81. See Ernst Haeckel, *The History of Creation*, 8th German ed., trans. revised by E. Ray Lankester, 4th ed. (London: Kegan Paul, Trench, Trubner, 1899), 2:437.

82. Blavatsky, *Secret Doctrine*, 2:7.

83. This is my count from the Theosophy Company's *Index to* THE SECRET DOCTRINE, 65.

84. Blavatsky, *Secret Doctrine* 1:306, 2:171. Double exclamation points are Blavatsky's. Blavatsky elsewhere (2:87n) cites as her source " '*The Pedigree of Man*,' by Ernest Haeckel, translated by Ed. B. Aveling." This work was probably Ernst Haeckel, *The Pedigree of Man and Other Essays*, trans. Edward B. Aveling (London: Freethought, 1883).

85. See, for example, ibid., 2:151, 153n, 154, 158.

86. Ibid., 2:189, 264, 190.

87. For Atlantis, the most important sources are probably W. Scott-Elliott, *The Story of Atlantis* (London: Theosophical Publishing House, 1896); Lewis Spence, *The Problem of Atlantis* (London: Rider, 1924), and the closely related *Atlantis in America* (New York: Brentano's, 1925); and Rudolf Steiner, *Atlantis and Lemuria*, trans. Agnes Blake (London: Anthroposophical Publishing, 1923), as well as, considerably later, Rudolf Steiner, *Cosmic Memory: Prehistory of Earth and Man* [*Aus der Akasha-Chronik*, orig. ed. ca. 1940], trans. Karl E. Zimmer (Englewood, N.J.: Rudolf Steiner Publications [1959]). For Lemuria, the most notable sources include the French archaeologist and physician (with an American wife) Augustus Le Plongeon, *Queen Moo and the Egyptian Sphinx* (New York: by the author, 1896); and the Anglo-American James Churchward, *The Lost Continent of Mu* (New York: Ives Washburn, 1926), as well as *The Children of Mu* (New York: Ives Washburn, 1931), and *The Sacred Symbols of Mu* (New York: Ives Washburn, 1933).

88. Edgar Cayce, in the Readings Research Department, comp., *The Edgar Cayce*

Readings, vol. 22, *Atlantis* (1987; rpt., Virginia Beach: Association for Research and Enlightenment, 1994), 23.

89. See Gina Cerminara, *Many Mansions* (1950; rpt., New York: William Morrow, 1968), 13–16.

90. Cayce, *Atlantis*, 25; see, also, 64, which duplicates the statement (emphasis in original).

91. Ibid., 30–31, 54, 61, 163.

92. Ibid., 65, 70. For Adam, see ibid., 67, 77.

93. [J. Gordon Melton,] "Atlantis," in J. Gordon Melton, Jerome Clark, and Aidan A. Kelly, *New Age Encyclopedia* (Detroit: Gale Research, 1990), 47.

94. Jim Robbins, "Psychic Raider of the Lost Ark," *New Age Journal* (Mar./Apr. 1995): 96.

95. I am indebted to Brian Wilson and Darryl Caterine for their research assistance.

Asian Religions in the United States: Reflections on an Emerging Subfield

THOMAS A. TWEED

By the end of the twentieth century Asian religions had become prominent in the American cultural landscape. Ninja Turtles, crime-fighting adolescent characters in children's cartoons and films, and Rafiki, the enigmatic baboon in Disney's *The Lion King*, meditated in the lotus position on screen. So did Bart Simpson, the animated star of the FOX television show, *The Simpsons*, who also studied Buddhist doctrines and puzzled over Zen *koans* in one 1990 episode. The Indian guru perched on the mountain to await inquirers had become a ubiquitous caricature in entertainment and advertising. A perfume was named *Samsara*; a rock band was named *Nirvana*. A film that contained a re-creation of the life of the Buddha played in theaters across the country. Avant-garde composers and abstract expressionist painters confessed Hindu, Taoist, and Buddhist influence and affiliation. So did icons of popular American culture — movie stars, rock singers, and sports heroes. At bookstores in shopping malls readers could peruse accomplished translations of many Asian sacred texts and purchase popularized accounts of yoga and meditation. Sitting at the computer, Americans could enter the "cybersangha" by joining one of several Buddhist discussion groups on the internet. Curled in bed they could tutor themselves in *The Tao of Golf* and *The Zen of Recovery*. As they traveled, they might encounter Hare Krishnas at the airport distributing almost free copies of the *Bhagavad Gita*. At the therapist's — and who didn't need therapy after all this? — they might be encouraged to try Buddhist mindfulness practice to reduce stress. Most important, in their neighborhoods, even in remote areas, they might encounter the visible presence of Asian religions in the more than 1,515 Buddhist centers and 412 Hindu centers. If they still remained unsure about Asian influence, they might be convinced by cover stories in *Time* and *Newsweek* proclaiming that the post-1965 immigrants, many of them from Asian lands, were radically changing the cultural terrain.[1]

While this Asian presence is not as new as the media would have us believe, it has not always been this way. When the first major survey of religion in the United States appeared a century and a half ago, in 1844, systematic trade with China and India had been going on for sixty years. For decades American Protestant missionaries had gone abroad to save "heathen" souls in Asia, and travelers had sent back their reports too. The first Asians to emigrate in large numbers, the Chinese, were beginning to arrive on American shores. Yet Asian religions were much less of a presence in the United States in the middle of the nineteenth century. It is not surprising, then, that Asians appeared in that first survey, Robert Baird's *Religion in America*, only as objects of Christian missionizing.[2]

But the cultural situation has changed, and so should our teaching and research. I decided that the best way to encourage change in the classroom and the study was not to offer a sustained case study, although we need many more of those too. Instead, because the subfield is so new and undeveloped, I thought it would be most helpful to offer reflections about what has been done and what might be done. The new subfield of Asian religions in America includes scholars trained primarily in Asian traditions as well as those whose main area of specialization has been American religions. I do not write exclusively, or even primarily, for those who already have expertise in this subfield, however. Rather, I write for those who study religion in North America but have little background in the history of Asian religions in the United States.[3]

I divide this chapter into three sections. I open by highlighting the diversity among Asian peoples and religions in the United States, trying to introduce readers to the topic and correct some widely shared misconceptions. Next, I assess the scholarship on Asian religions in America, focusing on Hinduism and Buddhism, and offer suggestions for future research. Finally, I consider the significance of the Asian presence for the teaching and writing of American religious history. Toward that end I identify three themes that arise from the study of Asian religions in the United States that offer illuminating angles of vision on the broader contours of the religious history of America.

Diversity: On Asians and Asian Religions

From the earliest American encounters with Asia, a major problem has been that diverse religions and peoples have been lumped together in the popular imagination. As one scholar has noted, "Throughout their history in this country, Asians have been struggling in different ways to help America accept and appreciate its diversity." The same has happened with their religions. Nineteenth-century interpreters regularly confused Hinduism and Buddhism, and fused all traditions outside Christianity and Judaism as "Oriental" religion. Almost everyone in America did this before 1840, and many did so for years after that. Even sophisticated interpreters made these mistakes. These problems persisted into the next century. For example, only a very small proportion of the Asian Indian immigrants who arrived in the first decades of the twentieth century actually were

Hindus, even though that was how they often were portrayed in the press at that time. A third of those Indian immigrants were Muslims, and most were Sikhs.[4]

It is crucial, then, to distinguish the multiple ethnic groups on the one hand from the many religious traditions on the other. Among the immigrants from Asia several groups have been most influential numerically and culturally—Chinese, Japanese, Indians, Sri Lankans, Koreans, Filipinos, Laotians, Thais, Cambodians, and Vietnamese. These immigrants affiliated with a range of religions when they arrived, including Hinduism, Buddhism, Islam, Sikhism, Zoroastrianism, Jainism, Shinto, and Christianity. Although most immigrants from Thailand are Buddhists and most from the Philippines are Catholics, there is no exact correspondence between nationality and religion. In many cases, the situation is quite complex. I already have mentioned the religious diversity among Asian Indians. There is a similar complexity among Vietnamese, for example. Although Roman Catholics constitute approximately 10 percent of the Vietnamese population, they are disproportionately represented among emigrants to America. As many as 29 to 40 percent of Vietnamese refugees in the United States affiliate with Catholicism. Most Vietnamese, in the homeland and in the diaspora, are Buddhists. To make it more complicated, some describe themselves as Taoist and Confucian, and influences from those traditions also have shaped the native and transplanted cultures significantly.[5]

Diversity also appears, of course, within each of the religious traditions themselves. To consider the two religions that I focus on here, there are multiple Hinduisms and Buddhisms. The very notion of unified traditions called "Hinduism" and "Buddhism" arose, to a great extent, as an imaginative construct of Western interpreters, especially during the eighteenth and nineteenth centuries. Within each of these so-called traditions multiple religious forms have appeared, varying significantly according to differences in nationality, ethnicity, region, gender, and class. Still obscuring much of this complexity, then, here I introduce readers who are unfamiliar with these religions to some of the forms that have found their way to the United States.[6]

Hinduism's diverse expressions have been especially difficult to classify. Many textbooks rely on the schema found to some extent in the *Bhagavad Gita* but which elite Hindus in the nineteenth century used as an apologetic device. That schema distinguishes three (or sometimes four) *margas* or paths to the religious goal—*karmamarga*, the path of action; *jñanamarga*, the path of knowledge; and *bhaktimarga*, the path of devotion. This classification, however, obscures the complexity of religion in India and the diaspora.

It is more useful to rely on Gerald James Larson's typology of the five major forms of Hinduism in the United States: (1) secular Hinduism, (2) nonsectarian Hinduism, (3) devotional (*bhakti*) Hinduism, (4) reformist-nationalist neo-Hinduism, and (5) guru-internationalist-missionizing neo-Hinduism. Secular Hindus, according to Larson, include mostly professional Indian males who do not affiliate with any religion, Hindu or other, but have been shaped by Hindu cultures. The devotional type, the third that he identifies, has been important in

India and America. Bhaktis' religiousness focuses on personal devotion to one or more deities in the Hindu pantheon — including Vishnu, Shiva, and the Mother Goddess in their various forms. This devotional religiousness might involve a range of beliefs and practices. Among the most important are the rituals of image worship (*puja*) in the home or the temple. As with one family I interviewed in northern California, members of the same multigenerational household each might ritually express primary devotion to different deities. That also is true in India. In the United States, however, other changes have occurred in temple worship. In India, temples are dedicated to a particular god or goddess, and they also enshrine his or her divine consorts and manifestations. In America, temples tend to be even more religiously eclectic. They often enshrine many unrelated deities as well in order to accommodate the regional, linguistic, ethnic, and religious diversity of Asian Indian devotees in America. For example, the Hindu Temple in Flushing, New York, was erected to honor the god Ganesh, the elephant-headed lord of auspicious occasions, but additional shrines for devotees of Vishnu and Shiva also were added. The Sri Venkateswara Temple in Pittsburgh, which was dedicated in 1977 and has since become a major pilgrimage site for North American Hindus, also necessarily accommodates multiple regional, linguistic, and devotional backgrounds.

As Larson notes, also among Americans shaped by Hinduism are "nonsectarian" Hindus who do not identify with any particular branch of Hinduism but who draw on a range of religious practices that originate in their native caste or region. "Reformist-nationalist neo-Hindus," a fourth type of follower in the United States, identify with one of the reform groups that arose before and after Indian independence in 1947. For example, the Ramakrishna Mission, which draws inspiration from the teachings of Ramakrishna Paramahmsa (1836–86), was founded by Swami Vivekananda in 1897. It promoted monistic Vedanta philosophy and advocated a program for social reform. Finally, small numbers of Asian Indians and larger numbers of American converts identify with "guru-internationalist-missionary neo-Hinduism." That category includes groups with twentieth-century Indian founders who sought to spread their teachings broadly in Asia and the West, including Transcendental Meditation and the Hare Krishna movement.[7]

A similar complexity characterizes Buddhism in the United States. The term "Buddhism" is relatively recent, perhaps three centuries old. Many forms of belief and practice have been associated with this pan-Asian religion. Sometimes the intrareligious differences are so significant that an outsider might wonder to what extent they arise from the same tradition. Sometimes all they seem to have in common is that practitioners proclaim that they take the life and teachings of Shakyamuni Buddha as normative in some way.

The best way to capture the diversity of Buddhist traditions that have been transplanted to the United States would be to describe fully followers' differences based on national, regional, ethnic, and class backgrounds. Since that is impossible here I rely on another schema that some followers and scholars have used to make sense of this complexity. They have distinguished three major forms of Buddhism, or three Buddhist "vehicles" — *Hinayana, Mahayana,* and *Vajrayana.*

The first form was named by its opponents, who called it the "small vehicle" or Hinayana. It is not surprising that this term offends many followers and scholars, who prefer other labels — *Theravada,* which means "Teaching of the Elders" and refers to the last surviving Hinayana sect, or "Southern Buddhism," which identifies the region of Asia in which it predominated. There are difficulties with all three of these labels, however. I will spare readers the intricacies of the terminological debates but use instead a more inclusive and accurate, and less offensive, designation for this first kind of Buddhism — *Nikaya* Buddhism (literally "sectarian Buddhism") — which alludes to the eighteen early Buddhist "schools" or "monastic orders." This Nikaya Buddhism described a gradual path of individual religious flourishing that was established in the first centuries after the Buddha's death. The original Buddhist community was entirely renunciant, with lay supporters of various degrees of dedication offering contributions. Later, within these monastic orders, various beliefs and practices developed that ultimately led to the proliferation of the eighteen sects or schools (*nikaya*). Since then, these sectarian lay Buddhists have followed the precepts of the Buddha, but they have not engaged in the same renunciations that lead more directly to nirvana, though they gain "merit" that might help them in future lives by supporting the monks and nuns. Nikaya Buddhism has had great influence in Southeast Asian countries such as Sri Lanka, Burma, Thailand, and Cambodia. In the United States, immigrants from South and Southeast Asia have brought forms of this sectarian Buddhism, and Insight (*Vipassana*) Centers for meditation that derive from Buddhist practices of those regions have attracted some converts.[8]

Mahayana Buddhists were those who dismissed their opponents as the "lesser" vehicle. Their "great" vehicle emphasized the active virtue of compassion as well as the reflective virtue of wisdom, which has been so highly valued by Nikaya followers. The ideal set out for Nikaya Buddhism was that of the *Arahant,* one who is free from all fetters, defilements, and impurities through the realization of nirvana and, so, free from all subsequent rebirth. Mahayanists, on the contrary, elevated the ideal of the *Bodhisattva,* the suprahuman being who combines both wisdom and compassion. It was the pursuit of this ideal of the Bodhisattva that was the distinguishing feature of the Mahayana sects and schools that predominated in East Asian nations like China, Korea, and Japan. And in the United States several forms of Mahayana have had significant influence. The first Asian immigrants, Chinese and Japanese, brought forms of Mahayana Buddhism, especially Pure Land, which focuses on devotion to Amida Buddha. Some more recent immigrants, like the Vietnamese, have transplanted their own forms of Mahayana as well. Zen, another Mahayana tradition, has drawn followers of Asian and European descent, and it has had the widest cultural impact in America of any Asian tradition.

A third Buddhist path to religious fulfillment, *Vajrayana* or the "Diamond

Vehicle," went further than the Mahayanists. Vajrayana Buddhists, or Tantric Buddhists, emphasized that the process to full realization could be briefer, even in this lifetime. Highlighting nondualism—the identity of *samsara* and *nirvana*, or the actual and the ideal—they also reconceived of the religious goal in texts called *tantras*. In their practice followers used sacred syllables (*mantras*) and paintings (*mandalas*). As with the other two major forms of Buddhism, this Tantric tradition had Indian roots; but it predominated in Tibet and Mongolia. In America, Tibetan Vajrayana traditions have attracted converts, though the number of Tibetan immigrants remains small. It is important to remember that although each of these three major Buddhist paths have predominated in a region, they also are found outside that area. For instance, Vietnam has Nikaya Buddhists as well as Mahayanists; and forms of Vajrayana have flourished in Japan alongside Mahayana traditions.

Buddhists in the United States have resisted and accommodated the American cultural context. Converts have transformed Buddhist traditions in significant ways, including opening them to greater participation by laity, especially women. Immigrants, who historically have had little sustained contact or cooperation with converts, have made their negotiations with American patterns too. Japanese Pure Land Buddhists, who sent missionaries to the United States in 1899, called their leaders "priests" and their buildings "churches." They founded Sunday schools and established Young Men's Buddhist Associations. By the first years of the twentieth century they sang Western-style hymns such as "Onward Buddhist Soldiers." The inattentive passerby might have mistaken them for good Methodists.[9]

More recent Buddhist immigrants have done their share of accommodating too, although most still conduct rituals in their native tongue. For example, like most Buddhists in America, the members of the *Chua Van Hanh* Pagoda in Raleigh, North Carolina, gather on Sunday mornings for collective rituals. As Baptists and Methodists elsewhere in Raleigh come together to read Christian scriptures, twenty or thirty Vietnamese meet in a small temple in a residential area to chant passages from Buddhist sacred texts. In Vietnam they might have come to the pagoda only on the first and fifteenth of the month, for major festivals such as Buddha's birthday, and when the troubles and joys of their lives moved them to offer petitions or give thanks. In the United States, however, they have accommodated American cultural and economic patterns to some extent. As the president of the North Carolina Buddhist Association told me, they worship regularly on Sundays now because work does not allow the old patterns. It does not hurt that doing so also helps them blend with their Protestant neighbors in one of the most religiously homogeneous states in the nation.[10]

Research on Asian Religions in the United States: An Assessment

Scholars have considered some of these diverse forms of Asian religions in the United States, especially in three main areas—religious and cultural encounter, European-American converts, and Asian-American adherents.[11]

Religious and Cultural Encounter

So far most of the research has analyzed religious and cultural encounters between Americans and Asians. The first of these contacts occurred in homes and
libraries as those in the North American continent read the reports of missionaries, travelers, diplomats, and traders. This was the nature of the encounter for the
Puritan divine John Cotton and the earliest colonists in America who had literary
contacts with Asian religions. Other articles and books tell important parts of the
story of contact and influence, but the best introduction to these intellectual
encounters from the colonial period to the progressive era is Carl Jackson's careful
study of *The Oriental Religions and American Thought*. He also offers a useful
guide to the literature on the history of this intellectual contact in his article,
"The Influence of Asia upon American Thought: A Bibliographical Essay," although that piece would need to be supplemented by a review of work published
since 1984.[12]

In some ways, America's intellectual encounter with Asian religions began in
1784. It was in that year that the first American ship landed in Asian ports and
systematic trade with China and India opened. The first accounts by travelers,
diplomats, and traders offered American readers impressions of Asian religions.
The published journal of Major Samuel Shaw, who participated in the first voyage to Asia, and the narrative of Amasa Delano, who traveled to China and India
in the 1790s, are key primary sources. But of the many secondary sources on
the commercial and diplomatic relations between the United States and Asian
nations, little of it deals directly with religion.

It is not surprising that the literature on foreign missions in Asia explores the
religious dimensions of the encounter more fully. Some of the earliest sources of
information for European and American audiences were the published accounts
of missionaries. These direct contacts began two years after the American Board
of Commissioners for Foreign Missions was formed in 1810, and they were carried
out with extraordinary vigor until 1920 or so, and, with some changes in aims and
means, continue to this day. A number of more narrowly focused studies shed
light on these developments, and books that aim to survey American foreign
missionary activity more broadly are especially useful, for instance, William R.
Hutchison's *Errand to the World* and Clifton Philips's *Protestant America and the
Pagan World*.[13]

There always is room for new stories told well, but I think two kinds of studies
on these topics would be especially welcome — further analyses of the *religious*
significance of commercial and diplomatic and travel contacts and more *theoretically* informed studies of all these transoceanic encounters. On the latter
point, a historical narrative that was shaped by categories drawn from, say, cultural studies and anthropology, might open new angles of vision on the processes
at work in these religious and cultural encounters.[14]

Most of the missionaries and travelers who sent back their reports about the
"heathens" abroad were religiously conservative by almost any standard, but religious liberals and radicals since the Enlightenment also have played an impor-

tant role in the encounters with Asia. In fact, much of the scholarly literature has focused on this. The Enlightenment fascination with Asian religions, especially Confucianism, was not as strong in the United States as it was in Europe, but a number of American intellectuals expressed interest, including John Adams and Benjamin Franklin. Unitarian writers of the first decades of the nineteenth century, such as Joseph Priestley and Hannah Adams, led the way in considering other traditions as well, including Hinduism and Buddhism. Later liberals and radicals — Unitarians, Transcendentalists, and Free Religionists — deepened the intellectual encounter. As early as the 1960s Sydney Ahlstrom and George Hunston Williams traced these developments, and more recently others have built on their work.[15]

Literary critics and religious historians have been fascinated by the American Transcendentalists and their interest in Asia. Frederick I. Carpenter's pioneering study, *Emerson and Asia*, appeared in 1930, and two years later Arthur E. Christy followed with *The Orient in American Transcendentalism*. Since then Roger Mueller, Carl Jackson, Thomas Tweed, Arthur Versluis and others have added characters and motifs to the narrative about the first- and second-cycle Transcendentalists. We are not yet to the level of sophistication and saturation that we have reached with the study of, say, Jonathan Edwards, but scholars planning to write more on Transcendentalism and Asian religions need to expand significantly the characters or shift considerably the approach to justify another study.[16]

The first scholars to explore Asian influences on the Transcendentalists and other religious liberals were specialists in literature, and that is not surprising since the impact from Asia has been significant in a number of areas of elite and popular culture. Information about Asian cultures and religions shaped the first genre of religious fiction in the United States, the Oriental tale. Mukhtar Ali Isani's unpublished dissertation and David Reynold's chapter on the topic remain among the few direct treatments of the Oriental tale. A number of briefer studies of individual writers — from Ralph Waldo Emerson and T. S. Eliot to Jack Kerouac and J.D. Salinger — have appeared. They trace Asian religious influences on later American poets and novelists; Beongcheon Yu surveys that topic in *The Great Circle: American Writers and the Orient*.[17]

Religious influences on American art, architecture, artifacts, and music are somewhat more difficult to trace, but art historians, folklorists, and musicologists have begun. The influx of first Chinese and later Japanese artifacts had its influence. Scholars who have written about the China trade have noted the impact on American domestic furnishings. Most scholars believe that Buddhist and Taoist principles shaped Japanese wood block prints in some ways, and American painters who participated in the vogue for Japanese things in the late nineteenth century — including James McNeill Whistler, Mary Cassat, and Winslow Homer — found themselves moved by what they saw. American painters in the twentieth century continued to turn to Asia for themes and techniques. The catalogue for the exhibition, "The Transparent Thread: Asian Philosophy in Recent American Art," explored the topic; but much more work remains to be done.

The same is true with music. Twentieth-century composers such as John Cage and Philip Glass have acknowledged that Asian religions have shaped their work in profound ways, but so far little scholarship has explored this. Even more surprising, there has been little sustained attention given the influence of Asian religions in popular music, especially rock and roll, during and since the 1960s. The same problems arise with most investigations of the religious significance of material culture and music: it can be a methodological challenge to extract meaning from nonverbal sources, and most scholars who have written on these topics have not been trained in religious studies.[18]

More work has been done on philosophical and theological encounters. Works already cited — those by Jackson and Ahlstrom — trace some of the early history of such encounters. Studies of individual thinkers explore these intellectual contacts, and Dale Riepe traced India's influence on American thought in a 1970 book. More recently, some Americans have "dialogued" with Hindus and Buddhists, exploring conceptual continuities and discontinuities. Although such encounters actually began earlier, many scholars date them from the World's Parliament of Religions of 1893, the meetings held in Chicago in conjunction with the World's Columbian Exposition. Recently a good deal of research on that intriguing event has begun to appear. One book was published in association with the Council for a Parliament of World's Religions, which organized an event in 1993 to celebrate the anniversary of the original meeting. In that work, *Dawn of Religious Pluralism*, Richard H. Seager has collected many of the speeches delivered at the nineteenth-century celebration. He also authored one of the books devoted to the Parliament. Eric Ziolkowski collected some Parliament speeches and later essays that attempt to assess the significance of the event. Other books, dissertations, and articles have considered the Parliament as well. Part of the significance of the Parliament was that Asian advocates of Hinduism, Buddhism, Confucianism, Jainism, and Zoroastrianism had center stage in American public space. That was important in its own right, but it also shaped the religious lives of some Americans in important ways.[19]

European–American Converts

Several of those Asian spokesmen — and they were men — would go on to draw European-American converts to Buddhism and Hinduism, and those converts have been the subject of some studies. Vivekananda, the most popular Asian speaker at the Parliament, toured the country, and his popularity and that of his message grew. In 1894 a journalist for the *Boston Herald* described the contents of a recent lecture in which Vivekananda outlined basic doctrines of Hinduism, especially the Vedanta tradition with which he affiliated. As with other accounts of the period, the writer for the Boston newspaper reported that interest was swelling: "The Brahmin monk has become a fad in Boston, as he was in Chicago last year, and his earnest, honest, cultured manner has won many friends for him." Whether it was his "cultured manner" or other factors that led to the interest, it seemed real enough. In the same year, 1894, Vivekananda established the first Hindu organization in the United States, the Vedanta Society; and three years later he established the Ramakrishna Mission in India. These groups have received some scholarly attention, and Carl Jackson has written a fine book tracing the history of the movement in America.[20]

Starting in the last quarter of the nineteenth century several thousand Americans of European descent also identified themselves with Buddhism, and some of that interest had been sparked by the Buddhist speakers at the Parliament, especially the Japanese Zen teacher Soyen Shaku and the Sri Lankan Buddhist, Dharmapala. As with converts to Vedanta Hinduism, Americans who found the tradition attractive were drawn in part by its alleged tolerance. Victorian American converts to Buddhism also were drawn by the claims that it was more scientific than Christianity. I told the story of these nineteenth-century converts in *The American Encounter with Buddhism, 1844–1912*. Parts of the story also appear in Rick Fields's engaging history of Buddhism in America and in assorted books, articles, and dissertations on some of the key figures, including Paul Carus, Ernest Fenollosa, and Lafcadio Hearn.[21]

Although much of the interest in Buddhism diminished among Americans after World War I or so, some of it continued quietly until the renewed interest of the 1950s and 1960s. This middle period remains understudied, and some of its key figures remain obscure. For example, Dwight Goddard traveled to China as a Protestant missionary and returned to the United States as a Buddhist advocate. A biography of Goddard, who led an intriguing life and influenced later converts, would contribute much.[22]

Some Americans of European descent who have identified themselves with Asian religions since the late nineteenth century have advocated a blend of Western occultism and Asian religions; others have joined new religious movements that claim some Hindu or Buddhist influence. Scholars have considered these developments, and Robert S. Ellwood has led the way. He has written on the Theosophical movement, which was founded in 1875, as well as other new religious movements with Asian influences. The Theosophical Society blended interests in Asian religions with spiritualism and other occult beliefs and practices. More recently, Stephen Prothero has offered a biography of one of the Theosophical Society cofounders, Henry Steel Olcott, who formally became a Buddhist in Sri Lanka in 1880. Various new religious movements in America with Asian influences have appeared since the 1870s. The Maharishi Mahesh Yogi's Transcendental Meditation Movement and the Rajneesh International Foundation received a great deal of attention in the press. Scholars, especially social scientists, have been more interested in other groups, for example, the Hare Krishna's (International Society for Krishna Consciousness) and Nichiren Buddhists (Soka Gakkai International and Nichiren Shoshu). The latter, Buddhist new religious movements transplanted from Japan, have been the subject of a number of scholarly articles. There also are a number of shorter pieces on the Hare Krishnas in the United States, and E. Burke Rochford has written an insightful book-length study. Scholars have made a good start on these topics, but new religious movements always are changing as old groups modify and new ones appear. One fruitful area of study is the New Age movement, which is important in late twentieth century America. More attempts to disentangle the Asian influences in New Age religiousness would be helpful.[23]

Asian–American Adherents

Asians have been arriving on American shores since the middle of the nineteenth century, just as waves of European immigrants were reshaping U.S. society and culture, and Asians — especially Chinese and Japanese — were a significant presence on the West Coast and in Hawaii. The history of this migration has been the subject of several studies, and the most comprehensive is Ronald Takaki's *Strangers from a Different Shore: A History of Asian Americans*. Articles and books on the pre-1960s emigrants from Asia have tended to focus on a particular group — the Chinese, Japanese, Indians, Koreans, or Filipinos — rather than being comparative; and most of this literature ignores or diminishes the role of religion. The best survey of the Chinese in America devotes only three pages exclusively to the topic, and the best overview of Japanese immigrants contains only one page exclusively on religion. No book-length study of the religion of first-wave Asian immigrants such as Chinese, Filipinos, and Koreans has appeared; but some scholars, mostly sociologists, have traced the history of Japanese Buddhists in the United States. There are a number of articles and unpublished dissertations on the topic, but the best sources are the seventy-fifth anniversary volumes published by the Buddhist Churches of America and Tetsuden Kashima's sociological analysis, *Buddhism in America: The Social Organization of an Ethnic Religious Organization*.[24]

The Chinese Exclusion Act of 1882 restricted migration from that nation, and the immigration act of 1924 essentially ended all Asian immigration. That changed, of course, with the revision of the immigration laws in 1965; and social and cultural changes followed. In 1960 there were fewer than one million persons of Asian descent in the United States; by the middle of the 1990s that figure climbed to more than seven million. Taken together, Asians have been the fastest growing racial or ethnic minority among immigrants, increasing 143 percent between 1970 and 1980 and 108 percent in the next decade. Scholars, and the media, have noticed these "new" immigrants; but their religious life has received less attention than their economic practices.[25]

Readers who want to understand the religious life of Asian immigrants and their descendants have some help, however. Two introductory textbooks include chapters on Hinduism and Buddhism in America, and these orient readers who are unfamiliar with the subject. Most teachers and researchers will want to supplement those works. An excellent bibliography on the religions of South Asians in the Americas has been compiled by John Y. Fenton, and that is the best place to start for the study of South Asian Sikhs, Muslims, Jains, Zoroastrians, and

Hindus. Fenton also wrote one of the two major studies of Hindus in America, *Transplanting Religious Traditions: Asian Indians in America.* Raymond Brady Williams authored the other, *Religions of Immigrants from India and Pakistan,* which also treats Muslims, Sikhs, Jains, Parsis, Jews, and Christians. No one has attempted a comprehensive narrative of the history of Hinduism in America, but three surveys of Buddhism have appeared. Understandably perhaps, most concentrate on American converts and none focuses on the religions of the post-1965 immigrant followers. Two of these books — by Emma Layman and Charles Prebish — were published in the 1970s, when the increase in converts seemed more noteworthy and before most observers had begun to notice the emerging patterns in immigration.[26]

Of all the neglected areas of research in this emerging subfield of American religious history, none needs attention more than Asian immigrant religion. Some scholars have made a start. Under the sponsorship of Diana Eck's Pluralism Project at Harvard, students have done historical and ethnographic work to document the changes in the American landscape, visiting Hindu temples, Muslim mosques, Jain temples, Zoroastrian communities, Sikh gurdwaras, and Buddhist centers. Other scholars have investigated particular congregations or temples in various urban areas. Fenton focused on South Asian developments in Atlanta, while Williams offered chapters on the same subpopulations in Houston and Chicago. The Hindu specialist Fred W. Clothey documented the dedication of the first major Hindu temple, in Pittsburgh, in a chapter and a video, just as Joanne Punzo Waghorne studied similar ceremonies at a temple in Maryland. Williams analyzed one Hindu community in Glen Ellyn, Illinois, for a collaborative project on American congregations. The geographer Surinder M. Bhardwaj has discussed pilgrimage to various Hindu sacred sites in the United States. Some studies of local Buddhist communities also have begun to appear. Eui-Young Yu treated Korean Buddhism in Southern California. The sociologist Paul Rutledge analyzed the Vietnamese Buddhist community in Oklahoma City, and the Buddhist specialist Paul Numrich dealt with Nikaya Buddhism as it is practiced by Sri Lankan and Thai immigrants at temples in Chicago and Los Angeles.[27]

We need many more case studies and much more comparison. We could profit from more studies of particular temples or from analysis of multiple centers in one urban area, such as Houston, Chicago, New York, or Los Angeles. For all such studies, however, scholars need to expand the sources and methods they use. Ethnographic as well as historical methods should be employed, as investigators attempt to reconstruct the religious life of a particular community. For historians who want to enter the subspecialty, that means getting training in other methods and languages; and for all who teach about American religion that means being open to insights from other fields — anthropology, folklore, sociology, and geography.

But to understand the broader patterns, these historical and ethnographic case studies should be placed in wider contexts. We need transnational studies that trace changes from the homeland to the diaspora. We need comparisons of the history of Asian religions in various Western nations. Most important, we need comparisons of the religions of Asian, African, and European migrants to the United States. I return to this last point in the final section as I consider the significance of the Asian presence for the study of religion in the United States.[28]

Significance for American Religious History: Three Themes

Readers might have been willing to follow my analysis this far, but some might wonder about the significance of the Asian presence for teaching and writing American religious history. So what? the skeptical reader might ask. Ultimately, readers will decide if anything is worth considering in all these developments. I thought that it might help, however, if I offered my own preliminary reflections on how attention to Asian religions in the United States might affect how we narrate the broader story in the classroom and in print. In most cases, what the Asian presence teaches us reinforces and deepens things we already know about American religion. In some instances, however, it illumines patterns that remain partially or wholly obscured when our focus is elsewhere. We see things in new ways.

Rather than attempt to renarrate American religious history here, I identify three themes or motifs that come into view when we focus on Asians in the United States, and these might be used to construct other narratives. I model my approach here on Jon Butler's in his essay, "Historiographical Heresy: Catholicism as a Model for American Religious History." There he correctly notes that most of the themes that have predominated in the historiography have been drawn from the experience of Puritanism — Calvinism, evangelicalism, democracy, declining religiousness, and American exceptionalism. Butler suggests that instead it might be useful to draw on six themes that emerge from the study of Catholicism — ethnic heterogeneity, spiritual heterogeneity, divine intervention, moral behavior, importance of place, and institutional authority. He employed those motifs in *Awash in a Sea of Faith*, which imaginatively renarrates U.S. religious history to the Civil War.[29]

If Butler advocated "heresy" by suggesting that we use Catholic themes to narrate the story, surely I will be consigned to historiographical hell for suggesting that we consider an Asian model. Nonetheless, I propose that three themes that emerge from the study of the Asian presence (although not only from that) illumine broader patterns in American religious history — place, identity, and contact.

Before turning to those three, however, it is worth noting another theme, diversity, which is important but hardly new. Diversity has been a guiding motif in the scholarly literature on American religions at least since Sydney Ahlstrom's encyclopedic survey, *A Religious History of the American People* (1972). Even earlier, mid-nineteenth-century observers from Europe and America noticed that multiple expressions of Christianity coexisted in the land. What changed by the end of the twentieth century was the extent of that heterogeneity. Not only have Asian immigrants brought multiple religions — not just diverse denominations of the same Christian tradition — but they also have come from various ethnic and national subpopulations. Among survey writers, Catherine L. Albanese stands out for her recognition of these emerging patterns. Her popular text, *America: Religions and Religion,* which originally appeared in 1981, contained a chapter on Asian religions. Some other scholars have noticed the Asian presence too. Yet attending to the history of Asian religions in America suggests that diversity is not just one feature of the religious landscape. It is the major one. Muslims, for instance, probably will soon surpass Jews as the second largest religious tradition in the United States, and Hindus and Buddhists combined could outnumber Jews soon too. By most counts, by the 1990s there were more Muslims than Episcopalians, more Buddhists than Quakers, more Hindus than Disciples of Christ. Attention to the Asian presence sensitizes us even further to diversity. But three other motifs, which have received less attention, seem especially promising as we think about how to narrate American religious history.[30]

Place

Some scholars already have explored to some extent the significance of place in American religious history. William Warren Sweet's influential survey, first published in 1930, developed Frederick Jackson Turner's insights about the role of the frontier in determining the character of Americans and their religion. Several decades later Edwin Gaustad's *Historical Atlas of Religion in America* alerted readers to the importance of locality, as have a number of studies on regional and local developments.[31]

Place is significant in other ways; and, to mention two, attention to Asians reminds us of the importance of domestic space and the significance of displacement. Until recently scholars have more frequently noticed public spaces, even though much work remains to be done on architecture and landscape in American religious history. As I noted, specialists also have begun to attend to sacred architecture. The construction of major Hindu and Buddhist temples, such as the Hindu Sri Meenakshi Temple in Houston and the Buddhist Hsi Lai Temple in Hacienda Heights, makes religious buildings more difficult to ignore. Even the natural terrain itself becomes sacralized not only through the construction of temples but also as the Mississippi, Monongahela, and the Rio Grande join the Ganges as sacred rivers for Hindus in America. As important, however, is the domestic environment. As in India, almost every Hindu in the United States will have a room or a space within a room for daily devotion (puja). So, too, with many immigrant Buddhists and converts. A Japanese Pure Land Buddhist in California might have a domestic altar with an image of Amida Buddha, who presides over the Pure Land; an American convert to Zen in New York City might have a corner in a bedroom reserved for daily seated meditation (*zazen*) that contains a meditation cushion, an image of the Buddha, and an incense bowl. It is natural to focus on what happens inside sacred public buildings; but much of religious life takes place in ordinary spaces. Hinduism and Buddhism, like other traditions, offer followers prescriptions about the use of food and sex, and so they shape what happens in kitchens and bedrooms as well. Scholars who have been influenced by social history and material culture studies in the past few decades have begun to consider private spaces, the artifacts that fill them, and the rituals that sacralize them. More attention is needed. The study of Asian religions reminds us of the importance of domestic religion to the story of America's religious past.[32]

The study of Asian immigrant experience also reminds us of the importance of displacement in American religious history. As Sidney Mead noticed, Americans have been "a people in movement through space." Both intracontinental and intercontinental migration have affected American history throughout. Martin Marty used the image of pilgrimage to focus his entertaining survey, *Pilgrims in Their Own Land,* and others have suggested that migration might be used as the central motif for stories of American religion. I agree. Considering how important displacement has been to Americans, however, the theme has been underemphasized. Displacement seems to be a common motif in the stories of many groups — American Indians, African Americans, German Jews, Hungarian Catholics, even British Protestants. In this regard, it can be helpful to consider both the religion of the homeland and the diaspora, and groups' mental maps of each. Of course, with Asian immigrants the narrator's focus shifts to the Pacific world. Some important differences appear when the story is told from there; but some similar cognitive, affective, and cultural processes are at work among immigrants. For instance, I have found striking parallels among first-generation Cuban Catholics and Vietnamese Buddhists in America. Both groups were forced from their natal land, and in different ways each uses religion to bridge the homeland and the new land. As one middle-aged Vietnamese man told me at a temple in North Carolina, "At first we were homesick and religion-sick, but now it's better since we have the pagoda." Similar patterns emerged among others who have been displaced, voluntarily or involuntarily, from their homelands. Scholars can become convinced of the importance of place — both domestic space and migratory movements — through the study of other groups, but awareness of the Asian presence adds to the sense that it might be one of the most illuminating motifs for the teaching and writing of American religious history.[33]

Identity

Where we are, or place, is related to who we are, or identity; and the latter is an illuminating motif as well. Ethnicity, class, and gender shape individual and collective identity, and in the past few decades scholars of religion in the United States have highlighted these. However, they have given much less attention to another contributing factor in religious identity — age. Age emerges as important in the story of both Asian-American adherents and European-American converts.

As with other traditions, religious rituals mark the shifts in the life cycles of indi-viduals — birth, maturation, marriage, childbirth, and death. That is as significant in a Buddhist funeral as in a Jewish bar mitzvah or a Christian baptism. Most converts to Asian groups in the twentieth century, as with most new religious movements in the United States, have been teenagers and young adults, those making the transition to adulthood. More important, Asian immigrants have pre-occupied themselves with intergenerational issues. To return to that Vietnamese pagoda in North Carolina, one fifty-year-old woman told me that the reason she participated so vigorously in the efforts to build the temple was the children. She worried that those born in the diaspora would not share the religious worldview of their elders, and she and other members complain that the children are more comfortable with English and know little about their inherited faith. The same is true in Hindu communities: temples are built in part to socialize the young and preserve the tradition. The study of Asian immigrant religion reminds us to consider the religious lives of children.[34]

At the same time, the transplanted symbols do not function only for the im-migrants' offspring. For those who came to the new land as children or young adults it means returning to youth, mother, and homeland. Even more so for the aged, who are, along with children, neglected by scholars. The Hindu temple in Pittsburgh, for example, was built not only for the children — although it was for them too. It also was for the grandparents. It established the new land as sacred and, at the same time, transported adults to the native country and its sources of sacrality. Of course, similar processes have occurred among other immigrant groups in America, and that is why age is one aspect of identity that would prove to be a helpful motif for new narratives.

Identity is important in another way. So far I have supposed that religious iden-tity was a relatively simple matter, as if people either affiliate with a single, unified religious tradition or they do not. As attention to the story of Asian religions in America reminds us, it is more complex in at least two regards. First, the combin-ing of religious traditions contributes to the complexity of religions. Haitian Catholics have been influenced by African cultural elements; Native American Catholics have been shaped by American Indian myths and rituals; Vietnam-ese Catholics are not entirely free of Confucian and Buddhist beliefs. In a similar way, Asian immigrants carry with them a complex and dynamic religion(s), al-ready formed by interactions among multiple traditions in their native lands. American converts, too, did not encounter a culturally isolated or religiously uni-fied tradition when they found "Hinduism" or "Buddhism" in the nineteenth century. Both traditions already had been shaped in Asia by Western beliefs and values. For instance, both the Hindu Vivekananda and the Buddhist Dharmapala had been influenced by Anglo-American Christian emphases on social activism, and that influence was evident in the reform minded movements they founded. As Buddhist studies scholars have noticed, the Buddhism that Americans en-countered through Dharmapala's teachings already had been "Protestantized" to some extent. So too twentieth-century converts have blended beliefs and prac-tices from multiple traditions. This is not only true of New Agers who might advocate both the healing powers of crystals and the efficacy of Vedanta Hindu philosophy. It also characterizes recent converts to traditional forms of Hinduism or Buddhism. American Jewish converts to Zen, for instance, bring to their adopted faith principles and practices from their preconversion lives and the surrounding culture.[35]

Attention to Asian religions in America not only reminds us that combination is common and significant, it also calls attention to another type of religious identity. Almost all scholarship — on immigrants and converts — presupposes that persons adhere to a tradition or they do not. Yet I have been struck by how many of the historical actors I have studied have fallen between traditions. Either they moved from exclusive devotion to one group after another, as Marie de Souza Canavarro did — she affiliated with, in turn, Catholicism, Theosophy, Nikaya Buddhism, Baha'i, and Vedanta Hinduism — or, more commonly, they simultaneously combined multiple religious influences. There are, for instance, those whom we might call nightstand Buddhists, who read books on Buddhist teaching and practice at night before bed and in the morning practice meditation as they learned it from one of the many how-to manuals. As I have suggested elsewhere, then, it might be helpful to focus on sympathizers as much as adherents. By "sympathizers" I mean those whose framework of meaning has been shaped in part by elements of a tradition but who blend those elements with beliefs and practices from another tradition. Most important, they fail to affiliate exclusively with the institutions of the religion with which they have some sympathy. These sympathizers might tell a pollster that they are Espicopalians or Methodists. They might say they incline toward Buddhism or Hinduism. Or they might report that they are not affiliated. In any case, they are an important part of the story of Asian religions in America; and I suspect that an interesting account of U.S. religion might be written by focusing on religious identity and concentrating on sympathizers, or dabblers, of various kinds.[36]

Contact

The story of America's religious past involves not only where we are, place, and who we are, identity, but also how we meet, contact. This third motif also arises from an Asian model and promises wider significance for narrating U.S. religious history. Contact has been a predominant theme in the writing of the colonial history of the Americas, especially in telling the story of African slaves and Native peoples. It also illumines much of the history of Asian religions in the United States, I suggest. The motif is helpful in exploring the encounters between Asians and Western travelers, traders, and missionaries, for instance. Here I highlight two other kinds of cultural and political contact.

In her analysis of travel writing about Africa and South America, Mary Louise Pratt introduced the term "contact zones" to describe the social and geographical sites of colonial encounters in which power and meaning were negotiated. The term also can be applied usefully to other contexts. For instance, politics, conceived broadly to include government and law, functions as a contact zone. Since

Robert Bellah's groundbreaking essay on civil religion in 1967, scholars have debated the nature and extent of a common religious tradition outside the churches and in the national political sphere. Some of the alleged features of this civil religion are a belief in the chosenness of the nation and the existence of a theistic god. To the extent that teachers and scholars take civil religion to be one unifying force in American religious history, it seems helpful to consider how, and whether, followers of Asian religions participate in this tradition. One obvious obstacle for Buddhists is that traditionally they do not accept theism, or belief in a personal creator. At the same, it is not self-evident that immigrants, or their immediate descendants, envision their adopted land on the model of ancient Israel, as a place chosen by god to establish a kingdom for god's chosen people. Whatever such a study of contact in the political zone might find, it would add to our understanding of American religious history more broadly.[37]

The legal system is another political zone of contact for Asian Americans. As with American Indians, African Americans, Roman Catholics, Mormons, and others, national and local laws have shaped the experience of Asians in crucial — and usually destructive — ways. Of course, observers since the early nineteenth century correctly have emphasized the importance of the separation of church and state in shaping American religious life, and attention to the story of Asians reinforces its centrality. Asian immigrants traditionally were not welcomed as were those from Europe. Racial and religious differences set them apart and inspired hatred and prejudice. They were ineligible for citizenship for a long time, and the government treated the Japanese, even those who had been in the country for generations, as aliens during World War II as they segregated them in camps. Even though some Japanese Americans also fought for the United States in that war, it was only recently that the Buddhist Churches of America, the Pure Land Buddhist group headquartered in San Francisco, legally was recognized as the first American institution outside the Judeo-Christian tradition that could certify clergy as military chaplains. Since the 1882 Chinese Exclusion Act, laws also have kept Asians from entering the nation. During the racist and nativist twenties, the immigration law of 1924 restricted immigration based on a national quota system that disfavored Asians. Only with the revision of immigration laws in 1965 did the legal situation change significantly for Asians immigrants. That new law, as I have suggested, was part of the confluence of forces that have changed the cultural landscape.[38]

Popular culture also might be conceived of as a zone of contact among religions and peoples. Scholars have explored this as a site with religious significance; but their focus, naturally enough, has been on Christian influences. Timothy Miller analyzed Protestant fiction such as *In His Steps*, while Colleen McDannell considered Catholic novels like *Aunt Honor's Keepsake*. McDannell and David Morgan have researched material culture, which has been understudied, with McDannell treating domestic furnishings and architecture and Morgan focusing on popular paintings such as Warner Sallman's *Head of Christ*. Peter Williams discussed religious influences in the *Reader's Digest* and the *National Enquirer*. Albanese analyzed the plots of fictional tales on television and in films, suggesting that Superman, the Lone Ranger, and Star Wars expressed traditional American Protestant themes such as millennial dominance and righteous innocence.[39]

In similar ways, I suggest, Hindu and Buddhist themes have begun to penetrate American popular culture, especially in recent decades. This can be seen in various cultural sites of contact — film, music, fashion, books, magazines, furnishings, advertising, and television. To take one example, *Star Wars* expresses Buddhist as well as Christian themes. In the second film of the trilogy, *Return of the Jedi*, Zen beliefs and practices are hinted at in the encounter between Yoda and Luke Skywalker. Yoda functions like a Zen master for his student, Luke. Yoda wears a monk's robe, speaks in koan-like riddles, and emphasizes harmony with "the Force."

I could mention many other sites of direct and indirect cultural contact, but among the most interesting are the many popular books on Taoism and Buddhism sold in bookstores across America. Limiting my search only to books with titles like "Tao of" and "Zen and," and not including translations of sacred texts or scholarly works, *Books in Print* lists more than sixty works on Taoism and more than one hundred on Zen. These popular books deal with almost all dimensions of human life — work, leisure, health, psychology, love, sex, parenting, food, and money. As with other religious groups in America that preach success, authors of these works promise increased effectiveness in the business world in the *Tao of Management* and *Zen and the Art of Creative Management*. Readers can nurture children better by practicing the *Tao of Motherhood* or *Zen and the Art of Changing Diapers*. For entertainment, they might consider the *Tao of Baseball* or *Zen in the Art of Climbing Mountains*. To increase mental and physical health, Americans can study the *Tao of Health, Sex, and Longevity* or *Zen Buddhism and Psychoanalysis*. Of course, the treatment of Buddhism and Taoism in these works often is superficial, even annoying or silly. Sometimes, however, these texts present intriguing applications of traditional Asian beliefs and practices to new contexts and purposes. In any case, we learn something about American religion and culture by examining these books and their readers, as well as other sites in popular culture where Americans encounter each other to negotiate meaning and power. As attention to Asian religions in the United States reminds us, explorations of popular culture as a site of religious contact might contribute to telling the story of American religion; and, as I have tried to suggest, other motifs that emerge from an Asian model — especially place and identity — promise wider significance as well. In this way and in others this new subfield can contribute to efforts to interpret the complexity of America's religious past.[40]

Notes

I would like to thank the scholars who commented on earlier drafts of this chapter, especially Martin Baumann, Carl Ernst, John Fenton, Jan Nattier, Charles Prebish, Stephen Prothero, James Sanford, Richard Seager, Joanne Punzo Waghorne, Raymond Brady Williams, and David Zercher. Of course, it's not their fault if errors remain.

1. Leland T. Lewis, *The Tao of Golf* (R and E Publishers, 1992). Mel Ash, *Zen of Recovery* (J.P. Tarcher, 1993). The film was titled *Little Buddha* and was directed by Bernardo Bertolucci. On the film, see Helen Tworkov, "Projecting the Buddha: On the Set with Bertolucci," *Tricycle: The Buddhist Review* (Summer 1993): 22–29. For an interesting example of the influence of that film, see the article in the Latino Catholic periodical: Ricardo Briz, "Sobre el film 'El pequeño Buda,'" *La Voz Católica*, 41 (June 24, 1994): 18. Another film that deals with Buddhism to a great extent is Oliver Stone's "Heaven and Earth." For Stone's reflections on the significance of the film, as the first American one to deal explicitly and extensively with Buddhism, see "Hell First, Then Heaven and Earth: An Interview with Oliver Stone," in *Tricycle: The Buddhist Review* (Spring 1994): 44–50. For evidence of significant Buddhist influence in music, see the lyrics to "Bodhisattva Vow" by the rap group, the Beastie Boys: "Adam Yauch of the Beastie Boys," *Tricycle: The Buddhist Review* 3 (Summer 1994): 30. Among celebrities who have confessed interest in or affiliation with Buddhism, for example, are Richard Gere, Patrick Duffy, Phil Jackson, Herbie Hancock, and Tina Turner. On this see "In with the Om Crowd," *New York*, June 6, 1994, pp. 30–34. Jackson describes his interest in Zen in Phil Jackson and Hugh Delehanty, *Sacred Hoops: Spiritual Lessons of a Hardwood Warrior* (New York: Hyperion, 1995), 43–58. On the "cybersangha" see Gary L. Ray, "A Resource Roundup for the Cybersangha," *Tricycle: The Buddhist Review* 3 (Summer 1994): 60–63. The figures for the number of Hindu and Buddhist centers in the United States are estimates based on several sources, especially the research conducted by Diana Eck and her students who are involved in the Pluralism Project. For this information, and ethnographic and historical information on many of these centers, see Archives, Pluralism Project, Philips Brooks House, Harvard University, Cambridge, Massachusetts. See also Diana Eck, ed., *On Common Ground*, CD-ROM (New York: Columbia University Press, 1997). One periodical, *Hinduism Today*, regularly publishes lists of Hindu centers in North America. Many, though not all, of the Buddhist centers are listed in Don Morreale, *Buddhist America: Centers, Retreats, Practices* (Sante Fe: John Muir, 1988). My estimate for Buddhist centers, derived from Pluralism Project figures, was confirmed in an interview with H. Ratanasara, president of the Buddhist Sangha Council of Southern California and president of the College of Buddhist Studies in Los Angeles. He has been involved in a study that aims to identify all Buddhist centers in the United States. Telephone interview with H. Ratanasara, Mar. 28, 1994. On Asian religious centers in rural areas, see Margaret L. Usdansky, "Asian Immigrants Changing Face of Rural USA," *USA Today*, Sept. 10, 1992. For some of the coverage in the press, see the special issue titled "The New Face of America: How Immigrants Are Shaping the World's First Multicultural Society," *Time*, Fall 1993. Jerry Adler, "The New Immigrants," *Newsweek*, July 7, 1980, pp. 26–31. See also the cover story on "The Immigrants" in the *New Republic*: Nathan Glazer, "The Closing Door: Is Restrictionism Unthinkable?" Dec. 27, 1993, pp. 15–20. On converts, see "Buddhism in America," *New York Times Magazine*, June 3, 1979, pp. 28–30, 93–99. "More Drawn to the No-frills Spirituality," *USA Today*, Aug. 10, 1994, pp. 1D-2D. "800,000 Hands Clapping," *Newsweek*, June 13, 1994, pp. 46–47.

2. Robert Baird, *Religion in America* (1844; rpt., New York: Harper and Row, 1970), 281–303. This volume is an abridged version of the revised edition of 1856. Book 8 contains almost no references to Asian religions in their own terms. Baird's concern was Christian missionary activity, not the "heathen" religions evangelists encountered.

3. As I note below, the term "Asian religions" is not at all clear. By that term I mean traditions that originated in South, North, and East Asia — such as Hinduism, Buddhism,

Jainism, Confucianism, Taoism, and Shinto. Other traditions with a significant presence in Asia originated in the "Middle East," including Zoroastrianism, Christianity, and Islam. These, by my definition, are not Asian religions. However, they are religions *in* Asia. Islam, of course, counts large numbers of adherents in Asia. In fact, the largest Muslim nations are Asian — Indonesia, India, Pakistan, and Bangladesh. On this, see John L. Esposito, ed., *Islam in Asia* (New York: Oxford University Press, 1987). Because of space restrictions, and at the request of the volume editors, I focus on Hinduism and Buddhism in this chapter. I also concentrate on the United States, but expanding the geographical contexts to include all of the Americas would be helpful. Some scholars already have done so. See John Y. Fenton, *South Asian Religions in the Americas: An Annotated Bibliography of Immigrant Religious Traditions* (Westport, Conn: Greenwood, 1995). I also need to say a word about my reference to the subfield of Asian religions in America. I refer primarily to this as a subfield of American religious history. However, much of the research has been done by scholars in history, sociology, and literature departments; and, more important, the subfield overlaps with the study of Asian religions. A good deal of the research, especially on recent immigrants, has been done by those trained primarily as specialists in Hinduism or Buddhism. The "subfield," then, overlaps a number of fields of study. Here I write primarily for those whose training and teaching focus on religion in the United States, although I hope that others might find it useful too.

4. Ronald Takaki, *Strangers from a Different Shore: A History of Asian Americans* (New York: Penguin Books, 1989), 473, 295.

5. Paul James Rutledge, *The Vietnamese Experience in America* (Bloomington: Indiana University Press, 1992), 47–49.

6. I am very grateful to Raymond Brady Williams and Joanne Punzo Waghorne for their insightful comments on earlier drafts of the section that follows on Hinduism. Readers who want an introduction to Hinduism might consult the overview by Alf Hiltebeitel: "Hinduism," in *Encyclopedia of Religion*, ed. Mircea Eliade (New York: Macmillan, 1987). There are a number of good introductory texts as well, including Klaus K. Klostermaier, *A Survey of Hinduism*, 2nd ed. (Albany: State University of New York Press, 1994), which might be the best introduction to the subject. See also Thomas J. Hopkins, *The Hindu Religious Tradition* (North Scituate, Mass.: Duxbury, 1971); and J.L. Brockington, *The Sacred Thread: Hinduism in Its Continuity and Diversity* (Edinburgh: Edinburgh University Press, 1981). Readers who want an introduction to Buddhism might consult the overview by Frank Reynolds and Charles Hallisey: "Buddhism," in Eliade, *Encyclopedia of Religion.* There also are a number of solid introductory texts, including Peter B. Harvey, *Introduction to Buddhism* (New York and Cambridge: Cambridge University Press, 1990); Richard H. Robinson and Willard Johnson, *The Buddhist Religion*, 3rd ed. (Belmont, Calif.: Wadsworth, 1982); and William R. LaFleur, *Buddhism* (Englewood Cliffs: Prentice Hall, 1988).

7. This helpful typology is found in Gerald James Larson, "Hinduism in India and America," in *World Religions in America: An Introduction*, ed. Jacob Neusner (Louisville: Westminster, 1994), 196–97.

8. I am indebted to Jan Nattier for helpful comments on my treatment of the three forms of Buddhism. It was she who suggested the term "Nikaya Buddhism."

9. Much more work needs to be done on Asian-American women and their religious practices. A few books and articles on female European-American Buddhist leaders and followers have appeared. For instance, see Sandy Boucher, *Turning the Wheel: American Women Creating the New Buddhism*, updated and expanded edition (1988; rpt., Boston:

Beacon, 1993), and Lenore Friedman, *Meetings with Remarkable Women* (Boston: Shambhala, 1987). Tensions between Asian-American adherents and European-American converts have been significant in recent years in Hindu and Buddhist communities. For one treatment of the issues among Buddhists see Charles S. Prebish, "The Two Buddhisms Reconsidered," *Buddhist Studies Review* 10 (1993): 187–206. One organization, the Buddhist Women's Network, has taken as one of its goals to unite European-American and Asian-American Buddhist women. On this group see "Findings and Footnotes," *Religion Watch* 9 (Nov./Dec. 1993): n.p.

10. My account of the ritual at the Vietnamese pagoda is based on fieldwork and interviews. The characterization of the president of the association, an older man who arrived in the United States in 1975, is based on his remarks to me in an interview: LN, June 26, 1994, Chua Van Hanh Pagoda, Raleigh, N.C. The text the Vietnamese chanted that Sunday was the Lotus Sutra. The next week they moved on to another Buddhist scripture. For one account of religion in North Carolina, see Grant Wacker, "A Tar Heel Perspective on *The Third Disestablishment*," *Journal of the Scientific Study of Religion* 30 (Dec. 1991): 519–25.

11. The assessment of the literature that follows is not exhaustive. Rather, my aim is to note some trends in scholarship, list some key sources, and identify some fruitful areas of research.

12. Carl T. Jackson, *The Oriental Religions and American Thought: Nineteenth Century Explorations* (Westport, Conn.: Greenwood, 1981). On Cotton's interest see Mukhtar A. Isani, "Cotton Mather and the Orient," *New England Quarterly* 43 (Mar. 1970): 46–58. Carl T. Jackson, "The Influence of Asia upon American Thought: A Bibliographical Essay," *American Studies International* 23 (Apr. 1984): 3–31.

13. William R. Hutchison, *Errand to the World: American Protestant Thought and Foreign Missions* (Chicago: University of Chicago Press, 1987); Clifton J. Philips, *Protestant America and the Pagan World: The First Half Century of the American Board of Commissioners for Foreign Missions, 1810–1860* (Cambridge, Mass.: Harvard University Press, 1969).

14. One possible model for a theoretically informed history of contact might be Mary Louise Pratt's *Imperial Eyes: Travel Writing and Transculturation* (London and New York: Routledge, 1992).

15. Sydney E. Ahlstrom, *The American Protestant Encounter with World Religions* (Beloit, Wis.: Beloit College, 1962); George Hunston Williams, "The Attitude of Liberals in New England toward Non-Christian Religions, 1785–1885," *Crane Review* 9 (Winter 1967): 59–89; Jackson, *Oriental Religions*, chs. 1–4, 6–7; Thomas A. Tweed, "An American Pioneer in the Study of Religion: Hannah Adams (1755–1831) and her *Dictionary of All Religions*," *Journal of the American Academy of Religion* 60 (Dec. 1992): 437–64; idem, introduction to *A Dictionary of All Religions and Religious Denominations*, by Hannah Adams, Classics in Religious Studies Series (Atlanta: Scholars Press, 1992), vii-xxxiv; idem, "'The Seeming Anomaly of Buddhist Negation': American Encounters with Buddhist Distinctiveness, 1858–1877," *Harvard Theological Review* 83 (1990): 65–92; Spencer Lavan, *Unitarians and India* (Boston: Skinner House, 1977); Arthur Versluis, *American Transcendentalism and Asian Religions* (New York: Oxford University Press, 1993).

16. Frederick I. Carpenter, *Emerson and Asia* (Cambridge, Mass.: Harvard University Press, 1930); Arthur Christy, *The Orient in American Transcendentalism* (New York: Columbia University Press, 1932); Roger Chester Mueller, "The Orient in American Transcendental Periodicals, 1835–1886" (Ph.D. diss., University of Minnesota, 1968); Jackson,

Oriental Religions, chs. 3, 4, 7; Thomas A. Tweed, *The American Encounter with Buddhism, 1844–1912* (Bloomington: Indiana University Press, 1992), 1–25; Versluis, *American Transcendentalism*.

17. Mukhtar Ali Isani, "The Oriental Tale in America through 1865: A Study in American Fiction" (Ph.D. diss., Princeton University, 1962); David S. Reynolds, *Faith in Fiction: The Emergence of Religious Literature in America* (Cambridge, Mass.: Harvard University Press, 1981), 13–68; Beongcheon Yu, *The Great Circle: American Writers and the Orient* (Detroit: Wayne State University Press, 1964). Two articles offer insights about the Beat movement and Asian religions: Carl T. Jackson, "The Counterculture Looks East: Beat Writers and Asian Religion," *American Studies* 29 (Spring 1989): 51–70, and Stephen Prothero, "On the Holy Road: The Beat Movement as Spiritual Protest," *Harvard Theological Review* 84 (1991): 205–22. For evidence of the continuing influence of Asian religions on American writers see the anthology of poetry, Kent Johnson and Craig Paulenich, ed., *Beneath a Single Moon: Buddhism in Contemporary American Poetry* (Boston: Shambhala, 1991).

18. Ellen Paul Denker, *After the Chinese Taste: China's Influence in America, 1730–1930* (Salem: Peabody Museum of Salem, 1985); Clay Lancaster, *The Japanese Influence in America* (New York: Walton H. Rawls, 1963); Society for the Study of Japonisme, *Japonisme in Art: An International Symposium* (Tokyo: Committee for the Year 2001, 1980); Warren I. Cohen, *East Asian Art and American Culture* (New York: Columbia University Press, 1992); Geri Gelbund and Geri De Paoli, *The Transparent Thread: Asian Philosophy in Recent American Art* (Philadelphia: University of Pennsylvania Press, 1990); Maurice Tuchman, ed. *The Spiritual in Art: Abstract Painting, 1980–1985* (Los Angeles: Los Angeles County Museum of Art; New York: Abbeville Press, 1986), 17–62; John Cage, *Silence: Lectures and Writings by John Cage* (1961; rpt., Middletown, Conn.: Wesleyan University Press, 1973).

19. Jackson, *Oriental Religions*; Ahlstrom, *American Protestant Encounter*; Dale Riepe, *The Philosophy of India and Its Impact on American Thought* (Springfield, Ill.: Charles C. Thomas, 1970); Grant Wacker, "A Plural World: The Protestant Awakening to World Religions," in *Between the Times: The Travail of the Protestant Establishment in America, 1900–1960*, ed. William R. Hutchison (Cambridge: Cambridge University Press, 1989), 253–77; Kenneth K. Inada and Nolan P. Jacobson, *Buddhism and American Thinkers* (Albany: State University of New York Press, 1984). To trace Buddhist-Christian dialogue since the 1980s, for instance, consult the issues of the annual journal, *Buddhist-Christian Studies*, which first appeared in 1981. Kenten Druyvesteyn, "The World's Parliament of Religions" (Ph.D. diss., University of Chicago, 1976); Larry A. Fader, "Zen in the West: Historical and Philosophical Implications of the 1893 Chicago World's Parliament of Religions," *Eastern Buddhist* n.s., 15 (Spring 1982): 122–45; Jackson, *Oriental Religions*, 243–61; Richard Hughes Seager, ed., *The Dawn of Religious Pluralism: Voices from the World's Parliament of Religions, 1893* (LaSalle, Ill.: Open Court Publishing, 1993); Richard Hughes Seager, *The World's Parliament of Religions: The East-West Encounter, Chicago, 1893* (Bloomington: Indiana University Press, 1995); Eric Ziolkowski, ed., *A Museum of Faiths: Histories and Legacies of the 1893 World's Parliament of Religions* (Atlanta: Scholars Press, 1993); Clay Lancaster, *The Invisible World's Parliament of Religions at the Chicago Columbian Exposition of 1893* (Fontwell, Sussex: Centaur Press, 1987). For a list of the major addresses at the Parliament, see Seager, *Dawn of Religious Pluralism*, 477–92.

20. "The Manners and Customs of India," in *The Complete Works of Swami Vivekan-*

anda, vol. 1 (Calcutta: Advaita Ashrama), 488–90; Carl T. Jackson, *Vedanta for the West: The Ramakrishna Movement in the United States* (Bloomington: Indiana University Press, 1994).

21. I might refer here to African converts as well as European, but African-American conversions to Asian religions, excluding Islam, seem to have been relatively recent, mostly since the 1960s. There is a significant presence of African Americans, for instance, among converts to Soka Gakkai in the United States. For a provocative analysis of race and Buddhism by an American Buddhist sympathizer of African descent, see bell hooks, "Waking Up to Racism," *Tricycle: The Buddhist Review* 4 (Fall 1994): 42–45. Tweed, *American Encounter with Buddhism*; Rick Fields, *How the Swans Came to the Lake: A Narrative History of Buddhism in America*, revised and updated (1981; rpt., Boston and London: Shambhala, 1986); Carl T. Jackson, "The Meeting of East and West: The Case of Paul Carus," *Journal of the History of Ideas* 29 (Jan.-Mar. 1968): 73–92; Lawrence W. Chisolm, *Fenollosa: The Far East and American Culture* (New Haven, Conn.: Yale University Press, 1963); Jackson Lears, *No Place of Grace: Antimodernism and the Transformation of American Culture, 1880–1920* (New York: Pantheon, 1981), 225–41; Beongcheon Yu, *An Ape of Gods: The Art and Thought of Lafcadio Hearn* (Detroit: Wayne State University Press, 1964).

22. For a brief overview of Goddard's life, see the entry in J. Gordon Melton, *Biographical Dictionary of American Cult and Sect Leaders* (New York: Garland, 1986), 99–100.

23. On the occult in America more generally, see the fine collection of essays, Howard Kerr and Charles L. Crow, eds., *The Occult in America: New Historical Perspectives* (Urbana: University of Illinois Press, 1983). A number of books and articles have appeared on new religious movements. For example, see Robert S. Ellwood and Harry B. Partin, *Religious and Spiritual Groups in Modern America*, 2nd ed. (Englewood Cliffs: Prentice Hall, 1988). That work is a collection of primary sources with background and analysis by the coeditors. For Robert Ellwood's analysis of the Theosophical movement, see *Alternative Altars: Unconventional and Eastern Spirituality in America* (Chicago: University of Chicago Press, 1979), 104–35. The best overview of Theosophy is Bruce F. Campbell, *Ancient Wisdom Revived: A History of the Theosophical Movement* (Berkeley and Los Angeles: University of California Press, 1980). Stephen Prothero, *The White Buddhist: The Asian Odyssey of Henry Steel Olcott* (Bloomington: Indiana University Press, 1996). On ISKCON see E. Burke Rochford Jr., *Hare Krishna in America* (New Brunswick, N.J.: Rutgers University Press, 1985), and David G. Bromely and Larry D. Shinn, ed., *Krishna Consciousness in the West* (Lewisburg, Pa.: Bucknell University Press, 1989). Two works begin to disentangle the Asian influences in the New Age movement: Andrea Grace Diem and James R. Lewis, "Imagining India: The Influence of Hinduism on the New Age Movement," in *Perspectives on the New Age*, ed. James R. Lewis and J. Gordon Melton (Albany: State University of New York Press, 1992), 48–58; and Ted Peters, *The Cosmic Self: A Penetrating Look at Today's New Age Movements* (San Francisco: HarperSanFrancisco, 1991). The latter contains scattered references to the influences of Asian religions. See the forty pages or so listed in the index under "Hinduism" and "Buddhism."

24. For one of the best studies of those European immigrants, see John Bodnar, *The Transplanted: A History of Immigrants in Urban America* (Bloomington: Indiana University Press, 1985). Bodnar makes passing references to Chinese and Japanese immigrants too. For a useful introduction to recent syntheses of immigration history see Dirk Hoerder, "Immigration and Ethnicity in Comparative Perspective," *Reviews in American History* 20 (1992): 575–79. Takaki, *Strangers from a Different Shore*. Takaki's fine text of 491 pages

contains only thirteen references to religion. For another helpful introduction to Asian-American immigration see Roger Daniels, *Asian America* (Seattle: University of Washington Press, 1988). Shih-shan Henry Tsai, *The Chinese in America* (Bloomington: Indiana University Press, 1986). David J. O'Brien and Stephen S. Fugita, *The Japanese American Experience* (Bloomington: Indiana University Press, 1991). Perhaps the best treatment of Chinese religions in the United States is L. Eve Armentrout, "Chinese Traditional Religion in North America and Hawaii," in *Chinese America: History and Perspectives, 1988* (San Francisco: Chinese Historical Society of America, 1988), 131–47. Buddhist Churches of America, *Buddhist Churches of America: Seventy-Five Year History, 1899–1974*, 2 vols. (Chicago: Nobart, 1974). Tetsuden Kashima, *Buddhism in America: The Social Organization of an Ethnic Organization* (Westport, Conn.: Greenwood, 1977). For developments in Hawaii, see Louise H. Hunter, *Buddhism in Hawaii: Its Impact on a Yankee Community* (Honolulu: University of Hawaii Press, 1971). A collection of essays on Koreans contains one chapter on religion, and that deals only with Christians: Hyung-chan Kim, "The History and Role of the Church in the Korean American Community," in *The Korean Diaspora: Historical and Sociological Studies of Korean Immigration and Assimilation in North America*, ed. Hyung-chan Kim (Santa Barbara: ABC Clio, 1977), 47–63. For a study of another early immigrant group see Joan M. Jensen, *Passage from India: Asian Indian Immigrants in North America* (New Haven, Conn.: Yale University Press, 1988).

25. One volume, which emphasizes legal restrictions and nativist reactions, collects useful primary sources concerning the history of Asian immigrants, especially the Chinese and Japanese: Philip S. Foner and Daniel Rosenberg, *Racism, Dissent, and Asian Americans from 1850 to the Present: A Documentary History* (Westport, Conn.: Greenwood, 1993). My data on Asian immigration is taken from reports of the U.S. Bureau of the Census. Three helpful statistical tables on Asian population growth since the 1960s are included in Masako Iino, "Asian Americans Under the Influence of 'Japan Bashing,'" *American Studies International* 32 (Apr. 1994): 29–30. On international migration before and, especially, after 1945, see Stephen Castles and Mark J. Miller, *The Age of Migration* (New York: Guilford, 1993). On religion and the new immigrants see the fine article by Peter Kivisto, "Religion and the New Immigrants" in *A Future for Religion?: New Paradigms for Social Analysis*, ed. William H. Swatos Jr. (Newbury Park, Calif.: Sage, 1993), 92–108. Somewhat more dated but still helpful is Morrison G. Wong, "Post-1965 Asian Immigrants: Where Do They Come From, Where Are They Now, Where Are They Going?" *Annals of the American Academy of Political and Social Science* 487 (Sept. 1986): 150–68.

26. The two textbooks, each with their own advantages and disadvantages, are E. Allen Richardson, *East Comes West: Asian Religions and Cultures in North America* (New York: Pilgrim, 1985), and Jacob Neusner, ed., *World Religions in America: An Introduction*. In the latter, the chapter on Hinduism, cited above, is by Gerald Larson. The chapter on Buddhism is by Malcom David Eckel. Fenton, *South Asian Religions in the Americas*. John Y. Fenton, *Transplanting Religious Traditions: Asian Indians in America* (Westport, Conn.: Praeger, 1988). See also Fenton's briefer overview, c.v. "Hinduism" in *Encyclopedia of the American Religious Experience*, ed. Charles H. Lippy and Peter W. Williams (New York: Scribner's, 1988). Raymond Brady Williams, *Religions of Immigrants from India and Pakistan: New Threads in the American Tapestry* (New York: Cambridge University Press, 1988). See also Raymond Brady Williams, ed., *A Sacred Thread: Modern Transmission of Hindu Traditions in India and Abroad* (Chambersburg, Pa.: Anima, 1992). Before the second wave of Asian Indian immigration a survey of Hindu groups in America ap-

peared that focused on American converts, the Ramakrishna movement, and religious encounter. It is more helpful than its hysterical, nativist title suggests: Wendell Thomas, *Hinduism Invades America* (New York: Beacon, 1930). Fields, *How the Swans Came to the Lake*. Emma McCloy Layman, *Buddhism in America* (Chicago: Nelson-Hall, 1976). Charles S. Prebish, *American Buddhism* (North Scituate, Mass.: Duxbury, 1979). Prebish also has written a briefer overview of Buddhism in America: c.v., "Buddhism" in *Encyclopedia of the American Religious Experience*.

27. Diana L. Eck and Susan A. M. Shumaker, "The Pluralism Project: A Preliminary Report," *Council of Societies for the Study of Religion Bulletin*, 21 (Apr. 1992): 35–37. Fred W. Clothey, *Rhythm and Intent: Ritual Studies from South India* (Madras: Blackie and Sons, 1983), 164–200. The film by Clothey is "Consecration of a Temple," color film, 45 min., Pittsburgh, 1981. Joanne Punzo Waghorne, "The Hindu Gods in a Split-Level World," in *The Gods of the City: Religion and the Contemporary American Urban Landscape*, ed. Robert A. Orsi (Bloomington: Indiana University Press, forthcoming); Raymond Brady Williams, "New Ethnics Take Their Turn: The Swaminarayan Temple in Glen Ellyn," in *American Congregations*, vol. 1, ed. James Lewis and James Wind (Chicago: University of Chicago Press, 1994); Surinder M. Bhardwaj, "Hindu Deities and Pilgrimage in the United States," in *Pilgrimage in America*, ed. Surinder M. Bhardwaj and Gisbert Rinschede, vol. 5 of *Geographia Religionum* (Berlin: Dietrich Reimer Verlag, 1990), 221–28; Eui-Young Yu, "The Growth of Korean Buddhism in the United States, with Special Reference to Southern California," *Pacific World: Journal of the Institute of Buddhist Studies*, n.s., 4 (Fall 1988): 82–93; Paul Rutledge, *The Role of Religion in Ethnic Self-Identity: A Vietnamese Community* (Lanham: University Press of America, 1985); Paul David Numrich, *Old Wisdom in the New World: Americanization in Two Immigrant Theravada Buddhist Temples* (Knoxville: University of Tennessee Press, 1996). For a mapping of the Buddhist temples in Seattle see "Fifty-three Temples in and around Seattle," *Tricycle: The Buddhist Review* 4 (Fall 1994): 46–47. For a directory of institutions in another urban area see Diana L. Eck, ed., *World Religions in Boston: A Guide to Communities and Resources* (Cambridge, Mass.: Pluralism Project, Harvard University, n.d.). For a social-scientific approach to the study of religion among new immigrants from Southeast Asia, see Ronald Burwell et al., "Religion and Refugee Resettlement in the United States: A Research Note," *Review of Religious Research* 27 (June 1986): 356–66. On Lao Buddhists in Toronto see Penny Van Esterik, *Taking Refuge: Lao Buddhists in North America* (Tempe: Arizona State University, Program for Southeast Asian Studies; Toronto: York University, Centre for Refugee Studies, York Lane Press, 1992).

28. Although no sustained cross-cultural comparative studies have appeared, the secondary literature on Asian religions in diasporic nations is beginning to build. Here I cite just a few secondary sources: Purusottama Bilimoria, *Hinduism in Australia* (Melbourne: Spectrum, 1989); Carolyn V. Prorok, "Patterns of Pilgrimage Behavior among Hindus of Trinidad," in *Pilgrimage in World Religions*, ed. Surinder M. Bhardwaj and Gisbert Rinschede, vol. 4 of *Geographia Religionum* (Berlin: Dietrich Reimer Verlag, 1988), 189–99; Ian P. Oliver, *Buddhism in Britain* (London: Rider and Company, 1979); Philip C. Almond, *The British Discovery of Buddhism* (Cambridge: Cambridge University Press, 1988); Paul Croucher, *Buddhism in Australia* (Kensington: New South Wales, 1989); Suwanda H. J. Sugunasiri, "Buddhism in Metropolitan Toronto," *Canadian Ethnic Studies* 21 (1989): 83–103; Martin Baumann, "Buddhists in a Western Country: An Outline of Recent Buddhist Developments in Germany," *Religion Today* 7 (1991): 1–4; Martin Baumann, *Deutsche Buddhisten: Geschichte und Gemeinschaften* (Marburg: Diagonal-Verlag, 1993).

29. Jon Butler, "Historiographical Heresy: Catholicism as a Model for American Religious History," in *Belief in History: Innovative Approaches to European and American Religion*, ed. Thomas Kselman (Notre Dame: University of Notre Dame Press, 1991), 286–309; Jon Butler, *Awash in a Sea of Faith: Christianizing the American People* (Cambridge, Mass.: Harvard University Press, 1990). In a persuasive essay, another scholar has proposed a Methodist model for narrating American religious history: Nathan O. Hatch, "The Puzzle of American Methodism," *Church History* 63 (June 1994): 175–89. For my own views on the writing of American religious history, see Thomas A. Tweed, introduction to *Retelling U.S. Religious History*, ed. Thomas A. Tweed (Berkeley and Los Angeles: University of California Press, 1997), 1–23.

30. Sydney E. Ahlstrom, *A Religious History of the American People* (New Haven, Conn.: Yale University Press, 1972); Catherine L. Albanese, *America: Religions and Religion*, 2nd ed. (Belmont, Calif.: Wadsworth, 1992), 283–323. My discussion of the number who affiliate with these religions and denominations is primarily based on the CUNY study. I will leave it to others more qualified than I to argue about the number of adherents. However, I join other scholars who suggest that the figures reported in the CUNY study seem quite low for some groups, including the non-Christian ones. That study reported only 527,000 Muslims, 401,000 Buddhists, and 227,000 Hindus. Barry A. Kosmin, in cooperation with Seymour P. Lachman, "Research Report: The National Survey of Religious Identification, 1989–90," Graduate School and University Center of the City University of New York, Mar. 1991. For a persuasive criticism of that study for its undercounting of many groups, see Robert S. Ellwood and Donald E. Miller, "Questions Regarding the CUNY National Survey of Religious Identification," *Journal for the Scientific Study of Religion* 31 (1992): 94–96. Kosmin and Lachman recently reported in another work that there were 800,000 Buddhists, and others estimate that they number one million. See Barry A. Kosmin and Seymour P. Lachman, *One Nation Under God: Religion in Contemporary American Society* (New York: Harmony Books, 1993). One estimate is much higher ("five to eight million"): Chrys Thorsen, "The State and Future of American Buddhism," in *Almanac of the Korean Buddhist Chogye Order of America: Kwan Um Temple 20th Anniversary, 1974–1993* (n.p.: n.d.), 140–42. Estimates for Muslims range as high as 8 million, from the Islamic Society of North America. Many observers suggest that there are at least 3.5 million Muslims in the United States, which would mean they now outnumber Jews or soon will. Hindus, as some have noticed, probably were undercounted in the original CUNY study because they are highly concentrated in a few areas of the country, and for other reasons.

31. William Warren Sweet, *The Story of Religion in America* (New York: Harper and Brothers, 1939). Edwin S. Gaustad, *Historical Atlas of Religion in America* (New York: Harper and Row, 1962). One useful overview of region and religion is Samuel Hill's "Religion and Region in America," *Annals of the American Academy of Political and Social Science* 480 (July 1985): 132–41. Until recently, much of the research on regional variation has focused on the South, and Hill and Donald Mathews have led the way. A number of local studies also have been published, mostly focusing on urban centers. For instance, see David G. Hackett, *The Rude Hand of Innovation: Religion and Social Order in Albany, New York, 1652–1836* (New York: Oxford University Press, 1991).

32. For an overview see Peter W. Williams, "Religious Architecture and Landscape," in Lippy and Williams, *Encyclopedia of the American Religious Experience*, 1325–39. For a fine study that considers church and domestic architecture, see Rhys Isaac, *The Transformation of Virginia, 1740–1790* (Chapel Hill: University of North Carolina Press, 1982). On the sacralization of American rivers, see Raymond B. Williams, "Hinduism in America,"

Christian Century, Mar. 11, 1987, pp. 247–49. That piece also offers insights about the significance of Hindu worship in temples and the home. On domestic religion among Christians, see Colleen McDannell, *The Christian Home in Victorian America, 1840–1900* (Bloomington: Indiana University Press, 1986), and A. Gregory Schneider, *The Way of the Cross Leads Home: The Domestication of American Methodism* (Bloomington: Indiana University Press, 1993).

33. Martin E. Marty, *Pilgrims in Their Own Land: 500 Years of Religion in America* (Boston: Little, Brown and Company, 1984); Sidney E. Mead, *The Lively Experiment: The Shaping of Christianity in America* (New York: Harper and Row, 1963), 7. On place and displacement see Thomas A. Tweed, *Our Lady of the Exile: Diasporic Religion at a Cuban Catholic Shrine in Miami* (New York and Oxford: Oxford University Press, 1997). Interview with DCN, male, aged 49, Chua Van Hanh Pagoda, Raleigh, N.C., June 26, 1994.

34. Interview with LN, woman, aged 50, Chua Van Hanh Pagoda, Raleigh, N.C., June 26, 1994. The literature on immigrants, Asians and others, is filled with references to intergenerational issues, but I also am grateful to Robert Orsi for reminding me of the significance of the religious lives of children.

35. Data, ed., *Complete Works of Swami Vivekananda*; George M. Williams, *The Quest for Meaning of Svami Vivekananda* (Chico, Calif.: New Horizons, 1974); Gananath Obeyesekere, "Personal Identity and Cultural Crisis: The Case of Anagarika Dharmapala in Sri Lanka," in *The Biographical Process*, ed. Frank E. Reynolds and Donald Capps (The Hague: Mouton, 1976). Bhikkhu Sangharakshita's *Anagarika Dharmapala: A Biographical Sketch* contains some useful information, but it is extremely sympathetic to its subject (Kandy: Buddhist Publication Society, 1964). More judicious treatments can be found in George Bond, *The Buddhist Revival in Sri Lanka* (Columbia: University of South Carolina Press, 1988); and Richard F. Gomrich, *Theravada Buddhism: A Social History from Ancient Benares to Modern Colombo* (London and New York: Routledge, 1988).

36. The term "sympathizer" might be most useful for analyzing the religious life of those who were shaped by occult or Asian traditions, but it also might illumine the beliefs and practices of those who dabbled with Deism in the eighteenth century or those who sympathized with Swedenborgianism in the nineteenth century. For an interpretation of the religious life of Marie Canavarro, see Thomas A. Tweed, "Inclusivism and the Spiritual Journey of Marie de Souza Canavarro (1849–1933)," *Religion* 24 (1994): 43–58. I appealed to the category "sympathizer" in my analysis of Buddhism in nineteenth-century America: Tweed, *American Encounter*, for example, 42–43.

37. Pratt, *Imperial Eyes*; Robert N. Bellah, "Civil Religion in America," *Daedalus* 96 (Winter 1967): 1–21.

38. Many of the relevant court decisions and laws, as well as varied responses to them, are collected in Foner and Rosenberg, *Racism, Dissent, and Asian Americans*. Thomas Pearson also has talked about the legal system as a "contact zone." See Thomas Pearson, "Santería in the Contact Zone," *Excursus: A Review of Religious Studies* 7 (Fall 1994): 5–14.

39. Timothy Miller, *Following in His Steps* (Knoxville: University of Tennessee Press, 1989); Colleen McDannell, "'The Devil Was the First Protestant': Gender and Intolerance in Irish Catholic Fiction," *U.S. Catholic Historian* 8 (Winter/Spring 1989): 51–65; McDannell, *Christian Home*; David Morgan, *Icons of American Protestantism: The Art of Warner Sallman, 1892–1968: An Exhibition Catalogue of Popular Religious Art* (Valparaiso, Ind.: Valparaiso University Press, 1994); Peter W. Williams, *Popular Religion in*

America (1980; Urbana: University of Illinois Press, 1989), 204–5; Albanese, *America*, 469–70.

40. *Books in Print, 1993–94,* (New Providence, N.J.: R.R. Bowker, 1994), 5:1557, 8: 6490–91, 8:7350–51; Bob Mesing, *Tao of Management* (New York: Bantam, 1992); Albert Low, *Zen and the Art of Creative Management* (Rutland, Vt.: Charles E. Tuttle, 1993); Vimala McClure, *Tao of Motherhood* (Willow Springs, Mo.: Nucleus, 1991); Sarah Arsone, *Zen and the Art of Changing Diapers* (Ventura, Calif.: Printwheel, 1991); Gordon Bell, *Tao of Baseball* (New York: Simon and Schuster, 1991); Neville Shulman, *Zen in the Art of Climbing Mountains* (Rutland, Vt.: Charles E. Tuttle, 1992); Daniel P. Reid, *Tao of Health, Sex, and Longevity* (New York: Simon and Schuster, 1989).

Make Room for the Muslims?

YVONNE YAZBECK HADDAD

Although Islam is one of the world's great religions, numbering nearly a billion believers, or about one-fifth of the world's population, it has not until very recently been associated with the United States. Recent events have drawn attention to the presence of Muslims in America and brought home the realization that Islam is not just a religion "of people over there." Rather, it is the religion of a growing number of Americans whose experiences, ideas, and organizational skills are beginning to have an impact on the larger Muslim world.

There are no accurate figures on the number of Muslims in the United States. Estimates provided by scholars and Islamic leaders show a great discrepancy, ranging from one to eleven million. The best assumption seems to be about four million people, making the American Muslim community larger than the Episcopal Church or the United Church of Christ. It is also estimated that by the first decade of the twenty-first century, the number of American Muslims will exceed that of those belonging to the Jewish faith. While initially Muslims welcomed the attention they received as part of the American mosaic, in recent years the often negative image that has been presented — of Muslims as a security or demographic threat — has had a chilling effect on the community.

The Muslims of America

Perhaps the most prominent feature of the Muslim population in North America is its diversity. The United States has Muslims from more than sixty nations who represent different linguistic, ethnic, tribal, sectarian, national, racial, educational, and cultural backgrounds.[1] The number of Muslims involved in organized religion and attending mosque services regularly is about 10 percent, with the majority unmosqued. Some join in the services for the two major Islamic holidays, *eid al-adha* (feast of sacrifice) and *eid al-fitr* (celebrating the end of fasting during the month of Ramadhan). Of those who are involved in the mosque movement some 29 percent are of Indo-Pakistani background, 29 percent are African American, and 21 percent are of Arab origin, with other nationalities constituting the balance. For the purpose of this study, Muslims in the United States will be discussed under three categories: immigrants, converts, and sojourners. While they represent somewhat differing concerns and interests, they all identify as Muslim and worship together when convenient. What they perceive as the prevailing negative feeling toward Islam in the United States today is helping to bring them together.

Immigrants

Muslim immigration to North America has come about in the last one hundred years, beginning in the 1880s.[2] The presence of Muslims in the population of the United States has been regulated during this century by American government policies pertaining to immigration and refugees. Early immigrants came from the Middle East and Eastern Europe. Continued Arab migration has more recently been supplemented by immigrants from the Indo-Pakistani subcontinent,[3] reflecting the changes in the immigration laws that repealed the Exclusion Act and specifically allowed a greater number of skilled and professional people ("the brain drain") from Asia to fill the needs of the expanding American economy.[4] Like other immigrants before them from all over the world, Muslims have come to the United States in order to take advantage of the benefits available in this country: economic and/or social enhancement, political refuge, and religious freedom. Also significant is the fact that there is a growing number of refugees who are seeking haven from sociopolitical and economic upheavals in their home countries.

The majority of the descendants of the first Muslim immigrants, now in their fourth and fifth generations, maintain some vestiges of ethnic and religious identity.[5] Significant Arab Muslim migration to the United States occurred in several waves. The first wave, 1875 to 1913, was composed mostly of uneducated and unskilled young men (some as young as thirteen years old) from the rural areas of what now constitutes Syria and Lebanon, then under Ottoman rule. The second wave, 1918 to 1922, followed World War I. It included a smattering of urban people, but the majority were relatives and friends of the earlier immigrants. By the time of the third wave, 1930 to 1938, American immigration laws confined immigration primarily to relatives of those already in the country who were naturalized citizens. The Muslims who came at that time to live with their relatives brought with them a new understanding of their own identity.

The fourth wave, 1947 to 1960, reflects America's assumption of its leadership role in the world. Immigrants began to include such people as North Africans and displaced groups from Eastern Europe fleeing communism, as well as children of the educated elites in various Arab countries, mostly urban in background, educated and Westernized prior to their arrival in the United States. Unlike the earlier immigrants, they did not perceive themselves as migrant laborers, eager to amass money to return home. These were the settlers, people who broke all ties to their previous homeland and came to the United States to make it their permanent home. They came to America in quest of a better life, higher education, advanced technical training, and specialized work opportunities as well as ideological fulfillment. Consequently, they attempted to carve out a niche for themselves in American society. While chain migration from rural areas of the Arab world continued in the fifties and sixties, the majority of the new immigrants were educated Westernized Arab professionals (Palestinians, Syrians, Iraqis, and Egyptians).

The fifth wave initiated by the change in immigration law in the sixties continued the flow of relatives but also opened up the immigration of Asian Muslims. The upheavals worldwide have brought a large group of refugees from all over the world fleeing various kinds of persecution including Chams from Cambodia, Kashmiris from India, Palestinians and South Lebanese from Israeli occupation, Iranians from the Islamic Republic, Kurds from Iraq and Turkey, Afghans from Russian occupation and later from Afghani civil war.

By 1972 intense migration of Muslims from Africa had begun. They are primarily of Indo-Pakistani background, whose families had migrated to Africa in the nineteenth and twentieth centuries. As traders and businessmen they were the backbone of the British African economy and civil administration of the empire helping to open up Africa for British colonization. When many African countries gained their independence in the sixties and seventies, the majority of these Muslims hoped to continue as residents of a new Africa. They soon realized, however, that the call for "Africanization" did not include them. Massacres such as those of Idi Amin spurred the exodus. They came to America from Uganda, Tanzania, Kenya, Mozambique, Zaire, and the Malagasy Republic. Others migrated from Pakistan, India, Bangladesh, Burma, Fiji Islands, Central Asia and in a second migration via Great Britain and Canada.

Most of the immigrant Muslim community in America are Sunni, although there are substantial Shi'a groups including Ithna Asharis,[6] Zaydis,[7] Alawis,[8] Isma'ilis,[9] and Druze,[10] as well as a flourishing Ahmadiyya[11] community that was established in the 1920s. Altogether they have organized more than 1,250 mosques/Islamic centers throughout the United States and developed over a thousand other Islamic institutions engaged in supporting parochial schools; publishing Islamic books, newspapers, and magazines; packaging radio and television programs; organizing political action committees; and providing *halal* food and proper dress. Most of these institutions are independent although they may function under the nominal influence of umbrella organizations such as the Federation of Islamic Associations,[12] the Islamic Society of North America,[13] the Islamic Circle of North America, and the Council of Masajid,[14] all of which include member mosques and organizations in Canada.[15] There are also several transplants of sufi groups.[16]

Converts

Converts, estimated to be about one-third of the community or some one million adherents, are predominantly from among the African-American population of the United States. Initially organized under indigenous leadership into sectarian forms of Islam such as the Moorish Science Temple[17] (formed by Noble Drew Ali in 1913) and the Nation of Islam (formed by Fard Muhammad and led by Elijah Muhammad in the early 1930s),[18] black Muslim sects continue to flourish among the underclass population of the ghettos of urban America, attracting members to such groups as the Nation of Islam under the leadership of Louis Farrakhan,[19] Ansaaru Allah,[20] the Five Percenters[21] and al-Rukn[22] gang of Chicago fame. The majority of the followers of Elijah Muhammad since his death in 1975 have moved into Sunni Islam. Malcolm X, the most famous of Elijah's followers, had left the Nation of Islam after performing the pilgrimage to Mecca and declaring its teachings to be deviant from Sunni Islam.[23] Under the leadership and guidance of Imam Warith Deen Muhammad some have joined mosques organized by immigrant groups.[24] Not all African-American converts were or are members of the Nation of Islam;[25] there are several independent small Sunni groups such as the Hanafis, the Islamic Party, Dar ul-Islam Movement, the Union of Brothers and Islamic People's Movement.[26] A recent development is the attraction by a growing number of blacks to revolutionary Shi'ite Islam and the establishment of several Ithna 'Ashari mosques under the leadership of African-American imams trained in Qum, Iran, in the 1980s.[27]

The conversion of African Americans to Islam in this century is generally referred to in the Muslim community as reversion rather than conversion to Islam. This language is perceived to be in line with the Islamic teaching that all human beings are born Muslim and that it is their parents who Judaize, Christianize, or Hinduize them. Thus to become a Muslim is to return to the original natural faith of all humanity created by God. On another level, many believe in what Clyde Ahmed Winters saw as a direct link of all African Americans in the United States to Islamic West Africa. For him, conversion to Islam is a reversion to ancestral identity.[28]

Muslims are encouraged by the conversion of Americans to Islam. Not only does it provide immigrants with the proof that Islam is viable for North American life, it also demonstrates to their children that Americans themselves are eschewing the values of the country because they deem Islam superior. Hence the repeated references in Muslim sources to the "first American convert" Muhammad Alexander Webb, who had been the American consul in the Philippines.[29] He represented Islam at the World's Parliament of Religions in Chicago in 1893 and was active in attempting to convert Americans to Islam. He opened a mosque in New York and published a periodical, the *Moslem World*, as well as several books.[30] Well-known sports figures (Muhammad Ali, Kareem Abdul Jabbar, and Ahmad Rashad) and entertainment figures (Yusuf Islam, formerly Cat Stevens) are highlighted in those publications. The latter gave up a successful musical career when he became a Muslim. He has become a special role model for young Muslims and is featured at annual conventions. The story of his conversion is sold on videotape throughout the Muslim world.

Estimates of white converts range from fifty thousand to more than ninety thousand. They include a few who are considered by the Muslim community to be opportunists, seeking employment or privileges from Muslims and Muslim countries. Some have converted for reasons of expediency such as Christian or Jewish men marrying Muslim women. The majority are deemed to be sincere seekers and genuine converts to Islam by those who associate with them. They come from a variety of religious traditions, and include even some ex-seminarians (both Catholic and Protestant). They also include a significant number of Jews. The majority are women who find Islam appealing because they believe they will be treated with respect and not as sex objects. Many indicate that they find Christian doctrines of incarnation and trinity implausible.[31] A significant number are attracted to groups formed around Sufi masters,[32] the largest and best organized being the Bawwa Muhaiyadeen Fellowship with headquarters in Philadelphia.[33]

Sojourners

Sojourners are those Muslims who are in the United States on a temporary basis. Some of them exercise important influence on immigrants and converts as they interact with them, while others remain quite marginal to American society.[34] Among the latter are the migrant laborers who come from different countries, the largest group coming from Yemen.[35] While some eventually settle in various parts of the United States, most see their identity in terms of their country of origin and maintain a marginal interest in participating in American public life. Their goal is to save money for their eventual return home.

A second marginal group are emigres who assume a temporary status in the United States, hesitating to put down roots while they wait for a change in their home governments. The largest émigré community comes from Iran.[36] The majority are assumed to be secularists and royalists awaiting the overthrow of the current Iranian regime and the assumption of power by Reza Pahlevi, the son of the former Shah. At first, Iranian immigrants were very reluctant to participate in organized religion and focused their energies on commercial and business activities.[37] More recently, with the awareness that they may be in the United States for a longer period than they anticipated and in response to individual and community needs, they have begun the organizing of Shi'ite worship groups. Recent political events in the Middle East have swelled the ranks of the émigré population with growing numbers of Lebanese, Iraqis, Afghans, and Kurds.

A third group of sojourners are the hundreds of thousands of students attending various institutions of higher learning throughout the United States. In many instances they have sought association with resident Muslims and attended their religious and cultural activities. Some have also volunteered to serve as language teachers in Islamic schools or as imams, guiding immigrant groups in the faith. Over the last forty years a significant number have opted not to return to their home countries and have sought employment in the United States.

Islamic student organizations are prominent in university towns across America. The Muslim Student Association (MSA), organized in 1963, has had a very significant influence on the definition of Muslim identity in the United States.[38] With ideological ties to the Muslim Brotherhood of Egypt and the Jamaati Islami of Pakistan, it has succeeded in creating the largest Muslim organization in the United States and Canada committed to developing a vibrant, authentic, and modern Islamic identity that supersedes ethnic and national allegiances. The importance of the MSA lies not only in its members' successful efforts at creating institutions such as schools and a large number of mosques/Islamic centers that have joined their organization (321 by 1984), but in the publication and dissemination of Islamic literature in English advocating their particular theological and cultural definition of Islam.[39]

The students who return home from the United States constitute a significant portion of the leadership of their countries. Their experiences in the United States shape their perceptions of America and its commitment to democratic and pluralistic ideals, as well as how it relates to Islam and Muslim minorities. This factor will continue to influence the response of Muslim countries to American foreign policy as the alumni of American colleges and universities translate their perceptions and experiences into policies. Meanwhile, these students constitute a hotbed of intellectual ferment about Islam and how it can and should respond to the challenges of life in the modern world. In this respect, the United States has replaced France as the primary center for Islamic intellectual reflection.

Also included among the sojourners are the itinerant missionaries who have come from all over the Muslim world. The largest number belong to the pietistic Tableeghi Jamaat (Group of Informers) who visit North America for what can be categorized as revival meetings primarily aimed at the faithful with a secondary effort to invite outsiders to join the community of believers.[40] Their influence goes beyond the estimated thirty mosques that follow their teachings. Their Islamic message tends to be isolationist, calling on Muslims to restrict their social interaction exclusively to those who share the same ideas and practices. They focus primarily on spiritual rearmament and the rewards of the hereafter; consequently, they are opposed to any political activity. Their regional meetings have been impressive in the number of participants they have been able to gather. (Some eleven thousand self-styled missionaries are reported to have attended their 1985 convention held in Columbus, Ohio.)[41]

The large contingent of diplomats from forty-four Islamic countries to the United States and the United Nations constitute an important link between temporary residents and the immigrant groups. A few of these diplomats have at times sought support for various causes in their home countries. Some have even financed periodicals advocating their interpretation of Islamic life and of current events.[42] This at times has served to replicate conflicts overseas among the more recent immigrants and their supporters.

Two international Islamic organizations, the Muslim World League and the Organization of Islamic Conference, are recognized by the United Nations as nongovernmental organizations. Both have diplomats at the United Nations. In the 1970s and 1980s, the Muslim World League had substantial involvement with Muslim organizations in the United States. One of its officials ran the Council of Masajid in North America (with a membership of 151 mosques/Islamic centers in 1985). It provided leadership (up to twenty-six imams serving in different mosques) and funds for Islamic activity in the United States (up to five million dollars a year) dedicated to the construction of mosque and school structures.

The steady flow of overseas tourists and relatives of immigrants is also an important source of information about intellectual, cultural, and religious trends in various Muslim countries. These Muslims provide input into Muslim life in America from the perspective of their home countries, including corrective commentary about what is Islamically proper, the organization of the community, and questions of identity.

American Scholarship and the Muslims

Until recently, the history and activity of the Muslim community in the United States has been seen as marginal or insignificant by the academic community and has been mostly ignored by historians of Islam and American religion.[43] Muslims searching for their history in the American context find that they have been depicted as insignificant "fringe" groups, outside the mainstream of American experience. Scholarship on Muslims in America, insofar as it exists, is very recent. Courses on American religion in the United States have generally tended to focus exclusively on Christianity and Judaism. Those dealing with Islam seldom include material on the presence of Muslims in North America.[44] Islam as a global religion is treated in the study of world religions, while area studies concentrate on the sociopolitical and economic factors that shape the various nations. Although some courses on Afro-American history may make reference to Black Muslims and those on religious sects discuss some of the Sufis, Islam continues to be taught on many campuses as an alien religion.[45]

There is a growing feeling among American Muslims that the story of the discovery of America has not been fully told. Some have attempted to reconstruct America's past by focusing attention on vestiges of Islamic presence and the unrecognized contribution of Muslims to American society. Promoters of Africanist perspectives believe that Muslims from Africa may have discovered America before the Europeans did, and in a significant manner helped the Spaniards in the early explorations.[46] This desire to participate in rewriting the American past appears to be motivated by the hope of participating in defining the American future. While reminiscent of Catholic efforts at the end of the nineteenth century,[47] Muslim discourse at the end of the twentieth century is the product of colonialism as well as the postcolonial, postmodernist experience. Some Muslim scholars question the motives that have obliterated reference to Muslim presence since the beginning of the American adventure. The absence of Muslims from the American record is attributed to the tendency of Europeans to exaggerate their own importance and see themselves as the acme of civilization, others suggest a willful intent that is grounded in the millennium-old Christian hatred and fear of Islam born out of the Crusades.

Since the mid-1980s the situation of scholarly neglect of Muslims in America has begun to change, with a significant number of scholars showing interest in the Muslim community.[48] A growing body of literature, including several bibliographies, is beginning to appear.[49] More Muslim scholars are now studying and writing on the experience of their community in North America.[50] The majority of the studies tend to be descriptive general surveys of Muslims[51] or studies of particular ethnic groups,[52] generally done by anthropologists. Immigrant groups that have been studied include Arabs,[53] Syrians,[54] Jordanians,[55] Iranians,[56] Lebanese,[57] Pakistanis,[58] Turks,[59] Palestinians,[60] and Egyptians.[61] More recently, a few scholars have concentrated on providing surveys of Muslims in particular metropolitan areas.[62]

While the immigrants came and continue to come of their own free choice, in the early history of America many Muslims were brought by force. A substantial number of the African slaves brought to American shores were of Muslim background.[63] The story of their conversion to Christianity has not been adequately explored as yet. While there have been some studies on the lives of a few distinguished Muslims who were enslaved in the United States, there is a great need for further research on this topic.[64] Allan D. Austin has published anthologies that include material about and by these early Muslims in the United States.[65]

The conversion of African Americans to Islam in the early part of this century can be seen primarily as a response to American racism and to the conditions of northern American urban centers to which the black population emigrated.[66] Black Muslims were defined as a threat by the FBI and the media,[67] and as alien by the scholars. Two important pioneering studies have shaped our perception of the phenomenon since the 1960s, influenced by the dominant headline-makers of the time such as the Black Panthers, black power, and Malcolm X. E.U. Eissien-Udom placed the black Muslims in the nationalist movement and C. Eric Lincoln in the black power movement. Later authors utilized other tools of analysis. Michael Parenti, for example, applied the Weberian thesis of charismatic leadership, Puritan ethics, and capitalism to explore the dynamics of Islam in the African-American community.[68] Building on Parenti's analysis a decade and a half later, Lawrence H. Mamiya used Weberian analysis to show that "Protestant" work ethic, frugality, and morality adopted by the African-American Muslims helped move them from a predominantly lower-class movement into the middle class.[69] Perry E. Gianakos argues that since most studies have been sociological in nature they have placed special emphasis on the "myths" of the group and have tended to emphasize the difference and distinctiveness. Even though Muslims who are black have been treated as alien to American social consensus and history, he says, they are "'as American as cherry pie,' . . . perhaps among the most American of Americans."[70]

Muslims overseas evidence a great interest in the fate of Muslims in the West in general and have written several studies on the Muslims of the United States. This interest is not restricted to the immigrant population and its survival in North America but extends to African-American Islam. While they have been excited by the prospect of "the return of African Americans" to their true faith, they have expressed serious reservations about the myths and teachings of the Nation of Islam. Their writings appear to have very little original information or research but are heavily dependent on the pioneering works of C. Eric Lincoln and Eissien-Udom. Zafar Ishaq Ansari has focused on the teachings of the Nation of Islam and identified the differences between the theology of the Nation and the doctrines of orthodox Islam.[71] These observers have great expectations that the reforms of Warith Deen Muhammad will mold the community into a replica of Islam overseas.[72]

Muslims and the American Experience

The majority (estimated at about 75 percent) of adult Muslims in the United States (excluding the African-American community) are foreign-born. Hence, their primary identity was formed overseas, and they continue to have ties with relatives and friends in other countries. Unlike what obtained in the last century, the old country is present to them in a very immediate way through the communication revolution. Not only can they fly to visit often, read the available foreign press, and listen to foreign broadcasts on shortwave radio, they can also be in daily touch through telephone, telefax, and increasingly, E-mail. American foreign policy toward Muslim countries is therefore interpreted through the insights of the nations from which they emigrated.

Since most of the early Muslim immigrants to the United States were from the Arab world, they were the first community to experience what is perceived as "the double standard" of the foundations of foreign policy. The Arab community in the United States became aware of the influence of Zionism on American policy in the 1940s.[73] They were frustrated by their inability to counter this influence given their small numbers and the fact they were dispersed throughout the United States and lacked the organizational structures and leadership to impact public policy. Their feelings of marginality were intensified by their inability to provide input into the shaping of American priorities, opinion, and foreign policy, or to influence the press to help correct what they perceived as the slanderous reports that were being published.[74] They realized that the often false information that was appearing in the press maligned them as a people as well as the heritage in which they took great pride. As a result a small group of American-born Muslim veterans of World War II, led by Abdullah Ingram, established the Federation of Islamic Associations as the first Muslim umbrella organization in North America then representing twenty-seven mosques and Islamic centers in the United States and Canada.[75] They became involved in gathering information, debating, and lecturing on issues of justice for the Palestinians.

The Arab-Israeli war of 1967 had a profound impact on the Arabs and Muslims living in the United States. From their perspective, it was an Israeli aggression on Egypt, Syria, and Jordan. American partisan depiction of the war was perceived as one-sided support for Israel. For many Muslims, it represented a moment of crisis when their faith and confidence in American justice and commitment to fairness and democracy were profoundly shaken. Muslims feel that United States support of Israel since 1967 through the vetoing of United Nations resolutions has allowed the occupation of Palestinian land through Israeli "aggression." It became apparent to Muslims worldwide that Israel and its wish list mattered more than international agreements and conventions.[76]

This experience helped bring about some organizational activity in the United States. Several Arab-American organizations were established to set the record straight. The American-Arab Anti-Discrimination Committee (ADC) was formed by James Aburezk, then senator from South Dakota, to combat prejudice against Arabs and Arab Americans.[77] Other groups include the Association of Arab-American University Graduates, Inc. (AAUG),[78] the American Arab Association (AMARA, successor to the defunct Eastern State Federation), and the National Association of Arab Americans (NAAA), which aims "to engage in political, social, cultural, and educational activities for the purpose of maintaining political action involvement in the United States." While the majority of the members of these organizations were Arab Christians, there was substantial Muslim participation. Their appropriation of the "Arab" designation is seen by some in the Islamic movement as divisive since it emphasizes nationalist or ethnic rather than religious identity and has left little room for identification by Muslims from Albania, Bosnia, Russia, Turkey, Iran, Pakistan, and other non-Arab Muslim countries.

The initial reaction of Muslim immigrants from non-Arab countries to these Arab organizations was very skeptical. Not only did the Arab Muslims come from countries where there is no freedom of speech and no room for political participation, the non-Arab Muslims felt that the Arabs were obsessed with Israel. An event that took place in a Montreal mosque is informative. When an Arab preacher during the Friday prayers began to talk about the Palestinian issue, six Pakistanis escorted him out of the mosque and informed him that politics has no place in the mosque. The burning of the Aqsa mosque in Jerusalem in 1969, as well as the experience of living in America, which provides what is perceived as unquestioned support for the state of Israel, transposed the Palestinian problem from an Arab issue into an Islamic cause.

Disenchantment with American foreign policy has led several Muslim groups — including the Salafis and the Tableeghi Jama'at, as well some in the African-American Muslim community — to advocate an apolitical stance. Others have been spurred to experiment with political activity. New Islamic political organizations have sprung up in different parts of the country. These include such organizations as the Muslim Political Action Committee (MPAC) in Los Angeles; the All America Muslim Political Action Committee (AAMPAC) in Houston; the United Muslims of America (UMA) in Sacramento and Los Angeles; the National Council of Islamic Affairs (NCIA); and the Islamic Society of North America Political Action Committee (ISNAPAC). Membership in these organizations still lacks experience in political activity, in working with the media, and in lobbying. No Muslim has been elected to national office.[79]

Non-Arab Muslims also have developed a range of national organizations that propagate a variety of international causes. For example, there are several political organizations that lobby for American aid to Pakistan. These include the Pakistani Federation of America (Chicago), the Muslim League of Voters (Chicago), the Friends of Pakistan Committee (New York), Pakistan Forum of USA (New York), and Pakistani-Political Action Committee (Michigan). Other organizations support the independence of Kashmir, and American intervention in Bosnia, Kurdistan, or Afghanistan, among other causes.

Of great concern to members of the Muslim community during the last decade has been the prejudice against Islam that seems to permeate American society at all levels, from the presidency to the editorial commentary in various newspapers to the concerns of ordinary citizens. An increase in such prejudice appears to have a direct relationship to the formation of the Islamic Republic of Iran. Diatribes against Islam have come from senior government officials such as President Ronald Reagan [80] and Vice President Dan Quayle.[81] Muslims have also been maligned by columnists,[82] academicians,[83] and media commentators.[84] Muslims living in North America are weary of being scapegoated for the activities of others overseas just as they resent the maligning of Islam in the American public forum. Increased incidents of harassment and attacks on individual Islamic institutions can often be directly connected with a public attack made by an American official against Muslim leaders overseas.

To Muslims, distortion of their history appears endemic to American society. They note the discrepancy between the proclaimed values of their new country and their experiences in their local environment, including schools,[85] courts,[86] places of residence and employment,[87] as well as the general ethos of the United States.[88] Depictions of Muslims by the image makers and opinion shapers in the popular culture, including literature,[89] textbooks,[90] the movies,[91] and the media,[92] are often painful. My survey of the literature on political correctness in the United States showed that not one list of protected communities considered the defamation of Arabs, Islam, or Muslims to be off-limits.

The often negative media portrayal of things Arab and Islamic is taking its toll on the Muslim community in the United States. The publication and dissemination of Salman Rushdie's The Satanic Verses,[93] and the accompanying press commentary about Muslim intolerance, has raised new questions: Will the Muslims of North America survive as a vibrant religious community? Will they be able fully and freely to participate in its religious mosaic and help in defining its future as a pluralistic society? Or will the children of the immigrants opt for an easy way out, identifying completely with their adopted country and abandoning the faith? And, as Rushdie is accused of doing, will they mock their own heritage and sacred values, using the idiom and precepts of the host culture? At present, the perceived demonization of Islam appears to be one of the important factors galvanizing the Muslim community. Attendance at mosques/Islamic centers and Sunday schools has increased. Muslims are listening to those who warn that America hates Islam and that the only option for Muslim survival is consciously to choose to be marginal and to reaffirm the Islamic identity of the community.

They seek to transform their current condition of oppression into a brighter future based on the achievements of the Islamic past, a past that is freed from the interpretations of the Orientalists.[94]

Arab and Muslim marginalization is apparent during political campaigns. The successful candidate for mayor in the city of Dearborn, Michigan (the city with the largest immigrant Arab community in America), ran on a platform promising to get the Muslims out. His hostility inspired graffiti in the city urging readers to "Be an American, kill an Arab." Politicians have also used other means to reinforce the increased alienation of American Muslims from the political process. Several candidates for political office, apparently afraid of being "polluted" by "Arab" money, refused and/or returned contributions from Arab Americans to their campaign.[95] This is seen by Arabs as a racist and prejudicial act as well as a means of disenfranchising the community. It was not until the election of 1988 that several Islamic political action committees were formed. In some cases, they joined the Rainbow Coalition in support of Jesse Jackson's candidacy for president.

With the coming of the Ayatollah Khomeini to power in Iran, American foreign policy has been perceived as increasingly hostile to Islam and Muslims.[96] This has been exacerbated by press depiction of events such as the Israeli invasion of Lebanon, American bombing of Libya, the Salman Rushdie affair, the bombing of the World Trade Center, and the Gulf War against Iraq.[97] At the same time, American policy tends to ignore the fate of persecuted Muslims whether in Kashmir, the Philippines, Chechnya, Azerbaijan, or Bosnia. This has convinced many that the American government does not place a prime value on human life or suffering when the victims happen to be Muslim.

The "Omnibus Counterterrorism Act of 1995" sponsored by the Clinton administration appears to be speedily making its way through Congress. It is perceived as targeting Muslims and Arabs in the United States, not only threatening their right to a fair trial but also restricting their ability to make charitable contributions to worthy causes overseas.[98] To Muslim and Arab observers, it appears that certain interests have succeeded in identifying Islam as the new demon for Americans to hate now that the forces of communism have been defeated. Questions are being asked whether the United States, the land of promised freedom of religion and of constitutionally guaranteed rights, can provide legal protection to, or has room for, Muslims.

The Oklahoma City bombing has once again made Muslim Americans worry about their security and the safety of their children. It is of great concern to them that Congressman Bill McCollum (Republican of Florida), was so quick to accuse Muslims of responsibility for the terrorism before any proof was available. Congressman McCollum in conjunction with Congressman Gary L. Ackerman (Democrat of New York) have recently sent a letter to all members of Congress urging them to vote for the anti-terrorism bill. Attached to the letter is a copy of the controversial television documentary entitled *Jihad in America*, prepared by Steven Emerson.[99]

Muslim sources see such an apparent obsession with Islamic movements to be part of an effort to create an enemy to take the place of the evil empire of communism. Muslims had a stake in the fall of the Soviet Empire. Muslims from all over the world were at the forefront of those who fought the Russian army in Afghanistan. Rather than American appreciation for fighting its proxy war and helping bring the Soviet Empire to its knees, however, they find that their position in the United States has become more tenuous because of what appears to them to be a smear campaign by Zionists. This includes the propaganda of the B'nai B'rith Anti-Defamation League, sometimes referred to by Arab Americans as "The Defamation League," since it has a history of defaming Arabs and Muslims.[100] The organization maintained a "black list" of scholars sympathetic to Arabs on American campuses and appears to have sponsored and supported spying on a variety of American organizations including those that are Arab and Muslim.[101] It has also issued several reports on Muslims[102] including African-American Muslims such as Louis Farrakhan[103] and the Al-Fuqra movement.[104]

These events have made Muslims realize that they are a community in jeopardy, encouraging their attempt to develop an Islamic response and to create Islamic institutions and discourse to counter the negative views of so much of the American public. This situation provides the historian of religion and the social scientist in America with an unusual laboratory condition for the study of a religion whose identity is being forged in a context in which its members experience a sense of alienation and victimization. Historians may point to the fact that Muslims are not the first religious group to face hostility in the United States; Mormons, Catholics, Jews, even Quakers and Presbyterians have suffered for their beliefs. What is unique about the current situation is the communication revolution that not only has facilitated the acquisition of information about Muslims by researchers but has also made it possible for the world to be an immediate eyewitness to events in America. It is also the case that this anti-Muslim campaign is taking place when issues of hate speech and political correctness have raised consciousness about creating tolerance in American society. What is most peculiar about the current affair is that of the apparent beneficiaries of the demonization, only one, namely conservative Christians, seem to be motivated by religious considerations.[105]

Muslims on the Americanization Path

The modernization and secularization of the Muslims of America began in the urban centers of their home countries, in Cairo, Damascus, Beirut, Tehran, Delhi, and Istanbul. While there are many studies that explore the influence of European thought on Islamic discourse in the nineteenth century, there has been no attempt to measure the influence of American missionary attacks on Islam in the creation of modern Islamic theological and ideological discourse. The French revolution had a measurable impact on Muslim intellectuals who visited Europe. Foreign protagonists of secularization and modernization in Islamic countries included both Christian missionaries who saw Islam as an impediment to the triumph of Christianity over the world by the end of the century, and the colonial bureaucrats who saw Islam as an obstacle to their efforts to modernize parts of the infrastructure in order to facilitate the utilization and domination of Muslim resources for the benefit of European nations.

American missionary activity, especially in inculcating American ideals in their educational institutions, had great influence on the graduates. By the 1920s missionary efforts included women's education, which aimed at fostering their liberation and thereby undermining Islam.[106] By the 1950s when the support of the American churches for the missionary endeavor petered out, missionaries were satisfied with secularizing the area. The nationalist ideals they had put forth emphasized a sense of peoplehood identified with a nation state, underscored by an ideology of shared culture, ethos, language, and history.[107]

With the departure of the missionaries and the end of the colonial period, new challenges to Muslims came from Marxism and Zionism. In combatting the claims of these ideologies to Muslim allegiance and space, Muslims developed their own ideology that had the imprint of the new struggle, especially on perceptions of self-definition. A careful analysis of the Islamist discourse during what Islamists call the neocolonial period of American hegemony and Israeli occupation of Palestine depicts Muslims as a community at risk. This community rejects what it perceives to be the "cages" prescribed by Europeans as manageable boundaries of nation-states and seeks transnational identity, evoking memories of ancient glory intentionally suppressed by the West. It seeks to redefine itself on its own terms. In reaction to the impetus of the West to bring about reform by divesting Muslims of Islam, they see that it is even more important to hold on to the faith, defending it not only against its detractors but also against those who harbor hatred for its tenets and seek to undermine its people's belief. Whereas the goal of the Islamists in the first half of this century was to modernize Islam, current Islamist thought seeks to Islamize modernity. In the American context this has been reinvigorated both by increased American involvement in Muslim nations and by the vagaries of American foreign policy. God — who has promised vindication to his people, say the Islamists — will surely fulfil his promise and create a just society where people are dedicated to faithfulness to his will for the world. God seeks one people, one order, the brotherhood of all humanity, surrendering to the one God who does not distinguish between humans based on color, nationality, or ethnic identity but guarantees equal justice for all.[108]

Following World War II, the United States became an important center of Muslim intellectual ferment.[109] Having replaced Europe as the dominant power in the third world it attracted a large number of students seeking technical and professional training. In an attempt to influence the future leadership of the third world, the United States encouraged the education of foreign students in the joys of capitalism and the evils of Marxism. In the process, American universities as well as some of the Islamic centers associated with them have become the locus for reflection and experimentation with a variety of Islamic worldviews.[110]

Earlier generations of Muslim students found in Europe, and especially in France, the model for a secular nationalism in which a range of identities was subsumed under the ideal of a single state. The Muslim experience of the United States appears to have created a different consensus. Despite the rhetoric of the separation of church and state, Muslims note that America is a religious society organized in churches with active congregations. The United States presents a special model of social organization focused on religious structures, whether these be churches or synagogues. A significant amount of social, cultural, and political activity is organized in these institutions. Following this model the mosques of the United States increasingly have become Americanized in administration and services, a development that appears to have international ramifications as students studying in the United States and participating in this new experiment may attempt to replicate their experiences in their homelands.[111] A case in point is the development of the "full service mosque" in Cairo, which provides comprehensive services such as Qur'anic study circles, counseling, tutoring of students, rooms for social events such as wedding receptions, financial support for the needy, and medical care. The leadership (mostly graduates of American universities) of the movement to restore the mosque to its original role, under way in various parts of the Muslim world, promotes a vision of the mosque as the center for organized community activities and not only for prescribed daily prayer, as its customary function had become. The model promoted is that of the mosque of the Prophet Muhammad in Medina where the community looked for guidance for all social, economic, political, and cultural matters.

Muslim students also experience American religion through the electronic church. Evangelical catchwords such as "born-again" Muslims, "salvation," and realizing the "Kingdom of God" on earth have become common in Islamic discourse. What is interesting is not only the fact that such affirmations are not traditional Muslim definitions of the faith but that the "new birth" to Islam occurs in the United States.[112]

Themes in American Islam

Several American developments in the sixties have had a profound impact on the shaping and transformation of the Islamist movement overseas as well as of the American Muslim community in the United States. Islamists are looking at America with new eyes and trying to learn from its lessons and to avoid the pitfalls into which they see it having fallen. From this perspective, for example, the Vietnam War demonstrated that a determined third-world people can withstand the "juggernaut of the mightiest nation" in the world. The hippie revolution proved the inadequacy of the American value system, which was rejected by its own young people. The feminist movement demonstrated that Western culture is not egalitarian and treats women not with respect but as sex objects. The black power movement through its revolutionary discourse exposed America's dark secrets of racism and slavery. And the legitimation of Zionism as a liberation movement justified American-Jewish identification with and commitment to the state of Israel, necessitating the crystallization of an Islamic identity under pressure-cooker conditions that demanded immediate results for a process that normally takes several generations to develop.

A variety of issues have surfaced as the community has attempted to define its Islamic identity vis-à-vis the American religious scene. While some of these issues are imposed on the community by the nature of American society, others characterize the constituent nature of the group itself as well as the parameters set by the scriptural foundations of Islam, parameters that are seen by some as non-negotiable.[113]

"Minorityness"

From the perspective of scholars overseas, Muslims of the United States are part of the larger category of worldwide minority Muslim communities, estimated at one-third of the Muslim population.[114] The status and welfare of Muslim minorities was a major concern of Professor Syed Zein al-Abdin of King Abd al-Aziz University, who established the Institute of Muslim Minority Affairs in Jeddah and began a journal devoted exclusively to issues of minorities and "minority-ness."[115] In a book published by the Institute, Moroccan Islamist M. Ali Kettani, who had lived in the United States for a period of time, discussed the realities of minority existence. Utilizing classical Islamic understanding of the issue, he attempted to reflect on the modern reality. For Kettani "minorityness" is determined not by the size of the community but by its weakness and powerlessness, a condition that he believed is incompatible with Islam. Islam works for the well-being as well as the social and political empowerment of a community. Muslims must not accommodate and acquiesce to those in power by accepting minority status as a permanent condition. Their "minorityness" is to be perceived as a challenge to the community, to seek to alter such a condition and transcend it. He counseled against integration and assimilation and called for the creation of separate colonies that try to keep themselves isolated from the dominant culture.

Kettani suggested that if a Muslim minority is unable to practice its faith, then its members have the options of either fighting back, *jihad*, or emigrating, *hijra*. These options follow the precedent of the practice of the Prophet Muhammad when confronted with persecution. "Emigration for one's belief is an act of religious merit; in some cases it is even a religious duty. Such a man is a *muhajir*, but not a refugee."[116] The term *muhajir* had been used by several generations of Arab immigrants in its generic meaning, one who emigrates from one place to another. For a growing number of Muslims, the term increasingly has been endowed with religious significance. It refers to one who consciously seeks to emulate the prophetic model, that is, leaving one's home in search of a new life where one can freely practice one's religion and its dictates. Thus immigrants must recognize that they are living in a condition of *hijra*. It signifies the structuring of life in a manner that does not give in to an oppressive power but posits a life of struggle to practice and maintain the prescriptions of Islam on both the individual and communal levels in the hope of establishing a righteous and just society.

The identity of *muhajirun* is that of immigrants, not pilgrims. Thus Muslims are not called to roam in the wilderness of North America in search of a corporate religious redemption, nor are they awaiting a new revelation that is particular to the venue in which they find themselves. Rather, they are a community that has responded to divine command, has armed itself with God's message, and has willingly assumed the task of establishing a just order. Muslims in America thus are immigrants in God's land. It is not the land of any particular group or nation. An immigrant is one who is always at home wherever he may find himself, ever vigilant, ever striving to realize justice in the world, not only in the land he has emigrated to, but also, even more important, in the one he left behind.

Separatists and isolationists among the Muslims feel that the suffering one experiences in living in a non-Muslim environment is a calling from God, who has commissioned Muslims to invite others to the straight path. From this perspective, they have been placed in the United States for a purpose, to help lead Americans away from their errant ways. While many of the immigrants have come to America for economic reasons, the separatists warn against being consumed by economic considerations and losing one's faith, what one Muslim leader called "the allurement of the dollar." For while it is permissible for Muslims to emigrate in the pursuit of better living conditions, it should not be at the cost of giving up the faith. The admonition is to return to poverty if the alternative is the loss of one's soul. "Should there be the least danger to faith go back to your native land or to any other place where there is the security of faith; go, and take your family, go even if you have to go on foot." [117]

There are significant differences between the interpretations of those who accept the isolationist position and those who, following the lead of Muhammad Abduh of Egypt whose opinion was dominant among Muslims in North America until the 1960s,[118] struggle to feel at home in America by being more accommodating. Thus Imam Abdul Rauf of the Washington Islamic Center counseled:

> The elements of Islamic culture, therefore may not be inherent in Islam. They are patterns of culture or a mode of life developed or adopted by a Muslim community. Therefore, when a Muslim moves into an alien culture, carrying with him his cultural heritage, he is at liberty to adjust to the host culture so long as he maintains the core of his religion, including all the specific Islamic tenets in all areas.[119]

Such flexibility, however, has now lost ground among some of those who are worried about compromising the purity of the faith. While the isolationists place a great premium on maintaining a halal kitchen, for example, the accommodationists argue that "any nourishing diet, any decent dress, and any type of architecture for their houses and mosques" [120] is acceptable if it does not violate the tenets of the prescriptions of the faith, since religion and culture are not one and the same thing.

In the last two decades, the conditions and problems of Muslim minorities have received increased attention from the various international Islamic organizations. The Muslim World League established a *Fiqh* Council representing all Islamic legal schools to address the variety of issues that face Muslim communities in the modern world, including the issue of minority life in a non-Islamic environment. The Council advocated the development of what is being called *fiqh al-darura* (jurisprudence of necessity) or *fiqh al-aqalliyah* (jurisprudence of minority) to address the issues that confront Muslim minorities.[121]

The Mosque Movement

The mosque movement, which began in earnest in the 1970s, is a voluntary association based on presumed common and shared values and beliefs. The mosque schools promote maintenance of religious and ethnic identity to preserve culture and provide instruction in values that promote upward mobility and maintenance of educational achievement. Brothers and sisters in the faith often serve the function of the extended family that one does not have in America. The mosque institutions face many challenges, paramount among them the fostering of Islam and its preservation in the next generation. Unlike earlier mosques, the new organizations do not represent ethnic minorities but rather are pluralistic groupings coping with a variety of cultures all believed to be genuinely Islamic at the same time that they exhibit cultural variations. The result is that the mosque today is not so much a transplant as a new creation with a revitalized function and role in society.

Muslim Women in America

The role of Muslim women and the family in the American context has received special attention from contemporary Muslim writers[122] as well as American scholars.[123] Part of the criticism of American culture on the part of Muslims over the past several decades has centered on the issue of women's roles and responsibilities. These roles have subtly changed and shifted over the years as more clearly defined Islamic expectations have been laid upon Muslim women.[124]

. The records of the early Muslim immigrants at the turn of the century show that Muslim women were very active in founding and operating Islamic institutions. In many cases they organized the fund-raising and took responsibility for the refurbishing of the mosques.[125] They sought Islamic education for their children, and many were involved in running the Sunday schools. Today young women are being taught that they have been endowed by God with the responsibility of maintaining an Islamic home and nurturing children in the faith, reinforcing the role of the woman as wife and mother.

The large number of white women converts to Islam has helped to enhance the image of Islam as one in which women have full and responsible roles to play. This has made the faith more attractive to college-educated American women. As they don Islamic dress and become involved in Islamic life, they affirm that the "dating and relationship games" of the dominant culture are not to be coveted, because the freedoms they provide can lead to perversion and pornography. The message is that Islam protects women. It respects them and honors them as major contributors not only to a wholesome family but to the creation of a better society.

For African-American women who convert to Islam, the new status not only provides a sense of liberation from being a sex object but in many cases is seen as a means of redemption for African-American society by providing a stable home-life in which the male is a full participant, the loving husband, the caring father, and the responsible provider. From this perspective, conversion to Islam is a revolutionary act that reverses what American society has done through its policies of social welfare to the African-American family and restores the sense of dignity to the African-American male.

Other concerns include the perception that the American press and the American academy do not display any sensitivity or appreciation of the Islamic understanding of the role and status of women in society. Rather, they appear to be engaged in an orgy of derision and distortion. What is more galling to many is the apparent defection of some Muslim women in the academy whose writings betray an apparent preference for Western standards. They are perceived as a product of self-hate and are accused of unwittingly aiding in the undermining of the Muslim community.

Muslim Intellectuals in America

The American experience has had an important influence in the shaping of Islamic ideas by Muslim intellectuals.[126] While Muslims since the tenth century have preferred to focus on the means of right conduct rather than on theological speculations, twentieth-century challenges have fostered reflection on issues of religion and identity, religion and the role of the human being, and Islam in the sociopolitical and economic sphere. The fact that many of the leaders of the Iranian revolution that brought Khomeini to power were alumni of American universities is often cited as an example of American intellectual influence. Of greater importance has been the development of revolutionary Islamic thought by two Arab thinkers whose worldviews have been greatly influential. Both the Egyptian Sayyid Qutb[127] (who lived in the United States from 1949 to 1951) and the Palestinian Isma'il al-Faruqi[128] (a Temple University professor who responded to American policies following the 1967 and 1973 Arab Israeli wars) were secular in their outlook before their American experience. Disenchantment with America's lack of justice and its support of Israeli infringement on the rights of Palestinians gave birth to a commitment to Islam as the answer to human suffering and the corrective to violations of human rights and international law.[129] Both writers emphasized the importance of Islamic unity. Both were concerned with the empowerment of the Muslim community as a necessary predicate to the salvation of the Muslim Umma. For both, the Qur'anic verse "Hold fast to the rope of God and do not separate" was an important commandment. They emphasized the need for the creation of an overarching ideology that can encompass the disparate national and cultural groups that constitute the worldwide Islamic community.

Isma'il al-Faruqi became an activist scholar who challenged other Muslim scholars throughout the Muslim world to seek a just path, to integrate their work with a commitment to re-Islamization of the world. He encouraged them to proclaim the good news from God that in the Islamic order there is no preference based on genetic inheritance, race, or creed, but that the new social, economic, and political order will serve to create justice and equality. He posited an Islam that seeks not only to reform the world but to transform it, a revolution committed to fairness and equity. He sought the renewal of American society by the application of Islamic teachings.

Two other prominent émigré scholars have had a profound influence on students from overseas. Both Seyyed Hossein Nasr[130] (from Iran) and Fazlur Rahman[131] (from Pakistan) came to the United States because of political turmoil in their home countries, which made it impossible for them to continue their work. In the United States they were free to develop their ideas away from the watchful eyes of security police. While Seyyed Hossein Nasr emphasized traditional Islam and Sufism,[132] Fazlur Rahman wrote on Islamic modernism.[133] Both scholars, in their own way, were disappointed with the shortcomings of American society and both sought to provide an Islamic answer to the problems of the age.

Education

The education of children has been of paramount importance to Muslim parents from the beginning in both the immigrant and the African-American Muslim communities.[134] Older immigrants when interviewed cite character building among the children as the primary reason for establishing mosques. Among the early immigrants, the need for a morally grounded education led some parents to send their children to Baptist and Catholic parochial schools. However, with the growth of the Muslim community, several hundred Sunday schools as well as about a hundred Muslim parochial schools have been established. The latter generally follow the curriculum mandated by the state but include instruction in Islamic teachings. There are constant efforts under way to upgrade these schools, especially with what is perceived as the collapse of discipline, the lack of moral instruction, and the chaos that reigns in many American public schools.

Culture

The conversion of blacks to Islam has been both an inspiration and a challenge to the Muslim immigrant community. There continue to be several points of difference between the immigrants and the converts that influence identity. Black converts have been severed from their historical roots as a consequence of the slave experience. They are attracted to Islam because it provides an authentic alternative identity. They generally view the immigrants as foreigners while they see themselves as American, not Americanized. They have become increasingly sensitive to the issue of defining the culture of Islam. While eager to adopt Islamic cultural traits, they are wary of immigrants who insist on including cultural baggage as part of the definition of Islam. The diversity of the immigrant Muslim culture raises questions about what is Islamically valid — is it Arab, African, Malaysian, Pakistani, or whatever? And if all are valid, why can there not be a new cultural expression, an American Islam? One former imam from the American Muslim Mission referred to the struggle for identity in the African-American community in the following words: "We have become cultural chameleons." The tendency has been to take seriously any one who claims to be an authority in matters of dress, food, greetings, and so on, only to be told later by others that such things are determined by local cultural definition and are not of the essential culture of Islam. Imam Warith Deen Muhammad has been resisting absorption by the immigrant groups if that means subservience to foreign leadership.

The present situation of Islam in America is fragmented. While Muslim communities struggle to realize Islam in their lives, Muslims continue to reflect their national, ethnic, and cultural preferences. The task is not easy; there is very little social mixing among the various ethnic groups, and intermarriages are almost nonexistent. It can best be described with the words of one Pakistani leader: "We worship together but then the Pakistanis go back to their curries and the Arabs to their kebabs." He could have added "and the African Americans to their soul food." The challenge of implementing Islam will be tested in practice when the black community is fully integrated into the mosque and when intermarriage, which at present is almost nonexistent, begins to take place.

Intermarriage is, in fact, one of the variety of new problems faced by Muslims in America. When Muslim men marry out of the faith, as they are permitted to do if their wives are Jews or Christians, it precipitates a crisis by increasing the number of Muslim women who cannot find husbands because they are not allowed to marry non-Muslims.[135] Many other issues engage the Muslim community in America, including whether it is necessary to implement Islamic law;[136] whether there is a proper way of living Islamic life in a non-Muslim environment;[137] whether Muslims can accommodate to the American economic system based on interest;[138] whether the pressure to promote religious dialogue is in accord with the necessity of propagating the faith;[139] whether the American experience dictates the development of a new kind of Islamic leadership;[140] whether to anglicize their names or hold on to distinctive Islamic names;[141] and whether American law guarantees full rights for the community.[142]

Prospects for the Future

It is clear that the Muslim community in the United States is marginal to the society; its importance, however, should not be viewed exclusively from the perspective of size, history, and power. Its potential for action and influence both in the United States and overseas exceeds what its size might indicate. Its members constitute the best educated per capita group in the world. It is strategically located with potential access to the American media, giving it opportunity to learn to understand as well as utilize the American political process in the interest of its ideals. It is well connected to worldwide networks of kinship and association. Its creative institutions and sophistication are significantly impacting Muslims from all over the world, especially students seeking higher education. It is ethnically and linguistically diverse, reflecting a microcosm of the world of Islam. Finally, its members live in a relatively free society where they are able to experiment with new models of organizational life and of theological and ideological interpretation.

The majority of Muslims in America today, however, do not subscribe to this kind of thinking. They continue to operate outside organized religion; a substantial number are college graduates who are integrated into the American professional class. Yet they too remain uncomfortable with what is perceived as the moral decadence of American society and the "double standard" in American foreign policy, as well as with the tendency of political leaders to describe America as a "Judeo-Christian" country. They hope for a better America, a place where the principle of separation of religion and state can really apply, and where people of all faiths can flourish and maintain their traditions without being subject to harassment and prejudice. Their goal is to work for the realization of America's potential within the framework of American ideals and values. At present this goal seems difficult to attain, as they experience hurt and disillusionment over the disparity between principled declarations and compromising actions by the American government.[143] They hope for the day when America can both admit and realize its nature as a multicultural and multireligious society, and that finally it can be proud of its identity as "Christian, Jewish and Muslim."[144]

A study[145] of five immigrant Muslim communities in the United States identifies five distinct Muslim worldviews or categories into which Muslims currently might be classified:

1. Liberals, who tend to be the most Americanized among the American-born children and grandchildren of immigrants who came at the turn of the century from Eastern Europe, Turkey, and the Middle East. Many appear to have assimilated into American society (including cases of conversion to Christianity). This group also includes the "unmosqued" secularists, nationalists, and socialists who came in the middle of the century from Eastern Europe and the Arab world. Participants in the mosque movement refer to them with derision as "born Muslims," a reference to their lineage rather than their faith commitment. Members of this group tend self-consciously to separate themselves from other Muslims whom they accuse of fanaticism and backwardness. The majority have generally not formed any religious organizations or associations; their concerns and energies are channeled through political, social, cultural, ethnic, and educational institutions.

2. Conservatives, who are Westernized but appear to adhere to the minimum

requirements of Islam dealing with personal piety, dietary restrictions, and pre-scribed practices. Identifying themselves as Muslim and American, they feel at home in American society but seek to remain faithful to the teachings of Islam. They can also be described as accommodationists.

3. "Evangelicals," who place great emphasis on the teachings of the Qur'an and the model of the Prophet Muhammad in defining the perimeter of faith. They are generally concerned with strict observance of the details of Islamic life, insisting on the importance of following the most minute prescriptions and proscriptions found in the legal books. They are isolationist in outlook and insist that the Muslim community must restrict its social interaction to Muslims, ex-cept when engaged in an effort of converting others to Islam. Some among the group refer to themselves as "born-again Muslims." They see themselves as trans-nationals, with no allegiance to any existing government, including that of the United States. They see the world in terms of the peoplehood of God and the peoplehood of Satan. Isolationism is the means employed to protect them from the realm of the Satanic.

4. Islamists, who utilize modern theological and organizational perspectives while affirming the necessity of adherence to the details of the practice of the faith. They are interested in the political dimension of Islam, insisting on the necessity of Islam's supervision of public life to insure obedience to the law of God, which is prescribed for all humanity. Consequently, they seek to establish governments committed to the supervision and implementation of Islam wher-ever possible. Islam is perceived as contending in America, seeking to eradicate the existent evil and transform it into a truly Islamic state. This vision tends to be a mirror image of the American way. They talk about one nation under God with liberty and justice for all; this nation, however, will be governed by Islam. Only when Islam rules society will there be justice. In a sense, they affirm divine im-perative to expand the domain of Islam.

5. The Sufis, organized in independent groups with allegiance to a different spiritual leader from overseas, focus on the spiritual dimension of Islam. They primarily attract "Anglo" converts. While members work hard to make a living, they renounce American obsession with the material aspects of life. Their main emphasis is on their relationship to God, the fellowship of the support group and the denial of selfishness. They eschew all political and economic theories affirm-ing the organizing of community as a fellowship of the believers. Such groups can be found in Texas, New Mexico, Pennsylvania, upstate New York, and California.

Meanwhile, slowly and in many cases imperceptibly, the children and grand-children of the immigrants will probably be formulating several new forms of American Islam to meet the needs of the variety of their constituents. The shape of the identity will continue to be formed by the reality of who the Muslims are when they come, the way American society treats them, and the input of Muslims from abroad.

The apparent orchestrated and persistent efforts at demonizing Islam and Muslims in the United States are increasingly acting as an important catalyst in forging a cohesive Islamic identity. The individuals and groups that perceive themselves to be the target of misinformation and stereotyping are being urged to participate in efforts to rectify the false accusations. The struggle to project the truth about Islam has fostered a sense of identity based on both past history of victimization and current perception of threat. The menacing accusations and the facile stereotypes are instigating further consciousness raising, including a reevaluation of the sources, a revitalization of the faith, and creative new ventures in combating what seem to them to be clear indications of Judeo-Christian hatred. In the process a more cohesive American Islamic community is slowly being formed. Will American pluralism make room for the Muslims?

Notes

1. Yvonne Y. Haddad, *A Century of Islam in America*, Occasional Paper No. 4 (Islamic Affairs Program, Middle East Institute, 1986).

2. Ibid.

3. Raymond Brady Williams, *Religions of Immigrants from India and Pakistan* (Cambridge: Cambridge University Press, 1988); Omar Khalidi, *Indian Muslims in North America* (Watertown, Mass.: South Asia Press, n.d.).

4. Farouk Ahmed Mohamed Shaaban, "Conditions and Motivations of the Migration of Talent from the Arab Countries into the United States" (Ph.D. diss., University of Illinois, 1972); A.B. Zahlan, "The Brain Drain: Lebanon and Middle Eastern Countries" (prepared for the United Nations Institute for Training and Research [UNITAR], 1969, mimeograph); A.B. Zahlan, "Migration Patterns of the Graduates of the American University of Beirut," In *International Migration of High-level Manpower*, by the Committee on the International Migration of Talent (New York: Praeger, 1970), 269–97; A.B. Zahlan, "The Problematique of the Arab Brain Drain," *Arab Studies Quarterly* 2 (1980): 318–31; Lafi Ibrahim Jaafari, "The Brain Drain to the United States: The Migration of Jordanian and Palestinian Professionals and Students," *Journal of Palestine Studies* 3 (1973): 119–31; Lafi Ibrahim Jaafari, "Migration of Palestinian Arab and Jordanian Students and Professionals to the United States" (Ph.D. diss., Iowa State University of Science and Technology, 1971); Mehrassa Farjad, "Brain Drain: Migration of Iranian Physicians to the United States" (Ed.D. diss., George Washington University, 1981); Thomas L. Bernard, "United States Immigration Laws and the Brain Drain," *International Migrations* 1:7 (Jan. 1969): 16–18.

5. Yvonne Yazbeck Haddad and Adair T. Lummis, *Islamic Values in the United States: A Comparative Study* (New York: Oxford University Press, 1987); Abdo A. Elkholy, *The Arab Moslems in the United States* (New Haven, Conn.: College and University Press, 1966); Abdo A. Elkholy, "Religion and Assimilation in Two Muslim Communities in America" (Ph.D. diss., Princeton University, 1960); Elaine C. Hagopian and Ann Paden, eds. *The Arab Americans: Studies in Assimilation* (Wilmette, Ill.: Medina University Press International, 1969); Umhau C. Wolf, "Muslims in the American Midwest." *Muslim World* 50 (1960): 39–48.

6. Abdulaziz Sachedina, "A Minority Within a Minority: The Case of the Shi'a in North America," and Linda S. Walbridge, "The Shi'a Mosques and their Congregations in Dearborn," in *Muslim Communities in North America*, ed. Yvonne Yazbeck Haddad and Jane Idleman Smith (Albany: State University of New York, 1994), 3–14, 337–58; Vernon Schubel, "The Muharram Majlis: The Role of a Ritual in the Preservation of Shi'a Identity," in *Muslim Families in North America*, ed. Earle H. Waugh, Sharon McIrvin Abu-Laban, and Regula Burckhardt Qureshi (Edmonton, Alberta: University of Alberta Press, 1991); Hamid Algar, *The Roots of the Islamic Revolution* (Markham, Ontario: Open Press, 1983). For a shi'ite response to questions about Islam by the imam of the Dearborn mosque, see Mohamad Jawad Chirri, *Inquiries About Islam* (Beirut: Islamic Center of Detroit, 1965).

7. The followers of the Zaydi tradition are predominantly from Yemen.

8. The Alawis are from Syria, Turkey, and Lebanon.

9. Azim Nanji, "Modernization and Change in the Nizari Ismaili Community in East Africa," *Journal of Religion in Africa* 6 (1974): 123–39; Fariyal Ross-Sheriff, "Elderly Muslim Immigrants: Needs and Challenges," in Haddad and Smith, *Muslim Communities*, 407–22; A. Esmail, "Satpanth Ismailism and Modern Changes Within It: With Special Reference to East Africa" (Ph.D. diss., Edinburgh University, 1972); Gardner Thompson, "The Ismailis in Uganda," in *Expulsion of a Minority: Essays on Ugandan Asians*, ed. M. Twaddle (London: Athlone, 1974); S. Walji, "History of the Ismaili Community in Tanzania" (Ph.D. diss., University of Wisconsin, 1974); Fariyal Ross-Sherif and Azim Nanji, "Islamic Identity, Family, and Community: The Case of the Nizari Ismaili Community," in Waugh, Abu-Laban, and Qureshi, *Muslim Families in North America*, 101–17.

10. Yvonne Yazbeck Haddad and Jane Idleman Smith, *Mission to America: Five Islamic Sectarian Communities in North America* (Gainesville: University Press of Florida, 1993), 23–48; Muhammad Said Massoud, *I Fought as I Believed* (Montreal: by the author, 1976); Nejla Abu Izzedin, *The Druze: A New Study of their History, Faith and Society* (Leiden, Holland: E.J. Brill, 1984); Sami Nasib Makarim, *The Druze Faith* (Delmar, N.Y.: Caravan Books, 1974); Abdallah Najjar, *The Druze*, trans. Fred I. Massey (Santa Barbara: American Druze Society Committee on Religious Affairs, [1984]); E. Toftbek, "A Shorter Druze Catechism," *Muslim World* 44 (1954): 38–42; E.D. Benyon, "The Near East in Flint, Michigan: Assyrians and Druze and the Antecedents," *Geographic Review* 24 (1944): 234–74.

11. For information on the Ahmadiyya movement, see Haddad and Smith, *Mission to America*, 49–78; Mirza Bahiruddin Mahmud Ahmad, *Way of the Seekers* (Washington, D.C.: Ahmadiyya Movement in Islam, n.d.); Muhammad Zafarulla Khan, *Ahmadiyyat: The Renaissance of Islam* (London: Tabshir, 1978).

12. The first Islamic organization that operated on a national scale. Established in 1952 by Muslims from different centers in the United States and Canada, mostly second- and third-generation Lebanese Americans who sought to coordinate their efforts to promote and maintain the Islamic faith and Muslim culture.

13. Established in 1982 as an umbrella organization with two constituencies: Muslim students on American campuses and the Islamic organizations that the alumnae of these campuses have established once they decided to settle in the United States. These include mosques, Sunday schools, publishing and investing concerns, as well as professional organizations such as the Islamic Medical Association, the Association of Muslim Social Scientists, and the Association of Muslim Scientists and Engineers.

14. Sponsored by the Muslim World League, it encourages cooperation among

mosques in the United States and overseas, and is concerned with the construction, furnishing, and maintenance of the structures.

15. For information on Islam in Canada, see Harold Barclay, "The Muslim Experience in Canada," in *Religion and Ethnicity,* ed. Harold Coward and Leslie Kawamura (Waterloo: Wilfred Laurier University Press, 1978), 101–13; Harold Barclay, "An Arab Community in the Canadian Northwest: A Preliminary Discussion of the Lebanese Community in Lac La Biche, Alberta," *Anthropologica N.S.* 10 (1968): 143–56; Harold Barclay, "A Lebanese Community in Lac La Biche, Alberta," in *Minority Canadians: Immigrant Groups,* ed. Jean Leonard Elliott (Scarborough, Ontario: Prentice-Hall of Canada, 1971), 66–83; Harold Barclay, "The Lebanese Muslim Family," in *The Canadian Family,* rev. ed., ed. K. Ishwaran (Toronto: Holt, Rinehart and Winston, 1976), 92–104; Harold Barclay, "The Perpetuation of Muslim Tradition in the Canadian North," *Muslim World* 59 (1969): 64–73; Khalid Bin-Sayeed, "Predicament of Muslim Professionals in Canada and Its Resolution," *Journal, Institute of Muslim Minority Affairs* 3, no. 2 (1981): 104–19; Yvonne Yazbeck Haddad, "The Impact of the Islamic Revolution in Iran on the Syrian Muslims of Montreal," in *The Muslim Community in North America,* ed. Earle Waugh et al. (Edmonton, Alberta: University of Alberta Press, 1983); Yvonne Yazbeck Haddad, "Islam in Canada," in *The Canadian Encyclopedia,* ed. James H. Marsh (Edmonton: University of Alberta Press, 1985); Yvonne Yazbeck Haddad, "Muslims in Canada: A Preliminary Study," in Coward and Kawamura, *Religion and Ethnicity,* 71–100; Daood Hassan Hamdani, *Muslims in Canada: A Century of Settlement 1871–1976* (Ottawa, Ontario: Council of Muslim Communities of Canada, 1978); idem, "Muslims in the Canadian Mosaic," *Journal Institute of Muslim Minority Affairs* 5, no. 1 (1983–84): 7–16; T. Aoki et al. *Canadian Ethnicity: The Politics of Meaning* (Vancouver, British Columbia: Center for the Study of Curriculum and Instruction, University of British Columbia, 1978); Baha Abu-Laban, "The Adolescent Peer Group in Cross Cultural Perspective," *Canadian Review of Sociology and Anthropology* 7 (1970); idem, "The Arab Canadian Community," in Hagopian and Paden, *Arab Americans*; idem, "The Arab Community in the Canadian Mosaic," *Rikka* 3 (1976): 30–31; idem, "Middle East Groups" (Ottawa, Ontario: Department of the Secretary of State, 1973); idem, *An Olive Branch on the Family Tree: The Arabs in Canada* (Toronto: McClelland and Stewart, 1980); Baha Abu-Laban and Faith T. Zeadey, eds. *Arabs in America: Myths and Realities* (Wilmette, Ill.: Medina University Press International, 1975); Sharon McIrvin Abu-Laban, "Family and Religion among Muslim Immigrants and Their Descendants," in Waugh, Abu-Laban, and Qureshi, *Muslim Families in North America*; Sharon McIrvin Abu-Laban, "Stereotypes of Middle East People: An Analysis of Church School Curricula," in Abu-Laban and Zeadey, *Arabs in America,* 149–69; Sadiq Noor Alam Awan, *The People of Pakistani Origin in Canada: The First Quarter Century* (Ottawa, Ontario: S.N.A. Awan [under the auspices of the Canada-Pakistan Association of Ottawa-Hull], 1976); Secretary of State, Canada, The Canadian Family Tree: Canada's Peoples (Don Mills, Ontario: Corpus, 1979); A *Salute to the Pioneers of Northern Alberta* (Edmonton, Alberta: Canadian Arab Friendship Association, 1973); Masadul Alam Choudhury, "An Occupational Distribution of Muslims in the Employed Labour Force in Canada: Estimates for 1978," *Journal Institute of Muslim Minority Affairs* 1, no. 2, and 2, no. 1 (1979–80); Asghar Fathi, "The Arab Moslem Community in the Prairie City," *Canadian Ethnic Studies* 5 (1976): 409–26; idem, "Mass Media and Muslim Immigrant Community in Canada," *Anthropologica N.S.* 15 (1973): 201–30; Huda Hayani, "Arab Women in Canada," *Arab Dawn* 4, no. 4 (1972): 9–10; Asghar Fathi and Hunter B. Smeaton, "Arabic-Canadian Periodical Publications," *Canadian Ethnic Studies* 5 (1976): 1–4; W. Murray

Hogben, "Marriage and Divorce among Muslims in Canada," Waugh, Abu-Laban, and Qureshi, *Muslim Families in North America*, 154–84. Abelmoneim M. Khattab, "The Assimilation of Arab Muslims in Alberta" (M.A. thesis, University of Alberta, Edmonton, 1969); Sheila McDonough, "Muslims in Montreal," in Haddad and Smith, *Muslim Communities*, 317–34; Louise E. Sweet, "Reconstituting a Lebanese Village Society in a Canadian City," in *Arab Speaking Communities in American Cities*, ed. Barbara Aswad (Staten Island, N.Y.: Center for Migration Studies and Association of Arab-American University Graduates, 1974), 39–52.

16. Frances Trix, "Bektashi Tekke and the Sunni Mosque of Albanian Muslims in America," Haddad and Smith, *Muslim Communities*, 359–80; Michael A. Köszegi, "The Sufi Order in the West: Sufism's Encounter with the New Age," in Michael A. Köszegi and J. Gordon Melton, eds., *Islam in North America: A Sourcebook* (New York and London: Garland, 1992), 211–22; Sheikh Muzzaffer Ozark, *The Unveiling of Love: Sufism and the Remembrance of God* (New York: Inner Traditions International, 1981).

17. For information on the Moorish Science Temple see Haddad and Smith, *Mission to America*, 79–104; E.E. Calverly, "Negro Muslims in Hartford," *Muslim World* 55 (1965): 340–45; A.H. Fauset, *Black Gods of the Metropolis* (Philadelphia: University of Pennsylvania Press, 1944); "A Moorish Temple Catechism," *Muslim World* 32 (1942): 55–59; Frank T. Simpson, "The Moorish Science Temple and Its 'Koran,'" *Muslim World* 37 (1947): 56–61.

18. The Nation of Islam was organized by Fard Muhammad in the early 1930s. After his disappearance, it was led by Elijah Muhammad until his death in 1975. C. Eric Lincoln, *The Black Muslims in America* (Boston: Beacon, 1961); E.U. Eissien-Udom, *Black Nationalism* (New York: Dell, 1962); Louis Edward Wright Jr., *The Political Thought of Elijah Muhammad: Innovation and Continuity* (Ph.D. diss., Howard University, 1987); Jabril Muhammad, *This Is the One Messenger Elijah Muhammad We Need Not Look for Another* (Phoenix: Truth Publications, 1971); Tynetta Muhammad, *The Comer by Night* (Chicago: Honorable Elijah Muhammad Educational Foundation, 1992); Rassoull Abass, ed., *The Theology of Time* (Hampton, Va.: U.B. and U.S. Communications Systems, 1992); Mala Halasa, *Elijah Muhammad* (New York and Philadelphia: Chelsea House, 1990). See the writings of Elijah Muhammad: *The Supreme Wisdom: Solution to the So-called NEGROE's Problem* (Newport, Va.: National Newport News and Commentator, 1957); *Message to the Blackman* (Philadelphia: Hakine's Publications, 1965); *How to Eat to Live* (Chicago: Muhammad's Temple of Islam No. 2, 1967); *The Fall of America* (Chicago: Muhammad's Temple of Islam No. 2, 1973); *Our Saviour Has Arrived* (Chicago: Muhammad's Temple of Islam No. 2, 1974); *The Flag of Islam* (Chicago: n.p., 1974); *The Time History of Jesus as Taught by the Honorable Elijah Muhammad* (Chicago: Coalition for the Remembrance of Elijah, 1992); *Accomplishments of the Muslims* (Chicago: Muhammad's Mosque No. 2, 1974).

19. Several leaders assumed the mantle of the leadership of sections of the Nation of Islam after the death of Elijah Muhammad, maintaining the name of the organization. The most prominent Nation of Islam is led by Louis Farrakhan. Mattias Gardell, "The Sun of Islam Will Rise in the West: Minister Farrakhan and the Nation of Islam in the Latter Days," in Haddad and Smith, *Muslim Communities*, 15–50; Mattias Gardell, "Countdown to Armageddon: Minister Farrakhan and the Nation of Islam in the Latter Days" (Ph.D. diss., University of Stockholm, 1995); Jabril Muhammad, *Farrakhan, the Traveler* (Phoenix: Phnx Sa and Company, 1985); Mattias Gardell, "Behold I Make All Things New," in *Questioning the Secular State: The Worldwide Resurgence of Religion in*

Politics (London: C. Hurst, and New York: St. Martin, 1995); Frances Daniel, "A Look at Minister Louis Farrakhan: America's Other Son," *N'Digo* 48 (Nov. 1993); Dennis Walker, "Louis Farrakhan and America's 'Nation of Islam': Black Millenarianism and Micronationalism in the U.S. Northeast," *Journal of the Pakistan Historical Society* 52, no. 3 (July 1994): 269–301. Cf. Louis Farrakhan, *Seven Speeches* (Chicago: Muhammad's Temple No. 7, 1974); *Three Speeches* (Brooklyn: East Publication, 1972); *A Torchlight for America* (Chicago: FCN Publishing, 1993); *Warning to the Government of America* (Chicago: Honorable Elijah Muhammad Educational Foundation, 1983); *The Meaning of the F.O.I.* (Chicago: Honorable Elijah Muhammad Educational Foundation, 1983); *The Announcement: A Final Warning to the U.S. Government* (Chicago: Final Call, 1989); "What Is the Need for Black History?" in *Black Where We Belong: Selected Speeches by Minister Louis Farrakhan*, ed. Joseph D. Eure and Richard M. Jerome (Philadelphia: PC International Press, 1989); Michael Hardy and William Pleasant, *The Honorable Louis Farrakhan: A Minister for Progress* (New York: Alliance, 1987).

20. Haddad and Smith, *Mission to America*, 105–36; for the teachings of this sect, see the writings of the founder: Isa Muhammad, *The Message of the Messenger is Right and Exact* (Brooklyn: Isa Muhammad 1979); *Racism in Islam* (Brooklyn: Isa Muhammad, 1982); *Al-Imam Isa vs the Computer* (Brooklyn: Isa Muhammad, 1982).

21. A splinter group from the Nation of Islam who believe that only 5 percent of humanity will be saved on the Day of Judgment. These will be exclusively members of their community. Yusuf Nuruddin, "The Five Percenters: A Teenage Nation of Gods and Earths," in Haddad and Smith, *Muslim Communities*, 109–32.

22. The courts convicted members of the gang of conspiracy to commit terrorist activities. It was shown at their trial that they were in contact with Qadhdhafi of Libya.

23. Spike Lee, *By Any Means Necessary: The Trials and Tribulations of the Making of Malcolm X* (New York: Hyperion, 1992); Julius Lester, "The Angry Children of Malcolm X," in *Black Protest Thought in the Twentieth Century*, 2nd ed., ed. August Meier et al. (Indianapolis: Bobbs-Merrill, 1971); Peter Goldman, *The Death and Life of Malcolm X* (New York: Harper and Row, 1973); Seyyed Ali Muhammad Ghaemi, "Malcolm X: Symbol of Struggle," in *Issues in the Islamic Movement*, ed. Kalim Siddiqui (London: Open Press, 1983), 85–89; John H. Clarke, ed. *Malcolm X* (New York: Collier, 1969); James H. Cone, *Martin and Malcolm and America: A Dream or a Nightmare* (London: Fount Paperbacks, 1993); John Henrik Clarke, *Malcolm X: The Man and His Times* (New York: Macmillan, 1969); Clayborne Carson, *Malcolm X: The FBI File* (New York: Carroll and Graf, 1991); George Breitman, ed., *The Last Year of Malcolm X* (New York: Schocken, 1968); Malcolm X, *On Afro-American History* (New York: Merit, 1967); idem, *Malcolm X Speaks* (New York: Grove, 1965); Malcolm X, with Alex Haley, *The Autobiography of Malcolm X* (New York: Ballantine, 1973); Alex Haley, "Interview with Malcolm X," *Playboy*, May 1963; George Breitman, ed. *By Any Means Necessary: Speeches, Interviews and a Letter by Malcolm X* (New York: Pathfinder, 1970); George Breitman, *Malcolm X Speaks* (New York: Grove, 1966); Archie Epps, ed., *The Speeches of Malcolm X at Harvard* (New York: William Morrow, 1968); Benjamin Goodman, ed., *The End of White World Supremacy: Four Speeches by Malcolm X* (New York: Merlin House, 1971); Lamin Sanneh, "Critical Reflections on the Life of Malcolm X," *Journal, Institute of Muslim Minority Affairs* 7 (1986): 331–40.

24. Raquel Ann Muhammad, "Black Muslim Movements After the Death of Elijah Muhammad" (Ph.D. diss., United States International University, 1980). For the writing of Warith Deen Muhammad, see Wallace D. Muhammad, *Challenges that Face Man*

Today (Chicago: W.D. Muhammad Publications, 1985); *An African American Genesis* (Chicago: Progressions, 1986); *As the Light Shineth from the East* (Chicago: W.D. Muhammad Publications, 1980); *Lectures of W.D. Muhammad* (Chicago: W.D. Muhammad Publications, 1978); *The Teachings of W.D. Muhammad (Elementary Level)* (Chicago: Elijah Muhammad Mosque No. 2, 1975); *The Teachings of W.D. Muhammad (Secondary Level)* (Chicago: Elijah Muhammad Mosque No. 2, 1976). Cf. Warith Deen Muhammad, *Prayer and al-Islam* (Chicago: Muhammad Islamic Foundation, 1982).

25. Mustafa El-Amin, *The Religion of Islam and the Nation of Islam: What Is the Difference* (Newark, N.J.: El-Amin Productions, 1991).

26. R.M. Mukhtar Curtis, "Urban Muslims: The Formation of Dar ul-Islam Movement," in Haddad and Smith, *Muslim Communities*, 51–74.

27. Sachedina, "Minority within a Minority," 3–14.

28. Clyde Ahmed Winters, "A Survey of Islam in the African Diaspora," *Pan-African Journal* 8, no. 4 (1975). Winters's other publications include "Roots and Islam in Slave America," *al-Ittihad* 8 (Oct.-Nov. 1976): 18–20; "Afro-American Muslims from Slavery to Freedom," *Islamic Studies* 17, no. 4 (1978): 187–90; "Islam in Early North and South America," *al-Ittihad* 14 (July-Oct. 1977): 57–67; "Origins of Muslim Slaves in the U.S.," *al-Ittihad* 21 (Spring 1986): 49–51.

29. Emory H. Tunnison, "Mohammad Webb, First American Muslim," *Arab World* 1, no. 3 (1945): 13–18.

30. Muhammad Alexander Russell Webb, *A Guide to the Names: A Detailed Exposition of the Moslem Order of Ablutions and Prayer* (New York: by the author, 1893); "The Influence of Social Condition," in John Henry Barrows, ed., *The World's Parliament of Religions* (Chicago: Monarch, 1894), 523–35; *Islam: A Lecture Delivered at the Framji Cowasji Institute, Bombay, India, Thursday Evening 10th November 1892* (Bombay: Bombay Gazette Steam Printing Works, 1892); *Islam in America: A Brief Study of Mohammedanism and an Outline of American Muslim Propaganda* (New York: Oriental, 1893); *Lectures on Islam*, Lahore, Pakistan: Mohammadan Tract and Book Depot, 1893); "Mohammed: The Most Misunderstood Messenger of God," *Minaret* 10, no. 2 (Spring 1989): 9–12.

31. Carol L. Anway, *Daughters of Another Path: Experiences of American Women Choosing Islam* (Lee's Summit, Mont.: Yawna Publications, 1996).

32. Köszegi, "Sufi Order in the West," 211–22.

33. Gisella Webb, "Tradition and Innovation in Contemporary American Islamic Spirituality: The Bawwa Muhaiyaddeen Fellowship," in Haddad and Smith, *Muslim Communities*, 75–108. For the teachings of their leader see M.R. Bawa Muhaiyaddeen, *Come to the Secret Garden* (Philadelphia: Fellowship Press, 1985); *The Wisdom of Man* (Philadelphia: Fellowship Press, 1980); *A Book of God's Love* (Philadelphia: Fellowship Press, 1981); *My Love You My Children* (Philadelphia: Fellowship Press, 1981); *The Golden Words of a Sufi Sheikh* (Philadelphia: Fellowship Press, 1982).

34. Ayad al-Qazzaz, *Transnational Links Between the Arab Community in the U.S. and the Arab World* (Sacramento: California Central Press, 1979).

35. Nabeel Abraham, "Detroit's Yemeni Workers," *MERIP Reports* 53 (1977): 3–9; idem, "National and Local Politics: A Study of Political Conflict in the Yemeni Immigrant Community of Detroit, Michigan" (Ph.D. diss., University of Michigan, 1978); idem, "Rejoinder to Detroit's Yemeni Works," *MERIP Reports* 60 (1977); idem, "The Yemeni Immigrant Community of Detroit: Background Emigration and Community Life," in *Arabs in the New World: Studies on Arab-American Communities*, ed. Sameer Y. Abraham and

Nabeel Abraham (Detroit: Wayne State University, Center for Urban Studies, 1983); Jonathan Friedlander, "The Yemenis of Delano: A Profile of a Rural Islamic Community," in Haddad and Smith, *Muslim Communities*, 423–44; Mary Bisharat, "Yemenis and Farmworkers in California," *MERIP Reports* 34 (1957): 22–26.

36. Michael M.J. Fischer and Mehdi Abedi, *Debating Muslims: Cultural Dialogues in Postmodernity and Tradition* (Madison: University of Wisconsin Press, 1990); Ron Kelley and Jonathan Friedlander, eds., *Irangeles: Iranians in Los Angeles* (Berkeley and Los Angeles: University of California Press, 1993).

37. In Los Angeles, where the largest group resides, they have published their own Yellow Pages: *The Iranian Directory Yellow Pages* (Los Angeles: Ketab Corporation, 1981, 1982, 1983, 1984).

38. Gutbi Mahdi Ahmed, "The Muslims of the United States," in Haddad, *Muslims of America*, 11–24.

39. Abul A'la Maududi, *The Role of Muslim Students in the Reconstruction of the Muslim World* (Kuwait: I.I.F.S.O., 1978).

40. For a study about the founder of the movement, see Abul Hassan Ali Nadwi, *Life and Mission of Maulana Mohammad Ilyas*, trans. Muhammad Asif Kidwai (Lucknow: Academy of Islamic Research and Publications, 1979).

41. The majority are recently naturalized American citizens who believe that every Muslim is a *muballigh* (informer, instructor) or a *da'iya* (missionary) whose duty is to invite others to the worship of the One God.

42. The *Muslim Star*, for a while controlled by a handful of people in the name of the Federation of Islamic Associations, published vicious articles attacking the Khomeini regime and supporting Saddam Husayn.

43. In the series, *Modern American Protestantism and Its World: Historical Articles on Protestantism in American Religious Life* (New York: K.G. Saur, 1993), editor Martin E. Marty included two essays on Islam in the African-American community in volume 9. Lawrence H. Mamiya, "From Black Muslim to Bilalian: The Evolution of a Movement," *Journal of the Scientific Study of Religion* 21, no. 2 (1982): 138–50, and Perry E. Gianakos, "The Black Muslims: An American Millennialistic Response to Racism and Cultural Deracination," *Centennial Review* 23, no. 4 (1979): 430–51.

44. Noted exceptions would be Professor Elmer Douglas of Hartford Seminary, who reportedly lectured to his classes on the subject in 1965. In the last decade, professors at several universities in California (Santa Barbara, UCLA, and San Diego), Duke University, University of North Carolina, Pennsylvania State University, as well as McGill University in Canada have introduced material on the Muslim experience in the United States.

45. When the centers for Middle East and Near Eastern studies were opened on various American campuses in the 1950s, only a handful of books on contemporary Islam were in print. These included Wilfrid Cantwell Smith, *Islam in Modern History* (Princeton: Princeton University Press, 1957); C.C. Adams, *Islam and Modernism in Egypt* (London: Oxford University Press, 1933); H.A.R. Gibb, *Modern Trends in Islam* (Chicago: University of Chicago Press, 1947); J.N.D. Anderson, *Islamic Law in the Modern World* (New York: New York University Press, 1959).

46. The Saudi Consul in New York in an interview with *al-Jazira* said that the Arabs were explorers. Columbus received his information from Arab navigators. A manuscript by al-Idrisi discovered in 1955 talks about an expedition by eight Arabs from Portugal that headed into the "Sea of Darkness." An African caliph in West Africa sent an expedition in

the fifteenth century; only one boat returned. The caliph then went with some of the explorers on the next expedition. This explains why blacks were discovered in America. Columbus took Arab navigators, some of whom were Mariscos who were forcibly converted to Christianity. His translator, Louis Torres, was a Marisco who spoke Arabic. He was able to converse in Arabic with the people of the Americas, some of whom were the Arapaho tribe who were descendants of the Arabs. Thus the Arabs preceded Columbus in the discovery of America. Abd Allah Ahmad al-Dari, *al-Wujud al-Islami fi al-Wilayat al-Muttahida al-Amerikiyya* (Jedda: Dar 'Ukaz li al-Tiba'a wa al-Nashr, 1983), 83–87.

47. For a discussion of Catholic history, see R. Laurence Moore, *Religious Outsiders and the Making of Americans* (New York: Oxford University Press, 1986), 48–71. Moore provides the following quote: "It was a Catholic monk who inspired Columbus with hope; it was Columbus and a Catholic Crew that first crossed the trackless main; it was a Catholic queen who rendered the expedition possible; and that it was a Catholic whose name has been given to the entire continent" ("Address to the Congress by Hon. Morgan J. O'Brien," in *Progress of the Catholic Church in America and the Great Columbian Catholic Congress of 1893* [Chicago: J.S. Hyland, 1987]).

48. Iftikhar H. Malik, "The Bilallians of United States," *Pakistan Journal of History and Culture* 2, no. 2 (1981): 24–34; Hasnain Walji, "Black Muslims: The Prodigals Return," *Afkār Inquiry* 4, no. 7 (1987): 54–55.

49. Sulayman S. Nyang, "Islam in the United States of America: A Review of the Sources," *The Search: Journal for Arab and Islamic Studies* 1 (1980): 164–82; Köszegi and Melton, *Islam in North America*; Winters, "Survey of Islam in the African Diaspora."

50. Thomas B. Irving, "The Islamic Heritage in the Americas," *Our Effort* 5, nos. 7–8 (1976); Ali M. Kettani, *Al Muslimun fi Euroba wa Amrika* (II Dar Idris, Iraq, 1976). Currently about a dozen graduate students are engaged in dissertation writing on the subject.

51. Mary Caroline Holmes, "Islam in America," *Muslim World* 16 (1926): 262–66; Andrew T. Hoffert, "The Moslem Movement in America," *Muslim World* 20 (1930): 309–10; Yvonne Haddad, "Islam in America: A Growing Religious Movement," *Muslim World League Journal* 9, no. 9 (1984); idem, "The Muslim Experience in the United States," *Link* 22, no. 4 (1979): 1–12; idem, "Muslims in America," in *Islam: The Religious and Political Life of a Community*, ed. Marjorie Kelly (New York: Praeger Press, 1984); Mehmed A. Simsar, "Muslims in the United States," *Twentieth Century Encyclopedia of Religious Knowledge*, vol. 2, ed. Lefferts A. Loetscher (Grand Rapids, Mich.: Baker Book House, 1955); Earle H. Waugh, Sharon McIrvin Abu-Laban, and Regula Burckhardt Qureshi, *Muslim Community in North America* (Edmonton, Alberta: University of Alberta Press, 1983); M. Arif Ghayur, "Muslims in the United States: Settlers and Visitors." *Annals of the American Academy of Political and Social Science* 454 (1981): 150–63; M.M. Aijian, "Mohammedans in the United States," *Muslim World* 10 (1920): 30–35; El Tigani A. Abugiedeiri, *A Survey of North American Muslims* (Indianapolis: Islamic Teaching Center, 1977); Lois Gottesman, "Islam in America: A Background Report," prepared for Institute of Human Relations, the American Jewish Committee, 1979; Akbar Muhammad, "Muslims in the United States: An Overview of Organizations, Doctrines and Problems," in *The Islamic Impact*, ed. Yvonne Yazbeck Haddad, Byron Haines, and Ellison Findly (Syracuse: Syracuse University Press, 1984), 195–218; Emily Kalled Lovell, "A Survey of the Arab-Muslims in the United States and Canada," *Muslim World* 62 (1973): 139–54; Sulayman S. Nyang and Robert Cummings, "Islam in the United States of America" (Report Submitted to the King Faisal Foundation, Riyadh, Saudi Arabia, 1983).

52. Kananur B. Chandras, *Arab, Armenian, Syrian, Lebanese, East Indian, Pakistani*

and Bangladeshi Americans: A Study Guide and Source Book (San Francisco: R and E Research Associates, 1977); J.K. David, "The Near East Settlers of Jacksonville and Duval County" (paper presented at the May 12, 1954, meeting of the Jacksonville Historical Society, Jacksonville, Fla.); M. Arif Ghayur, "Ethnic Distribution of American Muslims and Selected Socio-Economic Characteristics," *Journal of Muslim Minority Affairs* 5, no. 1 (1983–84): 47–59; Deborah L. Miller, "Middle Easterners: Syrians, Lebanese, Armenians, Egyptians, Iranians, Palestinians, Turks, Afghans," in *They Chose Minnesota: A Survey of the State's Ethnic Groups,* ed. J.D. Holmquist (St. Paul: Minnesota Historical Society, 1981), 511–30. Cf. Stephan Thernstrom, *Harvard Encyclopedia of American Ethnic Groups* (Cambridge, Mass.: Belknap Press of Harvard University Press, 1981), has entries on the following ethnic groups: "Afghans," 3–5; "Albanians," 23–28; "Arabs," 128–36; "Azerbaijanis," 171; "Bangladeshi," 172–73; "Bosnian Muslims," 184–86; "East Indians," 296–301; "Indonesians," 513; "Iranians," 521–24; "Kurds," 606–8; "Muslims," 732–33; "North Caucasians," 749–50; "Pakistanis," 768–70; "Tatars," 988–90; "Turkestanis," 991–92; "Turks," 992–96.

53. Ibrahim Habib Katiba and Farhat Ziadeh, *Arab-Speaking Americans* (New York: Institute of Arab American Affairs, 1946); Anthony P. Katarsky, "Family Ties and the Growth of an Arabic Community in Northeast Dearborn, Michigan" (M.A. thesis, Wayne State University, 1980); Yvonne Yazbeck Haddad, "Islamic Institutions in America: Adaptations and Reform," in Abraham and Abraham, *Arabs in the New World,* reprinted in James Zoghby, ed., *Taking Root, Bearing Fruit: The Arab American Experience* (Washington, D.C.: ADC, 1984); Mary Haddad Macron, *Arab Americans and Their Communities of Cleveland* (Cleveland, Ohio: Cleveland Ethnic Heritage Studies, Cleveland State University, 1979); Mary Haddad Macron, *A Celebration of Life: Memories of an Arab-American in Cleveland,* Anti-Discrimination Committee Report No. 7 (Washington, D.C.: ADC, 1982); Ernest McCarus, *The Development of Arab-American Identity* (Ann Arbor: University of Michigan Press, 1994); Beverlee Turner Mehdi, ed. and comp., *The Arabs in America, 1492–1977: A Chronology and Fact Book* (Dobbs Ferry, N.Y.: Oceana, 1978); Alixa Naff, "Arabs," in Stephen Thernstrom et al., eds., *Harvard Encyclopedia of American Ethnic Groups* (Cambridge, Mass.: Belknap, 1980), 128–36; Alixa Naff, *Becoming American: The Early Arab Immigrant Experience* (Carbondale: Southern Illinois University Press, 1985); Marlene K. Smith, "The Arabic-Speaking Communities," in Joan H. Rollins, ed., *Hidden Minorities: The Persistence of Ethnicity in American Life* (Washington, D.C.: University Press of America, 1981), 141–76; Michael Suleiman, "Arab Americans: A Community Profile," *Journal Institute of Muslim Minority Affairs* 5, no. 1 (1983–84): 29–35; Adele Linda Younis, "The Coming of the Arabic-Speaking People to the U.S.A." (Ph.D diss., Boston University, 1961); Nabeel Abraham, "Arabic Speaking Communities of Southeastern Dearborn: A General Overview" (Ph.D. diss., University of Wisconsin, Madison, 1975); idem, *Arabs in America: An Overview,* in *The Arab World and Arab Americans: Understanding a Neglected Minority,* ed. Sameer Y. Abraham and Nabeel Abraham (Detroit: Wayne State University, Center for Urban Studies, 1981); Abraham, "Detroit's Arab-American Community"; Sameer Y. Abraham, "A Survey of the Arab-American Community in Metropolitan Detroit," in Abraham and Abraham, *Arab World and Arab Americans;* Sameer Abraham, Nabeel Abraham, and Barbara Aswad, "The Southend: An Arab Muslim Working-Class Community," in Abraham and Abraham, *Arabs in the New World;* Ismael Ahmed, "Organizing an Arab Workers Caucus," *MERIP Reports* 34 (1975): 17–22; Abdeen Jabara, "Workers, Community Mobilized in Detroit," *AAUG Newsletter,* June 1974; Ibrahim Othman, "An Arab Community in the United States: A Study of the Arab-

American Community in Springfield, Massachusetts" (Ph.D. diss., University of Massachusetts, 1970); idem, *Arabs in the United States: A Study of an Arab-American Community* (Amman: Shashaa and the University of Jordan, 1974); Iris Sanderson, "Who Are the Detroit Arabs?" *Detroiter*, Sept. 1975, 28–32; Morroe Berger, "Americans from the Arab World," in *The World of Islam*, ed. James Kritzeck and R. Bayly Winder (New York: St. Martin's Press, 1959), 351–72; Barbara C. Aswad, ed. *Arab Speaking Communities in American Cities* (New York: Center for Migration Studies of New York, and Association of Arab-American University Graduates, 1974); Dan Georgakas, "Arab Workers in Detroit," *MERIP Reports* 34 (1975): 13–17; A.K.J. Germanns, "Arabic Literature in America," *Islamic Literature* 12, no. 2 (1966): 17–26; Atif A. Wasfi, "Dearborn Arab-Moslem Community: A Study of Acculturation" (Ph.D. diss., Michigan State University, 1964).

54. The term "Syrian" was used until the 1930s to designate immigrants from Syria, Lebanon, Palestine, and Jordan. Phillip K. Hitti, *The Syrians in America* (New York: George H. Doran, 1924); Louise Seymour Houghton, "The Syrians in the United States," *Survey* 26 (1911): 480–95, 647–65, 786–802, 957–68; James M. Ansara, "The Immigration and Settlement of the Syrians" (A.B. thesis, Harvard University, 1931); Afif Tannous, "Acculturation of an Arab-Syrian Community in the Deep South," *American Sociological Review* 8 (1943): 264–71; Najib E. Saliba, "Emigration from Syria," *Arab Studies Quarterly* 3 (1981): 56–67; Morroe Berger, "America's Syrian Community," *Commentary* 25 (1958): 314–23.

55. Ahmad Hammuda, "Jordanian Immigration: An Analysis of Migration Data," *International Migration Review* 14 (1980): 257–382.

56. Abdoulmaboud Ansari, "A Community in Process: The First Generation of Iranian Professional Middle-Class Immigrants in the United States," *International Review of Modern Sociology* 7 (1977): 85–101; Mehdi Bozorgmehr, "Social Differentiation, Chain Migration, and Sub-Ethnic Group Cohesion: The Case of Iranian Muslims in Los Angeles" (paper delivered to the Middle East Studies Association, 1984); Richard Z. Chesnoff, "Paris: The Iranian Exiles," *New York Times Magazine*, Feb. 12, 1984; Farah Gilanshan, "Iranians of the Twin Cities" (Ph.D. diss., University of Minnesota, 1983); Nassereh G. Golesorkhi, "Parent-Child Relations Among Exiled Iranian Families in Southern California: An Examination of the Impacts of Modernization and Forced Migration on Family Relations" (M.A. thesis, San Diego State University, 1983); K.C. Kim, H.C. Kim, and W.M. Hurh, "Job Information Deprivation in the United States: A Case Study of Iranian Immigrants," *Ethnicity* 8 (1981): 219–32; Jamshid Momeni, "Size and Distribution of Iranian Ethnic Group in the United States: 1980," *Iran Nameh* 2 (1984): 17, 21; Georges Sabagh and Mehdi Bozorgmehr, "Secular Immigrants: Religiosity and Ethnicity among Iranian Muslims in Los Angeles," in Haddad and Smith, *Muslim Communities*, 445–73.

57. Fuad I. Khuri, "A Comparative Study of Migration Patterns in Two Lebanese Villages," *Human Organization* 26 (1967): 206–13; Ralph Kepler Lewis, "Hadchite: A Study of Emigration in a Lebanese Village" (Ph.D. diss., Columbia University, 1967); Atif A. Wasfi, *An Islamic-Lebanese Community in the U.S.A.: A Study in Cultural Anthropology* (Beirut: Arab University, 1971); Milo Kay Campbell, "An Analysis of the Relationships between Self Concept and Sociological Receptiveness of Lebanese Ethnic Children in the Detroit Metropolitan Area" (Ph.D. diss., Wayne State University, 1972); Edward Wakin, *The Lebanese and Syrians in America* (Chicago. Claretin, 1974).

58. M. Arif Ghayur, "Demographic Evolution of Pakistanis in America: Case Study of a Muslim Subgroup," *American Journal of Islamic Studies* 1 (1984): 113–26; Salim Khan, "A Brief History of Pakistanis in the Western United States" (M.A. thesis, California State

University, Sacramento, 1981); idem, "Pakistanis in the Western United States," *Journal Institute of Muslim Minority Affairs* 5, no. 1 (1983–84): 36–46.

59. Barbara Bilge, "Voluntary Associations in the Old Turkish Community of Metropolitan Detroit," in Haddad and Smith, *Muslim Communities*, 381–405.

60. Patricia S. Maloof, "Medical Beliefs and Practices of Palestinian-Americans" (M.A. thesis, Catholic University of America, 1979). Lawrence Oschinsky, "Islam in Chicago: A Study of the Acculturation of a Muslim-Palestinian Community in That City" (M.A. thesis, University of Chicago, 1947); Elias H. Tuma, "The Palestinians in America," *Link* 14, no. 3 (1981): 1–4.

61. Samira Ahmed el-Sayed Mansour, "Cultural Change and the Process of Assimilation: A Study of the Assimilation of Egyptian Immigrants and Their Children Who Attend the Public School" (M.A. thesis, New York University, 1978); Kadri M. ed-Araby and Ibtihaj S. Arafat, "The Arab-Egyptian Muslim Community in New Jersey," in *The New Jersey Ethnic Experience*, ed. Barbara Cunningham (Union, N.J.: William Wise and Company, 1977), 168–78; Fathi Salaama Yousef, "Cross-Cultural Social Communicative Behavior: Egyptians in the U.S." (Ph.D. diss., University of Minnesota, 1972).

62. Edith Stein, "Some Near Eastern Immigrant Groups in Chicago" (M.A. thesis, University of Chicago, 1922); Ali Abdul Jalil al-Tahir, "The Arab Community in the Chicago Area: A Comparative Study of the Christian-Syrians and the Muslim-Palestinians" (Ph.D. diss., University of Chicago, 1952); idem, "Isolation, Marginality and Assimilation of the Arab Communities in Chicago to the American Culture," *Bulletin of the College of Arts and Sciences* [Baghdad] 1 (1956): 54–65; Marcia K. Hermansen, "The Muslims in San Diego," in Haddad and Smith, *Muslim Communities*, 169–94; Asad Husain and Harold Vogelaar, "Activities of the Immigrant Muslim Communities in Chicago," in Haddad and Smith, *Muslim Communities*, 231–57; Mark Ferris, "'To Achieve the Pleasure of Allah': Immigrant Muslim Communities in New York City, 1893–1991," in Haddad and Smith, *Muslim Communities*, 209–30; Steve A. Johnson, "The Muslims of Indianapolis," in Haddad and Smith, *Muslim Communities*, 259–77; Ron Kelly, "Muslims in Los Angeles," in Haddad and Smith, *Muslim Communities*, 135–67; Mariam Adeney and Kathryn DeMaster, "Muslims in Seattle," in Haddad and Smith, *Muslim Communities*, 195–208; Ishaq Y. Qutub, *The Immigrant Arab Community in New York City* (East Lansing, Mich.: n.p., 1962); Tamara Sonn, "Diversity in Rochester's Islamic Community," in Haddad and Smith, *Muslim Communities*, 279–92; Mary Lahaj, "The Islamic Center of New England," in Haddad and Smith, *Muslim Communities*, 293–315.

63. Thomas Bluett, *Some Memoirs of the Life of Job, the Son of Solomon* (London: Printed for R. Ford, 1734); Gilberto Freyre, *The Master and the Slaves* (New York: Knopf, 1971); George H. Calcott, "Omar ibn Said, A Slave Who Wrote an Autobiography in Arabic," *Journal of Negro History* 39 (1954): 58–63; Phillip D. Curtin, ed. *Africa Remembered* (Madison: University of Wisconsin Press, 1968); Douglas Grant, *The Fortunate Slave: An Illustration of African Slavery in the Early Eighteenth Century* (London: Oxford University Press, 1968); Joel Chandler Harris, *The Story of Aaron (So Named) The Son of Ben-Ali* (Boston: Houghton, Mifflin, 1896); Folarin Shyllon, *Black People in Britain, 1555–1833* (London: Oxford University Press, 1977).

64. Terry Alford, *Prince Among Slaves* (New York and London: Harcourt Brace Jovanovich, 1977).

65. Allan D. Austin, *African Muslims in Antebellum America: A Sourcebook* (New York: Garland, 1984). See also idem, *African Muslims in the New World: A Source Book for Cultural Historians* (Boston: Garland, 1981).

66. Erdman D. Benyon, "The Voodoo Cult Among Negro Migrants in Detroit," *American Journal of Sociology* 63, no. 6 (July 1937-May 1938); Morroe Berger, "The Black Muslims," *Islamic Horizons* 1, no. 3 (1964); Edward W. Blyden, *Christianity, Islam and the Negro Race* (London: W.B. Whittingham and Company, 1887); W.H. Burns, "The Black Muslims in America: A Reinterpretation," *Race* 5 (1963): 26–37; Calverly, "Negro Muslims in Hartford"; Pierre Crabites, "American Negro Mohammedans," *Muslim World* 23 (1933): 1968; Kevin Flynn and Gary Gerbart, *The Silent Brotherhood: Inside America's Racist Underground* (New York: Free Press, 1989); Jameela A. Hakim, "History of the First Muslim Mosque of Pittsburgh, Pennsylvania," in Köszegi and Melton, *Islam in North America*; John Howard, "The Making of a Black Muslim," in *Social Process in Minority-Dominant Relations*, ed. E.F. Dickie-Clark (New York: Free Press, 1968), 127–290; Lansinè Kaba, "Americans Discover Islam through the Black Muslim Experience," in Köszegi and Melton, *Islam in North America*, 25–33; Martha F. Lee, *The Nation of Islam, An American Millenarian Movement* (Lewiston, N.Y.: Edwin Mellen Press, 1988); Nicholas Lemann, *The Promised Land: The Great Black Migration and How It Changed America* (London: Papermac, 1992); C. Eric Lincoln, "The Black Muslims as a Protest Movement," in *Black History: A Reappraisal*, ed. Melvin Drimmer (New York: Anchor Books, 1969); C. Eric Lincoln, *Race, Religion and the Continuing American Dilemma* (New York: Hill and Wang, 1984); C. Eric Lincoln, "The Muslim Mission in the Context of American Social History," in *African American Religious Studies*, ed. G.S. Wilmore (Durham: Duke University Press, 1989); C. Eric Lincoln and Lawrence H. Mamiya, *The Black Church in the African American Experience* (Durham: Duke University Press, 1990); J.H. Laue, "A Contemporary Revitalization Movement in American Race Relations: The Black Muslims," *Social Forces* 42 (1964): 315–23; J.H. Laue, "Extremist Attitudes in the Black Muslim Movement," *Journal of Social Issues* 19 (1963): 75–85; Philip Norton, *Black Nationalism in America: The Significance of the Black Muslim Movement* (Hull: Hull Papers in Politics, University of Hull, Department of Politics, 1983); William Shack, "The Black Muslims: A Nativist Religious Movement Among Negro Americans," *Race* 3 (1961): 57–67; G.L. Watson, "Social Structure and Social Movements: The Black Muslims in the USA and the Ras-Tafarians in Jamaica," *Journal of British Sociology* 24 (1973): 188–204.

67. Kenneth O'Reilly, *Racial Matters: The FBI's Secret Files on Black America, 1960–1972* (New York: Free Press, 1989).

68. Parenti, "Black Muslims."

69. Mamiya, "From Black Muslim to Bilalian."

70. Gianakos, "Black Muslims," in Martin E. Marty, ed., *Native American Religion and Black Protestantism*, vol. 9 of *Modern American Protestantism and Its World*, 109.

71. Zafar Ishaq Ansari, "Aspects of Black Muslim Theology," *Studia Islamica* 53 (1981): 137–76.

72. 'Abd al-Wahab Ibrahim Abu Sulayman, *Munazzamat Elijah Muhammad al-Amerikiyya* (Jedda: Dar al-Shuruq, 1979).

73. Hatem I. Hussaini, "The Impact of the Arab-Israeli Conflict on Arab Communities in the United States," in *Settler Regimes in Africa and the Arab World*, ed. Ibrahim Abu Lughod and Baha Abu-Laban (Wilmette, Ill.: Medina University Press International, 1974), 201–22; Jacqueline S. Ismael and Tareq Ismael, "The Arab Americans and the Middle East," *Middle East Journal* 30 (1976): 390–405.

74. Janice J. Terry, "The Arab-Israeli Conflict in Popular Literature," *American-Arab Affairs* 2 (1982): 97–104.

75. Lovell, "Survey of the Arab Muslims in the United States and Canada"; Yvonne

Yazbeck Haddad, "FIA" (Federation of Islamic Associations), in John Esposito et al., eds., *Oxford Encyclopedia of the Modern Islamic World* (New York: Oxford University Press, 1995).

76. Yvonne Yazbeck Haddad, "Islamists and the 'Problem of Israel': The 1967 Awakening," *Middle East Journal* 46, no. 2 (Spring 1992): 266–85; Yvonne Yazbeck Haddad, "The Anguish of Christians in the Middle East and American Foreign Policy," *American-Arab Affairs* 26 (Fall 1988): 56–74; Yvonne Yazbeck Haddad, "Nationalism and Islamic Tendencies in Contemporary Arab-American Communities," in Hani Faris, ed., *Arab Nationalism: and the Future Arab World* (Belmont, Mass.: AAUG Press, 1987).

77. Its goal was to disseminate accurate information about the Arab-American community and struggle to hold American society accountable to its ideals, to combat stereotypes, and to sensitize American society to the legitimate rights of the Palestinian people.

78. M.C. Bassiouni, ed. *The Special Measures and some AAUG Public Action. The Civil Rights of Arab-Americans: The Special Measures* (North Dartmouth, Mass.: AAUG, 1974).

79. Two Muslim candidates who ran for congress were Bill Quraishi of California and Riaz Hussain of New York. Neither received endorsement from conservative Muslims. In Bill's case, the objection was to his appropriation of a Western name, perceived as a rejection of one's identity, while Riaz was faulted for not growing a beard.

80. In an interview with *Time* magazine, Reagan said, "Lately we have seen the possibilities of, literally, a religious war — The Muslims returning to the idea that the way to heaven is to lose your life fighting the Christians and the Jews" (*Time*, Nov. 16, 1980). Efforts by the Muslim World League Office in New York, the Council of Masajid, and the leadership of the Muslim communities in North America to correct this biased and inflammatory statement went unheeded. The president failed to acknowledge the real nature of Islam or the discriminatory nature of his statement. A request to receive a delegation of five Muslim religious leaders, including the director of the Muslim World League and the Imam of the mosque in Washington, went unheeded. *Muslim News* 1, no. 1 (Jan. 1981): 14.

81. In a 1990 speech at the Naval Academy, Quayle identified three evils that have challenged the West: "We have been surprised this past century by the rise of communism, Nazism and the rise of Islamic radical fundamentalism."

82. See, for example, Charles Krauthammer, "The New Crescent of Crisis: Global Intifada," *Washington Post*, Feb. 16, 1990. Cf. William F. Buckley, "Unfamiliar Foe among Us," *Washington Post*, Feb. 16, 1990, and July 8, 1993; Benjamin R. Barber, "Jihad vs. McWorld," *Atlantic Monthly*, Mar. 1992; Judith Miller, "The Challenge of Radical Islam," *Foreign Affairs* 72, no. 2 (Spring 1993): 42–56; Judith Miller, "The Islamic Wave," *New York Times Magazine*, May 31, 1992; Mortimer B. Zuckerman, "Beware of Religious Stalinists," *U.S. News and World Report*, Mar. 22, 1993; William Safire, "Islamic Extremists Exploit West's Havens and Forums," *Internation Herald Tribune*, Feb. 19, 1993; Daniel Pipes, "Fundamental Questions About Muslims," *Wall Street Journal*, Oct. 30, 1992.

83. See, for example, Bernard Lewis, "Roots of Muslim Rage," *Atlantic Monthly*, Sept. 1990, p. 47–54; Bernard Lewis, "Islam and Liberal Democracy," *Atlantic Monthly*, Feb. 1993, pp. 89–94. Amos Perlmutter, "Warp and Woof of a Malefic Fabric," *Washington Times*, Mar. 26, 1993.

84. Patrick Buchannan, "Rising Islam May Overwhelm the West," *New Hampshire Sunday News*, Aug. 20, 1989.

85. Ayad al-Qazzaz, "Images of the Arab in American Social Science Textbooks," in

Abu-Laban and Zeadey, *Arabs in America*, 113–32; Abu-Laban, "Stereotypes of Middle East Peoples"; Samir Ahmad Jarrar, "Images of the Arabs in the United States Secondary Schools Social Studies Textbooks: A Content Analysis and Unit Development" (Ph.D. diss., Florida State University, 1976); W. Griswold et al., *The Image of the Middle East in Secondary School Textbooks* (New York: Middle East Studies Association of North America, 1975); National Association of Arab Americans, *Treatment of the Arab World and Islam in Washington Metropolitan Area Junior and Senior Textbooks* (Washington, D.C., 1980); Barbara Aswad, "Biases and Inaccuracies in Textbooks: Depictions of the Arab World," in Abraham and Abraham, *Arab World and Arab-Americans*; Leonard Milton Kennedy, "The Treatment of Moslem Nations, India and Israel in Social Studies Textbooks Used in Elementary and Junior High Schools of the United States" (Ph.D. diss., Washington State University, 1960); Helen M. Kearney, "American Images of the Middle East, 1824–1924: A Century of Antipathy" (M.A. thesis, University of Rochester, 1976).

86. Hitti, *Syrians in America*, 88.

87. Khan, "Brief History of Pakistanis in the Western United States."

88. Shelley Slade, "The Image of the Arab in America: Analysis of a Poll on American Attitudes," *Middle East Journal* 35 (Spring 1981): 143–62; David D. Newsom, "The Arabs and U.S. Public Opinion: Is There Hope?" *American-Arab Affairs* 2 (1982): 61–68.

89. Edward Said, *Orientalism* (New York: Pantheon, 1978); Janice Terry, "Arab Stereotypes in Popular Fiction," *Arab Perspectives*, Apr. 1982; idem, "Arab-Israeli Conflict in Popular Literature"; idem, "Images of the Middle East in Contemporary Fiction," in *Split Vision: Portrayal of Arabs in the American Media*, ed. Edmund Ghareeb (Washington, D.C.: American-Arab Affairs Council, 1983), 315–26.

90. Glenn Perry, "The Arabs in American High School Textbooks," *Journal of Palestine Studies* 4 (1975): 46–58; al-Qazzaz, "Images of the Arab in American Social Science Textbooks."

91. Jack G. Shaheen, *The TV Arab* (Bowling Green, Ohio: Bowling Green State University Popular Press, 1984). Cf. Laurence Michalak, "The Arab in American Cinema: A Century of Otherness," *Cineaste* 17, no. 1 (1989): 3–9.

92. Edmund Ghareeb, "The Media and U.S. Perceptions of the Middle East," *American-Arab Affairs* 2 (1982): 69–88; Edmund Ghareeb, *Split Vision: The Portrayal of Arabs in the American Media* (Washington, D.C.: American-Arab Affairs Council, 1983); Mary C. McDavid, "Media Myths of the Middle East: The U.S. Press on the War in Lebanon," G. Neal Lendenmann, "Arab Stereotyping in Contemporary American Political Cartoons," Patricia A. Karl, "In the Middle of the Middle East: The Media and the U.S. Foreign Policy," and Jack J. Shaheen, "The Image of the Arab on American Television," in Ghareeb, *Split Vision*, 327–36; Jarrar, "Images of the Arabs"; Terry B. Hammons, "A Wild Ass of a Man: American Images of Arabs to 1948" (Ph.D. diss., University of Oklahoma, 1978); Michael C. Hudson and Ronald G. Wolfe, eds., *The American Media and the Arabs* (Washington, D.C.: Center for Contemporary Arab Studies, Georgetown University, 1980); Jack G. Shaheen, "The Arab Image in American Mass Media," *American-Arab Affairs* 2 (1982): 89–96; Jack G. Shaheen, "The Arab Stereotype on Television," *Link* 13, no. 2 (Apr./May 1980): 1–13; Nick Thimmesch, "The Media and the Middle East," *American-Arab Affairs* 2 (1982): 79–88; Aslam Munjee, "The Tyranny of the U.S. Media," *The Journal: Rabitat al-'Alam al-Islami* 7, no. 11 (1980): 59–62.

93. Salman Rushdie, *The Satanic Verses* (London: Viking, 1988).

94. Edward Said's *Orientalism* has received a great deal of attention from Islamists who saw its argument buttressing their assertion that the West is anti-Muslim. For the last two

years, Said has been trying to correct what he perceives as a misinterpretation of what he said, "*Orientalism* was mistakenly read as an anti-Western work and as an elevation of Islam, while in reality it should be read as a work revealing Orientalists' bias in their study of the Middle East and 'their chronic tendency to deny, suppress and distort the Orient.'" "Edward Said Lectures at AUB," *AUB Bulletin*, May 1995, p. 28; cf. Said, *Orientalism*.

95. These include Mayor Goode of Philadelphia, Congressman Joseph Kennedy of Massachusetts, and presidential candidate Walter Mondale. (It is worth noting that in two cases the donors were of Lebanese Christian background.)

96. Yvonne Yazbeck Haddad, "American Foreign Policy in the Middle East and Its Impact on the Identity of Arab Muslims in the United States," in Yvonne Yazbeck Haddad, *The Muslims of America* (New York: Oxford University Press, 1991), 217–35; idem, "Impact of the Islamic Revolution."

97. Edward W. Said, *Covering Islam: How the Media and the Experts Determine How We See the Rest of the World* (New York: Pantheon Books, 1981).

98. David Cole, Georgetown University law professor, among others have argued that the bill "is going to be targeted . . . first and foremost against Arabs and Muslims." Eyad H. Zayed, "The Counterterrorism Bill and Its Impact on our Community," *ADC Times* 16, no. 3 (May-June 1995): 3.

99. The letter, dated June 19, 1995, begins with the following paragraph: "In anticipation of the anti-terrorism debate, we would suggest that you take the opportunity to view the enclosed video entitled, 'Jihad in America.'"

While Connie Chung, Wolf Blitzer, and Steve Emerson advocated the possibility that the bombing was the work of Arab or Middle Eastern terrorists, even after it had become obvious that the primary suspects were not Middle Eastern, it was Steve Emerson who insisted on national television that the Muslims were responsible for the Oklahoma City bombing and that regardless of Muslim denial he will be proven right. Sam Donaldson of ABC News thought that the reporters were uncritical and were using statements of U.S. officials without verifiable evidence. "The U.S. Press: Achieving Balanced Coverage," *ADC Times* 16, no. 3 (May-June 1995): 4.

100. Paul Findley, *They Dare to Speak Out: People and Institutions Confront Israel's Lobby* (Westport, Conn.: Lawrence Hill and Company, 1985); Robert I. Friedman, "The Enemy Within: How the Anti-Defamation League Turned the Notion of Human Rights in Its Head, Spying on Progressives and Funneling Information to Law Enforcement," *Voice*, May 11, 1993, pp. 27–32; Dennis King and Chip Berlet, "ADLgate," *Tikkun*, July-Aug. 1993, pp. 31–36, 100–102; Rachelle Marshall, "Spy Case Update: The Anti-Defamation League Fights Back," *Washington Report on Middle East Affairs*, July/Aug. 1993, pp. 20, 85; Jeremy Kalmanofsky, "Defaming the Anti-Defamation League, *Moment*, Aug. 1993, pp. 40–43, 62–64.

101. For a list of organizations being spied on, see the fact sheet, "Is the A.D.L. Spying on You?" (n.p., n.d.).

102. ADL Backgrounder, "Hamas, Islamic Jihad and the Muslim Brotherhood: Islamic Extremists and the Terrorist Threat to America" (prepublication copy, Mar. 1993).

103. See, for example, the following publications by the Anti-Defamation League: *The Anti-Semitism of Black Demagogues and Extremists* (New York: Anti-Defamation League, 1992); *Jew-Hatred as History: An Analysis of the Nation of Islam's "The Secret Relationship Between Blacks and Jews"* (New York: Anti-Defamation League, 1993); *Louis Farrakhan: An Update* (New York: Anti-Defamation League, 1985); *Louis Farrakhan: The Campaign to Manipulate Public Opinion* (New York: Anti-Defamation League, 1990); *Louis Farrak-*

han: Continuing the Message of Hate (New York: Anti-Defamation League, 1988); Louis Farrakhan: In His Own Words (New York: Anti-Defamation League, n.d.).

104. Al-Fuqra: Holy Warriors of Terrorism (New York: Anti-Defamation League, 1993).

105. The beneficiaries include government officials and beltway experts who need an enemy in order to maintain their jobs, rulers of Arab countries who make enemies in order to justify their violation of the human rights of their opponents, Israel who needs to sell its service for continued aid, and the Christian right who need a new demon for the scenario of the last days. Yvonne Yazbeck Haddad, "The 'New Enemy'? Islam and Islamists after the Cold War," in Altered States: A Reader in the New World Order, ed. Phillys Bennis and Michel Moushabek (New York: Olive Branch, 1993), 83–94.

106. Missionary literature published by Fleming H. Revell Company in New York included such works as James L. Barton, Samuel Zwemer, and E.M. Wherry, eds., The Mohammedan World of Today (1906); E. M. Wherry, Islam and Christianity: The Irresponsible Conflict (1907); Annie van Sommer and Samuel M. Zwemer, eds., Our Moslem Sisters: A Cry of Need from Lands of Darkness Interpreted by Those Who Heard It (1907); and Robert E. Speer, Mission and Modern History (1904). Cf. Dr. and Mrs. Samuel M. Zwemer, Moslem Women (West Medford, Mass.: Central Committee on the United Study of Foreign Missions, 1926).

107. Yvonne Yazbeck Haddad, "The Authority of the Past: Current Paradigms for an Islamic Future," in The Authority of the Past, ed. Toby Siebers (Ann Arbor: Institute for the Humanities, University of Michigan, 1993).

108. Yvonne Yazbeck Haddad, "Operation Desert Shield/Desert Storm: The Islamist Perspective," in Beyond the Storm: A Gulf Crisis Reader, ed. Phillys Bennis (New York: Interlink Books, 1991).

109. Saad Eddin Mohamed Ibrahim, "Political Attitudes of an Emerging Elite: A Case Study of the Arab Students in the United States" (Ph.D. diss., University of Washington, 1968); Samira Mohammad Harfoush, "Study of Adjustment Problems and Attitudes of United Arab Emirates Undergraduate Students in the United States During the Fall of 1977" (Ph.D. diss., George Washington University, 1978); Abdulla Rashid Hagey, "Academic and Social Adjustment of Middle Eastern Students Attending Oregon Colleges and Universities" (Ph.D. diss., University of Oregon, 1968); Khalil Ismail Gezi, "The Acculturation of Middle Eastern Arab Students in Selected American Colleges and Universities" (Ph.D. diss., Stanford University, 1959); Fadlalla Ali Fadlalla, "Integration of Sudanese Students into the American Society: An In-depth Analysis of the Modern Problem of Alienation among Students in California" (Ph.D. diss., Claremont Graduate School and University Center, 1979); Mohammed Ahmed Rasheed, "Saudi Students in the United States: A Study of Their Perceptions of University Goals and Functions" (Ph.D. diss., University of Oklahoma, 1972); Khedair Saud al-Khedaire, "Cultural Perception and Attitudinal Differences Among Saudi Arabian Male College Students in the United States" (Ph.D. diss., University of Arizona, 1978); Horst Von Dorpowski, "The Problems of Oriental, Latin American, and Arab Students in U.S. Colleges and Universities as Perceived by these Foreign Students and by Foreign Student Advisors" (Ph.D. diss., Pennsylvania State University, 1977).

110. Herbert H. Williams, Syrians Studying Abroad: A Comparison of Factors Influencing the Number of Syrians Studying in the United States and Other Countries (n.p.: Institute of International Education, Research Program, 1952); Roland Max Kershaw, "Attitudes Toward Religion of Saudi Arabian Students in the United States" (Ph.D. diss., University of Southern California, 1973); Abdulrahman I. Ibrahim Jammaz, "Saudi Stu-

dents in the United States: A Study of Their Adjustment Problems" (Ph.D. diss., Michigan State University, 1972); Mohamed Ibrahim Kazem, "Prominent Values of Egyptian and American Students as Determined by an Analysis of Their Autobiographies with Educational Implications" (Ph.D. diss., University of Kansas, 1957); Saad Eddin Mohamed Ibrahim, "Interaction, Perception and Attitudes of Arab Students Toward Americans," *Sociology and Social Research* 55 (1970): 29–46; Gholamali Farjadi, "Economics of Study Abroad: The Case of Iranian Students in the U.S." (Ph.D. diss., New York University, 1980); A.J.M. Craig, "Egyptian Students," *Middle East Journal* 7 (1953): 293–99; Omaymah Ezzet Dahhan, "A Study of the Factors Influencing Future Plans and Career Goals of Arab Ph.D. Students in the United States" (Ph.D. diss., University of Texas, 1975); Lufty N. Diab, "Authoritarianism and Prejudice in Near-Eastern Students Attending American Universities" (Ph.D. diss., University of Oklahoma, 1957); Abdulrazzak Mohamed Salah Charbaji, "Academic and Social Problems Facing Arab Students on American Campuses" (Ph.D. diss., University of Northern Colorado, 1978); Adel Abdulla Bukhowa, "The Attitude of Arab Students in Colorado Toward Business and Industrial Firms in the United States" (Ph.D. diss., University of Northern Colorado, 1978); Mahmoud A. Saleh, "The Personal, Social, and Academic Adjustment Problems of Arab Students at Selected Texas Institutes of Higher Education" (Ph.D. diss., North Texas State University, 1979); Abdullah Saleh el-Banyan, "Cross-cultural Education and Attitude Change: A Study of Saudi Arabian Students in the United States" (Ph.D. diss., North Carolina State University, 1974); Isa Yacoub Azat, "The Nonreturning Arab Student: A Study in the Loss of Human Resources" (Ph.D. diss., University of Southern California, 1974); Khaled Ahmad M. Alyaha, "Constructing a Comprehensive Orientation Program for Saudi Arabian Students in the United States" (Ph.D. diss., University of Pittsburgh, 1981); Tuma Wadi Hazu, "The Effect of Cultural Affinity on Language Dominance of Arab Minority Students in Selected American Public Schools" (Ph.D. diss., Florida State University, 1982); Alyakdhan Talib al-Hinai, "Images, Attitudes and Problems of Middle Eastern Students in America" (Ph.D. diss., United States International University, 1977).

111. Yvonne Yazbeck Haddad, "Islamic 'Awakening' in Egypt," *Arab Studies Quarterly* 9, no. 3 (1987): 234–59.

112. This is especially true of some telecasts such as those of the now defunct PTL Club, Pat Robertson, and Jerry Falwell, who see the state of Israel as the fulfillment of Christian messianic hope. Their unabashed support of Israel regardless of the legality or justice of its policy and treatment of its Arab subjects is perceived as a confirmation of the "Judeo-Christian" conspiracy (or as some characterize it, the "Zionist-neo-Crusader" conspiracy against Islam).

113. John Obert Voll, "Islamic Issues for Muslims in the United States," in Haddad, *Muslims of America*; Yvonne Yazbeck Haddad, "Nationalism and Islamic Tendencies in Contemporary Arab-American Communities," in *Arab Nationalism and the Future Arab World*, ed. Hani Faris (Belmont, Mass.: AAUG Press, 1987).

114. Abdur Rehman Doi, "Duties and Responsibilities of Muslims in Non-Muslim States: A Point of View," *Journal: Institute of Muslim Minority Affairs* 8 (1987): 42–61; Thomas B. Irving, "Problems for Muslim Minorities and Millat," *Islamic Order* 2, no. 1 (1980): 60–63; A.K. Brohi, "Problems of Minorities," in *Muslim Communities in Non-Muslim States*, ed. A.K. Brohi (London: Islamic Council of Europe, 1980), 31–42. Other essays in Brohi's volume include Syed Z. Abedin, "The Study of Muslim Minority Problems: A Conceptual Approach," 17–29; Amadou Karim Gaye, "Muslim Minorities: A Framework," 1–6; M. Ali Kettani, "The Problems of Muslim Minorities and Their Solu-

tions," 91–107. Abul Hasan 'Al-Nadwi, *Muslims in the West: The Message and Mission* (Leicester, Eng.: Islamic Foundation, 1983).

115. The term has been coined by Syed Z. Abedin in his foreword to M. Ali Kettani, *Muslim Minorities in the World Today* (London: Mansell, 1986), xiii; Thomas B. Irving, "The Salvation of Muslim Minorities," *Journal, Rabetat al-'Alam al-Islami* 8 (June 1979): 27–31. For a longer discussion of the issue of minorityness, see Yvonne Yazbeck Haddad, "The Challenge of Muslim 'Minorityness': The American Experience," in *The Integration of Islam and Hinduism in Western Europe*, ed. W.A.R. Shadid and P.S. van Koningsveld (Kampen, The Netherlands: Kok, 1991).

116. Kettani, *Muslim Minorities*, 3.

117. Nadwi, *Muslims in the West*, 158.

118. His *fatwa* for Muslims living in South Africa legalizing the consumption of meat butchered for People of the Book (Christians and Jews) has been quoted as justification for not abiding by the restrictions of eating *halal* (properly butchered) meat. Abdu also issued a fatwa for Indian Muslims sanctioning cooperation with the British colonial forces despite the fact that they were not Muslim. In justification for his opinion, he cited the precedent of the Prophet and the early caliphs having cooperated with non-Muslims because of the benefit that would accrue to the Muslim community. "Isti'anat al-Muslimin bi'l-Kuffar wa-Ahl al-Bida' wa-al-Ahwa'," in Muhammad 'Amara, *al-A'mal al-Kamila li'l-Imam Muhammad 'Abdu: al-Kitabat al-Siyasiyya* (Cairo: al-Mu'assasa al-Arabiya lil-Dirasat wa'l-Nashr, 1972), 708–15.

119. Muhammad Abdul-Rauf, "The Future of the Islamic Tradition in North America," in *The Muslim Community in North America*, ed. Earle H. Waugh, Baha Abu-Laban, and Regula B. Qureshi (Edmonton: University of Alberta Press, 1983), 274.

120. Ibid.

121. This new development was brought to my attention by the Mufti of Oman in an interview in June 1990. He represents the Ibadi school of jurisprudence on the council. The justification for such an endeavor is the precedent set by the founder of the Shafi'i school of Islamic law who referred to the work he initiated in Egypt after leaving Baghdad as *"al-fiqh al-jadid,"* the new jurisprudence. (I am indebted for this information to Dr. Syed Saeed of the Institute of Islamic Thought in Herndon, Virginia.)

122. Gamal A. Badawi, *A Muslim Woman's Dress According to the Qur'an and Sunnah* (Plainfield, Ind.: MSA Women's Committee, n.d.); Regula Burkhardt Qureshi, "Marriage Strategies among Muslims from South Asia," in Waugh, Abu-Laban, and Qureshi, *Muslim Families in North America*, 185–213; Slaeem Qureshi, "The Muslim Family: The Scriptural Framework," in Waugh, Abu-Laban, and Qureshi, *Muslim Families in North America*, 32–67; Hammudah Abd al-Ati, *The Family Structure in Islam* (Plainfield, Ind.: American Trust, 1977); Muhammad Abdul-Rauf, *The Islamic View of Women and the Family* (New York: Robert Speller and Sons, 1977); idem, *Marriage in Islam* (New York: Exposition, 1972); Nouha al-Hegelan, *Women in the Arab World: Potentials and Prospects* (New York: Arab Information Center, n.d); Zahra Munir, "Being Muslim and Female," *Journal, Institute of Muslim Minority Affairs* 5, no. 1 (1983–84): 77–80; Na'im Akbar, "Family Stability among African-American Muslims," in Waugh, Abu-Laban and Qureshi, *Muslim Families in North America*, 213–231; Rabiyah Y. Abdul-Khabir, "Prevalent Problems in Muslim Marriages," *Al-Ittihad* 19, nos. 3–4 (1982): 15–26.

123. Marilyn Robinson Waldman, "Reflections on Islamic Tradition, Women, and Family," in Waugh, Abu-Laban, and Qureshi, *Muslim Families in North America*, 309–25; Barbara Aswad, "Attitudes of Immigrant Women and Men in the Dearborn Area Toward Women's Employment and Welfare," in Haddad and Smith, *Muslim Communities in*

North America, 501–19; *Arab Women: Potentials and Prospects* (New York: Arab Information Center, n.d.); Barbara Aswad, "Yemeni and Lebanese Muslim Immigrant Women in Southeast Dearborn, Michigan," in Waugh, Abu-Laban, and Qureshi, *Muslim Families in North America*, 256–81; Louise Cainkar, "Life Experiences of Palestinian Women in the United States" (paper delivered to Middle East Studies Association, Nov. 1985); idem, "Palestinian-American Muslim-Women: Living on the Margins of Two Worlds," in Waugh, Abu-Laban, and Qureshi, *Muslim Families in North America*, 282–308; Waugh, Abu-Laban, and Qureshi, *Muslim Families in North America*.

124. Munir, "Being Muslim and Female."

125. Safia Haddad, "The Woman's Role in Socialization of Syrian-Americans in Chicago," in Hagopian and Paden, *Arab Americans*, 84–101.

126. Sulayman S. Nyang and Mumtaz Ahmad, "The Muslim Intellectual Emigre in the United States," *Islamic Culture* 59 (1985): 277–90. For in-depth studies of three intellectuals see John L. Esposito, "Ismail R. al-Faruqi: Muslim Scholar-Activist," 65–79; Jane Idleman Smith, "Seyyed Hossein Nasr: Defender of the Sacred and Islamic Traditionalism," 80–95; and Frederick M. Denny, "The Legacy of Fazlur Rahman," 96–109; all in Haddad, *Muslims of America*.

127. Yvonne Yazbeck Haddad, "The Qur'anic Justification for an Islamic Revolution: The Views of Sayyid Qutb," *Middle East Journal* 38, no. 1 (Jan. 1983); idem, "Sayyid Qutb: Ideologue of Islamic Revival," in *Voices of a Resurgent Islam*, ed. John Esposito (New York: Oxford University Press, 1983).

128. Isma'il R. al-Faruqi, *Islam* (Niles, Ill.: Argus Communications, 1979).

129. Muhammad Shafiq, *Growth of Islamic Thought in North America: Focus on Isma'il Raji al-Faruqi* (Brentwood, Md.: Amana Publications, 1994).

130. Smith, "Seyyed Hossein Nasr," in Haddad, *Muslims of America*, 80–95.

131. Kenneth Cragg, "Fazlur Rahman of Karachi and Chicago," in his *The Pen and the Faith: Eight Modern Muslim Writers and the Qur'an* (London: George Allen and Unwin, 1985); Denny, "Legacy of Fazlur Rahman," in Haddad, *Muslims of America*, 96–108.

132. The following works are by Seyyed Hossein Nasr: *Traditional Islam in the Modern World* (London: Routledge and Kegan Paul, 1981); *Islam and the Plight of Modern Man* (London: Longman Group, 1975); *Islamic Life and Thought* (Albany: State University of New York Press, 1981); *Ideals and Realities of Islam* (New York: Frederick A. Praeger, 1967); *The Encounter of Man and Nature: The Spiritual Crisis of Modern Man* (London: George Allen and Unwin, 1968); *Knowledge and the Sacred* (New York: Crossroad, 1981); *Sufi Essays* (Albany: State University of New York Press, 1985).

133. The following works are by Fazlur Rahman: *Islamic Methodology in History* (Karachi: Central Institute of Islamic Research, 1965); *Prophecy in Islam: Philosophy and Orthodoxy* (London: Allen and Unwin, 1958); *Islam* (Chicago: University of Chicago Press, 1979); *Islam and Modernity: Transformation of an Intellectual Tradition* (Chicago: University of Chicago Press, 1982); *Major Themes in the Qur'an* (Minneapolis and Chicago: Bibliotheca Islamica, 1980).

134. E. Curtis Alexander, *Elijah Muhammad on African American Education: A Guide for African and Black Studies Programs* (New York: ECA Associates, 1981); idem, "Three Black Educators: A Study of the Educational Perspectives of Richard Allen, Elijah Muhammad, and Adam Clayton Powell, Jr." (Ph.D. diss., Columbia University, 1980); Kamal H. Ali, "Muslim School Planning in the United States: An Analysis of Issues, Problems and Possible Approaches" (Ph.D. diss., University of Massachusetts, 1981); Mehdi Razvi, "Cultural Values and Education in a Multicultural Society: A Muslim View," *Research Papers: Muslims in Europe* 17 (1983): 10–16; Kamal Ali, "Islamic Education in the United

States: An Overview of Issues, Problems and Possible Approaches," *American Journal of Islamic Studies* 1 (1984): 127–32; Noura Durkee, "Primary Education of Muslim Children in North America," *Muslim Education Quarterly* 5, no. 1 (1987): 53–81; Nimat Hafez Barazangi, "Parents and Youth: Perceiving and Practicing Islam in North America," in Waugh, Abu-Laban, and Qureshi, *Muslim Families in North America*, 132–47; Nimat Hafez Barazangi, "The Education of North American Muslim Parents and Children: Conceptual Change as a Contribution to Islamization of Education," *American Journal of Islamic Social Sciences* 7 (1990): 385–402; Ibrahim M. Shalaby, "The Role of the School in Cultural Renewal and Identity Development in the Nation of Islam" (Ph.D. diss., University of Arizona, 1967); Ibrahim M. Shalaby and H. John Chilcott, *The Education of a Black Muslim* (Tucson: Impresora Sahuaro, 1983); Abdullah Ghazi, "Problems of Religious Text Books and Instruction in North America," *Journal Institute of Muslim Minority Affairs* 5, no. 1 (1983–84): 67–70; Georgette Sesi, "The Middle Eastern Children in Detroit Public Schools" (M.Ed. thesis, Wayne State University, Detroit, 1973); Anis Ahmad, *Manual for Establishing Weekend Islamic Schools and Summer Schools* (Plainfield, Ind.: Muslim Student Association, [1979]).

135. Jon C. Swanson, "Mate Selection and Intermarriage in an American Arab Moslem Community" (M.A. thesis, University of Iowa, 1970); J.S. Nielsen, "Islam and Mixed Marriages," *Research Papers: Muslims in Europe* 20 (1983): 8–17; Dawud Assad, "Mixed Marriages," *Research Papers: Muslims in Europe* 20 (1983): 3–7; G. Harpigny, "Muslim-Christian Marriages and the Church," *Research Papers: Muslims in Europe* 20 (1983): 18–28; Rabiah Hakeem, "Cross-Cultural Marriages among Muslims: A Word of Caution," *Islamic Horizons* 14, no. 10 (1985); Ilyas Ba-Yunus, "Muslims in North America: Mate Selection as an Indicator of Change," in Waugh, Abu-Laban, and Qureshi, *Muslim Families in North America*, 232–49.

136. D.F. Forte, "Islamic Law in American Courts," *Suffolk Transnational Law Journal* (1983): 1–33; Ebrahim Sulaiman Sait, "Muslim Personal Law," in Brohi, *Muslim Communities in Non-Muslim States*, 109–24.

137. Akbar Muhammad, "Some Factors Which Promote and Restrict Islamization in America," *American Journal of Islamic Studies* 1, no. 2 (1984): 41–50; Monzer Kahf, *The Calculation of Zakah for Muslims in North America* (Plainfield, Ind.: Muslim Student Association, 1978); Ahmad Hussein Sakr, *Al-Khutab* (New York: Muslim World League, 1977); idem, *Dietary Regulations and Food Habits of Muslims* (New York: Muslim World League, n.d.); idem, *Cheese* (New York: Muslim World League, 1976); idem, *Fasting in Islam* (New York: Muslim World League, n.d.); idem, *Honey: A Food and a Medicine* (New York: Muslim World League, n.d.); idem, *Overeating and Behavior* (New York: Muslim World League, 1975); Mujahid al-Sawwaf, *Water in Islam* (New York: Muslim World League, n.d.); Yusuf al-Qaradawi, *The Lawful and the Prohibited in Islam* (Kuwait: I.I.F.S.O., 1984); Malik B. Badri, *Islam and Alcoholism* (Indianapolis: American Trust, 1976).

138. Ali F. Darrat, "Are Checking Accounts in American Banks Permissible Under Islamic Laws?" *American Journal of Islamic Social Sciences* 2 (1985): 101–4; Sulayman S. Nyang, "Muslim Minority Business Enterprise in America: An Economic Historical Perspective," *Search* 3, no. 2 (1982): 42–65; Raquibuz Zaman, "Banking, Investment, Insurance and Muslims in North America," *Journal, Institute of Muslim Minority Affairs* 5, no. 1 (1983–84): 71–76; Raquibuz Zaman, "Occupational Distribution of Muslim Minorities in North America" (unpublished paper prepared for the Seminar on the Economic Status of Muslim Minorities, King Abdulaziz University, Jedda, Nov. 1981); Monzer Kahf, *The Islamic Economy* (Plainfield, Ind.: Muslim Student Association, [1978]).

139. Marston Speight, "Christian-Muslim Dialogue in the United States of America," *Islamochristiana* 7 (1981): 201–10; Larry Poston, "The Future of *Da'wah* in North America," *American Journal of Islamic Social Sciences* 8 (1991): 501–11; Ahmad Hussein Sakr, "Islamic Dawa: Some Problems," *Journal: Rabetat al-'Alam al-Islami* 8 (June 1979): 14–16; Zaheer Uddin Nazim, *Manual of Da'wah* (Montreal: Islamic Circle of North America, 1983).

140. Earle H. Waugh, "The Imam in the New World: Models and Modifications," in *Transitions and Transformations in the History of Religions*, ed. Frank E. Reynolds and Theodore M. Ludwig (Leiden: E.J. Brill, 1980), 124–49; 'Abdur Rahman Shad, *Duties of an Imam*, revised by 'Abdul Hameed Siddiqui (Chicago: Kazi, 1978).

141. M.A. Qazi, *What's in a Muslim Name* (Chicago: Kazi, 1974); Sam Hamood, *Dying with the Wrong Name* (New York: Anthe, 1980).

142. Kathleen M. Moore, *al-Mughtaribun: American Law and the Transformation of Muslim Life in the United States* (Albany: State University of New York Press, 1995); Sidney Rahim Sharif, *Crime and Corrections: An al-Islamic Perspective* (Chicago: Kazi, 1983); Abdeen Jabara, "Operation Arab: The Nixon Administration's Measures in the U.S. after Munich," in *The Civil Rights of Arab-Americans: The Special Measures*, ed. M.D. Bassiouni (North Dartmouth, Mass.: Arab-American University Graduates, 1974).

143. Noor al Hussein, "Peace Efforts: Principles Versus Practices," *Arab-American Affairs* 8 (Spring 1984): 2–3.

144. While Islam recognizes Christianity and Judaism as monotheistic religions that may have veered astray, it considers Buddhism, Jainism, and Hinduism as polytheistic religions whose values are contrary to those revealed by God.

145. Yvonne Yazbeck Haddad and Adair Lummis, *Islamic Values in the United States: A Comparative Study* (New York: Oxford University Press, 1987).

A Century of Lakota Sioux Catholicism at Pine Ridge

CHRISTOPHER VECSEY

There is now a half millennium of written documentation regarding American Indian religions. Non-Indians from the first day of Columbian contact to the present — including explorers, missionaries, traders, ethnologists, historians, mythologists, missiologists, psychologists, New Agers, and others — have attempted to understand Native American religious expressions. In many times and places Indians themselves have attempted to make their religiousness understandable to those of us outside their native communities.

Hence, there is today a sizable accumulation of data, published and in archives, concerning American Indian symbolism, ceremonialism, spirituality, metaphysics, medicine, shamanism, oral tradition, eschatology, conversion and resistance to Christianity, syncretism, and the new religions that have punctuated Indian history over the past five centuries.[1]

Scholars of American religious history rarely have consulted these materials; nor have they considered the religious experiences of Native Americans a portion of their purview. These historians have focused their attention on Puritans, evangelicals, the theological dimensions of Christian traditions, church-state issues, the ethnic dimensions of New World religious immigration — the Jews, the Irish, and so forth — in short, the Judeo-Christian heritage in America. In such a context, the "primitive" or "tribal" religions of indigenous Americans have seemed more or less irrelevant.

On occasion denominational historians have written of Christian missionary efforts among the Indians, examining the goals, techniques, and effects of proselytizing. Almost invariably these studies have paid only passing attention to the recipients of missionizing, the Indians themselves, favoring instead the intrepid missionaries. In recent decades a more critical approach to Christian missions has interpreted these enterprises in the light of colonial, imperial, and nationalist aspirations and structures. Social scientists without sectarian allegiance — indeed, without any apparent love of religion—have condemned the black robes, short coats, and the bureaucrats associated with them, as agents of cultural and political devastation among the natives. Several Indian spokespersons, usually with Christian theological training, have challenged the remaining missionaries to amend their ways. Missiologists have asked searching questions of themselves. Still, the evangelists have received more ink than the Indians, whose adaptations of Christianity—for the most part—have been left unstudied by historians of American religious history.

At the same time, many scholars have devoted their careers to portrayal and analysis of American Indian religions. Grounding their study upon the voluminous reports of missionaries and others over the centuries who were in close contact with Native Americans, the first anthropologists and their successors for over a century now have tried to understand Indian religiousness. Their interest has not been in American religious history; rather they have used American Indians as case studies in the human condition, without explicit reference to United States culture or institutions.

For some ethnologists, Indian peoples constituted types of human communities: contrasts to urban, modern, or literate peoples; lower stages of evolutionary development; paradigms of *Gemeinschaft*, and the like. Indians fitted some niche in various theoretical models of human existence; thus, for example, Indians were said to be "animists," according to a scale of religious types.

A century ago Franz Boas began a tradition of fieldworking anthropology that eschewed, at least ostensibly, the evolutionism of his day. He and his legion of students and imitators entered Indian communities to gather data regarding every imaginable area of human culture: languages, kinship organization, tools and habitations, oral traditions, and so on. In the process, these ethnologists interviewed Indians regarding their religious concepts. They recorded Indian mythology and observed the patterns of religious ceremonialism. Sometimes religious specialists—medicine men and women, priests, conjurors, diviners, heads of sodalities—revealed the secrets of their trades. At other times common folk told of their representative lives: their rites of passage and initiation, their dreams and visions, their relations with the spirit world. From these ethnologies non-Indians have come to know the details of native religious life, and later generations of Indians have turned occasionally to these texts to learn how their forebears used to conduct their spiritual activities.

Building upon the work of the Boasians, social scientists in recent decades have turned again to theoretical models—how do religious elements function within societies; what are the underlying structures of mythological narratives; why are certain symbols found from one culture to another; when and under what conditions do people alter their religious patterns, and what elements persist, even during times of crisis. Modern students of Native American religions have sought meanings in the religious phenomena, not only regarding Indian culture but also concerning contemporary culture beyond Indian communities.

The last decade in particular has witnessed the growth of New Age interest in

American Indian religiousness. Americans (and Europeans and Asians as well) have hoped to gain something for themselves by appropriating aspects of Indian spirituality. In this context some historians of American religion have compared native and Euro-American ecological values, feminist principles, democratic ideals, and freedoms about sexual roles.

Little of this, however, has entered the mainstream of American religious history. For right or wrong, Native Americans remain peripheral to the study of religion in the United States. The late William G. McLoughlin's volumes on the Cherokees are examples, rarely matched, in which an American historian has scoured archives in order to document the changes in American Indian religion, including the adoption of Euro-American Christianity. The Cherokees did not necessarily become mainstream Christians; they maintained many of their native traditions. In McLoughlin's work, however, their story enters the mainstream of American religious historiography.

What follows here is a case study of American Indian persistence and change, focusing upon the Oglala Lakota (Sioux) people on the Pine Ridge Reservation in South Dakota, the second largest Indian territory in the United States. For a century Roman Catholic missionaries have made sustained and considerable efforts to alter the religious orientation and identity of the Pine Ridge Indians, particularly through the Holy Rosary Mission, established in 1888. Drawing upon the Holy Rosary archives at Marquette University, interviews with Lakotas and church personnel, and other sources, I am attempting to examine the range of Lakota responses to the mission efforts—a topic much in keeping with McLoughlin's interests and exemplary accomplishments.

Early Missionary Presence and Lakota Responses

Before the Christians arrived, the Lakotas expressed their traditional forms of religiousness, holding much in common with the other Teton (western) Sioux such as the Brule and Hunkpapa, and the Sioux further east: the several Yankton and Santee divisions.

For the Lakotas, religion constituted a means of making relatives; hence the term (*wacekiye*) for prayer and kinship address was the same; both were means of "invoking relationship."[2] The Lakotas cared deeply and persistently about communicating with the mysterious, powerful, awe-inspiring holy realm of being, the *wakan* world. The wakan revealed itself in its many aspects through natural phenomena and permeated the whole cosmos. In their religiousness the Lakotas attempted to bind themselves as relatives to the wakan beings, and above all to the supreme class of wakan beings, *Wakantanka*. They smoked pipes of sacred symbolism, the smoke serving as a medium of communication with the divine, the natural, and the human realms. Among their many myths they told narratives of a particular sacred pipe's origin: how the White Buffalo Calf Woman delivered it as a moral instruction; how its ritual created a kinship of people.

The Lakotas made themselves clean and proper before the wakan beings through the purification ceremony of the sweat lodge. They bound themselves in the commonality of the ordeal, sweating, singing, and praying together, ever invoking the phrase, "all my relations." In vision quests the Lakotas — particularly the men — sought direct communication with the holy ones under the guidance of trusted elders, in order to learn who they were and what they ought to become. These rites established lifelong personal relations with wakan beings and revealed something of the universe's structure and intent. Lakota girls came of age through the White Buffalo ceremony, which emphasized exchanges of gifts and the making of human relatives. Through this rite of passage young women bestowed the blessings of the wakan upon their communities.

In times of illness and other crises, the Lakotas elicited the help of the wakan beings through a conjuring ritual called Yuwipi. Medicine men derived their cures from the powers of wakan. The community members supported one another in order to persist as a people.

In the summer Sun Dance the Lakotas attempted the renewal of interrelations throughout the universe. They established a great lodge symbolic of the earth's central axis, joining this world with those above and below, and tried to orient themselves to this connective core of being. They fulfilled vows to the wakan beings and to each other, and made extended acts of generosity, suffering, and sacrifice, including rites of self-torture, so as to make themselves one with their fellow Lakotas and with their wakan ground of being. These rituals represented a greater matrix of ideas, images, behaviors, gestures, values, and relations, all designed at *wacekiye*, making all Lakotas relatives to one another and to the cosmos surrounding them. This matrix of religiousness was still functioning fully in the late nineteenth century, despite many years of contact with Christians.

Although Holy Rosary did not commence its operation until 1888, Catholic missionary contact with the Sioux had taken place as early as the 1660s, when the Jesuit Claude Allouez and Jacques Marquette had met eastern Sioux in what is now Wisconsin. In the eighteenth century other Jesuits found the eastern Sioux a difficult audience, and it was not until the 1840s that a Catholic priest made sustained evangelical interchange with the western, Teton Sioux, when the Belgian Jesuit Pierre DeSmet met them on his way to the Flatheads further west. He encountered the Oglala Lakotas for the first time in 1849, after they had just suffered a defeat from the Crows and were receptive to his spiritual powers. He baptized 239 Oglalas at the time, along with 280 Brules and 61 children of mixed descent.

Lakotas had already been in contact with Catholics for at least a century earlier, through relations with fur traders, most of French extraction. Father DeSmet became friendly with the new Lakota chief, Red Cloud, through the chief's French trader in-laws between 1865 and 1868. The fact that DeSmet was a French-speaking holy man made him especially beloved to the Sioux, and he was savvy in making use of his French connections to mixed-bloods to further his appeal to the Indians.

Red Cloud made a public appeal in 1876 for Catholic missions. He stated that when God sent His Son, Jesus, to the Whites, He had sent his daughter, Buffalo Calf Woman, to the Lakotas. The girl, Red Cloud said, had revealed that Indians would merge with Whites within the next ten generations; now it was time.[3] On a more mundane level, Red Cloud wanted priests and sisters to "teach our people how to read and write" the English language.[4] The chief recognized these skills as an adaptive "stratagem" for his Lakota relatives.[5] For him, Catholicism offered a means of enhancing his lineage organization, the traditional *tiyospaye*.

Jesuits received government approval in 1884 to open St. Francis Mission at Rosebud in 1886. When Mother Katherine Drexel donated sixty thousand dollars in 1887 for a Lakota institution at Pine Ridge, the Jesuits led by John B. Jutz, S.J., arrived with the wherewithal to establish something that would last among the Oglalas. The priests began a school, which they named after Drexel at first, and soon they had close to a hundred half-blood and Lakota students in grades 1–8, learning German, Latin, and later English — which is why some say that the Lakotas still speak with a German accent, having learned from German instructors. When the German Sisters of St. Francis of Penance and Christian Charity arrived in 1888, "The Indians called them Holy women, but asked if they were the four wives of the Blackrobe [Fr. Jutz]. The Sisters then explained to them they were not and came only for the sake of the Indians."[6]

The goals of the first missionaries were clear to themselves, and have been well described for the past century. They came to make Christians of the Lakotas, by bringing to them not only the Good News of the Gospels but also the institutions of Roman Catholicism. They meant to alter the fundamental conditions of Lakota existence: their family life, their economy, their spiritual orientation, their medicinal practices. Such was the basic "paradigm" of the early missionaries.[7] Father Florentine Digmann, one of the first Jesuits at Holy Rosary, criticized the habits of the Lakotas in the early years — "We had to do with little savages" who licked each other's plates — and he was determined to do away with the culture of Sioux savagery, God willing.[8]

At the same time, the Jesuits found worthy elements in Lakota culture. Almost all of the German Jesuits — Fathers Eugene Buechel, Placidus F. Sialm, Emil Perrig, Louis J. Goll, Florentine Digmann, and others — spoke Lakota, and they investigated Lakota religious concepts and practices in order to graft Christianity upon them. They perceived monotheistic aspects of Lakota theology — in the notion of a supreme class of wakan, named Wakantanka — and called the Christian God by that name. The priests taught about Catholic faith and institutions as if they were an outgrowth of Lakota religion: Eucharist was "holy food" (*yatapi wakan*); a church was a "sacred house" (*tipi wakan*); the devil was the evil mystery spirit (*wakansica*). The missionaries signified Catholicism as the "Black Robe prayer," using the traditional Lakota term, *wacekiye*. When the priests organized retreats for Lakota children, they referred to the meditative exercises as vision quests ("crying for a vision": *hamble iciyope*). So whereas the Jesuits found fault with many features of Lakota culture — what they considered the excesses of self-torture in the Sun Dance, the devilish conjuring of spirits in Yuwipi rituals, the superstitious prestige of medicine men — and thought condescendingly of the Indians as children in need of spiritual correction, they condoned, approved of, and even encouraged specific parts of traditional Lakota culture with which they were intimately familiar.[9]

The Jesuits established Sacred Heart Church in Pine Ridge agency in 1890, and by the 1930s there were more than thirty churches in various parishes throughout the various districts of Pine Ridge, all under the Jesuit control at Holy Rosary. When Red Cloud died in 1909, he received tribute from the missionaries: for inviting and protecting them, for converting so thoroughly to their faith. Father Placidus F. Sialm, S.J., one of the chroniclers of the mission in the 1930s, memorialized the chief: "Red Cloud is by far the most noble character of all the Sioux Nation, a leader and a statesman, not a medicineman like Sitting Bull with a double mind. Red Cloud deserved a monument and he got a nice outstanding tombstone in the Catholic Graveyard of Holy Rosary Mission. He died as a Christian and a Catholic and was buried with all the rites of the Catholic Church by Father Eugene Buechel."[10] Sialm failed to record Red Cloud's abdication speech of 1903, in which the chief vowed fidelity to the Sun (*Wi*) and his traditional religion in general. He said, "*Taku Skanskan* is familiar with my spirit (*nagi*) and when I die I will go with him. Then I will be with my forefathers. If this is not in the heaven of the white man, I shall be satisfied. *Wi* is my father. The *Wakan Tanka* of the white man has overcome him. But I shall remain true to him."[11] Notwithstanding, the Holy Rosary Mission School became known as Red Cloud Indian School in 1911.

Although attendance figures at Red Cloud are not exact, there were approximately 20,000 enrollees until 1958 when the boarding school was turned into a day school with perhaps another 10,000 since then. In the late 1880s, about 7,000 Lakotas lived at Pine Ridge; within twenty years a third of the Oglalas (ca. 2,300) were baptized Catholic. Within the first fifty years the priests baptized 7,500, marking half the Indian population in the Catholic ranks. By 1963 — seventy-five years after its founding — Holy Rosary had initiated more than 13,000 Indians into Catholic life. In its first 100 years Holy Rosary Mission has performed well over 20,000 baptisms, 2,000 marriages, and 1,500 funerals. Rapid City diocese today includes five Sioux reservations, with 60,000 Sioux, one-fourth to one-third of whom are nominally Catholic. These 15,000–20,000 constitute almost half the Catholics in the diocese. At Pine Ridge almost half of the 20,000 Lakotas are baptized Catholics.

Before the Jesuits and Sisters of St. Francis arrived among the Sioux there were already French, Irish, Canadian, and Mexican Catholics — traders, trappers, cowboys, "squawmen," and homesteaders — who introduced the Sioux to Catholic belief and ritual. By the 1880s many of these men who had been baptized and even received First Holy Communion in their youth, had married Sioux, and now had large families. "Through their children they came back to practice their religion, receiving here their second Communion and having their marriages revalidated."[12] Throughout the middle of the nineteenth century, "The anxiety of the 'squawmen' to have their children baptized begot a desire for the 'saving waters' in the natives and prepared the way for the missionaries."[13] Some of these men were influential with certain tribal leaders, and once the missions arrived, these Catholic non-Indians served as translators, catechists, sponsors, and provided "religious continuity" in the absence of priests and sisters.[14] Almost all the first pupils at the mission school were French or Mexican half-bloods; "the full-bloods were slow to come and when they did they were quick to leave."[15] The mixed-blood descendants were the first loyalists at Holy Rosary Mission. Today they are considered Sioux Indians, but they are of a special set of lineages — the Cliffords, the Pouriers, the Cunys, the Giagos, the Tibbits, and so forth. They are no less "Sioux" than the Black Elk family or other full-blood lineages, or those families of Mandan or Omaha origin who entered the tribe in earlier centuries and whose family trees are accounted for at Buffalo Woman ceremonies.[16]

The half-breeds were not the only ones to be baptized, and not the only ones to attend Holy Rosary Mission. At St. Cecelia's church in Kyle district was an old man named Apple, one of the first full-blood Pine Ridge Lakotas baptized in 1884 by a pioneer cleric, before Holy Rosary began. His son John Apple went to Holy Rosary School and became a devout Catholic. Medicine men converted; husbands followed their wives; parents followed their offspring; children followed their guardians. Some sought baptism after long periods of resistance. Some sought the faith following dreams: "Many people saw visions of Jesus or the saints which confirmed them in their faith or prepared them for death."[17]

Some of these converts needed to alter their marriages in order to receive baptism or communion. For example, Joe Big Head sought baptism but could not hurt the feelings of one of his wives by dismissing her — which he would have to do before becoming Catholic. Finally, he annulled his relation to the younger of the two, and all three of this menage received baptism. In the following years he could be found making the stations of the cross at the missions five times a week.[18]

If the Lakotas of the late nineteenth and early twentieth centuries were willing even to change their familial life in order to receive baptism and other sacraments, what techniques did the missionaries use to bring the Lakotas toward participation in Catholic life?

Father Digmann wrote that the Jesuits wanted the Lakotas to "forget camp life," so they taught them to sing Christian hymns in English (and Lakota) composed by Father Ravoux. Ravoux's little bilingual catechism was the Jesuits' first textbook in learning Sioux language, and the priests tried to impress the Indians by trying to learn their language. In addition, "To attract them to Church on Sundays, we offered the following inducement," a Magic Lantern show with colored biblical slides of Christ, the martyrs, but also some "funny ones." Digmann suggested that "the scheme worked well."[19]

He and his fellow evangelists augmented songs and slides with the use of a pictorial catechism, "The Road Picture" on which was visualized the rudiments of Catholic instruction: a road to heaven, and a road to the home of the devil.

Along the two paths the Indians could see God's creation, Adam and Eve, Noah, Abraham, Jesus, the church with its commandments and liturgy, featuring Mass on Sunday. There were illustrations of the seven capital sins, the seven sacraments, faith, hope, and love, the one, holy, universal and apostolic Catholic Church, purgatory, the communion of saints, and Luther leaving the good road for the bad one. Hence, the mission presented the Sioux with a Catholic worldview that set forth clear choices regarding belief, behavior, and loyalties: which road to take and which to eschew.[20]

Concurrently, the missionaries worked with the United States government in undermining the traditional religion. They did not forbid Indians their herbal medicines but "forbade them the use of the drum, the flute, the pumpkin-shells and sacred dances and songs, to which superhuman efficacy was ascribed." The priests confronted medicine men in the acts of curing: "We had a special eye on the sick, not to let them go without baptism. Several of these died soon after baptism and the opinion was spread by the medicine man that pouring on of water had killed them." Digmann described a confrontation with medicine men conjuring over a dying child: Digmann and a sister threw the curer's medicine bags out of the lodge and would not leave the child until the conjurers yielded.[21]

As an inducement toward conversion the missionaries made certain to provide food at Holy Rosary for those Lakotas interested in the Christian message, including sauerkraut for the first time on St. Valentine's Day 1889. At first the Indians disdained the Germanic food, but upon encouragement they tried it "and the ice was broken for the future."[22]

In order to establish their authority, the priests encouraged strict punishment of Lakota children. Lakota parents argued that they were not accustomed to doing such things; however, Digmann states that the "more sensible of them saw that our way was the right one." When three girls tried to burn down Holy Rosary in 1893, and one of them escaped jail and sought asylum with her parents, Digmann "insisted on unconditional surrender," and she was brought back by force "like possessed by the devil."[23]

The Indians may have been attracted by songs and pictures; they may have been lured by food or shelter. They were impressed by Christian charity and asceticism, and they perceived the Christian "God" as "Wakan Tanka."[24] It appears, however, that they were also motivated by fear regarding the afterlife. In a number of conversion episodes, the Sioux in the 1890s stated that they wished their souls to live after their death, and they regarded baptism as a means of assuring life after death. The priests then performed burials, with pageantry and crosses over the graves, replacing the Lakota practice of scaffold burial. By the 1890s some Lakotas were requesting baptisms and burials for their dead.

Joseph F. Busch, bishop of the Diocese of Lead (forerunner of Rapid City), wrote a letter around 1910 to the "Catholic Indians" of his diocese, warning of three "spiritual dangers": drinking, dancing, and divorce. The bishop condemned each one by threatening the Indians with sorrow "in Hell forever," unable to enter "the kingdom of Heaven."[25]

The priests and sisters had no sooner arrived, bringing with them a Christian eschatology, when the Ghost Dance swept across western America, including the Dakota Territory. Short Bull and other Sioux brought the Ghost Dance from the Paiute prophet Wovoka in Nevada, and adapted it to local contexts. Perhaps the missionaries' gospel of heavenly reward and Jesus' second coming was partially responsible for the Lakota participation in the Ghost Dance. Father Jutz, who was Holy Rosary Mission superior at the time, was an eyewitness to the dance. In his memoirs he described the economic, social, and political dissatisfaction of the Sioux in 1890, and the Ghost Dance's promises to eradicate whites and restore the old cultural and natural environment. He and other priests portrayed the dance itself: its frenzied singing, its pushing and pulling, the ecstasy of the dancers. At White Clay Creek, four miles from Holy Rosary, he entered the whirling circle in his religious habit, and when various Indians fainted — or died, in the Ghost Dance ideology — and revived, he asked them what they had seen in their swoon. He even offered to pay five dollars if they would tell him, but none would. Then he told them that there was no truth to their beliefs, that they were incapable of speaking with the dead through the medium of the dance. They would not heed him and resumed their dancing. During the Ghost Dance, the children at Holy Rosary "were just crazy over the Ghost Dance, and as soon as they thought they were not being observed, they danced it." The sisters took these frenzied children into the sick room at the mission to keep them from the hysteria.[26]

Pine Ridge Catholic Culture

Red Cloud Indian School constituted the principal means by which Holy Rosary attracted Sioux children, and thus their families, to Catholic culture. The mission inculcated the thousands of Lakota children who attended Red Cloud with a pervasive Catholic spirituality. The mission sponsored Corpus Christi processions, retreats, Rogation Days, Christmas feasts and pageants, Gregorian Masses with singing in Sioux language. There were Baptisms, Holy Communions, burials, the sayings of rosaries, as the Indians learned the liturgical forms of Catholicism. A mother superior wrote, "At Easter, 1906, many Indians came to see the first communion celebration of 46 children for the first time. They brought all their belongings and erected their tents where they would live for the next eight days. It looked like an entire village arose in one night."[27] They attended the Catholic rite of passage as if it were a Lakota ritual, with full family participation.

The missionaries attempted to deepen the faith of the initiated children with various methods of spiritual training. There was an attempt to present Catholic theology and spiritual experience unadulterated, and if we look at "A Retreat for Our Indian Children" conducted by Eugene Buechel in 1917, it is identical — although in Lakota — to retreat discourses delivered to non-Indians in Youngstown and Cleveland in 1907. He emphasized the elevation of the soul over the body, the types of sins we commit, the sacraments that save us, the judgment that comes after death, and the horrors of hell: its smells, sights, sounds are all horrible, but most horribly, it lasts forever; therefore, beware, use your time judiciously. He ended the retreat with a lesson upon the Prodigal Son, and reminded the children of our chance for forgiveness, God's love for us sinners, our hope, the Good News of the gospel. He told the Lakotas of a boy almost killed by snakes and reminded them that we are all close to death, and perhaps to hell: "We are not rocks, not bugs, not birds, not coyotes, not horses — we are men. Animals live and die and that's the end of them." We owe our lives to God, he said, belong to Him, are His property, and we must do His will, as if He were our employer and owner. In his many sermons Buechel emphasized the necessity of work; it was for him the means to compensate for our human sinfulness. It was our Christian penance and our duty to work, he told the Lakota children.[28]

The school spirituality focused partially upon death, particularly the death of young role models. Father Otto J. Moorman wrote obituaries in 1924 for two Sioux sisters, Esther and Grace, who died in 1922 and 1924 respectively, both at the age of twenty. Esther wanted to die and go to Jesus, and she persuaded her mother to release her to Him: "Esther, I told Jesus that I wish to keep you, dear, but that if He really wanted you He should take you now. I give you up to Him, Esther." Moorman commented, "When she spoke of her dreams of the Blessed Virgin, of the Angels, of the Child Jesus, whom the Blessed Mother had placed in her arms to caress for a 'long while' . . . I realized that here was truly a lily, a lily of the Sioux." Her sister Grace received communion daily, was saintly, and always kept her soul white. The priest recalled her possessing ruddy good cheer, "red with a thirst for martyrdom." To this day, some Lakota Catholics keep the memory of these pious women.[29]

To organize the pupils at Red Cloud into spiritual cadres, the missionaries formed a Young Women Society in the 1920s, a Holy Rosary Society in the 1930s, a Sacred Heart League in the 1940s, and members of these and other societies pledged to keep themselves "Right and Holy": "With God's help I promise to do all I can to save my soul. I wish to obey the Laws of God and of His Holy Catholic Church. Especially do I promise to Marry Right and Holy before the Catholic priest. I hate to think about a mixed marriage. And I strictly object against marrying in any other Church. So help me God and His Holy Gospel."[30]

But even at these sodality meetings, there could be subterfuge of the mission goals. Father Sialm wrote in the 1920s that sodality meetings were not necessarily spiritual in their purpose. The Indians used them for socializing, for staying up late and missing Sunday Masses. He noted that the members rarely met the rules for membership; even Protestants would show up! Indeed, he said, the meetings leaned toward Protestantism: "They dodge the priest. . . . Smart gangs don't like the priest so they may do as they please in these meetings.[31] The history of Red Cloud was a struggle for control over the behavior of Lakota youths.

In the church the priests made rules for the Lakotas who became altar boys: "No *slouchy* position *in Church . . . Hands & face* clean . . . *Hands* should be *joined* folded *before breast . . .* Movements on altar *not too fast*," as the Lakota boys had to learn a new spiritual language of gesture and posture.[32]

At the golden jubilee of Holy Rosary Mission, in 1938, the students performed a play, "The Princess of the Mohawks," in the mission auditorium, portraying the life of Kateri Tekakwitha. As early as 1931 a mission committee had organized on her behalf, and in 1935 a petition was sent to Pope Pius XI to advance her cause toward sainthood. Lakota girls had acted in "Coaina: The Indian Rose" in 1931, portraying a pious Algonquian Catholic girl. The play promoted devotion to the Virgin Mary and discouraged marriages between Catholics and traditionalists. Two years later the Holy Rosary students performed the life of Tekakwitha on Easter Sunday, and again in 1935 they put on another devotional drama about Tekakwitha, "Lily of the Mohawk." These thespian endeavors led to the 1938 production. The play, written by Joseph P. Clancy, told of the pure princess who resisted her stubborn pagan uncle's desire to marry her to a fierce medicine man, who prayed to the god of war. Kateri was saved by the blackrobe and taken off to the Christian reserve, Caughnawaga. Father Joseph A. Zimmerman, S.J., wrote of the Tekakwitha pageant, "Every feature was Indian, the cast of mission pupils, stage scenery painted by an Indian, Indian saint, Indian band playing Indian airs under its Indian leader, . . . and costumes of old tribal paraphernalia borrowed from our Indian homes. It is doubtful if this display of authentic regalia could be duplicated." [33] Nevertheless, a non-Indian produced the script, and the missionaries prompted the performance, which served the purpose of socializing the Lakota children and their families. They were meant to identify with the Christian Kateri and to condemn the pagan medicine man, the war ceremony, indeed, all of traditional Mohawk religion. Through such pageants the mission personnel attempted to create an "authentic" Indian history with which contemporary Lakotas could identify, on their journey toward Catholic American life. It was a fitting way to mark the first half century of progress at Holy Rosary.

Taking stock at the half century, Catholic publicists of the mission made the assessment that "Catholic education has been a success with the once war-like Sioux. . . . Who knows how many uprisings were prevented by educating the Indians?" [34] Rev. Louis J. Goll wrote in 1940 of the baptized Sioux: "They are not all saints, . . . but they are not a trifle less good than the average Catholic elsewhere . . . in the reception of the sacraments they surpass their white brethren. Four out of five who attend Mass also receive Holy Communion." He continued, "A careful study of parish records reveals the fact that during all these fifty years and more, only five per cent of the Catholic Indians gave up the faith in which they were instructed, to return to the old pagan superstitions of the medicine man or to embrace pagan cults of recent origin. Certainly not more than one per cent joined another Christian sect." [35] During the 1940s and 1950s the learning process continued with Forty Hours Devotions, May Day Crownings, Sodality Conventions, special devotion to the Sacred Heart of Jesus. Red Cloud students also worked in the gardens, played basketball, performed in the glee clubs, enjoyed picnics, watched approved films, and looked forward to fresh buns from the mission bakery. They joined sodalities, band, and choir, and performed their coursework. They took needlework, home economics, and shop. There are thousands of photographs of them over the century: at Catholic Congresses, praying at their bedsides, peeling potatoes, baking, butchering, singing, gardening, woodworking, shoemaking, cheerleading, attending Valentine's Day dances. Their hair and clothing styles were American, and changed as the American styles changed. The children in the photographs seem acculturated; however as Marla Powers points out, the traditional culture did not disappear. Many Lakotas walked two roads simultaneously, Sioux and American, although the photographs did not picture the Sioux road.[36]

Indeed, the Pine Ridge Sioux established patterns of "dual religious participation"[37] during the first half century of Holy Rosary, and many have persisted in those patterns to the present day, speaking the languages of Catholicism and traditional Lakota religiousness in alternating, compartmentalized sequences, suitable to varying circumstances. Holy Rosary Lakotas were Catholics in some situations, and traditionalists at other times. Lakotas sent their children to the Catholic school because of its food, its security, its charity. Adult Lakotas attempted to appropriate the spiritual powers of the church by participating in its rituals and structures. They did this, however, without necessarily eschewing aboriginal Sioux ways, especially since the Jesuits often characterized traditional Lakota faith as a primitive mode of Catholicism. Into the 1940s, Lakotas turned to Holy Rosary's Red Cloud School without necessarily turning away from their old ways.

By the early twentieth century most of the Lakotas belonged to one Christian denomination or another, with Catholic and Episcopal church organizations serving as the hubs of reservation neighborhood life, the tiyospaye. Government policy prohibited aboriginal rituals and social institutions. At the same time the Catholic missionaries encouraged Sioux adult participation in new rituals and institutions that were meant to replace the aboriginal forms and at the same time bind the new converts to Christian church life. The most important of these were the St. Joseph and St. Mary Societies, which met not only locally throughout the year but also in grand annual summer congresses. In this way a Lakota could join the Catholic Church, become a member of a men's or women's society, socialize with thousands of fellows at the summer encampment, all with the approval of the Holy Rosary authorities and government officials. Participation in these Christian institutions "was the source of the deepest solidarity and meaning of the Sioux people during the time that the 'reservation culture' flourished" until World War II.[38]

Rev. Francis M. Craft, the freelance missionary who served at Pine Ridge and Rosebud from 1883 to 1885, was inducted into the Omaha Society — a former warriors' society acquired from the Omaha in the 1860s. Craft saw that the Omaha Society of his day emphasized righteous conduct rather than military prowess; generosity and brotherhood were its virtues. He saw these as counterparts to Christian virtues; hence, he attempted to modify them to fit Christian teaching and ritual. His efforts led the way to the official formation of the St. Joseph Society among the Sioux.[39]

With the support of Bishop Martin Marty, the first St. Joseph and St. Mary sodalities were officially sanctioned among the Devil's Lake Sioux, North Dakota, in 1884. They were structured similarly to traditional men's and women's sodalities, with doorkeepers, visitors of the sick, waiters, heralds, hair cutters, horse traders, and so forth; however, membership was limited to Catholics married within the church, who had received First Communion. The members were known to observe the sabbath, to catechize their brethren, and to avoid polygamy and drunkenness. They were designed to be adult models of Christian virtue.[40]

The members of these mutual aid societies eschewed participation in native rituals abhorrent to Christianity. Instead, they spread the newly founded organizations to other Sioux communities in the 1880s. At each reservation those interested in joining applied to the local priests, and upon proving himself or herself a worthy Catholic — having received baptism, having learned basic prayers and church precepts, receiving communion regularly and attending Mass on Sundays and Holy Days of Obligation, respecting all church officials — the new members vowed to send their children to mission schools and to avoid Protestant services. The members performed corporal acts of mercy — visiting the sick, burying the dead, helping widows and orphans — and they abstained (or at least promised to abstain) from alcohol and superstitious customs.

In 1889 a Lakota asked Father Digmann for help in protecting the Omaha Dance and its brotherhood. The local agent was threatening to destroy it, charging that its nighttime dancing made the Indians unfit for "serious," steady work. Digmann replied: "'Nobody blames your society for helping one another, keep that up but true friendships exist only among those who worship the Great Spirit, come to Church.' Within myself I thought: 'This pagan society may turn out a basis for christian brotherhood (St. Joseph and Mary's Societies) and surely this was also Father Craft's idea. Go in with them in their door and lead them out to his.'"[41] The Catholic authorities thus aided in the formation of these sodalities and held the first Sioux Congress of sodality members in 1891, on the Fourth of July. Sun Dances at the summer solstice had been banned; the U.S. government had tried to replace them with patriotic, mock military gatherings; now the Catholic missionaries were providing their own version of seasonal liturgy. Three thousand Indians journeyed to Fort Yates on the Standing Rock Reservation, where the social functions of the banned Sun Dance — the gathering, the visiting, the feasting, the pledging, and even gambling — were celebrated. Bishop Marty had been reluctant at first to give too much room to the new sodalities of the 1880s, with their lay initiative; however, he wanted to rid Sioux reservations of the Sun Dances, and he saw Sioux Catholic congresses as direct replacements. Marty gave sermons about Jesus' hanging from a tree, in order to show the Sioux that the sacrifice of the Mass was a higher form of Sun Dance self-torture, with Jesus providing the salvific sacrifice for all humans.[42] In addition, the Ghost Dance of 1890 forced him to consider a means of gathering adult Sioux organizational force against such movements in the future. Moreover, he chose Independence Day in order to compete with the U.S. patriotic celebrations that allowed certain traditional dances, including war dances.[43] This first congress made the Pine Ridge Lakotas aware that their North Dakota relatives were more progressive — wearing short hair and the like. The Oglalas wanted to catch up and start their own St. Joseph and St. Mary Societies. One of them said at the time that he felt "like a child breaking through the shell. . . . The Blackrobes by their teaching have hatched me."[44]

Sioux who received baptism had a difficult life ahead of them. They were required to attend Mass; they were prohibited — at least publicly — from polygamy, the warpath, divination, superstitions, and consulting with medicine men. Their gentile relatives and friends ridiculed their Christian identity. The St. Joseph and St. Mary Societies provided a peer structure for mutual encouragement, under priestly guidance. Furthermore, these groups could lobby the reservation authorities against the old culture. As one priest noted, "an organized minority protected by law and a watchful police is a powerful factor in swaying public opinion."[45]

The congresses grew naturally from both Christian and Lakota institutions. The German Jesuits had promoted Catholic congresses in Germany, Austria, and Switzerland at midcentury, to foster devotion to God and church, to encourage Catholic schools, and to lobby for Catholic rights during the *Kulturkampf*. When those Jesuits emigrated to the United States, they initiated similar congresses among the Indians. For the Sioux, Catholic and Episcopal summer congresses served as traditional summer encampments; each tiyospaye traveled and camped as a unit, and pursued its goals of enhancing social solidarity, arranging intermarriages, and expressing religious values in common.

Each year the members set up camp with horses and tipis in the early days, wagons, tents, and autos as the century progressed. Each congress constructed a bower where thousands of delegates gathered. Criers greeted dignitaries, including bishops and papal representatives. Everyone shook hands solemnly, then proceeded to the magnificent Eucharistic processions, devotions to the Blessed Sacrament, hymnody in Sioux, Latin, and English, requiem services for those who had died during the year. Delegates gave speeches, passed resolutions (for example, against peyote use and divorce, or for greater federal funding for Catholic boarding school), put on plays about Catholicism's battle against paganism, and displayed the various sodality regalia.

At Holy Rosary Mission at one congress a Sioux Catholic said: "The new ways are better than the old. We have changed much and we owe all the improved conditions to the Black Gown. With my right hand I cling to the Cross, with my left I cling to the plow handle." At the 1933 meeting, Lizzie Whirlwind Soldier addressed the audience: "How shall a Catholic mother raise her children?" Ralph Eagle Feather expounded: "Why I became a member of the Catholic Church." At the fiftieth anniversary of Holy Rosary's founding in 1938, one of the old-timers recalled at the congress how hard it had been to adjust to the mission school: the alien blackrobes, the regimentation of days of the week: "Strange were the teachings of the new religion; the sign of the Cross was a subject for laughter and regarded as superstition by the pagan Indians." Sister Lucy, a native religious, addressed the congress in fluent Lakota and English. Everyone shook hands with her, and "it made everyone feel very happy." At the 1938 meeting there were 1,000 communions, 600 confessions, 83 confirmations, 6 first communions, and 1 baptism.[46]

Catholic Lakota Leadership

In the early twentieth century Bishop Stariha of South Dakota employed catechists as well as sodalities in order to solidify adult Sioux Catholic institutions. By 1909 he had thirteen paid and five volunteer native helpers, some of whom were interested in spreading the Catholic faith and its forms to other Plains Indians.[47] Between 1888 and 1932 twenty-three catechists worked at Pine Ridge — all men — including both half-breeds and full-breeds. These catechists — Ivan Star-Comes-Out, Joe Horn Cloud, Albert Long Soldier, and the others — held lay services in their locales when priests were not able to visit. They helped the priests pray over the sick; they taught them hymns and baptized in emergencies. Their main task was to "try to bring in as many converts as they can."[48] The catechists also served as the eyes and ears of the priests, informing on their tribesmen who persisted in aboriginal spirituality or peyote rituals, and counting all the Indians who attended Mass and received the sacraments.

Were any of the catechists prospective priests? Father Sialm, for one, doubted their ability to carry the administrative burdens of the priesthood, however useful they proved as helpers. In his "Retreat Notes" of 1930, the priest wrote rhetorically: Are there any Lakota doctors or lawyers? Why should we expect priests? He mentioned Nicholas Black Elk and other Lakota catechists, and asked if they were capable of running a farm, supporting a family: "What hope is there? Who is capable to manage his own household justly, reasonably — Christian like?" Drawing upon his forty-five years of experience at Red Cloud, he could not think of a single alumnus who, in his opinion, could serve well as a priest or brother: "What individual is there to be called!" He was aware of a girl or two who had become a tertiary of the Sisters of Saint Francis, staying at Holy Rosary, living and dying a good life. But what of boys? He found "very little love for sanctification in *any big boy*!" Where could he find the spirit of self-denial, the love of God for God's sake, the devotion to the Blessed Sacrament, the constancy of humility? What Lakota even had a family that encouraged and displayed those virtues, thus forming the priestly character in their children? He concluded that the Lakotas were simply not ready to produce a priest: "I should ask the question: Did the Gypsies have any priests of their tribe!" And even if the Lakotas were to produce a priest, where would he serve? At home his relatives would tempt and undercut him. Even one of the half-breeds was incapable of serving a non-Indian parish: "An Indian priest for whites! — Who will gladly accept!"[49] So for the first half century, and indeed to this day, there have been no Oglala Lakota Catholic priests, even though there have been Episcopalian priests (for example, Robert Two Bulls) and even a Russian Orthodox priest (Martin Brokenleg) from the Sioux. C.P. Jordan, a Rosebud Sioux fluent in Lakota, served as a priest at Holy

Rosary and is currently at St. Francis. Several Oglalas have been seminarians, including Gerald Clifford, and most recently, Emil Her Many Horses, but none has received full ordination.

One of the most prominent catechists at Pine Ridge was Nicholas Black Elk of Manderson. Born in 1863, he began his career as a medicine man at the age of seventeen. Although his wife joined the Catholic Church and three of his boys were baptized in the 1890s, Black Elk was not converted until 1904, when Father Joseph Lindebner, S.J., ejected him forcefully from a curing ritual. The legend has it that Black Elk was working with drum and rattle over a sick boy, when the priest arrived to provide last rites for the patient, already baptized. A struggle ensued between the two religious specialists, and Lindebner threw the Indian's sacred paraphernalia from the tent, grabbed Black Elk by the throat, saying "Satan, get out!"[50] Black Elk was so overwhelmed by the priest's power and authority that he received baptism himself two weeks later, on the feast of Saint Nicholas, from whom he took his Christian name.[51]

In the years that followed, Nicholas Black Elk became a catechist, earning five dollars a month, and proselytizing not only among the Sioux but also the Arapahos and Shoshonis. He and his second wife became pillars of Lakota Catholicism, with Black Elk appearing on the cover of the missionary journal *Indian Sentinel* in 1926, an image of the pagan-turned-Christian, rosary beads in hand. One missionary estimated that Black Elk brought at least four hundred conversions through catechetical duties. Father Westropp said of him, "Ever since his conversion he has been a fervent apostle and he has gone around like a second St. Paul, trying to convert his tribesmen to Catholicity. He has made many converts. . . . Though half blind he has by some hook or crook learned how to read and he knows his religion thoroughly.[52]

At the same time, he never abandoned his traditional Lakota worldview, as everyone knows who has read *Black Elk Speaks*, written by the poet John G. Neihardt, and *The Sacred Pipe*, by the scholar Joseph Epes Brown. As a result of these books, Black Elk the traditionalist Lakota holy man has become world-renowned.[53] When Black Elk converted, he vowed to have nothing more to do with his guardian animal; he is purported to have said, "No more screech owl."[54] Nevertheless, when John Neihardt arrived in 1930, seeking to interview an old-timer who remembered Custer's Last Stand and the Ghost Dance, Black Elk's traditionalism poured forth. On Decoration Day 1931 Nicholas Black Elk was noticeably missing from the Catholic Sioux Congress. He was with John Neihardt, relating his story.

When *Black Elk Speaks* was published in 1932, "the Jesuit priests at Holy Rosary Mission were shocked and horrified at the suggestion that one of their most valued catechists still harbored beliefs in the old Indian religion."[55] In 1933 when the catechist was run over by a team of horses and a wagon, he asked for last rites, and was granted them. Upon his recovery, he signed two documents now preserved in the Holy Rosary Mission archives in which he recanted and disavowed the contents of *Black Elk Speaks*.[56]

It would appear that when Black Elk was faced with possible death in the wagon accident, he promised to recant the book if the priest would give him last rites: "I called my priest to pray for me and so he gave me Extreme Unction and Holy Eucharist. Therefore I will tell you the truth." Just how much pressure was applied, we shall never know; however, it is clear that a quid pro quo took place. The recantation was apparently payment for Extreme Unction. Black Elk then stated that he was well aware of what St. Peter says of those men who forsake their faith (in 2 Peter 2). What Peter says is that those who accept Jesus and then reject Him are far worse than those who never accepted Him: the dog is returned to his vomit, the sow to her wallowing in the mire.

In the second document Black Elk blamed Neihardt for dwelling on the past, and accused the poet of inventing a paganized Black Elk. "Because I value my soul more than my Body I'm awful sorry for the mistake I've made," Black Elk concluded, and he reaffirmed the superiority of Catholicism over the Sun Dance, Ghost Dance, and Lakota medical practices. In both statements, Nicholas Black Elk was identified as a believing, normative, churchgoing Catholic.

And yet for the rest of Black Elk's life — he never served again as an active catechist after the *Black Elk Speaks* scandal although he remained an observant Catholic — the Indian involved himself publicly with presentations of traditional Lakota ritual, for example, appearing in Black Hills pageants and instructing Joseph Epes Brown regarding the seven sacred rites of the Oglala Sioux. Two years before his death in 1950 Black Elk told one man that "he had made a mistake in rejecting" his Lakota practices for Christianity. "Perhaps, after all, the Lakota religion would have been better for his people." [57]

Nicholas Black Elk was a "creative theologian" [58] who was able to understand each religious tradition in terms of the other. It would appear that, while thinking of the two faiths in terms of each other, he kept them separate in practice. He compartmentalized them. He did not substitute one entirely for the other; he maintained "a kind of theological bi-culturalism." [59] At Pine Ridge today some older people remember him as a catechist, whereas younger Lakotas know him through *Black Elk Speaks*. At St. Agnes Church in Manderson, the parish priests complains that everyone tries to turn Nicholas Black Elk into a "noble savage" when he was in fact a "man of faith" in Manderson. Across the road in the Catholic cemetery, "Chief Black Elk 1858–1950" is buried with other members of his family, supposedly with the pictorial catechism he used on his missionary journeys. At least one Catholic priest proposes that Black Elk be considered for sainthood, so holy and caring a man he was, and a Jesuit has documented Black Elk's lifelong Catholicism. [60] Yet his great-granddaughter Charlotte (and Gerald Clifford's wife) has his pipe, his amulets, the paraphernalia of his traditionalism, as well as a bag of tales about how Black Elk tricked various priests into thinking he was a thorough convert. Traditionalist Lakotas, traditionalist Catholics, and syncretists all draw upon Black Elk for justification and inspiration today. In the 1930s, however, his dual religiousness repelled the Holy Rosary authorities, and it helped end their experiment with Lakota catechists at Pine Ridge.

By World War II Holy Rosary personnel had decided that catechists were no longer necessary as part of the Catholicization process of the Lakotas. By then cars and paved roads made it easier for priests to get around by themselves, and the number of priestly vocations was large enough that catechists were superfluous. It was also felt that the catechists were not as trustworthy as helpers as it had been hoped — Nicholas Black Elk as the most prominent disappointment — and in the weakening of authority caused by the New Deal there was need to impose priestly, hierarchical, non-Indian authority over the Indians. An experiment in Catholic Indian leadership came to a close, and clericalism became a controlling force at the mission in the 1940s and 1950s. The missionaries charged then that the Sioux Indians were too "unstable" for Catholic leadership.[61]

After more than eighty years of Jesuit missions to the Lakotas at Pine Ridge, it was said two decades ago, "There has not been a single attempt on the part of the Sioux men to pursue office in the Church. . . . There is a deep inherited reticence on their part to put themselves forward as leaders."[62] Hence, the Jesuits in the Diocese of Rapid City proposed to begin a permanent diaconate program for Lakota men. They recommended that the Lakota community nominate candidates to the priests at Holy Rosary Mission, who would then approach the nominees, telling them of the community support. Bolstered by that vote of confidence, perhaps some would begin training. Their plan of study would include not only priestly formation, knowledge of church and Christ, but also the "Church's sacramental system and possible parallels with Indian sacramentals" such as vision quests, sacred pipe ritualism, and the like. The diaconate training program was to "stress Indian truths and ways that are good and beautiful which will enhance western Church's Theology."

According to the 1971 plan, these deacons were to perform many of the tasks formerly managed by the catechists: reading scriptures at Mass, leading prayer meetings, teaching religion classes, assisting priests with parish work. The deacons were trained to preside at wakes; assist at funerals; conduct devotions; give talks; provide instruction; take sacraments to the sick; assume some administrative functions; visit families, hospitals, and jails; and help with parish organizations. In 1975 this program went into effect, and a half dozen Oglala men have achieved the diaconate. The first American Indian deacon, Steven Levi Red Elk, was ordained in 1975 at Holy Rosary.

Despite the diaconate program of the past decade, Holy Rosary has not produced in a century of work the beginnings of a Lakota clergy. As one contemporary Jesuit writes, "Local Churches in many countries are able to boast of native clergy and lay leaders. The Indian communities of North America are a tragic exception."[63] The writer finds a paternalism in Holy Rosary's history that has never considered the locals ready to take over; there has never been enough trust in them. He recommends that there must be more trust and that there be more complete adult education programs, not only in priestly formations but also for lay leadership. There is no reason to think, he states, that the Lakotas at Pine Ridge (or any other Indian group, for that matter) are incapable of producing their own spiritual leadership.

Among the females there have been more vocations. Clara Condelario was the daughter of a Mexican father and Sioux mother. When both died she came to live at the mission with the sisters, one of the first girls at Holy Rosary Mission. She was the first Sioux girl to take a vow of chastity, and she belonged to the tertiary order of St. Francis, dying of tuberculosis in 1915 and being buried near the sisters in the Holy Rosary cemetery. Lucy Patton, another half-breed, took her tertiary vows in 1914, after fifteen years of schooling at Red Cloud.[64] At Pine Ridge there have been perhaps a dozen sisters from the native population in the first century.

Sister Genevieve Cuny, O.S.F., for several years a staff member of the National Tekakwitha Conference, has been a striking example of Lakota vocation in recent years. She attended Holy Rosary Mission for twelve years, coming from one of the prominent half-breed families on the reservation. Her Catholicism was already three generations deep at her birth, and she attests to receiving her faith not only from the sisters and priests but more significantly from her parents. Her parents were always praying, and she knew her prayers before ever entering Red Cloud School. Her parents were "like Jesus,"[65] always teaching to share, by example. She attended Sioux City College in Iowa and planned to marry, but after working for four years with the Franciscan tertiaries as a social worker, she decided to give her life to Christ. Only three or four Indian sisters were around when she made her decision; however, she has served as a model for other Sioux women as she has taught at Pine Ridge, Rosebud, and Standing Rock. Cuny views Lakota women as the active force of Catholicism at Pine Ridge. The women attend church services and take roles of leadership that reflect their economic status — women are more likely to have salaried jobs and are often the breadwinners these days. Lakota men suffer from acute unemployment (as high as 80 percent), alcoholism, and low self-esteem. Their "macho image," she suggests, prevents them from seeking God's help or forgiveness, and they seldom participate actively in Catholic liturgical life.[66] Tragically, she writes, Lakota men, suffering "serious social and psychological upheavals," perpetuate violence upon Lakota women.[67] As a result she has sought church and tribal protection for battered Lakota women, with the support of Sister Geraldine Clifford, O.S.F., also of Pine Ridge.

Rapid Social and Religious Change

Although it may have seemed to some that Holy Rosary remained cloistered from the changes of the 1940s, such was not the case. The coming of paved roads, the uses of automobiles, the installation of telephones were signs of modernity, and put an end to the seclusion of the mission. Like so many other Christian experiments — the reductions of Paraguay, the Canadian reserves of the seventeenth century, the praying towns in New England — there was an attempt on the part of the missionaries to keep the converts separate not only from their pagan tribesmen but also from influences of the secular world. At Pine Ridge, World War II intruded. Hundreds of Lakota men took part in the fighting. The United States usurped part of Pine Ridge — the area of Cuny Table (named for the family of Sister Genevieve) — for a bombing range. And for these and other reasons, many Lakotas moved from the reservation to urban areas like Rapid City and beyond. The rural, isolated Sioux became enmeshed in modern American culture, and the reservation was overrun by outside forces. The poor, uneducated Sioux became "the American lower-lower class, . . . the 'failure class.'"[68]

World War II seems a watershed, after which the mission held less prominent sway. Participants at the Catholic Sioux Congress found a slackening of spirit at their meetings. They noted that "The Second World War changed our men. They came back after seeing the world. . . . they couldn't live the same way." Furthermore, there was a bridling under the increased clerical control over all aspects of Catholic Lakota life in the 1940s. "In old days the people were the church. Then when things changed they no longer felt in control."[69] They experienced disaffection from the mission and from the church.

Many of the new social outlets were unhealthful to the Lakotas. Adult and juvenile delinquency increased in the postwar years. Drunkenness became common, and then epidemic. Innocents, especially women and girls, were "continually frightened and annoyed" by abuses. The police were not able to keep order, and bribery became common. In 1950 the Catholic Sioux Congress drew attention to these trends and passed a resolution to call to the attention of the tribal council on each reservation the great increase in disorderly and unlawful conduct among the people of the various reservations.[70]

Some Lakotas left the reservation to escape the disorder, traveling to Rapid City and elsewhere in search of jobs. Father Zimmerman went to Rapid City in 1949 in order to help Sioux from various reservations to adjust to urban life. Bishop William T. McCarty built Mother Butler Center as a chapel and social magnet for the Indians. Whatever the Sioux religious experience in Rapid City, urbanization was one factor that caused Father Bernard Fagan, S.J., to remark in the early 1960s that the number of Catholic Lakotas at Pine Ridge had been declining for a decade, even though the majority of Sioux continued to "die in the Church."[71]

World War II was one watershed; the Second Vatican Council of the early 1960s constituted a second. The first affected the Lakotas themselves directly; the second had its greatest immediate impact on the Catholic missionaries and other church personnel. Eventually, however, the effects were felt by the Lakotas themselves, and the ramifications persist to this day. In particular Vatican II reconsidered the attitude of Catholicism to non-Christian religious traditions, lessening the tone of condemnation toward them, and seeking reconciliation with members of other faiths. In the context of this panfaith ecumenism, the goal of missions became problematic. If Catholics were to respect religious orientations other than their own, the condemnation of those other religious traditions was out of place, and perhaps the whole missionary enterprise was outmoded, even wrongheaded.

In the 1960s the Holy Rosary staff evaluated and reevaluated its mission and procedures, and asked in searching ways — ways very much at odds with the first seventy-five years of Holy Rosary methods — what the real needs of the Lakotas might be. Holy Rosary Mission, like many other Catholic Indian missions, inaugurated a process of "inculturation." [72] The staff published traditional Sioux stories in Lakota language (*Ehanni Ohunkakan*) and English ("Lakota Stories") as part of curriculum development. They produced *A Lakota and English Hymnal* in 1972, which was meant to reflect Sioux as well as Catholic ceremonial traditions. Although it was recognized that many Lakotas possessed deep devotion to the Blessed Virgin Mary and preferred the rosary to any Lakota religious form — and that such traditional Catholics would be scandalized by these radical innovations (and many of them were indeed scandalized!) — certain priests decided to cross the boundaries between Catholic and Lakota religious experience.

In the late 1960s and 1970s, one Jesuit in particular set out to analyze not only Sioux religiousness but also its similarities and relationships to Christian forms. Father Paul Steinmetz taught at Holy Rosary during three summers in the mid-1950s, and when he was ordained in 1961 he received charge of the Oglala parish. He furbished the church there with murals of tipis, buffalos, thunderbirds, sun, moon, horses, and other natural phenomena. Benjamin Black Elk and other Lakota Catholics designed the church under Steinmetz's supervision, "expressing the Christian Trinity in Lakota religious symbols," [73] replacing the dove with an eagle, placing a pipe beneath the crucifix. Before long he bedecked Our Lady of the Sioux Catholic Church with an "Indian" Jesus hanging from the crucifix, a peace pipe, an eagle feather, and horse hair paraphernalia. The alter cloth read, "Wakan Wakan Wakan." An observer remarked that Father Steinmetz was "creating a revolution, returning to the Indians their own religious traditions. Surely, this was a Sioux, as well as a Catholic, place of worship." [74]

In 1965 Father Steinmetz began actively to use the pipe as a symbol of Christ, a gesture that some Lakotas rejected (why should *he* be entitled to employ a sacred pipe?) but others encouraged. Lakotas asked him to say Mass at the Pine Ridge Sun Dance in the same year, partially to help validate the traditional ceremonial in the face of harassment by Lakota Christians who blared gospel music during the rituals. For two years Steinmetz said Mass following the piercing rite, and in 1971 he prayed with the pipe at the Sun Dance, at the request of the Lakotas. He performed these syncretic acts because the Sun Dancers were Catholics; he saw no good cause to keep their dual religious identities separated.

In 1973 Steinmetz introduced a pipe ceremony at the Catholic Sioux Congress, and its use lasted until around 1980. Steinmetz wrote in 1969, "One starting point in the blending of the traditional Sioux Religion and the Christian Religion would be to transform the Sacred Pipe into a Christian prayer instrument." For him the pipe was a "type of Christ," since Jesus mediates perfectly between humanity and God, as the pipe mediates "in an imperfect way. . . . The Pipe, then is the great Sioux foreshadowing of Christ in His Priestly Office." [75] If the pipe could be purified and exorcised, it could become, in Steinmetz's view, a means to Christ, not the hindering pipe the early missionaries condemned. Steinmetz asked: "When you have taken the Pipe into the Catholic Church, you have taken in the essential good of their religion. Does this mean that we need to take in all their religious values without careful examination? No, some of these must be purified or even rejected." [76] The priest reported that some Lakotas objected to the use of the pipe because they had always learned from the missionaries that the pipe was impure; Steinmetz told them that he was "baptizing" the pipe so long condemned by priests to be now an instrument of Catholic prayer. One Catholic full-blood who at first was against the use of this pagan device decided he "wanted to be the godfather" of the pipe for Christian use. [77] Steinmetz saw the use of the pipe as a means of reaching the many Sioux who were presently "leading double lives," going through sweats or vision quests while maintaining Christian lives, but feeling guilty about their bireligiousness. [78] In classes he taught at Red Cloud he praised Indian heroes; in church he told the legend of the White Buffalo Calf Woman. He encouraged some young Lakota men to engage in vision quests and advised them about their spiritual experiences. He prodded Lakota Catholics to "interpret Christianity through the symbols of their own heritage, rather than sacrifice their old beliefs and . . . Indian identity." [79] More than one Lakota expressed gratitude, as did Ben Black Elk, that Father Steinmetz had made it possible for Indians to practice traditional and Catholic rituals openly and in peaceful communion with one another, without fear of being unfaithful to Catholicism.

When asked if he was fostering paganism, Steinmetz replied that he was doing what Jesus did in substituting the Mass for the Jewish Paschal meal; he was fulfilling, not destroying the Sioux religion. For Steinmetz, Jesus was the fulfillment not only of Judaism but also of Lakota religious tradition. He wrote that Lakota religion is "pre-Christian" in the sense that it prepares one for Christianity. [80] Lakota religion can exist, he said, in a Lakota Catholic, continuously preparing the person for the "deeper understanding" of Christian faith. Such was the Jesuit's perception of inculturation. Quoting the Lakota Catholic, Edgar Red Cloud, Steinmetz wrote: "When the Indians knew Mother Earth, they knew the Blessed Virgin Mary but they did not know her by name." [81] More crucially, for Steinmetz, the Lakotas knew aboriginally of Jesus through their sacred pipe, without yet enunciating His name. By combining the pipe and Christ, the priest hoped to fashion a profoundly fulfilling Lakota Catholicism at Pine Ridge.

Steinmetz and other Jesuits may have wanted to syncretize the pipe and Christ, but many Sioux preferred to keep the two forms of religious practice separate. They did not mind comparing them, and understanding one in terms of the other, but in practice they wanted them segregated. [82] It was one thing to compare the Christian rite of Confession with the Lakota sweat lodge; both have similar functions: to purify, to bring a person back into right relations with the holy and with humans. Nevertheless, one should not perform Catholic confession in a sweat lodge.

There were many Sioux who resisted the liturgical innovations of the past decades, others who adopted them for a while, until Steinmetz and other Jesuits moved on. Some feared that syncretism and dialogue promoted by Jesuits would undermine their traditional Lakota religious identity. Some Jesuits accused Steinmetz and his cohorts of fostering paganism and watering down the uniqueness of Christianity. There were also many Jesuits at Pine Ridge who regarded liturgical reform as irrelevant to the Sioux crises of the 1970s. The American Indian Movement (AIM) takeover at Wounded Knee in 1973 led some mission observers to focus not so much on religious as political, social, and economic issues. Robert A. White, S.J., writing in the midst of Wounded Knee II, depicted intense Sioux poverty and alienation. He found among the Indians a culture of despair that constituted for the church and the government a "crisis" of policy. The Sioux insisted on remaining Indian; they rejected the melting pot. They wanted to make their own decisions and not be dependent on Whites. They were bitter and did not want to be anthropological museum pieces. There were tensions among the various classes of Sioux, but among them all there was yearning for autonomy — from the United States and from the Catholic Church. He found over the years since World War II "the gradual de-Christianization of the Sioux . . . people," and observed that "the Sioux made a remarkable acceptance of Christianity, something most sincere, and they integrated this into their lives. Their Christianity was built into the rhythm of life of the reservation culture from 1900 to 1940 and when this collapsed the institutions of reservation Christianity collapsed with it." [83] The average age at Pine Ridge, White stated, was fifteen. These young Indians were poor and aimless. They were not guided by Christian norms, or any religious norms for that matter. They avoided religious leaders, both Catholic and Lakota, and constituted a "culture of excitement — seeking the thrill of the moment." He doubted that the church and the American government knew how to treat these disaffected Sioux. Furthermore, the tragedy of the Sioux was not that the young did not attend Mass. It was that they did not have faith in the universe; they had no hope; they practiced little love. That is, they lacked the attitude of religiousness that the missions tried and failed to instill. The aboriginal Sioux culture had religiousness galore, not only in form but in attitude. "But in the lower-class, alienated culture the Indian is de-religionized and de-humanized in the process." White argued that rather than trying to revive some old Sioux gestures in Catholic worship, the church must try to answer the questions raised by contemporary Sioux culture.

White noted that in the early years of Holy Rosary, the St. Joseph and St. Mary Societies, the congresses, the catechists were all institutions that worked with Sioux kinship communities, giving local neighborhoods a chance to organize and help themselves. They were community-builders at local, tribal, and even pantribal levels. But after the 1930s the church neglected and even undermined the local autonomy of Sioux communities in favor of regimentation and clericalism. Following the lead of some Latin American base communities, White encouraged church-supported, lay Indian-leadership programs. He argued that the church should provide funding, training facilities, and support for Indian Catholics who wanted to serve and organize their people, who were willing to dedicate themselves but who did not necessarily want to be priests. He even argued in favor of ordaining Lakota men as priests who were chosen for leadership by the Catholic Indian community. Such programs would have the effect of building community without emphasis on building church hierarchy. In effect, White argued for a Sioux liberation theology, and for several years he attempted to foster an effectively liberating Lakota base community, through the American Indian Leadership Council.[84]

Recent Reflections

One hundred years after the foundation of the South Dakota missions, church personnel are vigorously engaged in asking of themselves whether institutions such as Holy Rosary are meeting the ideals set forth, for example, in Pope Paul VI's 1975 encyclical, "Evangelization in the Modern World." The Jesuit John Hatcher reminds us that today as a century ago the church is still considered missionary by nature: compelled to preach the good news, even to those who already have religious traditions of their own. These peoples have a right to hear the Christian word, to have their religious traditions completed, but not destroyed, by Christianization. He notes that the role of mission is to establish a community of believers, a church. Hatcher concludes that the missionaries must admit the injustices of the past and seek forgiveness from the Sioux, effecting a "reconciliation" between Holy Rosary personnel and Pine Ridge Catholic population, both of whom represent the Church.[85]

Although virtually all of the Indians at Pine Ridge are nominally Christian, there is in reality a range of religious orientations on the reservation. First, there are the Catholic Lakotas who have felt encouraged to Indianize their liturgy, as well as participate in Sioux religiocultural ceremonies. These are the Lakotas about whom William Powers speaks when he describes "dual religious participation."[86] Black Elk's great-granddaughter Charlotte says that her people were able to become Christians without leaving behind their Lakota traditions. They are good Christians, insofar as they have a relationship to Jesus, but not in the sense of identifying themselves exclusively as Catholics.[87] This bireligious mode is perhaps the normative stance among the Lakotas. Among this group there are those who compartmentalize their religious practice, even though the religious ideas from each tradition may interpenetrate each other, and there are those who syncretize their religious practice; the former tend to be those who are more embedded in traditional worship; the latter feel comfortable with Catholic worship but like the old-time Sioux ambience in their Christian liturgy.

Gerald Clifford—coordinator of the Black Hills Steering Committee, an accountant with an engineering degree—is one Lakota Catholic who embraces both religious traditions without trying to combine them. He is a "Lakota Sioux Indian activist who is also a practicing Catholic." Between 1962 and 1968 he studied to be a priest in the Camaldolese Hermitage in California and the Benedic-

tine Theologate in Rome, leaving short of final ordination when his mother died
and his father needed his help. Gerald chose to honor his kinship responsibilities
and aid his father in a time of crisis; he realized that it would be "irresponsible
for me not to come home," and so he quit the seminary.[88]

He did not reject his Catholic faith; however, after nearly six years of studying
and practicing Christian spirituality, he returned to Pine Ridge and discovered
Black Elk Speaks, in which he found his own native spirituality. He joined Father
Bob White's American Indian Leadership Council, which met each weekend to
create a plan for restructuring Lakota society: to take over the schools, create
Lakota colleges, run native businesses and law enforcement, and to revitalize
Lakota spirituality. The council brought him together with Charlotte Black Elk;
they married in 1969. For over two decades he has chosen to express his religiousness through Lakota forms: sweats, pipe ceremonies, the Sun Dance. At the same
time, he continues to participate in Catholic liturgical life: lovingly, but not without ambivalence. He recalls whippings from the Jesuits at Red Cloud School. He
claims that the priests discouraged Lakota men from pursuing religious vocations.
He sensed Jesuit condescension toward Lakota adults. Nevertheless, he identifies
himself as a Catholic, and several years ago he helped establish a Rapid City
diocesan Office of Native American Concerns.

Second, there are non-Catholic Christians: primarily Episcopalians and Con-
gregationalists; however, there are now thirteen Christian denominations at Pine
Ridge, in addition to Half Moon and Cross Fire peyotists. The relations among
these groups is relatively friendly, even ecumenical, although more so among the
older denominations than the newer ones. Among the Lakotas themselves, there
is less differentiation among the various Christian bodies than there is among
non-Indians.

Third, there are those who have been baptized but who want nothing to do
with Christianity. These are born-again pagans who have attempted to return to
native religious practice, or to neotraditional forms, and they oppose the Catholic
use of their Sioux traditions. Indeed, they are anti-Christian in their tone.

There are strong Lakota feelings against Catholicism and Christianity in general. To many Indians at Pine Ridge Christianity has been and continues to be
the White Man's religion, accepted, understood, and rejected as such. When
there are resentments against the whites — as there are to this day — the whites'
religion shares in the onus. For the Lakotas all non-Lakota institutions, including
all those of the Catholic Church, are peripheral to their existence and impinge
on their autonomy and identity as Lakotas. Their major frame of reference is
their Lakota relational community, and Holy Rosary Mission is perceived as a
looming intrusion to that community.[89] Lakota children receive their education
from Red Cloud; however, "they never set foot in a church again."[90]

Resentment still exists over the decades in which whites refused to permit traditional religious practices — even among those who have forever eschewed those
practices. Since traditional Lakota religious practice — with its emphasis on everyday behavior and its effect on relatives — was so embedded in community life,

the impingements were not only on liturgical form but on the very way of life of the Lakotas, and Lakotas still resent white Christians for destroying that way of life. Many Lakotas perceive Christianity as the cause, not the cure, for contemporary Lakota social woes.

Many of these resentments have been expressed through militant organizations like AIM. Even those only tangentially touched by AIM have felt themselves more radically disassociated from Christianity, even though they were probably baptized in their infancy or youth. So Wallace Black Elk, Black Elk's putative grandson, spent the mid-1980s preaching to the Indians and non-Indians alike, both on and off the reservations, about the salvific, New Age strength of Lakota religion. He and his wife, Grace Spotted Eagle, ran sweat lodges and self-help workshops based on semitraditional Indian lore, teaching non-Indians how to make flesh offerings and conduct vision quests, in order to find a spiritual life superior to Christianity.[91]

At the same time there are Lakotas who are attempting to follow a religious way of life that they refer to as the Good Red Road. It is based on Black Elk's teaching in *Black Elk Speaks*, and it entails a syncretism apart from Catholic authority. Leona Bull Bear is a middle-aged Lakota woman living in Kyle, married to a man who studied for the diaconate. She was studying the Bible, but a few years ago she and her husband decided that they needed to participate in Lakota religious life, practice the Lakota sacraments, get in touch with Lakota spirits. Her husband now speaks directly with the spirits. They have not turned their backs on Catholicism completely, but for now they pay attention to their Lakota ways. For her the Good Red Road is roughly equivalent to the Way of Christ, only with specific Indian content. In her view the Lakota spirits can be dangerous, and one must be very careful not to be harmed along the Good Red path. On the other hand, she reports, Good Red Road adherents favor sweats to confession because they cannot trust priests to keep secret what they hear in the confessional. With the sweats one speaks silently and privately to the spirits and one is purified.[92]

Finally, Lakotas, particularly older Lakotas, still engage in Catholic rituals; indeed, there are traditional Sioux Catholics; many, but not all, of these are mixed-bloods. For several generations their families have engaged in Catholic institutional life and identification, and even today many of these prefer the Latin Mass of their youth to an Indianized liturgy.

They attend Sunday masses at Sacred Heart Church in Pine Ridge. They place twenty-dollar bills in the offertory basket and greet each other and strangers with friendly "Peace" embraces. Their Mass has no explicit Indian references, except to living and dead members of the immediate community. There are yellow-black-white-red cloths hanging, some Southwest bowls, a picture of an Indian hunter, and a painting of Kateri Tekakwitha, but the priest conducts the service according to standard non-Indian form. At St. Agnes in Manderson, Father Joseph Sheehan, S.J., officiating, the scene is similar. A quiet crowd puts singles rather than twenties into the collection plates; these are poorer folks than the

Lakotas at Pine Ridge. There are some "Indian" designs of the sun, moon, lightning, a tipi, behind the altar; however, the service itself is normative Catholic. After Mass everyone retires to the Tekakwitha Hall behind church for doughnuts and coffee.

Many Oglalas who have attended Red Cloud, like Tim Giago, criticize the mission. "The system was wrong, and the system has changed, but too late for too many." These Indian critics say that the teachers whipped them. They refused to let the Indians speak their language. They erased individuality with militaristic discipline. They isolated the pupils from their families: "I still remember being strapped severely by Mr. John Bryde, who became a priest. In my time he was school principal at Holy Rosary Mission."[93]

Agnes Picotte, an educator formerly at the University of South Dakota at Vermillion, and a full-blood Oglala who attended Red Cloud School from the age of five, complained bitterly in 1978 that everyone who had authority at Holy Rosary was "not of my culture."[94] If her parents were allowed to visit, they had to deliver her back to the school by dinnertime and then depart. As a child, she wondered, "Could it be that they were not capable of taking care of me?" She wept by herself, away from the disapproving sight of the sisters. She wept from loneliness and from an acute sense of inferiority, realizing herself and her parents to be "incapable" of authority or autonomy. She claimed that the mission programmed Indians to fail by usurping control over the upbringing of the generations.

The primary critique of the mission — that it took over Sioux parental functions — is also a compliment to the place. Given the poverty and the dissolute character of Lakota society in the twentieth century, some Lakotas are grateful to Holy Rosary for the food, shelter, and other services.[95] Even Charlotte Black Elk notes that in spite of the "mission bashing" that goes on among the Indians, there is a great deal of mutual respect between the present mission staff and the contemporary Lakota community.

Indeed, graduates of Holy Rosary school speak grateful praise for the school. Eilleen Tibbits Jelovich graduated from Red Cloud in 1945, growing up as one of ten children to mixed-blood parents on the reservation. When she graduated, she left for Washington State, where she had a sister and other acquaintances who had attended the mission school. She had been "weaned" from her parents, nine months per year all those years, and she wanted to "better myself" by leaving the reservation. There was "too much heartache" at Pine Ridge, and Red Cloud provided her with the means to escape. She married a non-Indian, worked in white society, had children, and returns only occasionally. She is what anyone would call acculturated, and that is what she wanted as a graduate in 1945. She is happy for her education and for her choice to leave. "I had to sacrifice something — being close to my parents," but she is glad she did. "It makes me madder than hell" she says, to hear Lakota children complain that the missions destroyed the Indians. "It was the best thing that ever happened to us." Throughout the centennial celebration of Holy Rosary in 1988 one frequently heard that the staffers were strict or "mean" and the punishments were plentiful (kneeling on hands, whipping, and so forth) but that the results were good. One woman says that "it made me strong." They wish that Lakota children today had this kind of discipline, but it has not existed on the reservation since the 1970s.[96]

Jelovich has "stayed with" her Catholicism. She raised her children in Catholic schools and is glad to see that they are coming back to Catholic liturgical structures, after a "hippie" phase, now that they are parents. A widow, she works as a cook for a parish rectory, and although she is a post-Vatican II Catholic — picking and choosing which elements of the modern church to embrace or reject — she is little different from any other middle-aged middle-class Catholic woman in America today. She and others at the centennial reunion are Catholic Indians who have ceased participation in Indian religious forms. They converted and became mainline Catholics. Jelovich's mother went through six grades at Red Cloud; she completed all twelve grades. Her mother stayed on the reservation; she left. A study of Lakota Catholics today is not complete if her life story is omitted, even if it is a pattern only for a minority of Red Cloud alumni.

Indeed, an evaluation of Holy Rosary's first hundred years at Pine Ridge requires attention to a spectrum of viewpoints — including those of Father Steinmetz as well as Father Digmann, Sister Cuny as well as Mr. Giago, Ms. Black Elk as well as her famous forebear. There are old Lakota women today who say the rosary daily in their homes. There are mixed-bloods, proud of their white and Indian heritage and their Jesuit education. There are married couples, graduates of Red Cloud School, who argue with each other over whether to celebrate Christmas and other Christian holidays. There are many faces and many voices of Lakota Catholicism, a century after the founding of Holy Rosary Mission.

One of the most profound of the Catholic Lakotas in the 1990s is Sister Geraldine Clifford, O.S.F. Sister Geraldine was born on the Pine Ridge Reservation, grew up at Holy Rosary, daughter of Robert Clifford (the athletic director and coach) and Geraldine Swallow Clifford, who taught in the grade school at Red Cloud. Presently Sister Geraldine teaches psychology at Oglala Lakota College on Pine Ridge and runs the St. Francis Home for Children, which she founded several years ago. For thirty years she served her order, the Franciscan Sisters of Charity, away from her home community. She trained novices and served as provincial superior at the motherhouse in Denver. Only recently was she "permitted" to return to her land and people, and she expresses regret at the decades of "deculturation" she underwent. She appreciates the "fine education" she received from the sisters at Holy Rosary and from Jesuits at advanced institutions such as Loyola in Chicago and Fordham in New York. Nevertheless, she wishes that her training had not meant assimilation to white life and alienation from her kinfolk — the very people she most wishes to serve. It is now her project to overcome the cultural loss and serve her fellow Oglalas.[97]

Prayer is a powerful force in Sister Geraldine's life, helping her to reach toward God's transcendence. She has absorbed the contemplative works of St. Teresa of Avila and St. John of the Cross, and she attempts to combine the "charism" of their prayer techniques with the ameliorative effects of apostolic social action, in order to live a helpful life of prayer. She and her brother Gerald — a former seminarian and more recently a Sun Dancer — attended an international convocation of Franciscan prayer in 1992, at which he prayed with a Lakota pipe, at his sister's urging. As a Catholic she has aspired to prayerful contemplation; however, the model she has followed most assiduously has been that of her Lakota grandmother, who raised herself to relation with the divine through traditional Lakota spirituality. Sister Geraldine tells people that the Lakotas were religious contemplatives who prayed to God before becoming Christians. Today Sister Geraldine is attempting to achieve the levels of prayer once attained by her Lakota kin.

At Red Cloud Indian School the authorities kept her apart from Lakota culture. Her parents worked for Red Cloud, lived at Red Cloud, and yet they were treated like other Indian parents when it came to visiting their children. The priests and sisters regarded all Indian parents as intruders and dangerous influences. The goal of the boarding school was to break contact with the parents' culture, even if that culture was Catholic. The children belonged to the school, and Geraldine's parents were permitted only occasional personal contact with their children, sitting on benches in the hallways. In the summers, Red Cloud arranged for her to work off the reservation; hence she rarely saw her parents, indeed hardly knew them after early childhood. As a result, she says, she became "completely acculturated."[98]

She did not experience beatings or other overt violence at Red Cloud, but her brothers did, including from Father John Bryde, who wrote so eloquently about Indian acculturative psychology. By the 1950s the Sisters of St. Francis were "sending to Siberia" — that is, to Indian missions — their problem sisters. As a result, these sisters "acted out" their personal maladjustments upon the girls, including Geraldine's younger sister, who attempted to run away from the school and received a strap-lashing. Their mother was horrified, but in their father's view, "The Jesuits could do no wrong." Sister Geraldine comments that the Jesuits performed their tasks with "intensity and thoroughness." The result of their effective work was to "annihilate our culture."[99]

When Geraldine was at Red Cloud, the Franciscan sisters did not allow Indians into their order. They told her as a youngster that she was "too close to paganism," because her grandparents had been gentile Lakotas; even though her parents were Catholics, she could not enter a novitiate when she first felt a religious vocation.

Her two aunts, Esther and Grace, were the saintly girls memorialized by the priests at Holy Rosary when they died in their youth. Both wanted to become Franciscan sisters but were refused admittance. Geraldine bore a striking resemblance to one of her aunts, and her vocation was understood by Lakotas and Holy Rosary personnel as a fulfillment of the deceased aunt's wish to take the veil. For a time, strictures interfered.

The rule changed; she joined the order, and in her years of training she almost never went home to Pine Ridge. The process of deracination from her family and culture, begun at boarding school, was completed. She found in the sisterhood a community that accepted her, and even elected her to positions of authority and responsibility. She has remained certain of her vocation, and she has continued to love her order. Despite her criticism of the alienating process by which she gained her training, she has never wavered in her prayerful love and service for God as a sister.

In the 1980s Sister Geraldine attended a meeting of the Association of Native Religious and Clergy, a support group for Indian sisters, brothers, and priests. Other sisters were telling how much racism they faced in their orders; she testified gratefully that she had never experienced bigotry from her sister Franciscans. Upon consulting with members of her order, and upon reflection, however, Sister Geraldine realized that the sisters treated her as if she were white because she acted exactly like a white. She was struck with the realization that through boarding school and novitiate she had "ceased to be an Indian," at least in the eyes of others.[100]

She determined to move back to Pine Ridge and regain her relations with her sisters, brothers, and extended family. She wanted to be with her people and help them if she could, after thirty years of absence. The Franciscan sisterhood permitted her this goal; the question was, what would she do on the reservation? She did not want to live at Holy Rosary ("a ghetto," she called it). She did not wish to serve the chancery office in Rapid City. She decided instead to teach at the Lakota-operated community college and to create a shelter for abused Lakota children. She and another sister built a nine-bedroom house where the children could live with her, in a family setting. She did not cut ties with the Franciscans; indeed, she has served two recent years as provincial, and she is now spiritual director for Franciscan novices, who come to Pine Ridge to receive her guidance. Neither did she eschew contact with her alma mater; in fact, she is a member of the board of directors of the Red Cloud School. Her primary ministry, however — one might say, her prayer, her religiousness, her *wacekiye* — is to create a web of relations for needy Lakota children, serving as their foster parent, their grandmother and guardian. In the process she is reestablishing her own Lakota identity.

It has not been easy. In trying to learn Lakota language, for example, she experienced great frustration. Her teacher was Father Jim Green, S.J., and she felt resentment that this Jesuit could speak with facility the language of her forebears, while she stumbled through it. She rued that it was his mission forebears who prevented her from speaking Lakota as a child, when she was a Red Cloud student. Now the Jesuits favor the teaching of Lakota language and culture at the school, while most Lakota board members think it impractical to teach the things of the past. They want their children to learn skills that will overcome contemporary poverty.

The Pine Ridge Reservation constitutes the poorest county in the United States, with 63 percent of the population living in poverty according to Census Bureau standards. The annual per capita income is $3,417, and the Tribal Chairman refers to the constituency as a fifth-going-on-sixth-generation welfare state.

This poverty causes Father Joseph Sheehan at Wounded Knee to comment: "I don't know what I would be if were an Indian. I think I would be an alcoholic." [101]

Sister Geraldine Clifford regrets that in the midst of this poverty Lakota youths have little or nothing to hope for; theirs is the culture of empty excitement, of cowboys and sports, of alcohol and abuse. In this context most Lakota youths want nothing to do with religion. They take their religion courses at Red Cloud; however, prayer means nothing to them. When they leave school, they abandon the church.

These are the children Sister Geraldine is trying to reach. She says that it does not disturb her so much that baptized Lakota youngsters refuse to embrace Catholic spirituality, would that they embraced traditional Lakota religion. Her sorrow is that they embrace nothing. They have no prayer, no spiritual relations, no human commitment.

So, in 1992 she took her foster children to witness her brother Gerald — the former seminarian — enact a Sun Dance at the summer solstice. She and the children danced at the periphery of the Sun Dance grounds, in support of his prayer.

Notes

1. See Åke Hultkrantz, *The Study of American Indian Religions*, ed. Christopher Vecsey (New York: Crossroad, 1983), and "A Decade of Progress: Works on North American Indian Religions in the 1980s," in *Religion in Native North America*, ed. Christopher Vecsey (Moscow: University of Idaho Press, 1990), 167–201.

2. Raymond DeMallie, ed., *The Sixth Grandfather: Black Elk's Teachings Given to John G. Neihardt* (Lincoln: University of Nebraska Press, 1984), 301.

3. Donald R. Thompson, "A History of Holy Rosary Indian Mission from its Beginnings to the Present" (M.A. thesis, University of Denver, 1953), 86.

4. Ross Enochs, "Lakota Mission: Jesuit Mission Method and the Lakota Sioux, 1885–1945" (Ph.D. diss., University of Virginia, 1993), 37.

5. William K. Powers, *Beyond the Vision: Essays on American Indian Culture* (Norman: University of Oklahoma Press, 1987), 112.

6. Sisters of St. Francis, "Chronicles," Holy Rosary Mission Records, 1888–1969, Marquette University Memorial Library, Department of Special Collections (hereafter HRMR), 1.

7. Harvey Markowitz, "Catholic Mission and the Sioux: A Crisis in the Early Paradigm," in *Sioux Indian Religion. Tradition and Innovation*, ed. Raymond J. DeMallie and Douglas R. Parks (Norman: University of Oklahoma Press, 1987), 113–37.

8. Florentine Digmann, S.J., "History of St. Francis Mission, 1866–1922," HRMR, c. 1922, p. 4.

9. See Enochs, "Lakota Mission," 135, 142–46, 154–59, 174–76, 190–97, 205.

10. Placidus F. Sialm, S.J., "The History of Holy Rosary Mission, Pine Ridge, South Dakota, 1888–1932," HRMR, 1930s, p. 83.

11. Quoted in James R. Walker, *Lakota Belief and Ritual*, ed. Raymond J. DeMallie and Elaine A. Jahner (Lincoln: University of Nebraska Press, 1991), 140.

12. Digmann, "History of St. Francis Mission," 13.

13. Sr. Mary Claudia Duratschek, O.S.B., *The Beginnings of Catholicism in South Dakota* (Washington, D.C.: Catholic University of America Press, 1943), 15.

14. Mark G. Thiel, "Catholic Sodalities among the Sioux, 1882–1910" (manuscript in author's possession, 1989), 3.

15. Sr. M. Florence Southall, O.S.F., "The Work of the Jesuit Fathers and the Franciscan Sisters among the Teton-Sioux of South Dakota," HRMR, 1964, p. 44.

16. Charlotte Black Elk, "Oral History and Traditional Religion" (presentation at the conference, "Two Roads: A Century of Christian Missions among the Lakota," Holy Rosary Mission, Pine Ridge, S.D., Aug. 2–4, 1988 [hereafter "Two Roads"]).

17. John Edward Hatcher, S.J., "Paul VI's *Evangelization in the Modern World* and the Mission to the Sioux Indians of South Dakota: Theory and Praxis" (Sacred Theology Licentiate thesis, Regis College, 1987), 83.

18. Henry Ign. Westropp, S.J., "In the Land of the Wigwam: Children's Lecture on the Jesuit Missions in S. Dakota," HRMR, n.d., pp. 9–10.

19. Digmann, "History of St. Francis Mission," 6.

20. See Henry Grotegeers, S.J., "Instruction by Means of the Two Roads," HRMR, 1931.

21. Digmann, "History of St. Francis Mission," 8.

22. Ibid., 16.

23. Ibid., 19, 38.

24. Gordon MacGregor, *Warriors Without Weapons: A Study of the Society and Personality Development of the Pine Ridge Sioux* (Chicago: University of Chicago Press, 1951), 92.

25. Red Cloud Indian School Records, Series 1/1, Box 1, Folder 3, HRMR, 1869–1988.

26. John B. Jutz, S.J., "Historic Data on the Causes of the Dissatisfaction among the Sioux Indians in 1890: The Ghost Dance Religion," *Woodstock Letters* 47 (1918): 313–27. For a view of the dance from St. Francis Mission, see Emil J. Perrig, S.J., "Diary, 1886–1909," St. Francis Mission Records, Marquette University Memorial Library, Department of Special Collections.

27. "Holy Rosary Special Centennial Edition, 1888–1988," *Lakota Times*, Aug. 2, 1988, p. 3.

28. Eugene Buechel, S.J., "A Retreat for Our Indian Children," HRMR, 1917.

29. Otto J. Moorman, S.J., "A Lily of the Sioux," and "The Rose of the Sioux," HRMR, 1924.

30. Local Sodalities Records, 1909–86, HRMR.

31. Local Sodalities Records, 1909–86, HRMR.

32. Red Cloud Indian School Records, Series 1/1, Box 2, Folder 1, HRMR.

33. John M. Scott, S.J., *High Eagle and His Sioux* (St. Louis: n.p., 1963).

34. Sr. M. Serena Zens, O.S.B., "The Educational Work of the Catholic Church among the Indians of South Dakota" (M.A. thesis, University of South Dakota, 1936), 56. See also, Thompson, "History of Holy Rosary Indian Mission," 84.

35. Rev. Louis J. Goll, S.J., *Jesuit Missions among the Sioux* (Saint Francis, S.D.: Saint Francis Mission, 1940), 69.

36. Marla Powers, "The Boarding School: A Photoethnography" (presentation at the conference, "Two Roads," Aug. 3, 1988).

37. William K. Powers, "Dual Religious Participation: Traditional Religion vs. Christianity" (presentation at "Two Roads," Aug. 2, 1988).

38. Robert A. White, S.J., "Christianity on the Reservations," HRMR, 1965, p. 2.

39. Thiel, "Catholic Sodalities," 6.

40. Ibid., 8.
41. Digmann, "History of St. Francis Mission," 19.
42. Enochs, "Lakota Mission," 86.
43. Thiel, "Catholic Sodalities," 11.
44. Digmann, "History of St. Francis Mission," 28.
45. Goll, *Jesuit Missions*, 38.
46. See reports of the Catholic Sioux Congress for the years 1920, 1933, and 1938, HRMR, 1920–88.
47. Thiel, "Catholic Sodalities," 31.
48. Westropp, "In the Land of the Wigwam," 8.
49. See Placidus F. Sialm, S.J., "Retreat Notes," HRMR, 1930–32.
50. DeMallie, *Sixth Grandfather*, 14.
51. Throwing doubt on this story is the account in Michael F. Steltenkamp, S.J., "No More Screech Owl: Lakota Adaptation to Change as Profiled in the Life of Black Elk," HRMR, 1987, pp. 91–97.
52. Henry Ign. Westropp, S.J., *In the Land of the Wigwam*, (Pine Ridge, S.D.: Holy Rosary Mission, 1910), 12.
53. William K. Powers, "When Black Elk Speaks, Everybody Listens," in Vecsey, *Religion in Native North America*, 135–51.
54. See Steltenkamp, "No More Screech Owl."
55. DeMaille, *Sixth Grandfather*, 58.
56. Red Cloud Indian School Records, Series 1/1, Box 1, Folder 5, HRMR.
57. DeMaille, *Sixth Grandfather*, 72.
58. Clyde Holler, "Black Elk's Relationship to Christianity" (paper presented at the American Academy of Religion annual meeting, Dallas, 1983).
59. Holler, "Black Elk's Relationship to Christianity."
60. Interviews with Rev. Camillus Cavagnaro, O.F.M., by author, Aug. 3–6, 1988, Pine Ridge, S.D.; Michael F. Steltenkamp, S.J., *Black Elk: Holy Man of the Oglala* (Norman: University of Oklahoma Press, 1993).
61. Robert A. White, S.J., "Church Imposed Uniformity," *Great Plains Observer*, Aug. 1969, p. 14.
62. Diocesan Permanent Diaconate Program, May 28, 1971, in Diocesan Permanent Diaconate Programs Records, HRMR.
63. Hatcher, "Paul VI's *Evangelization in the Modern World*," 91–92.
64. Sisters of St. Francis, "Chronicles, 1888–1969," 38.
65. Sr. Genevieve Cuny, O.S.B., "Leadership and Professional Development in the Light of the Native American Experience," *Tekakwitha Conference Newsletter* 6, no. 5 (1987): 6–8.
66. Interview with author, Aug. 8, 1986, Bozeman, Mont.
67. See "Report on Indian Work and Applications for Aid Presented to the Commission for the Catholic Missions among the Colored People and the Indians" (Bureau of Catholic Indian Missions, Department of Special Collections, Marquette University Memorial Library, 1979).
68. White, "Christianity on the Reservation," 2.
69. Catholic Sioux Congress, Feb. 15, 1983, in Minutes of the Catholic Sioux Congress, 1920–88, HRMR.
70. Catholic Sioux Congress, 1950, Minutes, HRMR.

71. Southall, "Work of the Jesuit Fathers and the Franciscan Sisters among the Teton-Sioux of South Dakota," 90.

72. Robert Hilbert, S.J., "Contemporary Catholic Mission Work among the Sioux," in *Sioux Indian Religion: Tradition and Innovation*, ed. Raymond J. DeMaille and Douglas R. Parks (Norman: University of Oklahoma Press, 1987), 144.

73. Paul B. Steinmetz, S.J., *Pipe, Bible and Peyote among the Oglala Lakota* (Stockholm: Almqvist and Wiksell International, 1980), 37.

74. Dabney Otis Collins, "A Happening at Oglala," *American West* 6, no. 2 (1969): 16.

75. Paul B. Steinmetz, S.J., "Explanation of the Sacred Pipe as a Prayer Instrument," *Pine Ridge Research Bulletin* 10 (1969): 20.

76. Steinmetz, "Explanation of the Sacred Pipe as a Prayer Instrument," 20–21.

77. Ibid., 21.

78. Ibid., 21.

79. Collins, "Happening at Oglala," 16.

80. Steinmetz, *Pipe, Bible and Peyote*, 160 n. 2.

81. Ibid., 161.

82. Ben Black Bear Jr., "Dialogue between Medicine Men and Priests" (presentation at the conference, "Two Roads," Aug. 4, 1988).

83. Robert A. White, S.J., untitled manuscript, c. 1973, HRMR.

84. See White, "Church Imposed Uniformity" and "The Crisis among the Sioux Today," n.d., HRMR.

85. Hatcher, "Paul VI's *Evangelization in the Modern World*," 144.

86. See Powers, "Dual Religious Participation."

87. Elk, "Oral History and Traditional Religion."

88. Catherine Walsh, "The Eucharist and the Sweat Lodge: A Lakota Sioux Speaks Out on His Journey" (manuscript in author's possession, n.d.).

89. Martin Brokenleg, "Use of the Lakota Language in the Missionary Process" (presentation at the conference, "Two Roads," Aug. 3, 1988).

90. Quotation by Sr. Geraldine Clifford in a telephone interview with the author, Oct. 16, 1991.

91. See Wallace H. Black Elk and William S. Lyon, *Black Elk: The Sacred Ways of a Lakota* (San Francisco: Harper and Row, 1990).

92. Interview with Leona Bull Bear by author, Aug. 4, 1988.

93. Tim A. Giago Jr., *The Aboriginal Sin* (San Francisco: Indian Historian Press, 1978), viii, 2.

94. Red Cloud Indian School, Workshop/Seminar, Audiotapes, 1978, HRMR.

95. Powers, "Dual Religious Participation."

96. Interview with Eilleen Tibbits Jelovich by the author, Aug. 5, 1988.

97. Interview with Sr. Geraldine Clifford by the author, Oct. 16, 1991.

98. Interview with Sr. Geraldine Clifford by the author, Aug. 9, 1992.

99. Ibid.

100. Ibid.

101. See Peter T. Kilborn, "Sad Distinction for the Sioux: Homeland is No. 1 in Poverty," *New York Times*, Sept. 20, 1992, p. 1.

Contributors

CATHERINE L. ALBANESE is a professor of religious studies at the University of California at Santa Barbara. She is the past president of the American Academy of Religion and the author of, among other books, *Sons of the Fathers: The Civil Religion of the American Revolution, Corresponding Motion: Transcendental Religion and the New America*, and *Nature Religion in America: From the Algonkian Indians to the New Age.*

WALTER H. CONSER JR. is a professor of religious studies and history at the University of North Carolina at Wilmington. He is the author of *Church and Confession: Conservative Theologians in Germany, England, and America, 1815–1866*, and *God and the Natural World: Religion and Science in Antebellum America* and is coeditor of *Experience of the Sacred: Readings in the Phenomenology of Religion.*

JAY P. DOLAN, a professor of history at the University of Notre Dame, is the past president of the American Catholic Historical Association and the American Society of Church History. He is the author of *The Immigrant Church: New York's Irish and German Catholics, 1815–1865*, which received the John Gilmary Shea Award, *Catholic Revivalism: The American Experience, 1830–1900*, and *The American Catholic Experience: A History from Colonial Times to the Present*, and is coeditor of *New Dimensions in American Religious History.*

YVONNE YAZBECK HADDAD, a professor of the history of Islam and Christian-Mulsim relations at Georgetown University, is the past president of the Middle East Studies Association. She is coauthor of *Islamic Values in the United States* and *Mission to America: Five Islamic Sectarian Communities in North America*, editor of *The Muslims of America*, and coeditor of *The Oxford Encyclopedia of Islam in the Modern World.*

ROSEMARY SKINNER KELLER, an academic dean and a professor of church history at Union Theological Seminary in New York City, is the author of *Patriotism and the Female Sex: Abigail Adams and the American Revolution* and *Georgia Harkness: For Such a Time As This* and is coeditor of *In Our Own Voices: Four Centuries of American Women's Religious Writings, Women and Religion in America: A Documentary History*, and *Women in New Worlds: Historical Perspectives on the Wesleyan Tradition.*

DONALD G. MATHEWS, a professor of history and American studies at University of North Carolina at Chapel Hill, is author of *Slavery and Methodism: A Chapter in American Morality, 1780–1845*, and *Religion in the Old South* and coauthor of *Sex, Gender, and the Politics of ERA: A State and the Nation.*

ALBERT J. RABOTEAU, Henry W. Putnam Professor of religion at Princeton University, and DAVID W. WILLS, a professor of religion at Amherst College, are coeditors of *Afro-*

American Religion: A Documentary History Project, an undertaking funded by the Lilly Endowment. Associate editors are RANDALL K. BURKETT, associate director of the W.E.B. Du Bois Institute for Afro-American Research at Harvard University; WILL B. GRAVELY, a professor of religious studies at the University of Denver; and JAMES MELVIN WASHINGTON, who was a professor of church history at Union Theological Seminary before his death in 1997.

JONATHAN D. SARNA is Joseph H. and Belle R. Braun Professor of American Jewish history at Brandeis University. He is the author of *Jacksonian Jew: The Two Worlds of Mordecai Noah*, which was nominated for the National Jewish Book Award. He also is coeditor of *Jews and the Founding of the Republic* and *Ethnic Diversity and Civic Identity: Patterns of Conflict and Cohesion in Cincinnati Since 1820* and coauthor of *Religion and State in American Jewish Experience.*

STEPHEN J. STEIN is a chancellor's professor of religious studies at Indiana University. He is the past president of the American Society of Church History, the author of *The Shaker Experience*, which received the Philip Schaff Prize, and the editor of Jonathan Edwards's *Apocalyptic Writings.*

THOMAS A. TWEED is an associate professor of religious studies at the University of North Carolina at Chapel Hill. He is the author of *The American Encounter with Buddhism, 1844–1912: Victorian Culture and the Limits of Dissent* and *Our Lady of the Exile: Diasporic Religion at a Cuban Catholic Shrine in Miami* and the editor of *Retelling U.S. Religious History.*

SUMNER B. TWISS, a professor of religious studies at Brown University, is coauthor of *Comparative Religious Ethics: A New Method* and coeditor of *Genetic Counseling: Facts, Values, and Norms, Experience of the Sacred: Readings in the Phenomenology of Religion,* and *Religion and Human Rights.*

CHRISTOPHER VECSEY is a professor of religion and Native American studies at Colgate University. He is the author of *Traditional Ojibwa Religion and Its Historical Changes, Imagine Ourselves Richly: Mythic Narratives of North American Indians,* and the forthcoming three-volume work, *American Indian Catholics.* He is the editor of *Religion in Native North America.*

Index